STRANGERS TO THEMSELVES:
THE BYZANTINE OUTSIDER

Society for the Promotion of Byzantine Studies

Publications
8

STRANGERS TO THEMSELVES:
THE BYZANTINE OUTSIDER

Papers from the Thirty-second Spring Symposium of Byzantine
Studies, University of Sussex, Brighton, March 1998

edited by
Dion C. Smythe

ASHGATE
VARIORUM

Aldershot • Burlington USA • Singapore • Sydney

Published by Variorum for the Society for the Promotion of Byzantine Studies

Ashgate Publishing Limited
Gower House, Croft Road
Aldershot, Hampshire GU11 3HR
United Kingdom

Ashgate Publishing Company
131 Main Street
Burlington, Vermont 05401
USA

Ashgate website: http://www.ashgate.com

ISBN 0–86078–814–8

British Library Cataloguing-in-Publication Data
Strangers to Themselves: the Byzantine Outsider. Papers from the Thirty-second
Spring Symposium of Byzantine Studies, University of Sussex, Brighton, March
1998. – (Society for the Promotion of Byzantine Studies Publication: 8)
1. Byzantine Empire – Civilisation – Congresses
I. Smythe, Dion II. Society for the Promotion of Byzantine Studies
949.5′013

US Library of Congress Cataloging-in-Publication Data
The Library of Congress Catalog Card Number has been preassigned as :
00 – 130354

This volume is printed on acid-free paper.

SOCIETY FOR THE PROMOTION OF BYZANTINE STUDIES — PUBLICATION 8
Printed and bound in Great Britain by MPG Books Ltd, Bodmin, Cornwall

Contents

vi   CONTENTS

Editor's Preface

As symposiarch of the thirty-second Spring Symposium – outsider by name and outsider by nature – I find myself with a happy task of thanking the many people who enabled the 'symposium that almost didn't happen' to take place. I blame Liz James, myself. She e-mailed me with the rash suggestion of a second symposium at Sussex, and failed to bring me down with a tackle when I lifted the ball and ran. She persuaded the authorities at the University of Sussex that an invasion of Byzantinists for the second year running would be a good idea; she drew together (all the while protesting that the symposium was nothing to do with her) the local team without which 'Strangers' would have been impossible. Her 'Advice and Anecdotes' have helped greatly in bringing this volume to final fruition, though she bears no responsibility for its faults, errors and omissions.

It is a *topos* of these introductions to say that the symposia are the results of team-work. As we now know, just because something is a *topos* does not make it empty of meaning. Karen Wraith was local organizer: like the Byzantine title *mystikos*, it hides its meaning well. Karen Wraith was the person who made the symposium work: all the little problems that are never so little just vanished. Without her the symposium could not have taken place. Bente Kortegård Bjørnholt was her admirable second in command, who led her local troops to victory. Many of these local troops are known only to themselves and God, but honourable mention and my sincerest thanks go to Bev Barstow, Ed Davis, Martin Dench and David Felton who turned out yet again to stand and wait.

Thanks beyond measure are also due to the many charitable trusts and foundations that enabled the symposium to take place. Support was received from the British Academy, the Hellenic Foundation, the Leventis Foundation and Variorum (a division of Ashgate Publishing Limited). Their generous support of the Spring Symposia, now extending over many years, enables the work of these conferences to continue. As symposiarch of Sussex '98, I am grateful also to the Society for the Promotion of Byzantine Studies, who agreed to underwrite the conference should it fail to break even. There was no need for Jubilee remission; and for that I thank all those who registered, paid and occupied the rooms that had been pre-booked and bought the mugs and t-shirts, all of which helped pay for the event. Without symposiasts inside, symposia are as nothing.

I envisioned 'Strangers' as an exploration of the ways in which the concept of 'outsider' could be used to explore issues in Byzantine studies. Speakers were asked not to focus on lists of foreigners, but to play with the concept in new and divergent ways. They took me at my word. I thank all the speakers who came to Brighton willing to venture something new. The papers presented here give some flavours of what we talked about, what we discussed and what we heard. Those readers who turn to the concluding paper by Robin Cormack expecting to find 'the answer' will come away disappointed: there is no single answer and to expect one is to miss the point. One has to be outside the question in a way to see its relevance. What I hope emerged at 'Strangers 98' and what is clear in this collection of papers, is that the concept of the outsider and outsiderness can provide interesting avenues of exploration through Byzantine studies.

The production of a volume is always a daunting undertaking. I am grateful to John Smedley, Ruth Peters and Kirsten Weissenberg (all three great exponents of *sang-froid* and dispatch) at Ashgate Publishing Limited for all their help and willingness to deal with missed deadlines, slow working, Spanish practices of all sorts and naïve questions. I also wish to record my thanks to Robin Cormack as Chairman of the SPBS executive and Elizabeth Jeffreys as series editor and chair of the SPBS publications committee for their staunch support. The final debt is to Daniel Farrell who compiled the index.

Dion C. Smythe
just outside the
City of London
December, 1999

Abbreviations

AnalBoll	*Analecta Bollandiana*
B	*Byzantion*
Blockley, *FCH*	R.C. Blockley, *The Fragmentary Classicizing Historians of the Later Roman Empire* (Liverpool, 1981–3)
BMGS	*Byzantine and Modern Greek Studies*
ByzFors	*Byzantinische Forschungen*
Bsl	*Byzantinoslavica*
BZ	*Byzantinische Zeitung*
DOP	*Dumbarton Oaks Papers*
EHR	*English Historical Review*
Jones, *LRE*	A.H.M. Jones, *The Later Roman Empire* (Oxford, 1964).
JÖB	*Jahrbuch der Österreichischen Byzantinistik*
JRS	*Journal of Roman Studies*
JThS	*Journal of Theological Studies*
ODB	*Oxford Dictionary of Byzantium*, ed. A. Kazhdan, 3 vols (Oxford and New York, 1991)
P&P	*Past and Present*
REB	*Revue des études byzantines*
Stein II	E. Stein, *Histoire du Bas-Empire*, vol. 2 (Amsterdam, 1949).
TM	*Travaux et mémoires*

For all other abbreviations, consult *JÖB*, and the main English-anguage Greek lexica (LSJ, Lampe, Sophocles)

Plates

1. The 'Other' in Byzantium

Margaret Mullett

Had a symposium on the Byzantine outsider been held in France, there is no doubt that the 'Other' would have dominated discussion. A symposium in Sussex on the Byzantine outsider promised more eclectic – if not less prejudiced – approaches. After all, we all know what an outsider is, don't we? Someone who doesn't quite fit in, not one of us, a bit of a rebel perhaps, a loner.[1] We might have said forty years ago 'an Angry Young Man', in celebration of Colin Wilson's instant best-seller, perhaps the true progenitor of the symposium. This book, *The Outsider*, a study of Barbusse, and Camus, Hesse and Dostoevsky, T.E. Lawrence, Van Gogh and Nijinsky, Blake and Kierkegaard,[2] was deeply affected by the existentialist milieu out of which emerged Simone de Beauvoir, who in *The Second Sex* first introduced many academic feminists to the concept of alterity, to the idea of woman as not the subject of academic inquiry, but as the object, the Other.[3] She did this with her famous accusation of sexism against Levinas's *Time and the Other* which – as his editor Hand says – 'appears to offer a male-oriented discourse', as he brings the Subject out into alterity to meet work, death, eros and fecundity.[4] He was indebted to Husserl and Heidegger and ultimately to Freud; but

---

[1]   For more rigorous definitions, see D.C. Smythe, 'Byzantine perceptions of the outsider in the eleventh and twelfth centuries: a method' (Unpublished PhD thesis, St Andrews, 1992).

[2]   C. Wilson, *The Outsider* (London, 1956).

[3]   S. de Beauvoir, *Le deuxième sexe* (Paris, 1949), tr. H.M. Parshley, *The Second Sex* (Harmondsworth, 1972).

[4]   De Beauvoir, *Second Sex*, 16 and n. 1; E. Levinas, 'Le temps et l'autre', in J. Wahl, ed., *Le choix, le monde, l'existence* (Grenoble and Paris, 1947), tr. R.A. Cohen, *Time and the Other* (Pittsburgh, PA, 1987); S. Hand, *The Levinas Reader* (Oxford, 1989), 38; J. Llewellyn, *Emmanuel Levinas; the Genealogy of Ethics* (London, 1995), esp. 98–99; C. Davis, *Levinas: an Introduction* (Cambridge, 1996), esp. 38–47; I am grateful to Dr Stephen Kelly for advice here.

From *Strangers to Themselves: The Byzantine Outsider*, ed. Dion C. Smythe. Copyright © 2000 by the Society for the Promotion of Byzantine Studies. Published by Ashgate Publishing Ltd, Gower House, Croft Road, Aldershot, Hampshire, GU11 3HR, Great Britain.

postmodern French feminists through Lacan have come to terms with the
concept, and indeed with Levinas.[5] We may still be shocked when we
come upon this sexist discourse, especially in its least explicit forms: the
interpolated first sentence of the *ODB* entry on women, 'the Byzantine
attitude towards women was ambivalent', appears again, almost
verbatim, in Cavallo's anthology *The Byzantines*, placing in question the
status of the exercise as a whole.[6] Who are these Byzantines? we ask. Are
these male Byzantines? Or did female Byzantines collude in their ascribed
status, so marginalized as to be off the map? Or just the Byzantines who
have left us a record? This is a major methodological problem of the
symposium theme: how do we arrive at 'the Byzantines' for whom there
is an 'Other'? (Anthropologists have recently become cautious about
generalizing from a few subjects to a whole community,[7] and this is an
issue which goes to the heart of historical method as well.) But the Other
for Levinas is not just the feminine (or the female), and its priority is at
the basis of his philosophy: he is endlessly obligated to it and responsible
for it.[8] For Edward Said, however, the Other involves detachment and
exteriority: orientalists (in Said's sense) comment on the oriental with a
certainty that these (orientalist and oriental) are watertight compart-
ments: the orientalists make of themselves – or Said makes of them –
outsiders.[9] In a way, the intellectual or artist as outsider is not an
unfamiliar concept, though it is one that Wilson abandoned in his book as
too easy.[10]

But this exteriority is not what in English we regard as an outsider,
though we are notoriously unenthusiastic about intellectuals: our
outsider is far more like John Italos in Anna Komnene's *Alexiad*. He was a
powerful arguer, with his fists as well as with his tongue, and

---

[5] T. Moi, *Sexual/Textual Politics: Feminist Literary Theory* (London, 1985), 98–99; see for
example, L. Irigaray, 'Così fan tutti', *Ce sexe qui n'en est pas un* (Paris, 1997), 85–101; tr. C.
Porter (Ithaca, New York, 1985), 86–105. See Davis, *Levinas: an Introduction*, 140 on a
feminist reading of Levinas.

[6] *ODB*, III, 201; A.-M. Talbot, 'Women', in G. Cavallo, ed., *The Byzantines* (Chicago
and London, 1997), 117.

[7] For example A.P. Cohen, *Self Consciousness. An Alternative Anthropology of Identity*
(London, 1994), ix: 'I squirm with some discomfort'.

[8] See for example Levinas, 'Beyond intentionality', in A. Montefiore, ed., *Philosophy in
France Today* (Cambridge, 1983), 112–113.

[9] E.W. Said, *Orientalism. Western Conceptions of the Orient* (London, 1978; reprinted
Harmondsworth, 1995).

[10] Wilson, *Outsider*, 14–15.

neither his defective pronunciation nor the clipping of sounds
escaped the notice of most people and the better educated accused
him of vulgarity. It was this that led him to string his arguments
together with dialectic commonplaces. They were by no means
exempt from faults of composition and there was in them liberal
sprinkling of solecisms.

He fares no better in the *Timarion* where Pythagoras snubs him and he
gets into a fight with Diogenes the Cynic.[11] What is not ultimately clear is
why he is picked upon. It is surely not because of his heresy – though it
might be a more Byzantine approach to lampoon a representative of a
perceived minority than to apply the stereotypes Jeffrey Richards studies;
Richards follows Gilman in interpreting these stereotypes of leprosy,
disease, sodomy and witchcraft in terms of the self and the Other.[12] But is
Italos mocked because of his perceived provincialism? The boy from the
backwoods? (Alexios Komnenos, also from the sticks, in Paphlagonia,
made very good, is sneered at only by twentieth-century Byzantinists[13]).
Or is his problem ethnicity? Perceptions of certain westerners in
Byzantium are explored below by David Jacoby.[14] Or was he seen more
like poor patriarch Tryphon, who inadvertently signed his own
resignation, because of inadequate literacy skills?[15] Snobbery, prejudice,
discrimination, a sense of personal and cultural superiority, all
concomitants of labelling as we know it.[16]

---

[11] Anna Komnene, *Alexiad*, V.viii, ed. B. Leib, 3 vols (Paris, 1937–45), II, 32–337;
Timarion, ch. 43–44, lines 1077–1121, ed. R. Romano, *Timarione*, Byz et NeoHellNeap 2
(Naples, 1974), 88–89.

[12] J. Richards, *Sex, Dissidence and Damnation: Minority Groups in the Middle Ages*
(London and New York, 1990); S.L. Gilman, *Difference and Pathology: the Stereotypes of
Sexuality, Race and Madness* (New York, 1985).

[13] L. Clucas, *The Trial of John Italos and the Crisis of Intellectual Values in Byzantium in the
Eleventh Century*, Misc.Byz.Monac. 26 (Munich, 1981), esp. 3–8.

[14] See Jacoby, below 129–147.

[15] John Skylitzes, *Synopsis historion*, ed. H. Thurn, *Synopsis historiarum, editio princeps*
(CFHB, 5, Berlin and New York, 1973), 226–227.

[16] H.S. Becker, *Outsiders: Studies in the Sociology of Deviance* (New York, 1963); J.I.
Kitsuse, 'Societal reaction to deviant behavior', *Social Problems* 9 (1962), 247–256; E. Lemert,
'Stuttering and social structure in two Pacific island communities', in E. Lemert ed., *Human
Deviance, Social Problems and Social Control* (Englewood Cliffs, NJ, 1967), 183–206; D. Matza,
Becoming Deviant (Englewood Cliffs, NJ, 1969); E. Goode, 'On behalf of labeling theory',
Social Problems 22 (1974–75), 570–583; A. Liazos, 'The poverty of the sociology of deviance:
nuts, sluts and preverts', *Social Problems* 20 (1972–73), 103–120; M. Freilich, D. Raybeck, J.
Savishinsky, eds, *Deviance: Anthropological Perspectives* (New York, Westport, CT and
London, 1991).

The organizers of the symposium set a visual puzzle, by choosing as the conference poster fol. 1(2bis)[v] of the Paris Homilies of John Chrysostom (Coislin 79). What we see here in these richly luxurious pages is the charmed circle of Byzantine rule: the Almighty who crowns and legitimates his vice-gerent who crowns and so legitimates the *augousta*, who is essential to the empire. What could be more on the inside track? How can Nikephoros and Maria (or Michael and Maria[17]), be outsiders? Maria of Alania was of course a Georgian princess, one of the marriers-in whose acculturation was discussed at the symposium by Barbara Zeitler. But these marriers-in, it has been argued, were essential to the development of Byzantine culture in the period.[18] Maria was also of course a woman, and vulnerable as a mother, though she was one of those who turned that vulnerability into strength in the 1080s.[19] She was a serial bride, which might have been difficult at some periods,[20] and she is regarded by some writers to have taken the veil, though it has to be said it did not cramp her style very much.[21] If we regard this as Michael VII, we see an emperor who lost out to a usurper and was to live out his life as metropolitan of Ephesus in the monastery of Manuel in Constantinople, a loser if not an outsider.[22] If we regard him as

---

[17] Paris. Coislin 79, fol. 1 (2bis). The illustration was apparently first of Michael and Maria, then after the change of regime was cut out and pasted into a new frame, relabelled as Nikephoros and altered to make his face look older. In contrast, fol. 1 (2bis)[v] was a 'new' picture of Nikephoros. See H.C. Evans and W.D. Wixom, eds, *The Glory of Byzantium* (New York, 1997), 182 and 207–209.

[18] E. Jeffreys, 'Western infiltration of the Byzantine aristocracy: some suggestions', in M. Angold, ed., *The Byzantine Aristocracy, IX–XIII centuries*, BAR Int ser. 221 (Oxford, 1983), 202–210; see D. Smythe, 'Women as outsiders', in L. James, ed., *Women, Men and Eunuchs: Gender in Byzantium* (London, 1995), 149–167 at 158f. on Maria as insider.

[19] M.E. Mullett, 'Alexios Komnenos and imperial renewal', in P. Magdalino, ed., *New Constantines: the Rhythm of Imperial Renewal in Byzantium*, SPBS 2 (Aldershot, 1994), 257–267; B. Hill, 'Alexios I Komnenos and the imperial women', in M. Mullett and D. Smythe, eds, *Alexios I Komnenos*, I, *Papers*, BBTT, 4.1 (Belfast, 1996), 37–54.

[20] J. Beaucamp, *Le statut de la femme à Byzance (4e–7e siècle)*, I, *Le droit impérial*, Travaux et mémoires, Monographies 5 (Paris, 1990), 226–238; A.E. Laiou, *Mariage, amour et parenté à Byzance aux XIe–XIIIe siècles*, Travaux et mémoires, Monographies 7 (Paris, 1992), 12–13; see also Beaucamp, below, 87–103.

[21] She is shown as receiving panegyric and endowing monasteries in the early 1080s, Theophylact, *Paideia basilike*, ed. P. Gautier, *Théophylacte d'Achrida: discours, traités, poésies*, CFHB 16/1 (Thessalonike, 1980), 185–193; bringing up Anna in the late 1080s to early 1090s, *Al.*, III.1.4, ed. Leib, I, 105, and being suspected of involvement in the Diogenes conspiracy in 1094, *Al.*, IX.viii.2, ed. Leib, II, 179.

[22] Zonaras, *Epitome historion*, XVIII.19, ed. T. Büttner-Wobst, CSHB (Bonn, 1897), III, 723.

Nikephoros Botaneiates, he describes himself in a message to the Komnenoi in Anna's history as a lonely old man with neither son nor brother nor relative; when the Komnenos brothers took over the city he was taken to the Peribleptos from Hagia Sophia and tonsured:

> Such is the way of fortune: when she wishes to smile on a man she exalts him on high, crowns him with a royal diadem, gives him sandals of purple; but when she frowns instead of the purple and the crown she clothes him in ragged garments of black. And this was the fate of Botaneiates now. When he was asked by one of his friends if he found the change tolerable, he replied: 'abstinence from meat is the only thing that worries me: the other matters cause little concern.'[23]

What we can say about all of them is that if the manuscript is to be dated to either side of 1078, three years later they were all three out of the inner circle of empire, Michael in the Manuel, Nikephoros in the Peribleptos, Maria in an alternative court at the Mangana, making up to her adopted son the new emperor, then progressively slipping from power as Alexios and John ceased to need her.[24] If Cheynet has made us see usurpation or attempted usurpation as the cornerstone of the Byzantine political way of life, the transience of empire was revealed long ago by Guilland's lists of the fates of Byzantine emperors.[25] We should also bear in mind the dependence of our historical record on disgraced or exiled politicians: we think not just of Kantakouzenos exploring his past in the light of a new identity, but Anna in Kecharitomene, Zonaras in Hagia Glykeria, Kinnamos out of office, Niketas excluded from Constantinople and voicing an exile culture are the norm not the exceptions.[26] Even the most

---

[23] *Al.*, III.i.1, ed. Leib, I, 103–104.

[24] M.E. Mullett, 'The "disgrace" of the ex-basilissa Maria', *BS* 45 (1984), 202–211.

[25] J.-C. Cheynet, *Pouvoir et contestations à Byzance 963–1250*, ByzSorb 9 (Paris, 1990); R. Guilland, 'Le destinée des empereurs de Byzance', *EEBS* 24 (1954), 37–66.

[26] For Kantakouzenos see D.M. Nicol, *The Reluctant Emperor: a Biography of John Cantacuzene, Byzantine Emperor and Monk, c. 1295–1383* (Cambridge, 1996); for Anna, still G. Buckler, *Anna Comnena; a Study* (Oxford, 1929); for Zonaras, I. Grigoriadis, 'Linguistic and literary studies in the *Epitome Istorion* of John Zonaras' (Unpublished PhD thesis, St Andrews, 1996), for Kinnamos, R. Macrides and P. Magdalino, 'The fourth kingdom and the rhetoric of hellenism', in P. Magdalino, ed., *The Perception of the Past in Twelfth-Century Europe* (London, 1992), for Niketas Choniates, A. Kazhdan, *Studies on Byzantine Literature of the Eleventh and Twelfth Centuries*, Past and Present Publications (Cambridge, 1984), ch. VII, 256–286, and Kazhdan's extensive but unpublished commentary on Niketas. There is a

frequently used source of our most cherished visualizations of the
Byzantine way of life, the Madrid Skylitzes, has been shown to be an
outsider's view, what a group of artists in Norman Sicily thought went on
in Byzantium.[27]

So should we see our symposium icons as individuals, or as
representative of a group? Snapshots or group portraits?[28] Should we
compare Maria or Nikephoros or Michael to those Byzantines who we all
have an inkling are not just the most characteristic, like Kekaumenos, let
us say, or Neophytos or Symeon the New Theologian?[29] There is some
doubt whether as historians we should be doing this labelling anyway,
and even if we internalize what we can reconstruct of the Byzantine value
system, we have our own prejudices to deal with. Kekaumenos, let us
admit, has more than a flavour of 'Disgusted, Tunbridge Wells' about
him; can anyone be so suspicious of mushrooms, doctors, friends,
bureaucrats let alone symposia? We find it much easier to accept
Galatariotou's characterization of him as a man who felt he was just
about to break at the seams than to accept Kazhdan's assumption that his
fears as expressed in the *Strategikon* can be used to posit a generalized
Byzantine culture of fear.[30] But here is the rub, Cohen's crux: to generalize
from an exception, an eccentric, an outsider, looks highly dubious. If it
was embarrassing for Cohen as an anthropologist to look back on his
early work and realize he had generalized from seven informants,[31] to
posit a culture of fear from a single informant is not best practice in

---

sense of course in which – even in Byzantium – 'all political careers end in failure' and in
their rewriting.

[27]   For the Skylitzes manuscript, see A. Grabar and M. Manoussacas, *L'illustration du
manuscrit de Skylitzes de la Bibliothèque nationale de Madrid*, Bibliothèque de l'Institut
hellénique d'études byzantines et post-byzantines de Venise 10 (Venice, 1979); for the
dating, N.G. Wilson, 'The Madrid Skylitzes', *Scrittura e civiltà* 2 (1978), for its Sicilian nature
see I. Ševčenko, 'The Madrid ms of Skylitzes in the light of its new dating', in I. Hutter, ed.,
Byzanz und der Westen. Studien der Kunst des europäischen Mittelalters, Österreichische
Akademie der Wissenschaften, Phil.hist. Kl., Sitzungsberichte 432 (Vienna, 1984), 117–130;
a Belfast project, with partners in Melbourne and Sussex, will examine aspects of
interculturality and perception of display as well the basic issues of narrative; cf. now R.
Cormack, 'Lessons from "The glory of Byzantium" ', *Dialogos* 5 (1998), 27–39 at 32.

[28]   As suggested by Robin Cormack at the symposium.

[29]   See below, Greatrex, 215–228 on Procopius as an example of this approach.

[30]   On Kekaumenos see C. Galatariotou, 'Open space/closed space: the perceived
worlds of Kekaumenos and Digenes Akritas', *Alexios I Komnenos*, I, 302–328; A. Kazhdan
and G. Constable, *People and Power in Byzantium: an Introduction to Modern Byzantine Studies*
(Washington, DC, 1982), 36 and below, Roueché, 203–214.

[31]   Cohen, *Self Consciousness*, ix.

history either. But it is harder for us than for the anthropologist: he can go back and ask the others – or record what the Others told his wife[32] – whereas we are stuck with Kekaumenos and can only attempt to construct for him a context, which Charlotte Roueché does below.[33] How about Symeon the New Theologian? It took a long time to detach him from an apparently seamless hesychast tradition, and make him an outsider who needed to be rehabilitated by an enthusiastic pupil;[34] it took another stage before John McGuckin showed us the Symeon who was an aristocratic monastic founder, at the heart of late tenth-century court life and politics.[35] Or Neophytos of Cyprus: here Galatariotou presents him not as the cranky outsider his writings and patronage suggest[36] but as the outsider who is the quintessential Brownian holy man, required by society to stand outside the norms of society, and in particular needed because of the evils of Cyprus at the time, long after the holy man had proved redundant in Constantinople.[37]

This is another option, a structural-functionalist view. Should we see Michael/Nikephoros and Maria as necessary outsiders in a rather similar way? It is only a matter of time, I think, before the prevalence, the almost structural prevalence, of usurpation in Byzantium is set in the anthropological context of stranger-kings.[38] Even if we jib at that idea, we may concede that an emperor is set apart from the populace through his court, ringed by eunuchs who are themselves made strange, marked by

---

[32] See Cohen's discussion, *Self Consciousness*, 80–90, of recent reassessment of John Campbell's fieldwork for *Honour, Family and Patronage: a Study of Institutions and Moral Values in a Greek Mountain Community* (Oxford, 1964) following the publication of J.K. Campbell, 'Fieldwork among the Sarakatsani 1954–55', in J. de Piña-Cabral and J.K. Campbell, eds, *Europe Observed* (Basingstoke, 1992), 148–166.

[33] See below, Roueché, 203–214.

[34] I. Hausherr, 'Paul Évergétis a-t-il connu Syméon le Nouveau Théologien?', *OCP* 23 (1957), 58–79.

[35] J.A. McGuckin, 'Symeon the New Theologian (d.1022) and Byzantine monasticism', in A. Bryer and M. Cunningham, eds, *Mount Athos and Byzantine Monasticism*, SPBS 4 (Aldershot, 1996), 17–36.

[36] His autohagiography is matched by peculiarities of iconography and architecture such as angelic ascent with shared wings, and the placing of his special chamber *vis-à-vis* the Ascension in the vault; see R. Cormack, *Writing in Gold* (London, 1985), 229–251.

[37] C. Galatariotou, *The Making of a Saint: the Life, Times and Sanctification of Neophytos the Recluse* (Cambridge, 1991).

[38] See for example forthcoming work by Declan Quigley predicated on M. Sahlins, *Islands of History* (London and New York, 1987).

the initiation or installation rituals which are imperial ceremony.[39] What we see in Coislin 79 is a visual iteration of that installation, and also the legitimation of usurpation and erasure in this palimpsest[40] image. But why Maria? Why is the Other needed as well as the Subject in this most basic scene of imperial iconography?

All this depends on how you view outsiders, and what kind of theory you read. Smythe's labelling theory is primarily sociological, concerned with the largest of units, but if we look at smaller groups anthropology offers various insights into ethnicity, liminality, assimilation, the performative *egoismos* of Herzfeld and the new reflexivity which sees the anthropologist in the field as magician, trickster, outsider;[41] to psychology we owe concepts of the Self and the Other, the anatomy of the smallest unit of all;[42] all of these disciplines have claims on the concept of identity and all of us need to engage with this concept. As outsiders like Said's orientalists, we may think we can spot an outsider – but when we start to look at what they have themselves to say we are forced to rethink. Everyone is an insider when you examine her personal network. It is only when you begin to add to that network the networks of others that the picture becomes harder to read.[43] If we take for example a diagram of

---

[39] Classically M. Fortes, 'On installation ceremonies', *Proceedings of the Royal Anthropological Institute* (1968), 5–19.

[40] In the sense that the image of the emperor has been altered, not in the sense of a scraped and rewritten manuscript.

[41] On ethnicity see for example R. Jenkins, *Rethinking Ethnicity: Arguments and Explorations* (London, Thousand Oaks and New Delhi, 1997); on liminality, T.M. Wilson and H. Donnan, eds, *Border Identities: Nation and State at International Frontiers* (Cambridge, 1998); for *egoismos*, M. Herzfeld, *The Poetics of Manhood: Contest and Identity in a Cretan Mountain Village* (Princeton, 1985); on reflexivity with anthropologist as magician, K. Hastrup, 'Writing ethnography: state of the art', in J. Okely and A. Lock, eds, *Anthropology and Autobiography* (London, 1992); as trickster, V. Crapanzaro, *Hermes' Dilemma and Hamlet's Desire: on the Epistemology of Interpretation* (Cambridge, 1992). The paper of Stephenson, below, 239–251, owes something to these approaches, as well as to B. Anderson, *Imagined Communities: Reflections on the Origin and Spread of Nationalism* (London and New York, 1983).

[42] See for example J. Lacan, *Écrits* (Paris, 1966), tr. A. Sheridan, *Jacques Lacan, Écrits, a Selection* (London, 1977), especially ch. 2, 'The function and field of speech and language in psychoanalysis', ch. 5, 'The agency of the letter in the unconscious or reason since Freud', and ch. 9, 'The subversion of the subject and the dialectic of desire in the Freudian unconscious'. The paper of Simeonova, below, 223–238, touches on issues of the self.

[43] Contrast figs 2 and 3 in M. Mullett, *Theophylact of Ochrid: Reading the Letters of a Byzantine Archbishop*, BBOM 2 (Aldershot, 1997), 192, 195.

twelfth-century letter-writers in Byzantium,[44] we see that there seem to be some authors hardly connected to any of those best connected of letter-writers. Yet when we look closer we see that most of these are monks, and if we look in monastic *typika* of the period we discover that monks are in some cases expressly forbidden to carry on correspondences;[45] it is unlikely that correspondence between the monastery and the world would have been the norm when letters do exist. The slightest knowledge of ideology may quickly undermine what appears to be empirical observation.

So it is probably worth exploring, briefly, whether the Byzantines thought at all in these terms of exteriority, of exclusion, of ins and outs. They talk of course of an inner and an outer learning, of St Anthony's inner and outer Mountain, of inner and outer narthekes leading the faithful towards the sanctuary, from which some are excluded. They also think in terms of concentricity, of pupils as a *kyklos* around a great man or a patroness, or of rhetors as a *choros*, rather like the dancers in an eleventh-century psalter in the Vatican.[46] Concentricity is certainly one way the Byzantines thought about cosmology,[47] and in the *Alexian Komnenian Muses* there is a clear image of the emperor in the City at the centre, the empire around, and beyond that the encircling barbarians:

> At that suit of armour the Celt trembles,
> The Norman, seeing the support it gives
> shortens canvas and timidly sails back,
> at this the Persian and the whole breed of the Scythians,
> at this the nations of the Arabs shudder,
> at this the Abasgian, the audacious Keltiber
> and the Indian race and the army of the Maurousioi
> and the throng lying opposite on parallel sides,
> at the north wind and at the south pole;
> and they say the Ethiopians lie opposite.[48]

---

[44]   M.E. Mullett, 'Theophylact through his letters', Fig. IIa (Unpublished PhD thesis, Birmingham, 1981), II, 825.

[45]   For example *Hypotyposis* of Evergetis, 902–903, ed. P. Gautier, 'Le typikon de la Théotokos Évergétis', *REB* 40 (1982), 5–111 at 65–67.

[46]   Vat.gr.752, 1058–59, Miriam's dance, see *Glory of Byzantium*, fig. 142.

[47]   Vat.gr.1291, fol. 9r: Ptolemy's geography: the zodiac, see A. Cutler and J.-M. Spieser, *Byzance médiévale 700–1204* (Paris, 1996), fig. 30.

[48]   *Mousai*, I.272–281, P. Maas, ed., 'Die Musen des Kaisers Alexios I', *BZ* 22 (1913), 348–367 at 356; R.H. Jordan and C.E. Roueché, eds and trs, *Alexios I Komnenos*, II, BBTT, 4.2 (Belfast, forthcoming).

What we are offered in pictures is rather different, the world-view of Kosmas Indikopleustes,[49] who manages to appear to combine extreme political orthodoxy with extraordinary cosmological eccentricity. Does this make him another outsider – or is his just one Byzantine viewpoint among many? Perhaps the middle Byzantine microcosm[50] is as close as we can get to a thoroughly orthodox world-view, with Pantokrator in the dome, Virgin in the cave, feast scenes in vaults and saints on walls.[51]

There are other kinds of spatial representation Byzantines went in for: a ladder shows the progression upwards, step by step, of ascetics towards the divine, assailed by temptations and *logismoi*, and overshadowed by patrons, and some drop off.[52] Ascending scales, of virtues,[53] of human relationships from slave–master up to brother–brother,[54] from trivium to quadrivium to theology, or rhetoric to psalter to epistle to gospel,[55] exist, just as downward models are also found. The emperor tramples on

---

[49] Sinai.gr.1186, fol. 66r, ed. W. Wolka-Comus (SC, 141, Paris, 1968), 186; cf. *Through Byzantine Manuscripts* (Greek Ministry of Culture, Athens, 1995), fig. 32.

[50] T. Mathews, 'The sequel to Nicaea II in Byzantine church decoration', *Perkins Journal* 42 (1988), 11–21.

[51] Kokkinobaphos homilies, Vat.gr.1162, 2v: the microcosm, see Cutler and Spieser, *Byzance*, fig. 293.

[52] Sinai: Klimakos icon, see Weitzmann, *The Icon* (London, 1978), pl. 25.

[53] Various Byzantine virtue-systems coexist: the ancient imperial virtues of panegyric (*andreia, dikaiosyne, phronesis, sophrosyne*, supplemented in *parainesis* by *sophia, praotes, philanthropia* and above all by *eusebeia*) have a close parallel in the novel, for example Eustathios Makrembolites, *Hysmine and Hysminias*, II.1–7: *phronesis, ischus, sophrosyne* and *themis*. But there are also Christian virtues, the three theological (*pistis, elpis, agape*) as well as the four cardinal. Klimax distinguishes between natural virtues (*eleemosyne, agape, pistis, elpis*) and those which are beyond nature (*agneia, aorgasia, tapeinophrosyne*), some of which do not seem to us like virtues at all but practices (*proseuche, agrypnia, nesteia, katanyxis*). In Klimax's ladder, the early rungs 3–6 are occupied by fundamental virtues (*hypakoe, metanoia, mneme thanatou, penthos*), ascending through rungs 7–23, which are the control of various vices, to the more advanced virtues of the higher rungs, 24–26, *praotes, tapeinophrosyne, diakrisis*, which enable the move into *physike* with *hesychia, proseuche, apatheia* and, at the very top, *agape*. This itself owes a great deal to Evagrios, both the progression from *praktike* through *physike* to *theologia* and the importance of the *praktike* stage for acquiring virtues, through resistance to the eight *logismoi*. See A. Louth, *The Origins of the Christian Mystical Tradition. From Plato to Denys* (Oxford, 1981), 100–113.

[54] For example Nicholas Kataskepenos, *VCyril*, 9.2, ed. E. Sargologos, *La vie de saint Cyrille le Philéote, moine byzantin (†1110)*, SubsidHag 39 (Brussels, 1964), 73.

[55] *Taxeis eis ta ekklesiastika offikia*, J, L, M, N, O, ed. J. Darrouzès, *Recherches sur les offikia de l'église byzantine*, AOC 11 (Paris, 1970), 555, 563, 566, 568, 571.

conquered peoples,[56] the heretic grovels at the feet of the synod,[57] as the resurrection sets the tone with Hades vanquished by the triumphant Christ.[58] Discrimination, the separation of sheep from goats,[59] observed by Campbell among the Sarakatsanai as applying to their gender-system,[60] is found in the Byzantine love of systematizing and listing. No other historians may have to deduce the organization of a bureaucracy from four seating plans for banquets – but we should be grateful that it was so important to note that the *strategos* of Kephallenia ranked above the *strategos* of Cherson, in that *taxis* which was represented in ceremony and to its practitioners ensured the continuity of a civilization.[61] Social exclusion[62] is demonstrated at its most final in representations of the Last Judgement[63] from the eleventh century on, which draw on various of the conceptualizations we have observed: the binary discrimination of sheep and goats, left and right; the vertical downward implications of the triumph over evil, the tidy pigeonholing of sinners by *taxis* or orders of society (bishops here, women there) or by category of sinners, by vice or, as Richards might say, by minority group.[64] Here are usurers, who succumbed to avarice; here are fallen women, who succumbed to the demons of *porneia*. Not here the circles of Dante's hell, or the confusion of Timarion's, or the joyful democracy of Moschos's vision of hell, where you might find yourself conveniently able to use a bishop as a leg-up.[65]

---

[56]   Marc.gr.17, fol. 3r: Basil Psalter, see Cutler and Spieser, *Byzance*, fig. 254.

[57]   Vat.gr.1613, fol. 108: Arius at Nicaea, see C. Walter, *L'iconographie des conciles dans lat tradition byzantine*, AOC, 13 (Paris, 1970), frontispiece.

[58]   A.D. Kartsonis, *Anastasis: the Making of an Image* (Princeton, 1986).

[59]   Ravenna, S. Apollinare Nuovo, see A. Grabar, *Byzantium from the Death of Theodosius to the Rise of Islam* (London, 1966), fig. 165.

[60]   Campbell, *Honour, Family and Patronage*, 31: 'women and goats are conceptually opposed to men and sheep'.

[61]   On the four *taktika*, see N. Oikonomidès, *Les listes de préséance byzantines des IXe et Xe siècles*, Le monde byzantin (Paris, 1972).

[62]   See L. Leontidou and A. Afouxenidis, 'Boundaries of social exclusion in Europe', in R. Hudson and A.M. Williams, eds, *Divided Europe* (London, 1998), 255–268, and the work of the Centre for Analysis of Social Exclusion, LSE, London. I am grateful to Graham McFarlane and (through him) Piero Vereni for advice here.

[63]   Torcello: west wall, see *Glory of Byzantium*, 437.

[64]   See G. Prinzing, 'Zu den Minderheiten in der Mäander-Region während der Übergangsepoche von der byzantinischen zur seldschukisch-türkischen Herrschaft (11. Jh.– Anfang 14. Jh.)' in P. Herz and J. Kobes, eds, *Ethnische und religiöse Minderheiten in Kleinasien. Von der hellenistischen Antike bis in das byzantinische Mittelalter*, Mainzer Veröffentlichungen zur Byzantinistik 2 (Wiesbaden, 1998), 153–177, for the 'minorities' approach.

[65]   John Moschos, *Pratum spirituale*, ch. 44, PG, 87.3, col. 2900A.

But models of exteriority also exist. Wherever there are walls, someone is outside them, in the wilderness.[66] The Long Wall in Thrace said to approaching barbarians, 'you're not inside yet'. City walls said to country-dwellers, 'this is what civilization is all about'. And monastery walls mark off what may be more an alternative society than a Kazhdanian microcosm of the world outside. St Basil said,

> There is but one escape from all this: separation from the world altogether. But withdrawal from the world does not mean bodily removal from it, but the severance of the soul from sympathy with the body and the giving up of city, home, personal possessions, love of friends, property, means of subsistence, business, social relations and knowledge derived from human teaching, and it also means the readiness to receive in one's heart the impressions engendered there by divine instruction.[67]

And *typika* suggest that what is envisaged by founders – in their prescriptive dreams – is a small enclosed community where the ways of the world do not prevail, and the laws of the state are less real than instructions over frequency of bathing or fasting on a feast-day in Lent.[68] Human relationships undergo a kind of atrophy inside a monastery: the complex bonds necessary for survival in outside life (of consanguines and affines, ritual kin and spiritual kin, patrons, clients and friends, lords and servants[69]) form a threat to the simple society of a monastic community,

---

[66] See below Ševčenko, 75–86, for a neatly reversed model in which the outsider ascetic strays into the insider world of the wilderness of the beasts.

[67] Basil, ep. 2, ed. and tr. R.J. Deferrari, *The Letters of St Basil* (Cambridge, MA, and London, 1961), I, 10–11.

[68] See the forthcoming J.P. Thomas and A.C. Hero, eds, *Byzantine Monastic Foundation Documents*, 4 vols, DOS 35 (Washington, DC, 2000). See www.doaks.org/typ000.html for electronic pre-publication.

[69] On various personal relations in Byzantine society see for ritual kinship, R. Macrides, 'The Byzantine god-father, *BMGS* 11 (1987), 139–162; fictive kinship, 'Kinship by arrangement: the case of adoption', *DOP* 44 (1990), 109–118; spiritual kinship, R. Morris, 'The political saint in the tenth and eleventh centuries', *Vorträge und Forschungen*, 42 (1993), 385–402 and H.J.M. Turner, *St Symeon the New Theologian and spiritual fatherhood*, Byzantina neerlandica 11 (Leiden and New York, 1990), 109–118; personal patronage, M.E. Mullett, 'Patronage in action: the problems of an eleventh-century bishop', in R. Morris, ed., *Church and People in Byzantium* (Birmingham, 1990), 125–147; friendship, M.E. Mullett, 'Byzantium: a friendly society?', *P&P* 118 (1987), 3–24, P. Hatlie, 'Friendship, politics and other disappointments during the Byzantine Iconoclast age' and M.E. Mullett, 'Friendship in Byzantium: genre, topos and network', both in J. Haseldine, ed., *Friendship in Medieval Europe* (Thrupp, 1999), 137–152; 166–184. For erotic relations see L. James, ed., *Desire and*

where *hegoumenos* and office-holders, novices and tonsured, spiritual father and spiritual son, are the small differentiations in a community where each member has taken on a new identity with a monastic name.[70] Only occasionally do marks of rank or kinship from the world outside impress themselves upon the community, or special friendships threaten the smooth running of this simpler cosmos – there is (with very few exceptions) no Byzantine equivalent to the spiritual friendship of the twelfth-century monastic West: spiritual love in Byzantium was directed from the Christian to God alone.[71] The social life of monasteries may sometimes be sensed in episodes of a saint's life, like Theodora of Thessalonike or Lazaros of Galesion,[72] but only Dirk Krausmüller has managed to exploit the shadowy catechetical sources to show the pecking order of *diakoniai* and *megaloschemai*, of the offices and ranks of the counter-culture.[73] Even the idea of community has its limitations in Byzantium: a sense of belonging was discouraged in Byzantine monasteries, and saints regularly are seen to move on when they become too much at home or too much loved by the abbot.[74] The best recent book on monasticism has been described by its most intelligent reviewer as 'an outsider's view':[75] perhaps this is what is needed, an outsider's view of professional, though perhaps not always high-achieving, outsiders.

Yet what also comes over from these prescriptive texts is the ability of the founder or patron in little ways to overturn norms, to step out of the

---

Denial in Byzantium, SPBS 7 (Aldershot, 1999). I hope soon to publish a (long-maturing) study of the detection of relationship in eleventh- and twelfth-century rhetorical texts.

[70] On monastic names see my introduction to M. Mullett and A. Kirby, eds, *Work and Worship at the Theotokos Evergetis*, BBTT 6.2 (Belfast, 1998), 1–20, esp. 10–17; on the importance of naming, see R.A. Alford, *Naming and Identity: a Cross-Cultural Study of Naming Practices* (New Haven, 1987).

[71] I intend to devote a separate study to this complex problem, but see M. Mullett, 'From Byzantium, with love', *Desire and Denial*, 1–22; 'Friendship in Byzantium', *Friendship in Medieval Europe*, 166–184.

[72] For Theodora see A.-M. Talbot, *Holy Women of Byzantium: Ten Saints' Lives in English Translation*, Byzantine Saints' Lives in Translation 1 (Washington, DC, 1996), 159–237; for Lazaros see the forthcoming volume by Richard Greenfield in the same series.

[73] See D. Krausmüller, 'The monastic communities of Stoudios and St Mamas in the second half of the tenth century', in M. Mullett and A. Kirby, eds, *The Theotokos Evergetis and Eleventh-Century Monasticism*, BBTT 6.1 (Belfast, 1994), 67–85.

[74] For example, *Bios kai politeia kai merike thaumaton diegesis tou hagiou kai thaumatourgou Nikonos myroblytou tou Metanoeite*, 12–15, ed. D.F. Sullivan, *The Life of St Nikon*, Archbishop Iakovos Library of Ecclesiastical and Historical Sources 14 (Brookline, MA, 1987), 58–66.

[75] R. Morris, *Monks and Laymen in Byzantium 843–1118* (Cambridge, 1995), review J. Munitiz, *JHS* 117 (1997), 268.

frame, to impress an individual stamp on a group of like-minded people. All patrons can buy this ability: the portraits of Theodore and Elene Gabras in St Petersburg State Library ms 291 show it very clearly.[76] But also Nancy Ševčenko has shown us how kicking over the traces on occasion, stepping over the bounds like the movie-star in *The Purple Rose of Cairo*, is something the most saintly of Byzantines could do.[77] Why the Gabrades have shown us themselves in no-nonsense 'warts & all' mode, the kind of provincial *archontes* we would otherwise have had to invent, is a question for the art historian as well as the historian. Why they showed themselves outside the frame (while taking full advantage of the spiritual intercession and support represented inside the frame) may be another order of question, and its answer, self-assertion combined with their wish to be both in and out of the text, goes to the heart of the concerns of this volume. For similar opportunities not to conform are limited in Byzantium: angry young men do not press upon our consciousness: Ptochoprodromos in his various personae must come as close as we can get; Robin Hood would not have stood much of a chance where emperors in ideology (and in crusader representation at least[78]) were the primary protectors of the poor and oppressed.[79] Even emperors had little scope for manoeuvre, when expectations of their role and behaviour were recalled to them frequently in imperial rhetoric and in *parainesis*,[80] and when day after day was taken up with mind-crippling ceremony. Transgression has been seen in the ability of imperial women to step over the gender lines – or gendered codes of sexual morality, in the amiable lunacy of holy fools, and hesychasts *vis-à-vis* coenobitic communities.[81] But examples in the literature are thin and the methodology underdeveloped.[82]

---

[76] Fols 2v and 3r, see A. Cutler and J.-M. Spieser, *Byzance médiévale, 700–1204* (Paris, 1996), 328–329, pls 258–259.

[77] N. Ševčenko, 'Contact between holy figures and the faithful as represented in Byzantine works of art', in A. Guillou and J. Durand, eds, *Byzance et les images* (Paris, 1994), 255–285.

[78] For example on the cover of the Melisende psalter; see H.C. Evans and W.D. Wixom, eds, *The Glory of Byzantium* (New York, 1997), 388.

[79] R. Morris, 'The powerful and the poor in tenth-century Byzantium', *P&P* 73 (1976), 3–27.

[80] On the difference see M. Mullett, 'The imperial vocabulary of Alexios I Komnenos', *Alexios I Komnenos*, I , 379–384.

[81] See for example C. Barber, 'The imperial panels at San Vitale: a reconsideration', *BMGS* 14 (1990), 19–42; D. Krueger, *Symeon the Holy Fool: Leontius's Life and the late antique city*, The Transformation of the Classical Heritage 25 (Berkeley, 1996), ch. 4, 57–71.

[82] L. Garland ed., *Conformity and non-conformity in Byzantium. Papers given at the eighth conference of the Australian Association for Byzantine Studies*, ByzForsch, 24 (Amsterdam, 1997)

Were things different, far from the *omphalos* of the *oikoumene*? Are there provincial values in Byzantium, if we can escape from the tadpole model of Byzantium, with a very big head and a very small tail?[83] Victor Turner would persuade us on the other hand that liminality is the crucial space, and Fredrick Barth that frontiers are where identities are forged, because there they are tested against others.[84] We should look to frontier society – if we can find it! The Corinth plate[85] may not be Digenes, but then Digenes may not be truly a borderer, at least a borderer of the historic Byzantine frontier with the Arabs, but an exile or a representative of the wrong border, in southern Italy.[86]

If opportunities for non-conformity were slight, opportunities for responding to it were manifold, and labelling is only one way. The Other may be confronted, and not just in war: in the eleventh and twelfth centuries, the largest single body of writing comes under the heading of religious polemic; the same must be true of the seventh. Set-piece disputations seem to be part of the life of the court, with theologians on hand to keep the empire's end up.[87] Reference to missionary activity is sparse; when it does appear, it is in the guise of disputations, as much as in the fruit of evangelism, baptism. Polemic eloquence is pictorial as well as verbal.[88] Or the Other can simply be left out, ignored, as happens to Jews in Byzantine historical narratives. We know that there was a flourishing community of Jews in Kastoria in the eleventh and twelfth

---

does not advance the subject beyond H.G. Beck, 'Formes de non-conformisme à Byzance', *Bulletin de l'Académie Belge*, ser. 5, 65 (1979), 313–329; there is no introduction, and of the contributors, only D. Smythe, 'Outsiders by *taxis*: perceptions of non-conformity in eleventh- and twelfth-century literature', 229–249, addresses the theoretical and methodological issues.

[83] See P. Magdalino, below, 149–150, for the New Yorker's view of the world.

[84] V. Turner, *The Forest of Symbols: Aspects of Ndenbu Ritual* (Ithaca, 1967), 93–111 and F. Barth, *Ethnic Groups and Boundaries: the Social Organisation of Culture Difference* (London, 1969), esp. 15–16; 122–134.

[85] See *Glory*, 254.

[86] E. Jeffreys, 'The Grottaferrata version of Digenes Akrites', in R. Beaton and D. Ricks, eds, *Digenes Akrites: New Approaches to Byzantine Heroic Poetry*, KCL 2 (Aldershot, 1993), 26–37; see also her new edition, *Digenis Akritis: the Grottaferrata and Escorial Versions*, Cambridge Medieval Classics 7 (Cambridge, 1998).

[87] See A. Cameron, 'Texts as weapons: polemic in the Byzantine dark ages', in A.K. Bowman and G. Woolf, eds, *Literacy and Power in the Ancient World* (Cambridge, 1994), 198–215.

[88] K. Corrigan, *Visual Polemics in the Ninth-Century Byzantine Psalters* (Cambridge, 1992); J.C. Anderson, 'Marginality in the ninth-century Byzantine psalters', written for E. Schwartz, ed., *Encountering the Other* (forthcoming, now to appear in a Festschrift).

centuries: Ann Epstein has tried to interpret some of the paintings of the Mauriotissa there in this light; Anna Komnene spends a great deal of her narrative around Kastoria with the Normans – yet notoriously she refers to Jews only three times. As Nicholas de Lange puts it, 'the presence of Jews in Byzantium has been overlooked', a modest expression of this kind of religious and cultural exclusion.[89] The Other can be written out in more subtle ways: Nicholas Kataskepenos in his life of Cyril Phileotes very cleverly avoids embarrassment for his readership in his handling of a typology of Elijah and the behaviour of the Komnenian imperial women. Far from the managing geniuses, termagants and assertive wives of Zonaras and Choniates, these women do not rant over the deathbed of their husbands or push their men scornfully into rebellion; they are seen feeding the sick saint by hand with a cup, or addressing him only in the characteristic words of the *Apophthegmata patrum*: father, give me a word.[90] They behave in fact more like the only one of their number who made it to the *Synaxarion* of Constantinople, the Hungarian Piroska-Eirene-Xene.[91] Otherwise the Other can be investigated and tracked down, in the ethnographies of Agathias and Constantine Porphyrogennetos, or appropriated as in Tzetzes's glorious boast of ancestry.[92] We engage with them on this literary level, but with how many of them? How badly skewed is our view of Byzantine society by our dependence

---

[89] Anna Komnene, *Al.*, VI.v.10, ed. Leib, II, 54 (*skala* of Jews in Constantinople); *Al.*, VII.iii.4, ed. Leib, II, 96 (Zedekiah last of the dynasty); *Al.*, XI.vi.9, ed. Leib, III, 32 (First Crusaders kill Jews and Muslims); none of these is relevant to Jewish communities in the Byzantine Empire, for which we must consult Benjamin of Tudela, ed. and tr. M.N. Adler, *The Itinerary of Benjamin of Tudela* (London, 1907); A. Epstein, 'Frescoes of the Mauriotissa monastery near Kastoria: evidence of millenarianism and anti-semitism in the wake of the first crusade', *Gesta* 21 (1982), 21–29, though it does not completely convince, amply reveals the historians' deficiency; on the implications see below, N. de Lange, 105–118.

[90] See B.N. Hill, 'Alexios I Komnenos and the imperial women', in Mullett and Smythe eds, *Alexios I Komnenos*, I, 37–54 for the stereotype; M.E. Mullett, *Death of a Genre*, forthcoming, for the spin.

[91] For Eirene, see *Synaxarion* of Constantinople, AASS, Nov.Prop. (Brussels, 1902), cols 887–890; G. Moravcsik, *Die Tochter Ladislaus des Heiligen und das Pantokrator-Kloster in Konstantinopel* (Budapest and Constantinople, 1923); M. Mathieu, 'Irène de Hongrie', *B* 23 (1953), 140–142; M. Živojinović, 'Le prologue slave de la vie de l'impératrice Irène', *ZbRad* 8 (1964), 483–492.

[92] For example Agathias, *Historiai*, II.23–31, ed. R. Keydell, *Agathiae Myrinaei historiarum libri quinque*, CFHB 2 (Berlin, 1967), 56–67; Constantine Porphyrogennetos, *Excerpta de legationibus*, see J. Shepard and D. Lee, 'A double life: placing the *Peri presbeon*', *BS* 52 (1991), 15–39; for Tzetzes, see P. Gautier, 'La curieuse ascendance de Jean Tzetzès', *REB* 28 (1970), 207–220.

on a written record? Who owned it,[93] and how fictional was the most apparently sober account?[94] Even pictorial narrative rarely stands alone, so much that the lack of an inscription can be in itself, like something left out of an encomium, more important than what is included. Two cases are the narthex panel in Hagia Sophia and the Vatican 666 portraits of Alexios I where the Fathers are named but he is not (the author is simply left out).[95] Some have tried to detect literacy levels by checking spellings in original documents on the assumption that the Byzantines were particularly finicky about orthography. But were they? Inscriptions on highly precious works of art suggest another story.[96] I mentioned earlier the sad tale of patriarch Tryphon who excluded himself from office by his illiteracy – but when reading is pictured as sitting on a high throne and listening to a monk who stands and reads from a lectern,[97] and writing as a flow diagram from the inspiring Holy Ghost through the dictating St John to the penning Prochoros,[98] we surely have to ask who is excluded from the experience on these grounds – and reconsider our interpretation of the significance of literacy skills in Byzantine society.

On occasion we indeed persuade ourselves that Byzantium was far from a persecuting society,[99] that heresy is all relative and it would be so easy to err a little too much on the other side,[100] that settled people and nomads can occupy the same territory (and with the second even welcomed by the first),[101] that lepers are provided with spacious and

---

[93] See below, J. Baun, 47–60.

[94] See below, R. Beaton, 179–188 for a consideration of Bakhtin's adventure-time.

[95] See discussions in R. Cormack, 'Interpreting the mosaics of S. Sophia at Istanbul', *Art History* 4 (1981), 139; P. Magdalino and R. Nelson, 'The emperor in Byzantine art of the twelfth century', *ByzForsch* 8 (1982), 124–126.

[96] J. Waring, 'Byzantine monastic libraries in the eleventh and twelfth centuries' (Unpublished PhD thesis, Belfast, 1998), 24–25.

[97] Paris homilies of John Chrysostom, fol. 1(2bis)r, the monk Sabas; see *Glory*, 82.

[98] Dionysiou 588, fol. 225v; see *Treasures of Mount Athos* (Thessalonike, 1997), 199.

[99] See R.I. Moore, *The Formation of a Persecuting Society* (Oxford, 1987).

[100] Certainly one explanation of the apparent surge in intellectual heresy under Alexios is the excessive enthusiasm of the polemicists against heresy: the cases of Neilos the Calabrian and Eustratios of Nicaea can both be read as failures in debates with the Armenians. For the alternative view see (first) R. Browning, 'Enlightenment and repression in Byzantium in the eleventh and twelfth centuries', *P&P* 69 (1975), 3–23.

[101] S. Vryonis, 'Cultural diversity and the breakdown of Byzantine power in Asia Minor', *DOP* 29 (1975), 1–20 and A.A.M. Bryer, 'Greeks and Türkmens: the Pontic exception', ibid., 113–148; *Diegesis merike*, ed. P. Meyer, *Die Haupturkunden für die Geschichte der Athosklöster* (Leipzig, 1984), 163–184 at 163.

comfortable leprosaria,[102] that gypsies, the ultimate outsiders, have unexpected defenders in pillars of court and church society,[103] that there were ways of getting away with murder in twelfth-century Constantinople.[104] Yet Byzantines did castrate children[105] and mutilate rebels, if only to eliminate them from competition.[106] They did whitewash icons,[107] burn books and (once)[108] a Bogomil. Perhaps a major task of this volume is to discover the limits of this postulated tolerance. We shall find certainly many examples of petty snobbery,[109] of delight in freaks of nature,[110] of a heightened sense of the pecking order, of a highly competitive sense of *asteiotes*[111] which shows Alexios I Komnenos – that man who had no time for rhetoric[112] – wincing when his home team of theologians failed to put up an adequate show against the visiting side.[113] And high-handed banishment to monastery or exile when anyone became a nuisance, in each case excluding them from the empire as conventionally defined.[114]

---

[102] A. Philipsborn, 'Hiera nosos und die Spezial-Anstalt des Pantokrator-Kranken-hauses', *B* 33 (1963), 223–226; T.S. Miller, *The Birth of the Hospital in the Byzantine Empire* (Baltimore, 1985) adds nothing.

[103] Nikephoros Gregoras, *Romaike Historia*, VIII.10, ed. L. Schopenus, CSHB (1829), 348–349 on the virtues of gypsies. I am grateful to Karin White for pointing me in this direction.

[104] R. Macrides, 'Killing, asylum and the law in Byzantium', *Speculum* 63 (1988), 509–514.

[105] See S. Tougher, 'Byzantine eunuchs: an overview with special reference to their creation and origin', in James, ed., *Women, Men and Eunuchs*, 168–184, esp. 170, 175–177, 178–180.

[106] E. Patlagean, 'Byzance et le blason pénal du corps', *Sodalitas* 6 (Rome, 1984), 405–426.

[107] Or at least the Khludov psalter represents them as so doing, see Cormack, *Writing in Gold*, fig. 45; fig. 39 shows in detail the alternative technique of excision and replacement.

[108] See Balsamon, *Comm in Nomokanon*, X.25, PG, 104, col. 1111.

[109] P. Magdalino, 'Byzantine snobbery', in M. Angold, ed., *The Byzantine Aristocracy*, 58–78.

[110] Even of the human variety; see Madrid Bib.Nac.vitr.26–2, fol. 131 b, c, ed. Grabar and Manoussacas, figs 159–160 for the siamese twins.

[111] P. Magdalino, 'In search of the Byzantine courtier', in H. Maguire, ed., *Byzantine Court Culture from 829 to 1204* (Washington, DC, 1997), 141–165 at 145–146.

[112] See even as recently as M. Angold, 'Alexios I Komnenos: an afterword', *Alexios I Komnenos*, I, 416.

[113] A. Amelli, 'Due sermoni inedite di Pietro Grosolano, archivescovo di Milano', *Fontes Ambrosiani* 4 (1933), 35f.; H. Bloch, 'Monte Cassino, Byzantium and the west in the earlier Middle Ages', *DOP* 4 (1946), 163–224 at 224.

[114] For monasteries as prisons and exile-places see J.M. Hussey, 'Byzantine monasticism', *CMH*, IV.ii (Cambridge, 1967), 161–184; E. Evert-Kappesowa, 'L'archipel de Marmara comme lieu d'exile', *ByzForsch* 5 (1977), 23–34.

How Byzantines – any Byzantines – defined themselves is another matter, and there is so much more work to do here. This issue of identity has followed us from Bryer's Wiles lectures through the St Andrews and Australian considerations of the ancient past in Byzantine consciousness, to Copenhagen.[115] It surfaces in two recent modern Greek conferences on Macedonian cultural identity, and in the King's meeting on Byzantium in modern Greek identity.[116] Paul Magdalino long ago pointed us to the Menandrian categories of *patris* and *genos*, and the modern Greek categories of honour and shame;[117] Bryer makes us rethink the boundaries between religious identity, language and ethnicity.[118] Individuals must seldom – except in the pages of Gregory Dialogos – have been given the opportunity to step outside their bodies and examine their 'self',[119] though the important work being done now in various centres on dreams and visions will allow us to step back ourselves from preconceived concepts of the self in Byzantium.[120] Issues of gender and orientation follow; Liz James's book demonstrated firmly that gender in Byzantium is still an issue, and suggested that there were only two of them;[121] and we may

---

[115] P. Magdalino, ed., *The Perception of the Past in Twelfth-Century Europe* (London, 1992); G. Clarke with B. Croke, R. Mortley and A. Emmett Nobbs, eds, *Reading the Past in Late Antiquity* (Canberra, 1990); K. Fledelius and P. Schreiner, eds, *Byzantium: Identity, Image, Influence. XIX International Congress of Byzantine Studies*, 2 vols (Copenhagen, 1995).

[116] P. Mackridge and E. Yannakakis, eds, *Ourselves and Others: the Development of a Greek Macedonian Cultural Identity since 1912* (Oxford and New York, 1997); J. Burke and R. Scott eds, *Byzantine Macedonia*, ByzAus (Melbourne, forthcoming); D. Ricks and P. Magdalino eds, *Byzantium and the Modern Greek Identity*, KCL 4 (Aldershot, 1998).

[117] P. Magdalino, 'Honour among *Romaioi*: the framework of social values in the world of Digenes Akrites and Kekaumenos', *BMGS* 13 (1989), 183–218.

[118] A.A.M. Bryer, 'The Crypto-Christians of the Pontos and Consul William Gifford Palgrave of Trebizond', *Deltio Kentrou Mikrasiatikon Spoudon* (Athens, 1983), 13–68; 363–365.

[119] For example Greg.Dial., I.12.2, ed. A. de Vogüé, tr. P. Antin, SC 260 (Paris, 1979), II, 114.

[120] Work on Byzantine dreams and visions, slow off the mark compared with recent work on classical and late antique dreams, was encouraged by the classic article of G. Dagron, 'Rêver de Dieu et parler de soi. Le rêve et son interprétation d'après les sources byzantines', in T. Gregory, ed., *I sogni nel medioevo*, Lessico Intelletuale Europeo 35 (Rome, 1985), 37–55, and by the patient labours of Steven Oberhelman; the volume D.I. Kyrtatas, ed., Ὄψις ἐνυπνίου (Heraklion, 1993) includes Byzantine material. Work is currently under way in Minnesota, in London with Charles Stewart, in Cambridge and Nijmegen with Robin Cormack and an Anglo-Dutch seminar, Birmingham with the work of George Calofonos and Belfast with the doctoral work of Margaret Kenny.

[121] James, ed., *Women, Men and Eunuchs*; for the two genders, see S. Tougher, 168–184 contra K. Ringrose, 'Living in the shadows: eunuchs and gender in Byzantium', in G. Herdt, ed., *Third Sex, Third Gender* (New York, 1994), 85–109.

after the 1998 New York conference on the Queer Middle Ages be less inclined to follow Foucault and Halperin rather than Richlin and Brooten on issues of sexual identity in pre-modern societies.[122] We should try to look at self-consciousness, in Cohen's sense, and at Kazhdan's postulated development of individualism in the wake of the vogue for autobiography in the middle Byzantine period. Yet autobiography has its own special traps: the ins and outs of the copying and appropriation of text in Byzantium could lead to the mindless plagiarism of autobiographical material and the original contribution of timeless truths.[123] Once we can reach the individual, we must look beyond: role relations enable individuals to locate themselves in a limited way within a community, and we must continue to collect scrupulously every example of how Byzantines defined themselves in relation to others, without which we cannot hope to understand any of these relationships, which form the spokes reaching out from the individual to the circumference of society.

---

[122] The greatest single contribution of M. Foucault, *History of Sexuality*, 3 vols was to present the concept of homosexuality as a modern construct; D. Halperin in *One Hundred Years of Homosexuality* (New York, 1990) developed this idea, showing the great gulf between ancient and twentieth-century attitudes, and joined other classicists, for example J. Winkler, *The Constraints of Desire* (New York, 1990); D. Halperin, J.J. Winkler and F. Zeitlin, *Before Sexuality: the Constructon of Erotic Experience in Ancient Greece* (Princeton, NJ, 1989), to characterize ancient sexuality more in terms of active/passive, penetrator/penetrated than erotic orientation towards the same or the opposite sex, the act rather than the person or the concept. A. Richlin, 'Not before homosexuality: the materiality of the cinaedus and the Roman law against love between men', *Journal of the History of Sexuality* 3.4 (1993), 523–573 and B.J. Brooten, *Love between Women: Early Christian Responses to Female Homoeroticism* (Chicago, 1996) have both highlighted the limitations of this approach, Richlin by concentrating on the existence of a recognizable homosexual type (the male penetrated by choice), Brooten by showing that the concept of orientation was used in ancient astronomical literature. This revisionism is still a long way, however, from the confident approach of J. Boswell, *Christianity, Tolerance and Social Welfare: Gay People in Western Europe from the Beginning of the Christian Era to the Fourteenth Century* (Chicago, 1980). See James, ed., *Desire and Denial* for fuller treatment of these issues, esp. papers by D. Smythe, S. Tougher and M. Mullett.

[123] For the rise of the individual see A. Kazhdan and A.W. Epstein, *Change in Byzantine Culture in the Eleventh and Twelfth Centuries*, Transformation of the Classical Heritage 7 (Berkeley, 1985), 197f.; for a survey of Byzantine autobiography see M. Angold, 'The autobiographical impulse in Byzantium', *DOP* 52 (1998), 225–257; for an example of religious autobiography, J. McGuckin, 'The luminous vision in eleventh-century Byzantium: interpreting the biblical and theological paradigms of St Symeon the New Theologian', *Work and Worship at the Theotokos Evergetis*, BBTT 6.2 (Belfast, 1998), 90–123; for autobiography and letters, Mullett, *Theophylact*, 281–288. See below R. Jordan, 61–73, for the Phoberou *typikon*'s rather surprising borrowing patterns.

This chapter has played with concepts of the Outsider and the Other, of minorities and marginalization, of identity and community, of conformity, dissidence and deviance, conversion and assimilation, of liminality and bordering, of ethnicity, gender, heterodoxy and *taxis*, of social exclusion and of alternative societies. It has touched on certain polarities: capital and province, centre and margin, norm and divergence, legal and illegal, heresy and orthodoxy, the settled and the nomad, the city and the desert, the civilized world and the wilderness, virtue and vice, literacy and illiteracy. But it has left unexplained so far the symposium title: 'Strangers to themselves'. This title clearly acknowledges the influential work of Julia Kristeva,[124] in which she looks at the history of foreignness in Europe, bringing with her the sense of being as it were an immigrant in the midst of post-structuralist Paris, as Theophylact would put it, a metropolitan, and, strange to say, a Bulgarian.[125] The phrase finds a curious echo in Theophylact's near contemporary and Maria's foster-daughter and Michael's potential daughter-in-law, Anna Komnene. When she describes at the very end of the *Alexiad* the effect on her of the death of Nikephoros Bryennios, she says

> I plunged into an ocean of despair; finally, only one thing irked me – that my soul still lingered on in my body. It seems to me that if I had not been made of steel, or fashioned in some other hard, tough substance, a stranger to myself, I would have perished at once. But living I died a thousand deaths.[126]

L'étranger, the stranger, the foreigner, has a particular resonance in Byzantium, for whatever identity anyone assumed, the identity of a *xenos* was common to all. All Byzantines were exiles from Paradise and might hope to return there at the end of the world, but until then, 'say always that you are a *xenos*'.[127] Julia Kristeva does in fact touch on this issue, that we are all foreigners and that the foreigner is within us. What is most fearful to us in the stranger may be the very quality we do not want to

---

[124] J. Kristeva, *Étrangers à nous-mêmes* (Paris, 1988), tr. L.S. Roudiez, *Strangers to Ourselves* (New York, 1991).

[125] Cf. Theophylact, ep.G4, to Maria, ed. P. Gautier, *Théophylacte d'Achride, II, Lettres*, CFHB 16.2 (Thessalonike, 1986), 41.58–60.

[126] Anna, *Al.*, XV.xi.22, ed. Leib, 242, S, 514: Καὶ εἰ μή, ὡς ἔοικεν, ἀδαμαντίνη ις ἦν ἢ ἄλλης τινὸς φύσεως διάπλασις ... καὶ ξενίζουσα, κἂν ἀπωλόμην εὐθύς ...

[127] A saying of *abba* Olympios, Moschos, *Pratum spirituale*, ch. 12, PG, 87.3, col. 2861B; see below, J. McGuckin, 23–38.

recognize in ourselves. Only by recognizing this, that the barbarians are within, can we guard against racism and xenophobia.[128] This is not a matter of the barbarians being 'some kind of a solution', or indeed of 'inventing the barbarian' as an aid in self-definition, or an ironic reversal of verities as a rhetorical strategy.[129] It is something that would have been instantly recognized in twelfth-century Byzantium, where complaints about barbaric surroundings were the perquisite of senior churchmen vying with one another in a recognizable exile discourse to make the most attractive of sees sound like the back of beyond. Michael Choniates capped them all by being able to quote Euripides, *Orestes* 485 straight: 'I have become a barbarian here for so long in Athens'. This fear of literary infelicity, of *agroikia*, is shared by the civil servants who plead – more feebly – pressure of work, not the monstrous accompaniments of episcopacy: 'the Harpies overturn my books'.[130] This fear of alterity, that it is within, is what Anna in her grief and disappointment was also trying to express, and what we should keep in mind through all the papers of this volume: that we are strangers to ourselves and so to the Byzantines we study.

---

[128] Kristeva, *Strangers*, esp. 191–195.

[129] C.P. Cavafy, Περιμένοντας τοὺς βαρβάρους, ed. G.P. Savvides, *K.P. Kabaphe, Poiemata*, I, *1896–1918* (Athens, 1963), 107–108; E. Hall, *Inventing the Barbarian: Greek Self-Definition through Tragedy* (Oxford, 1989).

[130] Michael Choniates, ep. 28, ed. S. Lampros, Μιχαὴλ Ἀκομινάτου τοῦ Χωνιάτου τὰ σωζόμενα, 2 vols (Athens, 1879–80), 44; Theophylact, ep. 29, ed. P. Gautier, *Théophylacte d'Achrida: Lettres*, CFHB 16/2 (Thessalonike, 1986), 225; M.E. Mullett, 'Originality in the Byzantine letter; the case of exile', in Littlewood, ed., *Originality*, 39–58 for the twelfth-century imagery; Mullett, *Theophylact*, 274–276 for the overall attitude to exile and the Other.

scabury

2. Aliens and Citizens of Elsewhere:
Xeniteia in East Christian Monastic Literature

John McGuckin

How intriguing it is, when one looks at the religious literature, to find the Christian Greeks developing the same concept that has elicited the interest of us post-moderns for our conference topic on the 'Outsider', or the notion of being 'Aliens to themselves'. Not only had the Byzantines considered it, but from an early stage had taken it to a pitch beyond anything comparable in the prior Greco-Roman philosophical or rhetorical tradition, before subjecting it to several variations around a central theme, and rendering it, finally, as a stock theme of all later monastic literature. Such an apotheosis is reflected in the way the notion achieves the status of a chapter to itself in that veritable manual of Byzantine ascetical theology, John of Sinai's *Sacred Ladder*. *Xeniteia*, that state of being foreign or other, even in one's own locality, what we could best describe as the position of living unattached, as a stranger would in that antique time and social condition, or the more interesting analogous (and highly paradoxical) inner state of being distant even to one's intimate self, that reflects upon itself in an exaggerated solitude – if not a uniquely Byzantine theme, is certainly taken to a uniquely specific peak in this literature.

Xeniteia is clearly a regularly used, and seemingly important, concept in early Christian monastic texts, especially those of the Egyptian desert tradition. It has often been rendered in the secondary literature as 'exile', which, in other linguistic contexts, it could possibly connote; but the use of this translation 'exile' occludes certain key aspects of a fuller appreciation of what is going on when the monastic writers apply the term to the burgeoning forms of *ascesis* near the Nile: first that the concept of exile, *per se*, is very much a minor aspect of a more complex set of

associations; and second, that the technical term for exile[1] is almost
entirely absent from the Christian literature.

Doubtless those who adopted the ascetic lifestyle and came to reflect
so intently upon the nexus of related ideas were hardly the sort who
could even hope to attract the dubious distinction of a sentence of exile in
the normal order of affairs. They were, in the main,[2] people who lived
beneath that kind of legal radar. The standard and perfectly respectable
words for exile were *exoria* (the banishment of, usually, political
prisoners) or *periorismos* (confinement or house arrest). *Periorismos*
brought benefits to the state if applied as a preliminary to *exoria*, for
under the terms of confinement the offender's property was confiscated,
whereas in the case of the banishment of *exoria*, the condemned retained
rights to domestic property.[3] The only recorded case I could find of a true
legal exile being interpreted in the spiritualizing monastic–ascetic sense
was the odd reference in the much later *Life of St. Theodora of Arta*. This
Vita is unusual in several respects, not least because it may be the only
record of a female Byzantine saint from the whole of the thirteenth
century. Here the application is far from straightforward. The tradition is
so late, and so clearly dominated by traditional Byzantine monastic *topoi*,
that the (real) *exoria* suffered by Theodora is transmuted into a spiritual
xeniteia by the hagiographer. Theodora's husband, Michael II Komnenos
Doukas, regnant at Epiros between 1231 and 1267–68, was (we are told)
bewitched and seduced by an aristocratic 'sorceress' at court,[4] and so
drove away his legitimate wife penniless.[5] The rare motif is appropriate
for the equally rare example of a royal female hagiography, but indicates
how the rhetorical tradition has, by this period, turned full circle. Driven
out in *exoria*, Theodora transforms it into the *xeniteia* of the (more
standard) ascetical heroine. Like one of the most famous of the female

---

[1] Precisely, that is, a legal punishment imposed on a citizen in the *polis*-dominated
society of Late Antiquity before the barbarian invasions.

[2] Evagrios is an obvious exception: and one needs to keep in mind that many of the
commentators on this lifestyle (such as Palladios at Constantinople) were indeed city-based
citizens to whom physical exile from the city was a regularly witnessed event.

[3] Symeon the New Theologian received both sentences from Basil II in the early
eleventh century. His hagiographer Nicetas Stethatos softened the scandal by describing
the *periorismos* as the saint's retreat into *hesychia* – evidently once one was socially elevated
enough to attract a real exile, the term was thought too controversial to apply in a
spiritually symbolic sense.

[4] Charmingly designated by the hagiographer as 'gangrene'.

[5] A.M. Talbot, ed., *Holy Women of Byzantium* (Washington, DC, 1996), 331–332.

penitents,[6] living off wild herbs and wandering in the wilderness, she achieves sanctification and even excels the ancients, for her suffering was innocent. It is clear that one had to excel (or be made to seem to, by a good hagiographer) purely in terms of monastic celibate canons, to make the grade in the honours of the church in the thirteenth century.

In earlier Christian times, however, when the legal punishment of exile was really, properly, and harshly applied to prominent believers (such as under the terms of the Diocletianic suppression of the third century), then the memory was a bitter one. Certainly no one then thought it a fit subject for spiritual allegorization. The Roman Church had no second thoughts about how to regard its *Papas* when he was exiled from his see by imperial prescript: though a confessor for the faith, another must be elected to his place as the true successor, for an exile was unable to head a corporation under the terms of the law, and such an incapacity rendered the episcopal function void.[7]

There is little surviving papyrological or archaeological data from this period precisely on this subject,[8] but what there is, again, makes no symbolic glorification or allegorization of the exile proper. The status of Confessor was accorded (like that of the *Lapsi*) only in the aftermath of the suppression of churches, as part of the Christian efforts at social and disciplinary reconstruction.

In Antiquity, exile was a fearful punishment; the thought of leaving home a frightening prospect. The British Church's early penitential canons continued the self-same antique attitude into the seventh century and beyond. The Penitentials of Theodore (1.2.16) and Egbert (para.3)[9] set exile as the penalty for the worst of 'uncontainable' crimes: parricide,

---

[6]   The hagiographer is obviously trying his hardest to evoke the totally non-apposite Life of St Mary of Egypt, and use Theodora's sufferings as her *causa sanctitatis*.

[7]   For this reason Diocletian favoured the penalty after 303.

[8]   There is an allusion to a third-century 'possibly-Christian' woman sent into exile from Alexandria, found in a papyrus cache at the Great Oasis in Egypt, in 1890. Compare Grenfell Hunt, *Greek Papyri* II (Oxford, 1897); cf. text and discussion in: *Dictionnaire d'Archéologie Chrétienne et de Liturgie* (henceforth *DACL*), vol. 4.1 (Paris, 1920), col. 663. It is, however, a confusing instance, and modern commentators take it to be a reference to a mummy rather than to a real person: cf. A. Lukaszewicz, *Journal of Juristic Papyrology* 28 (1998), 85–94; and S. Llewelyn and A. Nobbs, *Akten des 21 Int. Papyrologenkongress* (Berlin, 1997), 613–630.

[9]   Compare H. Leclercq. *DACL* 1 (Paris, 1922), col. 963: *'exilium'*. See also A. Guillaumont, 'Le dépaysement comme forme d'ascèse dans le monachisme ancien', *Annuaire de l'École pratique des hautes études. Vième section: Sciences Religieuses* 76 (1968–1969), 31–58.

incest and clerical adultery. We may recall, for example, that Columbanus's great missionary endeavours came about as the result of his *ascesis* of exile, though it was a sentence he received initially *qua* penitent for the blood he had shed. Nowhere, then, while exile was still a real legal penalty that could be (or was being) faced by Christians, did anyone choose to allegorize it spiritually.

Again, no one connects the term, or hardly so, with what might be thought to be the 'obvious' spiritual symbols of the Exile of Israel (either understood as the time of servitude in Egypt, or the sojourn in the desert). This fact is noteworthy, and explicable largely on the grounds that the supposedly close connection of the Exile of Israel to the notion of a spiritual state of the 'Golden Age' (as hinted at but not explicated in some prophetic texts such as Hosea) is a rather modern hermeneutic. The Byzantine tradition was far more ready to regard the Exile as a state of the passive captivity of the Elect People (a passivity that carried the usual negative, not positive, allied associations); and similarly, the journey of the exiles through the desert is almost unanimously interpreted as a symbol of wandering and testing (usually a testing that resulted in lamentable failures). It connoted for Byzantine interpreters how the old era was destined to give way to the true Golden Age – the desert is left behind for the Promised Land. The people once elect have now been replaced by the truly elect: the Greek *ethnos* in a Christian *imperium*. Nowhere is there the hermeneutical basis for focusing on the concept of the Exile itself as a positive symbol.[10]

The idea of Israel's progress through the desert as a blue-print for the faithful Jew's advance towards true righteousness was certainly part of Philo's philosophical re-reading of the biblical narratives, and something that was even brought onto centre stage for Christians by Origen. His teeming intelligence, however, did not rest content with merely one symbolic meaning for the 'Exile of Israel', and so in many texts he invested it with subtle Christological and ecclesiological patterns, while in others (and the famous *27th Homily on Numbers* is a case in point) the exile's progress is developed in a Philonic manner, to become a detailed pattern of an individual soul's progress towards deification.

---

[10] In a Western, post-Reformation context, and increasingly in European and American exegesis of the modern era, the Exile became used in other more positive ways as symbolic of a time of spiritual liberation and simplicity where God 'spoke directly' to his journeying people, and dwelt among them intimately in the tabernacle. The view appeals to texts such as Hosea 2:14–16.

Many of the subsequent patristic writings take up this Christological and ecclesiological hermeneutic, connecting exilic images such as the sea, the cloud, and the manna, with the Christian sacraments of initiation; but the spiritual allegorization of the exilic journey as some form of blue-print for the soul's mystical advance is enthusiastically propounded only by Origen and his most dedicated intellectual heirs: Gregory Nazianzen, Gregory of Nyssa, Evagrios and Didymos. It is the latter part of this chain that probably explains why such a hermeneutic has all but been scoured from the desert monastic tradition on *xeniteia*, as represented in the *Apophthegmata* or the *Ladder* of John of Sinai; we may list it as one of the many casualties of the early fifth-century Origenist controversy.

For reasons such as these, we ought to be very careful in our English translation. Exile is by far the most favoured rendering of *xeniteia* in modern versions and commentaries on the Byzantine ascetical literature. The recent Boston edition of John's *Sacred Ladder*[11] even has a footnote to the effect that although the word *xeniteia* is an obvious synonym for 'pilgrimage', for consistency's sake the translation of 'exile' will be used throughout. The point is, however, that it is *not* an obvious synonym for anything like this at all, except to a modern mind steeped in biblicisms to the extent that the frequent biblical pairing of stranger with sojourner comes to mind in a creative association. Such a (fairly common theme) appears especially in two late New Testament texts that directly allude to *xeniteia*: Hebrews and 1 Peter. But once again (and it is only *prima facie* surprising), this biblical tradition of *xeniteia* theology has next to no bearing or impact on the way it is used in the Byzantine ascetical texts.[12]

One is tempted, in the face of such an enigmatic concept, and certainly under the aegis of such a theme as ours, to turn instead to a post-modern lexicon and render *xeniteia* as 'alienation'. But although 75% of the United Kingdom population, according to a recent newspaper survey, are supposed to be currently experiencing 'metaphysical alienation' allied with a sense of 'spiritual vacuity' in the face of the impending millennium, we must none the less rein in our modern apocalypticism sufficiently to note that no such sense whatsoever of the loss of confidence in the self or ambiguity of identity is traceable in the ascetical rhetoric surrounding *xeniteia*. Despite much interesting work in the last

---

[11] *The Ladder of Divine Ascent. St John Climacus.* Holy Transfiguration Monastery (Boston, 1991). It is an extensive re-edition of Lazarus Moore's 1959 translation of the same.

[12] There is a rare exception in the manner that *xeniteia*, as the pathetic state of being 'foreign', is applied in relation to Ex.2.22 in the *Acts of Xanthippe*, to evoke sympathy for the infancy of Jesus spent in Egypt. But this has little, if any, impact on the larger tradition.

few decades on the difficult socio-economic contexts of the system of
agricultural small-holding along the Nile valley, and their relation to the
establishment of micro-subsistent monastic hermit colonies on the one
hand or the larger cenobitic production communities on the other (such
as those of Pachomios, or Shenoudi), the monastic literature gives no
trace that I can see of *xeniteia* understood in the sense of survival
psychology.

In a recent and sensitive study Douglas Burton-Christie called
xeniteia[13] 'One of the most evocative terms in early Monasticism'.[14]
Unfortunately, that is more or less all that he had to say on the matter.
Both Peter Brown and Graham Gould have given more attention to this
term in their work on Egyptian desert monasticism. Brown noted how
much of the apophthegmatic material related to anger-limitation, and the
maintenance of good relations in the early desert literature. He argued
that this was a clear reflection of the ubiquity of tensions in the village
communities of the Nile fellahin in Late Antiquity. Brown sees the quest
for *autarkeia*, and what he terms 'social death',[15] as a reflected aspiration of
the independent small-holders of the valley set against one another in
open competition for very limited resources. Graham Gould's later study
of the concept of desert community points out, with proper caution,[16] how
unwise it is to push that macro-argument to become an all-embracing
social explanation for ascetic attitudes among these particular Christian
communities. There is, after all, still little evidence that Christianity was
anything like a majority consensus in this area at this time (more to
suggest that it was not), nor much to convince us that such a form of
ascetic *hesychia* (at least of the lavriotic and eremetical types) would
actually provide a better option for a small-holder at 'wits-end farm'.

Gould's study of the term *xeniteia*, a subsection of his study focused on
desert community, has noted how regularly the term[17] is paired with
'silence'. The twinning of the notions, he says, 'could be converted to
serve as a shorthand for attitudes necessary as a condition of good
relationships'.[18] Gould sees the stress of living in the difficult physical
conditions of the Nile semi-desert as requiring careful regulation of social

---

[13]   Which he translates as 'exile'.
[14]   D. Burton-Christie, *The Word in the Desert. Scripture and the Quest for Holiness in
Christian Monasticism* (Oxford, 1993), 139.
[15]   P. Brown, *The Making of Late Antiquity* (Cambridge, MA, 1978), 88–89.
[16]   G. Gould, *The Desert Fathers on Monastic Community* (Oxford, 1993), 185.
[17]   He too translates it as 'exile'.
[18]   G. Gould, *The Desert Fathers*, 165.

mores; withdrawn taciturnity is seen as being able to defuse flashpoints of dispute. His monograph works very closely with the apophthegmatic tradition, and concludes on the basis of the majority usages within those sources that pair together *xeniteia* and 'silence' that the term *xeniteia* is fundamentally one that connotes the spiritual symbol of withdrawal – that inner passivity that marks the mind of the monk as one withdrawn from the cares, passions and ambitions of the world. The general terms of this analysis are surely clear and correct, but there are points, it still needs to be noted, even in the apophthegmatic materials themselves, where such a symbolistic reading of *xeniteia* is by no means applicable,[19] which have been footnoted in Gould's treatment rather than being assessed in the main text.[20] Accordingly, in two studies on the subject[21] he states a clear disagreement with P. Rousseau[22] who, in his study on Pachomios, had postulated that *xeniteia* was probably, originally, an advice to primitive monastics (by elders who preceded them) just to set up on their own and go off somewhere sufficiently distant. The later monastic tradition, particularly the forms of cenobitism favoured by the Latin Church, certainly came to regard such 'rootlessness' with particular horror, and listed the *gyrovagi*, or wandering monks, as one of the worst forms of low-life. The later Greek tradition called such as these *kabiotai* (rovers) or, when it wanted to be particularly scornful, *boskoi* (nomadic grazers). But these wanderers were exactly those who had gone off from their domicile to become *xenoi*, foreigners of no fixed abode. It is surely worthy of note, then (at least as a sign of some tradition-conflict surviving in the texts), when we find the monastic rhetorical argument urged upon us that those who literally adopt a life as *xenoi* must not be accorded the honour of having achieved monastic *xeniteia*.

Rousseau suggested that the later monastic cenobitic tradition had transmuted this relatively primitive stage of wandering into something else, effectively suppressed it by changing *xeniteia* into the symbol of an inner state, in the course of monasticism's settling down as an organized and regulated (canonical) Christian lifestyle. This argument has much to

---

[19] See for example: Apoph. Bessarion, 1.12; Daniel 5; James 1; and The Greek Anon. Series of Apophthegmata (no. 250). F Nau, ed., 'Histoire des solitaires égyptiens', *Revue d'Orient Chrétien* 12 (1907); 13 (1908); 14 (1909); 17 (1912); and 18 (1913).

[20] G. Gould, *The Desert Fathers*, 163–165 *passim*.

[21] G. Gould, *The Desert Fathers*, 163; and G. Gould, 'Moving On and Staying Put in the *Apophthegmata Patrum*' in E.A. Livingstone, ed., *Studia Patristica* 22 (Leuven, 1989), 237.

[22] P. Rousseau, *Ascetics, Authority, and the Church in the Age of Jerome and Cassian* (Oxford, 1978), 43–44 and 48–49.

commend it, *pace* Gould's dismissal, though one needs to distance oneself from any fixed presupposition that the progress from wandering 'monastic' life to organized ascetic-community lifestyles represented any form of invariable institutional development either in Egypt or elsewhere. Here Gould is surely right in questioning Rousseau's macro-theory of monastic organization patterns, but in the later of his two studies[23] he seems to me to miss something of Rousseau's positive point, in so far as he himself contains *xeniteia* too strictly within the notions of wandering and solitude (as follows from his consistent reading of the term as an inner moral attitude). In other words, I think we ought not to suppose too readily that what was at issue in the apophthegmatic warnings about literal *xeniteia* was primarily an anxiety about monks going off into solitude prematurely. We need also to take seriously how the spread of monastic 'lore'[24] must have attracted both aspirants and monastic 'researchers'. Visitors such as Egeria, Palladius, a Basil of Caesarea or the other varied forms of temporary non-monastic clients who came to consult the masters in the desert colonies were one kind of intrusion. But such literary visitors were usually aristocratic and well able to pay their way. Even on a smaller level of patron–client relationship, the offering of bread for services rendered to occasional visitors could offer sustenance enough to offset the disruption experienced. On the other hand, a seasonal increase in the population of temporary monks, who might well be expecting to draw on the very limited annual resources of the smaller colonies, and able to offer only their labour as a contribution, could have disastrous effects on the ability to sustain a balanced annual economy.

To pull back a little from speculative reflection, and to consider the term itself in the context of the whole gamut of its rhetorical development, may help us to clarify something more of what was going on. This literary consideration is a foundational analysis not yet sufficiently provided in the studies. One thing is clear enough. The term did not originate with the Christians, and despite Origen, or perhaps because of him, it never assumed the mantle of a developed biblicism in any of the possible routes it could have taken towards such a stature in Christian rhetorical use – the Exile of Israel, the estrangement of the patriarchs, the paradigms of the life of Jesus or the missionary hardships

---

[23]   G. Gould, *The Desert Fathers*, 163–164.

[24]   And the apophthegmatic tradition represents this rhetorical spreading of the lore just as much as it represents a putative early stage of monastic organization or a manual for monks' behaviour. One could instructively compare, for example, the rhetorical *telos* of Palladius's *Lausiac History* with that of John of Sinai's *Ladder*.

and endeavours of the apostles. Even though we glimpse occasional biblical reminiscences, no hermeneutical tradition along any of these lines is associated with the Christian application of the term *xeniteia*. In itself, this is a very odd and interesting thing.

For me it is also the chief indicator to suggest that *xeniteia* is largely rhetorical in its origin, that it is obviously a Greco-Roman political concept. By Late Antiquity it had entered the stock repertoire of philosophical aphorisms attributed to Democritus the Philosopher.[25] When the first Christian writers adopt it, it is unquestionably from a large available pool of late Stoicizing aphoristic wisdom. The writer of Hebrews, in his resonant phrase 'Here we have no abiding *politeia*',[26] is repeating, for effect, what he has just said earlier: that all human beings are foreigners (*xenoi*) and passers-by on the face of the earth.[27] The application in 1 Peter 2.11 amounts to exactly the same. Such is also the usage of Clement of Alexandria,[28] who describes the sojourn of all the saints on earth as a *xeniteia*. The selfsame is found in the *Letter To Diognetos* 5.5, in a brilliantly applied paradox that brings out the purest form of the politico-ethical rhetorical archetype.[29]

Political de-racination, therefore, is the rhetorical archetype used in the religious literature as an image of how the thinking person (that is the religious and moral person in a Neo-Stoic context) ought to live. A certain detachment from the affairs of life is in order; it is needful for all. Such a moral generalization must have had particular appeal to the early Christian writers, especially the Diognetos author and Clement of Alexandria, philosophically inclined moralists who were conscious of how their religious aspirations were increasingly bringing them into conflict with the majority society's ideas of what constituted good citizenship.

It is, of course, this rhetorical trunk of Neo-Stoic 'detachment theory' that continues to bud forth throughout the whole Byzantine ascetical tradition about *xeniteia*, but specific and proper developments occur that make it necessary to seek an alternative translation for the word, to go beyond the generic sense of 'exile' or mere de-racination. For the moment let us settle on the more bland rendering of 'expatriation' – living in the condition of being foreign or alien among one's neighbours. Such a state

---

[25] Fifth century BC. Compare H. Diels and W. Kronz, eds, *Fragmenta*, vol. 2, 40.6.

[26] Hebrews 13:14.

[27] Hebrews 11:13.

[28] *Quis Dives Salvetur*, 36.2, PG 9, 642; also *Stromateis* 4.26, PG 8, 1376.

[29] Ὁ ἐκλεκτὸς ὡς ξένος πολιτεύεται. *Ep. Diogn.* 5.5.

might indeed dwindle one's capacity and range of powers among those neighbours (the notion of the poor, alienated exile); on the other hand it might not (the expatriate may have much greater visibility and much greater access to power than the native neighbour).

In Byzantine ascetical usage, the term *xeniteia* has come, quite clearly, to be de-politicized. Its original semantic context, in the earliest Christian period, was still rooted in the conditions of the Hellenistic city-state, and Christian use of the idea had predominantly followed the path charted by the Neo-Stoic ethical tradition which applied such a political symbol, in the cause of an urban moral *paranesis*, to connote the way in which a good man ought to be detached from the grasping affairs of the world. But by the time of the Byzantine monastic writers such a background context had become antiquated, and the moral usage had become non-resonant through over-generalization.

Evagrios still wants to contrast urban life's difficulties with desert life's freedoms, but to make his point the term *xeniteia* is no longer sufficient for him. He has to turn instead to the psalmist to provide his picture of undesirable urban violence. In this revealing passage, *xeniteia*, or voluntary expatriation, is quite specifically and concretely meant. To achieve that *hesychia* essential for wisdom it is necessary, Evagrios tells his readers, to get up and leave. It does not matter whether it is one's town or one's hermit cell: 'get up and leave' is his advice:

> If you find yourself growing strongly attached to your cell, leave it. Do not cling to it. Be ruthless. Do everything in your power to attain stillness (*hesychia*) and freedom from distraction, and struggle to live according to God's will, battling against your invisible enemies. If you cannot attain stillness where you live now, consider living in expatriation (*xeniteia*) and try to make up your mind to go. Be like an astute merchant. Make stillness your criterion for testing the value of everything and choose always what contributes to it. Indeed, I urge you to welcome expatriation. It frees you from all the entanglements of your own locality and allows you to enjoy the blessings of stillness undistractedly. Do not stay in a town, persevere in the wilderness, for the Psalm says, 'So I would wander far off and dwell in the desert' (*Ps.* 55.7). If possible, do not visit a town at all, for there you will find nothing of benefit, nothing useful,

nothing profitable for your way of life. To quote the Psalm again,
'I have seen nothing but violence and strife in the city' (*Ps.* 55:9).[30]

There we have the advice of a consummate philosopher and rhetorician,
who had to flee for his life from Constantinople in 383. He goes on to
describe *xeniteia* as the 'foremost (πρωτή) of the radiant glories of the
ascetic conflicts', 'foremost' in the sense of the acme of achievement. This,
too, is a significant rhetorical indicator. By the end of the Christian
rhetorical chain of advice on this matter, and let us take the *Sacred Ladder*
to represent that 'end' of the chain, the achievement of *xeniteia* is still the
'first' of virtues, but now no longer '*prote*', simply primary. The unstated,
but loud, implication of the structure of the ladder, that veritable manual
of ascetical *praxis*, is that *xeniteia*, as step three on the lower rungs, is but a
beginner's *ascesis*. It is something to achieve that sets the rest in motion.
This is the chief tone of most of the material collated together by John of
Sinai in that third section of the *Ladder* devoted to the term.

There, fifteen aphorisms concern the entrapment of kin-affection,
which has to be cut off in case it draws the 'expatriate' back to his old
condition.[31] Attachment to family is seen as the chief cause of collapse in
the early stages of monastic commitment. To have the attitude of a true
expatriate, John teaches, can harden the novice's resolve. Apart from this
treatment, the *Ladder* merely mentions *xeniteia* five or six more times as a
generic symbol for moral detachment.[32] In other words, for John, *xeniteia*
is now rhetorically synonymous with the proper monastic mentality. By
this stage it is pointless asking what *xeniteia* contributes to monastic
spirituality. It has been utterly flattened out in the course of a brief but
vibrant Christian twist of the Greco-Roman moral rhetoric tradition, as
the church forged a newly precise language of *ascesis*. It has simply
become synonymous with 'entrance into the monastic state', and those
leave-takings that new beginnings require. It is for this reason that the
Ladder adds in warnings about feelings of homesickness for lost kin or the
daily temptation to return to one's family.

This synonymity of *xeniteia* with monastic stability is certainly not the
context of Evagrios, however. His fixed goal was *sophia*. Yet we make a
large mistake if we take him too literally when he advocates withdrawal.
He does so, for example, chiefly for a rhetorical end – a *theoria* rather than

---

[30] Evagrios (formerly attributed to Nilus of Ancyra), *Ad Eulogium* 2, PG 79, 1096.
[31] *The Sacred Ladder* 3.2; 3.3; 3.4; 3.7; 3.8; 3.10; 3.11; 3.12; 3.14; 3.16; 3.17; 3.20; 3.23; and 3.27.
[32] *The Sacred Ladder* 3.5; 3.6; 3.22; 24.28; and 28.25.

a *praxis* – and that end (*telos logikos*) of achieved Wisdom is witnessed, in part, precisely by the text he produces to demonstrate his mastery of the inner life. In his published Discourses (*Logoi*) that miraculously survived both imperial and ecclesiastical hostility, we see the recommendation of quiet (non-verbal) estrangement precisely as what it is in his own case: the process of a philosopher–theologian who moves toward a more purified and thus more potent form of discourse. It is, if you like, comparable to Gregory of Nazianzen's 'Silent Lent', the pre-paschal fast of more or less that same year as Evagrios fled from Constantinople. For the whole forty days Gregory 'fasted from words' on his private estates; yet it was one of the most famously voluble silences in Christian history, recounted to us in the exquisitely crafted rhetoric of his poetry. In this sense, as with Evagrios, silence is about assuming the right to teach. If Evagrios was not always heard with deference in the monastic assemblies where, perhaps, his Coptic was not as fluent as that of others who regarded the *xenos* with suspicion, then in his textual *Logoi*, at least, he was heard internationally, and in the end heard through the centuries.

To be silent in such a case is to speak the loudest of all. This specific rhetorical move, an advocating of the right of the spiritual master to direct others, is what I would mark out carefully as the first specifically Christian contribution to the theory of philosophic *xeniteia*. *Xeniteia* and silence, then, are first connected in the context of the claims to authoritative discourse. With Evagrios that claim was backed up literarily. It shares the same paradoxical character of the paranetic tradition on *xeniteia* expressed in the Letter of Diognetos, though in this case the political idiom has been superseded. The same rhetorical argumentation can be found in the later orations and poems of Gregory Nazianzen, Evagrios's one-time teacher.

If Evagrios taught authoritatively through his *Logoi*, however, others in that Egyptian milieu, and who used the Coptic tongue, needed a more vocal avenue for authoritative teaching. In this case it is ultimately no surprise, though at first puzzling, to see how many of the references to *xeniteia* in the apophthegmatic tradition, stretched between Evagrios in the fourth century and John of Sinai in the seventh, are connected with making *xeniteia* issue forth not in wise teaching, but in abiding silence.[33]

---

[33]   The material Gould focused on, describing the *logia* as 'few but significant ... '

Abba Tithoes, for example, says: '*Xeniteia* means a man should keep his mouth shut.'[34] And when Abba Longinos asked Abba Lucius if he should follow his desire to go into *xeniteia*:

> The old man said to him, 'If you do not control your tongue, you will not be in *xeniteia* wherever you go. Control your tongue here, and you will.'[35]

Abba Agathon is reported to have said:

> Keep the mindset of a foreigner (*xenos*) so as to overcome carelessness in speech.[36]

So how can one deduce that *xeniteia*, as Evagrios indicated, is a springboard to authoritative discourse (a claim on the part of someone to be fitted for the task of the master-teacher), when the evidences of this nexus of *logia* seem so clearly against such an idea? Well, two things need to be kept in mind. The first is that not all the warnings against speech, when set in tandem with the concept of *xeniteia*, are so peremptorily given as the above appear to be. There are several others which suggest a mood quite like that of Evagrios's point. One of these comes from Abba Isaiah, who thereby proves his quality as guiding-master to the disciples who are in the process of being taught by him:

> One of us asked, 'What is *xeniteia*, father?' And he said, 'Be silent, and in every situation say, "Who am I?" Wherever you dwell, do not get involved with anyone over any business at all. This is *xeniteia*.'[37]

Similarly, the rock of the rhetorical sub-text is not quite covered by the tide in the *Logion* ascribed to Poemen:

> A brother asked Abba Poemen, 'How ought I to live in the place where I dwell?' The old man said to him, 'Have the mindset of a

---

[34]   *Apoph. Patrum*, Tithoes 2, *PG* 65, 429.

[35]   *Apoph. Patrum*, Longinos 1, *PG* 65, 256.

[36]   *Apoph. Patrum*, Agathon, *PG* 65, 108–109.

[37]   Abba Isaiah, *Logos* 6.6Bb, in R. Draguet, ed., 'Les V recensions de l'Asceticon syriaque d'Abba Isaie', *Corpus Scriptorum Christianorum Orientalium* 293, *Scriptores Syri* 122, (Louvain, 1968).

foreigner (*xenos*) in the place where you dwell so as not to desire to parade your wisdom before you. Then you will have rest.'[38]

Three of the aphorisms on *xeniteia* collated together in Section Three of the *Sacred Ladder* also preserve this character of the connection between seeking to be a stranger and unknown, and yet having always the potential to be recognized as someone decidedly public, whether from the quality of one's inner condition or from the authoritative leadership one might command as a 'patriarch' and teacher:

> He is in *xeniteia* who has knowledge but still sits like one of foreign speech, amongst a people of a different tongue.[39]

Or again:

> Hide your noble birth, and do not glory in your distinction, lest you be found to be one thing in word, and another in deed.[40]

Or lastly:

> Sometimes the Lord has brought much glory to the man who has gone into *xeniteia* after the manner of the patriarch [Abraham]. But even if the glory is God-given, still it is an excellent thing to deflect it from oneself with the shield of humility.[41]

Such texts suggest to me that the first stage of the particularly 'Christian' monastic literature on *xeniteia* was represented in a pure form by Evagrios, and ran on dilutedly in a few other apophthegmatic texts. To sustain such a point, I would like to come back to that core body of material in the apophthegmatic tradition which says explicitly, and precisely: '*Xeniteia* means for a man to keep his mouth shut!' Far from contradicting our thesis, this sustains the point that *xeniteia* (even with a command to silence) is ultimately about the claim to the power of authoritative discourse. What I mean thereby is that the text does not equate *xeniteia* with everyone's need to be silent – but insists rather on the

---

[38] Poemen, *Logion* 4, *Greek Apophthegmata Supplement*, in J.C. Guy, ed., 'Recherches sur la tradition grecque des Apothegmata Patrum', *Subsidia Hagiographica* 36 (Brussels, 1962 and 1984), 30.

[39] *Ladder*, 3.13.

[40] *Ladder*, 3.19.

[41] *Ladder*, 3.21.

hearer's requirement to be silent. In this tradition the listener must 'shut up' while receiving the authoritative discourse of the *logion* of a now long-dead master: a *logion*, needless to say, which has been carefully edited or translated into Greek and presented in the memorizable form of alphabetical aphorisms. It may not be quite the free spirit of an Evagrios any more, but it is certainly more approachable by a wider readership, and more practical as a guidance manual. The *Vita* of John Klimakos also suggests the same thing – for he assumed the *hegumenate* of Sinai, we are told, only after having been criticized for being too ready to discourse (to visitors to his cell). In response he closed his doors to all the brethren for over a year, and gave no more *logoi* until he was petitioned by the Sinai community to become their chief teacher. His text, the *Ladder* itself, issued from that elevation as an expression of his right to authoritative discourse. The rhetor's claim to authoritative discourse is still very much present: proven by long prior *praxis* of silent reflection and acute discernment, it now issues forth in the form of an authoritative and closing (if not already closed) literary canon, for a time when the ready supply of living masters has dwindled. Paradoxically, the last stage of the tradition, represented in the *Apophthegmata* by the common-sense Coptic masters rather than by the acute rhetorically trained philosopher– theologians like the Cappadocians or Evagrios, is precisely the one that was reclaimed by the Greek translators and collators such as Palladios or John of Sinai (the 'Scholastic'), re-imparted to Byzantium to launch a spiritual tradition that was to outlast Late Antiquity and survived as an ascetical *Grundschrift* in a world that hardly remembered any more the philosophical and rhetorical postulates of that era that first gave it birth.

Our conclusions, then, are as follows. The state of *xeniteia* in the New Testament and earliest Greek Christian writers is but a continuation of the Neo-Stoic *topos* of moral detachment. In the first movement to appropriate the term for a new discourse among Christian ascetics, philosophically trained and competent rhetors, especially Evagrios, developed the notion of being an expatriate, to signify detachment from the world, but added in to the monastic tradition the specific elements of recommending the physical act of wandering, as a defence of *hesychia*. It was something that rose out of the particularity of Evagrios's own condition: the paradox of a withdrawn figure of international fame. For him, *xeniteia* is important as a fundamental preparatory *ascesis*. Silence is the essential prelude to true spiritual discourse. The later apophthegmatic tradition certainly irons out much of this sub-text, though never quite levels it. The great *abbas* in the aphoristic collections equated *xeniteia* with silence, not to stifle the rhetorical claim to authoritative discourse but to control the pedigree and succession of that discourse – the line of masters and disciples. The disciple must be silent; the master continues to speak with great force, even when he recommends that it is better not to.

In the end, and already visible by the time of the *Sacred Ladder*, the concept of *xeniteia* is flattened out with a new meaning that thinks it has gone back to the original sense of the word: it is moving off to foreign parts (at least metaphorically understood now). By this time, however, the Christian sense of etymology is astray. This was not the original force of the word at all, and is not a re-pristination of meaning as much as a newly forged meaning within the tradition. To continue to use the word in the monastic literature where it had a now customary place, the ascetic tradition re-assigned it to a rather lowly task: part of the encouragement of novices in the early stages of leave-taking not to grieve too much about leaving their kin.

The history of the tradition in this respect is more complex than might at first emerge from a narrow collation of the *logia*. How typical of the Byzantine, who valued discourse and locality so highly, that the symbol of *xeniteia* (being an expatriate) meant not so much a permanent acceptance of awkward silence among a people of foreign tongue, but part of an energetic work that heralded the publication of an authoritative discourse – in Greek of course. The Byzantine ascetical teacher belonged to an international tradition, one provided at first by the solid foundations of an ancient philosophical culture and soon afterwards by a shared set of expectations among Christian ascetic communities. Such a *Homo Byzantinus* did not stay *xenos* for long, no matter where he might find himself geographically.

3. Byzantine Asceticism –
a Stranger to the Church?

Janet Rutherford

We are used to thinking of Byzantine ascetics against the paradigm of the great monastic theologians who played such a large part in the development of Orthodoxy. The weight given to their activities, both by political historians interested in the consequences of schisms, and by ecclesiastical historians interested in tracing the development of Christian doctrine, has made this inevitable. But how representative were prominent monastic theologians of wider ascetic culture? Were monastic communities in general really interested in doctrine at all, and if so, what kind of doctrine? To assess this it is necessary to consider not only the literature produced by monk theologians and preserved by 'the Church' as the cornerstones of Orthodoxy, but also the literature which was preserved by ascetic communities themselves. Work is currently in progress examining extant monastic *brebia* and noting the books they mention,[1] and it will be interesting to examine the results this produces. But such inventories are relatively few, and will only provide partial evidence for the life of other monastic communities. A complementary, and more widespread source of evidence for the literature which practising ascetics used is provided by the extent of manuscript survival. With reference to this type of evidence I would like to examine the works of two ascetics who, though living at different times and engaged in different types of composition, produced works which had a wide and enduring appeal for monastic communities both in their own day and continuously to the present. My excuse for linking two authors who differ both in period and genre is that one of them valued and made extensive use of the other.

---

[1] See, for example, the work by Judith Waring, 'Byzantine monastic libraries in the eleventh and twelfth centuries' (Unpublished PhD thesis, Belfast, 1998).

From *Strangers to Themselves: The Byzantine Outsider*, ed. Dion C. Smythe. Copyright © 2000 by the Society for the Promotion of Byzantine Studies. Published by Ashgate Publishing Ltd, Gower House, Croft Road, Aldershot, Hampshire, GU11 3HR, Great Britain.

To start with, however, we should take a moment to recall that Byzantine asceticism was generally characterized by an obstinate conservatism in the propagation of its own practical, as distinct from specifically theological, literature. Despite his condemnation on theological grounds, for example, Evagrios's practical instruction on prayer was jealously preserved by ascetics, who either attributed it to Neilos and circulated it pseudonymously,[2] or where applicable translated it into Syriac.[3] There is in these Evagrian works little that bears directly on contemporary doctrinal debates, but much on the theory and practice of prayer, and it is this which is significant: while the Christological debates raged, and despite the monastic associations of many of the participants, the bulk of the non-biblical and non-liturgical literature guarded and transmitted by monks did not address Trinitarian theology at all. Arians and Monophysites may be cast as villains in apophthegmata, but the moral of the story usually bears on the dangers of pride and disobedience rather than the details of Trinitarian relationships.

It is important to note that this non-participation in Trinitarian and Christological dogmatic development was not confined to ascetics, or indeed to clergy, of less education or eminence than the figures whose names are familiar to us. In other words, it is not simply a case of the generality of monks not being able to keep abreast of affairs which occupied their more sophisticated brethren. Aeneas of Gaza in the late fifth century, for example (admittedly a layman and philosopher), occupied himself not with what we have been accustomed to believe were the prevailing theological concerns of his day, but with composing a very elegant dialogue, in a Platonic style, on the immortality of the soul and the reality of resurrection life. The much-neglected fifth-century theologian Diadochos of Photike also provides evidence of there being more pressing issues for working ascetics than Trinitarian or Christological Orthodoxy. A bishop in fifth-century Epiros and an ascetic, Diadochos wrote a major theological treatise whose concepts owed much to Aristotle and whose style much to classical models.[4] In addition to his evident education, he was not so much of a recluse as to have no knowledge of contemporary affairs outside his diocese. He signed, and may have been the author of, a letter to Leo I from the bishops of Epiros

---

[2]   As the treatise 'On Prayer', PG 79, 1165–1200.

[3]   As 'The Gnostic Centuries', A. Guillaumont, ed., PO 28.

[4]   100 Kephalaia Gnostika, in the critical edition by E. des Places, Oeuvres spirituelles de Diadoque de Photice (Paris, 1966).

on the death of Proterios of Alexandria.[5] His work was known in Africa at a very early stage, perhaps even in his lifetime.[6] Yet his theological treatise was built upon an understanding of the relationship between the persons of the Trinity which would have been more at home in the third century than his own, to judge from our usual understanding of the history of doctrinal development.[7]

The preoccupations of historians have had an unfortunate impact on Diadochos's reputation. Because he wrote in a sophisticated and somewhat convoluted style, it has not been easy to grasp his meaning; but an isolated and passing reference to Christ not being 'of one confused nature' preserved him for dyophysite orthodoxy.[8] In fact, the composition of the person of Christ plays no part in his developed theology. This is not to say, however, that Diadochos was not concerned about heresy, or indeed about relationships between the persons of the Trinity, because he was; he wrote to address a heresy. But the heresy he refuted concerned the practice of prayer, as we shall see. A theory of the operation of the Godhead on the human condition was essential to him since his subject matter was the presence of grace in the soul.

For Diadochos, understanding our fallen condition is inextricably linked to understanding Christ's saving achievement. Humanity's creation 'in the image of God' involved the soul in a continuum of being which emphasized our innate kinship with God. The unknowable Father patterned humanity after His own *Logos*, His essential rationale and perfect likeness, manifest in creation. Subsequent to the Son's Incarnation and consequent to one's baptism, the Spirit conveys the presence of the *Logos* to the soul as the light of illumination, re-integrating it and re-orientating it towards its source and pattern, restoring its form 'in the likeness' of Christ through the prayer 'Lord Jesus'. Thus, there is an effulgence of luminous being flowing from the Father, manifest in the Son, and conveyed into the divinely patterned soul by the Spirit. Diadochos's theory of salvation was equally anachronistic. Christ's saving achievement came through his example among us, and through being the pattern for our creation and restoration. Although his theories are not identical to those of any other author, Diadochos has more in

---

5   Mansi, *Concilia*, VII, 619A.

6   See 'Diadoque de Photike et Victor de Vita', *REB* 45 (1943), 225–232.

7   See J. Rutherford, 'Sealed with the likeness of God', T. Finan, ed., *Studies in Patristic Christology* (Dublin, 1998), 67–83.

8   'Sermon on the Ascension', in critical edition by E. des Places, *Oeuvres spirituelles* (Paris, 1966).

common with Eusebios of Caesarea, or indeed Clement of Alexandria, than with the Trinitarian theorists of his own day. In many respects this is not surprising: the tendency in the development of Trinitarian theology was to emphasize the otherness of creature from Creator, in order to safeguard the Son as being a full and equal person within the Godhead. For those whose business was to find God in prayer, and pattern themselves on Christ, the growing emphasis on the radical difference between God and the human soul cannot have been helpful. Earlier emphases on Christ as the Father's manifest presence among us, and the *Logos* as God's ordering and sustaining presence within creation, would have been much more congenial.

Diadochos was, however, as I have indicated, interested in heresy, and it was to counter heresy that he wrote. But the heresy which concerned him was one which threatened the practice of prayer rather than our understanding of the composition of the Godhead. The broad movement we know as Messalianism taught that the devil remains in man even after baptism; consequently Messalians regarded the unceasing prayer enjoined on us by St Paul to be a perpetual, and demonstrative, penance. In addition, they cited the presence of *logismoi* in the mind during one's attempts to pray as evidence of the devil's continuing indwelling presence in the soul. This heresy, affecting one's understanding of prayer, and consequently one's efforts to pray validly, was an immediate danger to practising ascetics in a way that Trinitarian and Christological heterodoxy was not. Yet collections of *logoi* with Messalian associations contained much valuable insight on prayer which ascetics were reluctant to give up. These writings themselves were zealously preserved pseudonymously, like those of Evagrios; in this case under the name of Makarios. I have indeed argued that Diadochos's driving force in arguing against Messalian interpretations of the experience of prayer was his desire to preserve the useful instruction of these writings, and their distinctive language of the emotional consequences of praying, without their underlying theology.[9] His theories of the nature of the soul, its damage due to Adam and its experience of grace through Christ, were developed to explain the true significance of spiritual experience in prayer: the soul remains damaged after baptism, but not inhabited by Satan.

---

[9] J.E. Rutherford, 'An Imperative of longing: apprehending God in the 100 Kephalaia Gnostika of Diadochos of Photike' (Unpublished PhD thesis, Belfast, 1996).

Diadochos's importance to practising ascetics is known to us partly through the number of extant manuscripts of his work, and its eventual inclusion in the *Philokalia* of Nikodemos.[10] But in addition, his work also makes up a significant proportion of a *florilegium* which itself came to be valued by ascetics from the eleventh century onwards. The *Synagoge* of Paul Evergetinos has also been neglected in terms of the evidence it provides of day-to-day asceticism out of the glare of doctrinal controversy.[11] Eleventh-century Constantinopolitan monasticism is associated in most people's minds with Symeon the New Theologian and his radical claims to spiritual authority.[12] Yet what evidence we have, even from his own hagiographer, does not suggest that Symeon was representative of anyone but himself.[13] As a monastic organizer he was not a success, and his community at St Mamas did not flourish after his departure. By contrast the monastery of the Theotokos Evergetis was not only a success itself; it served as a pattern for other communities, both through the *Hypotyposis* of its second founder Timothy, and through the *Synagoge* and *Katechetikon* of its first founder Paul.

The *Synagoge* itself had a very wide influence, and upward of 80 manuscripts are still extant. These range in date from the eleventh century to the eighteenth (when the first printed edition was made), evidence of its widespread and continuing appeal to practising ascetics. That it was valued as a working text and not merely preserved as an esteemed volume is evidenced within the manuscripts themselves. At times scribes were careless about clearly marking the beginnings of new chapters, or new source authors within chapters. Here almost invariably the same hand or a second has gone back and added marginal markers for chapters or authors. In addition marginal lemmas for Paul Evergetinos's own glosses are commonly made, but not uniformly between manuscripts. A table of chapter titles is usually provided at the beginning of each volume. All these things, and corrections made in the text, indicate that the work was used as a source book for the many ascetical subjects Paul discusses; it was important to be able to look a

---

[10]   *Philocalia*, St Nikomemos of the Holy Mountain (Athens, 1963), vol. 1.

[11]   See M. Mullett and A. Kirby, eds, *The Theotokos Evergetis and Eleventh-Century Monasticism* (Belfast, 1994) and M. Mullett and A. Kirby, eds, *Work and Worship at the Theotokos Evergetis* (Belfast, 1997).

[12]   See J. McGuckin, 'The luminous vision in eleventh-century Byzantium', in Mullett and Kirby, *Work and Worship*, 90–123.

[13]   See Nikitas Stethatos, 'Life of Symeon the New Theologian', I. Hausherr, ed., with a French translation by G. Horn, *Orientalia Christiana* 12 (1928).

topic up, and find its number in the volume without too much trouble. More than once, a scribe has had to go back and add chapter numbers where he had only given titles.

The *Synagoge* therefore struck some nerve in Byzantine monasticism. It filled a gap in useful instructive literature, and this can tell us much about the real day-to-day theological interests of large numbers of Byzantine monks. Two things stand out in this respect. One is the selection of authors that Paul made for his work. Unlike the *Philokalia*, for example, Paul did not incorporate whole works into his collection. Based on what must have been an intimate personal knowledge of his source authors, he intricately selected and edited passages to illustrate hypotheses of his own composition. Thus Paul's own hypotheses and selectivity provide evidence of what many Byzantine ascetics wished to preserve for their own edification. Both these aspects tell us interesting things. Paul's supporting texts come predominantly from apophthegmata and lives of ascetics, together with other literature from the golden age of desert monasticism: Cassian, Palladios, Ephraem, Isaac. There is little that is later in date than the *Dialogues* of Gregory the Great, themselves of practical rather than theological import. Theologians represented in the *Synagoge* are Maximos and Diadochos, theorists on the practice of prayer.

As far as the subject matter of Paul's hypotheses is concerned, there is also a marked emphasis on 'how to', from the physical and logistical concerns of community life, developing in the last volume to prayer and spiritual leadership. Because he wrote so shortly after Symeon the New Theologian, Paul's silence on the subject of deriving authority from spiritual experience is significant, as is his explicit instruction to avoid doctrinal debate and 'pseudonymous writings' completely.[14] His emphasis on the simple and humble reading of Scripture is also significant, in view of the use Symeon made of scriptural paradigms for his own claims.[15] Yet in accordance with his own instruction, even in the aftermath of Symeon and at a time of increased tension with the papacy, Paul makes no reference to any doctrinal controversy or schism of any period. The odd Arian in apophthegmata is sufficiently ancient to be a mythical beast; and Paul's glossed apophthegm concerning Messalians is illustrative of the error of pride.[16] His intricate editing of both Mark the Monk and Diadochos excised all mention of their respective anti-

---

[14] *Synagoge*, Hypothesis IV.18.
[15] *Synagoge*, Hypotheses IV.16–17.
[16] *Synagoge*, Hypothesis IV.8.

Messalian baptismal theologies.[17] Interestingly, work done on Paul's *Katechetikon* by Barbara Crostini Lappin has also shown his deliberate excision of references to the iconoclast debate from those catecheses of Theodore Studios he borrowed.[18] To judge from the widespread and enduring influence of Paul's works, we must assume that he provided the things that many Byzantine ascetics regarded as helpful for what they wanted to be about; and as I have said, the evidence of manuscripts of the *Synagoge* suggests that monks not only preserved such texts for their image value, but also used them.

What then are we to conclude about the relationship between the generality of Byzantine ascetics, both educated and not, and doctrinal Orthodoxy? The evidence we have does not suggest heterodoxy, but rather a consuming interest in other things. We cannot suppose that Orthodoxy was not important to ascetics' understanding of themselves, but the constituent details of Orthodox doctrine did not greatly impinge on their lives. This has implications also for our assessment of the significance of the conventions of ascetic literature and the ascetic *bios*. We must be careful in looking back from our own agnostic and image-ridden day and assessing what was or was not a *topos* of ascetic life, to say nothing of what was 'only' a *topos*. The evidence of the *Synagoge* and the works it draws upon suggests that, if anything, Trinitarian Orthodoxy was a *topos* for those trying to get on with the nitty-gritty of prayer, while the subject matter of desert monastic literature was of real practical concern for them. Ultimately we may ask whether our notion of *topoi* fits Byzantine psychology or self-understanding very well at all. In the case of asceticism, Orthodoxy was affirmed liturgically and was perhaps primarily a statement of kinship within a religious culture, whereas the conventional terminology of ascetic literature was the familiar working context for life within that culture. I suggest that Orthodoxy was the theological context for *bios* within the prevailing religious culture, within which conventions of ascetical language were used, more widely than we may be accustomed to think, for genuine attempts to draw near to God.

---

[17] See M. Cunningham, 'Creative selection? Paul of Evergetis's use of Mark the Monk' and J. Rutherford, 'Diadochos of Photike and the Structure of the Synagoge', both in Mullett and Kirby, *Work and Worship at the Theotokos Evergetis*, 134–142 and 152–165.

[18] B. Crostini Lappin, 'Originality and dependence in the *Katechetikon* of Paul of Evergetis: some examples of catecheses adapted from Theodore of Studios', in M. Mullett, ed., *Founders and Refounders in Byzantine Monasticism* (Belfast), in preparation.

4. Middle Byzantine 'Tours of Hell': Outsider Theodicy?

Jane Baun

In the classic twentieth-century statement of the outsider, Camus's *L'Étranger*, the hero's gradual alienation from society culminates in a courtroom, during a trial that proceeds virtually as if the accused himself were not present. In a little-known Byzantine vision of the otherworld from around the turn of the tenth century, the *Apocalypse of Anastasia*, the climax also occurs in a courtroom. The judge is Christ and the court is in heaven, but the trial is as grim and inexorable as Meursault's; the judge, just as oblivious of the defendant and as deaf to the pleas of the defence.[1]

Mankind is on trial. The prosecutors before the throne of God are three women, *Agia Kyriake*, *Agia Tetrade* and *Agia Paraskeve*, who represent the feast and fast days of Sunday, Wednesday and Friday. The charges are: failing to abstain from work, lighting ovens, and strolling through the streets on Sundays; eating meat and cheese, and engaging in sexual relations on Wednesdays and Fridays. All three woman complain of the defilement they suffer at the hands of faithless humanity. After each complaint, a disembodied 'Voice', presumably that of God, pronounces a thunderous curse upon those who work on Sunday, and who fail to fast on Wednesdays, Fridays, and before receiving Holy Communion. Those who persist in their evil ways, it promises, will inherit eternal fire. Finally the Theotokos, the Mother of God, speaks for the defence:

> Master, you should not hear the entreaty of holy Friday and holy Wednesday, and destroy the works of your hands, but you should send forth a sign, so that they might see and believe.[2]

---

[1]   Rudolf Homburg, ed., *Apocalypsis Anastasiae* (Leipzig, 1903), 12–16.

[2]   *Anastasia*, 15.4–6.

From *Strangers to Themselves: The Byzantine Outsider*, ed. Dion C. Smythe. Copyright © 2000 by the Society for the Promotion of Byzantine Studies. Published by Ashgate Publishing Ltd, Gower House, Croft Road, Aldershot, Hampshire, GU11 3HR, Great Britain.

Deaf to the pleas of his mother, Christ turns his face away. Mary exclaims, 'Is there no one to help the sinners?!' Her cry activates a mass *proskynesis*:

> ... all fell on their faces before the throne of God: the angels and archangels, prophets and apostles and martyrs, crying out and saying, 'Master, have mercy on the sinners, and do not destroy the works of your hands'.[3]

No response comes from the throne. The plea is left hanging in the air, the fate of mankind in the balance. Anastasia and the angel proceed matter-of-factly to their next venue, a punishment zone of fiery lakes and pits. Will God destroy the works of his hands? We are left uncertain, and also with the suspicion that this drama of accusation and intercession is ongoing.

Camus considered an ordinary secular court, with human judges, most expressive of alienation for modern Western European society. Our tenth- or eleventh-century Byzantine author chose a heavenly court, staffed with divine personnel, and this choice has disturbing implications. The author's clear conviction that the judge has not the slightest interest in pleas for mercy, not even those of the Theotokos, is all the more chilling because this is truly the supreme court, whose verdicts are irrevocable and eternal.

The *Apocalypse of Anastasia*'s tableau of the Creator disowning and threatening to annihilate his creation signifies the ultimate in alienation – not just from society, but from the very source of one's being. What could underlie such a drastic perspective on sin and judgement? This paper argues that it is the experience of outsiders, of the socially excluded and ecclesiastically alienated, that informs – whether deliberately or subliminally – much of the moral imagination of Middle Byzantine apocryphal revelations such as the *Apocalypse of Anastasia* and a sister text, the *Apocalypse of the Theotokos*.[4]

Both apocalypses narrate journeys to the otherworld. They are early medieval (ninth- to eleventh-century) reworkings in Greek of the Late Antique genre, popular among both Jews and Christians, of the 'tour of

---

[3]   *Anastasia*, 15.11–16.2.

[4]   Both texts are discussed in detail in a forthcoming monograph on medieval Greek apocryphal texts, based in part on my doctoral dissertation (Princeton, 1997).

hell'.[5] The Late Antique apocalypses were attributed to biblical authority figures – prophets, scribes and apostles, such as Baruch, Enoch, Peter and Paul. In contrast, the two early medieval visions are both attributed to women. Is the change in attribution only coincidental? The earlier, 'male', texts generally reinforce a patriarchal and autocratic *status quo*, both in heaven and on earth. The later texts work within the same imaginative and interpretative structures, but to very different ends. Each, under the pressure of its unique social environment, imbues the conventions of the 'tour' genre with new meanings, and in particular with a tension wholly lacking in the earlier texts. I shall argue that the two 'female' apocalypses not only adapt the 'tour' genre, but ultimately subvert it, shifting its emphasis from the revelation of 'insider' secrets by authority figures to an expression of 'outsider' grievances through characters of more ambiguous status.

To this end, we shall first establish the nature of the 'tour' genre in general, and the basic features of two Late Antique exemplars, the *Apocalypses* attributed to Peter and to Paul. We shall then contrast the *Apocalypse of the Theotokos*, with its strong element of protest against otherworld punishments, examining it in the context of contemporary changes in the Byzantine penal code. Finally, we shall return to the *Apocalypse of Anastasia*, which, in its infusion of class tensions, completes the process of informing the genre with 'outsider' concerns.

In the two medieval texts, we may just glimpse what it was to be on the receiving end of the resurgent administrative, fiscal and judicial discipline of the Isaurian and Macedonian dynasties. Few other sources supply us with this perspective. The land legislation of the Macedonian emperors provides hints, but as Rosemary Morris has shown, its biblically flavoured rhetoric finally speaks most eloquently of Constantinople's attempts to break the power of the magnates, rather than of the realities or thought world of the humble.[6] Some saints' lives, such as the ninth-century *Life* of Philaretos the Merciful, offer anecdotal detail of the lives of those alienated by poverty, disease, military obligations, landlords, tax collectors, and other authority figures.[7] If we seek, however, a sense of the imaginative structures through which the alienated understood their lives, the various transformations of

---

[5] See M. Himmelfarb, *Tours of Hell: An Apocalyptic Form in Jewish and Christian Literature* (Philadelphia, 1983).

[6] R. Morris, 'The Powerful and the Poor in Tenth-Century Byzantium: Law and Reality', *P&P* 75 (1976), 3–27.

[7] M.-H. Fourmy and M. Leroy, eds, 'La Vie de S. Philarète', *B* 9 (1934), 85–170.

apocryphal 'tours of hell' deserve careful observation. The flexibility of the genre enabled, even encouraged, each new copyist to adapt the text to his or her own circumstances, while the underlying stability of the genre's structure and imagery throws such changes into high relief.

Evelyne Patlagean, the first to consider medieval Greek apocrypha with the eye of a social historian, coined the phrase 'normative fiction' for this kind of text.[8] The category encompasses a variety of types, from chain letters to apocalypses to saints' lives such as those of Basil the Younger and Andrew the Fool. Such texts may possibly preserve traces of actual historical or visionary experience, but are essentially fictions, cast in traditional religious genres, intended to reinforce moral and canonical norms. Whose articulation of these norms is being represented? Patlagean suggested we see the hand of a commissioning pastor or bishop, purposing to scare his flock sinless. I am here proposing that in the apocalypses' imaginative transformations we may also be able to sense an articulation, however indirect, of the outlook of the flock itself – of those on whom the norms were being imposed.

In the Theotokian and Anastasian apocalypses, the controlling theme is of the estrangement of man from God and from society by sin. The long arm of government and orthodoxy, personified in God the Father and the Son, is a terrifying arm of judgement and retribution, alienating the sinner from all possibility of divine compassion and forgiveness. The idea that mankind is estranged from God by sin is of course not new; it pervades the prophets, psalms, and histories of Israel. Canonical and apocryphal texts that grapple with problems of divine justice and mercy have a long history in Jewish literature. The 'tour of hell' apocalypses of the intertestamental period provided an ideal forum for such questions: most early otherworld tourists plead with a stern God to favour clemency over punishment, no matter how terrible the sin.[9]

Christians, adopting the genre with enthusiasm, continued both the debate and the practice of attribution to Biblical heroes. Not surprisingly, the earliest explicitly Christian otherworld journeys, of the second and

---

[8] E. Patlagean, 'Byzance et son autre monde. Observations sur quelques récits', in *Faire croire. Modalités de la diffusion et de la réception des messages religieux du XIIe au XVe siècle* (Rome, 1981), 201–221.

[9] See Richard Bauckham, 'The Conflict of Justice and Mercy: attitudes to the damned in apocalyptic literature', *Apocrypha* 1 (1990), 181–196.

third centuries AD, feature the apostles Peter and Paul.[10] It is worth examining these texts briefly, in order to highlight the formal similarities and thematic divergences between them and their medieval descendants.

Peter's vision begins with the disciples gathered around the Lord on the Mount of Olives – an insider group if ever there was one.[11] They ask Jesus for a teaching about the end of the world, and he obliges. Peter is so horrified at the terrible fate of the sinners that he exclaims it would have been better for the sinners if they had never been born. Christ rebukes him, warning him not to think himself more merciful than God. Peter is then shown the deeds that invited the terrible punishments. Persuaded that the sinners have got what they deserved, he is silent for the rest of the text. God's terrible justice is accepted.

Paul is not so easily cowed. He groans, weeps, pleads and argues with God throughout his journey, and gets results. The *Apocalypse of Paul* introduces a new generic feature: concessions. Jesus for Paul's sake grants all the sinners respite from punishment on Sundays.[12] (The story gets better in the telling: in one later Armenian version of the apocalypse, at the fervent prayers of Paul and the Theotokos, God releases all the sinners from torment and destroys the places of punishment – the *apokatastasis!*[13])

Paul questions God, and wrests concessions from God's Son, but he does so as an insider, receiving favours for sinners because of his personal friendship with Christ. Peter and Paul are 'team players'; neither ultimately questions the structures of the otherworld. They are, after all, the twin pillars of the church; they have something to lose by defying God. It will take two women, neither of whom has anything to lose, and the passage of around six centuries, to turn the genre upside down, to inspire texts that challenge the fundamental structures and principles of the otherworld. The gender inversion of the protagonists, from male authority figures to women, is the first step in the subversion of the genre, since the authority of women is always ambiguous. The *Apocalypse of the Theotokos* builds on Mary's moral standing within the church as an intercessor – but as we shall see, the position of female intercessors is

---

[10] *Peter* and *Paul* cited here from the translations of M.R. James, as reprinted in J.K. Elliott, ed., *The Apocryphal New Testament* (Oxford, 1993), 593–615 (Peter); 616–644 (Paul). Greek text of *Paul* in K. Tischendorf, *Apocalypses Apocryphae* (Leipzig, 1866), 34–69.

[11] Elliott, *ANT*, 600–612.

[12] Elliott, *ANT*, 639; §44.

[13] L. Leloir, transl., *Apocrypha Apostolorum Armeniaca*, Corpus Christianorum, Series Apocryphorum 3 (Turnhout, 1986), vol. 1, 171–172; version 4, §35.

more ambivalent than it might seem. The heroine of the *Apocalypse of Anastasia* is precisely a 'nobody', a generic nun, from an unnamed convent in an unidentified place.

Let us look more closely at the *Apocalypse of the Theotokos*, a direct descendent of Paul's apocalypse, composed probably around the ninth century.[14] Its close relationship to *Paul* helps to underscore its idiosyncracies – idiosyncracies that suggest the articulation of 'outsider' ideas.

How can the Mother of God be an outsider? Mary would seem the consummate heavenly *insider*, the advocate eternally poised at the right hand of Christ, as proclaimed in homilies, ivories, processional crosses, mosaics, templon screens and wall paintings all over Orthodox Byzantium.[15] Two images in particular would have been familiar to the Middle Byzantine Christian: the Deesis composition, featuring 'Christ enthroned between Mary and John like an emperor enthroned between interceding courtiers',[16] which began to dominate templon screens and provincial apses in this period; and the Theotokos *Paraklesis*, in which Mary, holding a prayer scroll, pleads with Christ for mankind.[17] A ninth-century mosaic of the *Paraklesis* image survives in Thessalonike's St Demetrios church: Mary's features appear red and distorted with grief, and her scroll reads 'Lord God, hear the voice of my prayer, for I pray on behalf of the world'.[18]

Mary does have full access to the throne, but in the popular imagination she, unlike most courtiers, uses her insider rank to be an advocate for outsiders. As we shall see below, one especially tormented group of sinners in her apocalypse makes this point explicitly, reciting a litany of famous (male) visitors – including Paul – who had never bothered to stop and ask after them. The desperate, whether excluded by economic misfortune, illness, low social status or the evil eye, have always gravitated to Mary's intercessory powers, even as today they flock to Lourdes, Fatima, Guadeloupe, Tinos and Medjugorje.

---

[14] M.R. James, ed., *Apocalypse of the Theotokos*, in *Apocrypha Anecdota*, Texts and Studies 2/3 (Cambridge, 1893), 115–126. See R. Bauckham, 'The Four Apocalypses of the Virgin Mary', in *The Fate of the Dead: Studies on the Jewish and Christian Apocalypses* (Leiden, 1998), 332–362.

[15] Sirarpie Der Nersessian, 'Two Images of the Virgin in the Dumbarton Oaks Collection', *DOP* 14 (1960), 74–75.

[16] Annemarie Weyl Carr, 'Deesis', in *ODB* (Washington, DC, 1991), 599–600.

[17] Der Nersessian, 78–80.

[18] G.A. and M.G. Soteriou, *He Basilike tou Hagiou Demetriou Thessalonikes* (Athens, 1952), 195–196, pl. 66.

The exact nature of Mary's position as an insider is complicated, and has been constantly subjected to redefinition. Being an intercessor does not of necessity signify insider status, especially for women within patriarchal structures. Paul Strohm has suggested, for example, that the intercessory role of later medieval English queens developed as their actual authority declined, and was contingent upon 'exclusion from the centers of mundane authority'.[19] Mary's intercession fits uncannily well into the patterns noted by Strohm. She is portrayed in her apocalypse as one whose normal sphere lies outside the male power centres of the otherworld, into which she bursts as a *femina ex machina*, able to force changes precisely because she comes from without.

Does Mary's intercession make her apocalypse a subversive text? Not necessarily. In the medieval English examples, intercession actually functions within the texts in submissive and total support of patriarchal autocracy.[20] Yet, Strohm notes, 'any such structure can be captured and redirected from within',[21] and I believe that this process can also be discerned within the Theotokian apocalypse.

Mary's vision, like that of Peter, begins on the Mount of Olives. Desiring to see the otherworld, she prays, 'In the name of the Father, Son and Holy Spirit, let the Archangel Gabriel descend, so that he may inform me concerning the punishments.'[22] The Archangel Michael descends with a company of angels, and all exchange a series of poetic greetings, multiple *khairetismata*, in the formal style of an *akathistos* prayer.

Mary has clout: she commands archangels and they come (though why Michael instead of Gabriel remains obscure). Notice, however, that all is at her initiative. She is not swept up, on God's initiative, to see the heavens, as were Paul, the prophets, or even Anastasia. Alone among all the otherworld tourists known to me, Mary is portrayed as having to ask for admittance, a significant departure from the norm. She is not invited into the otherworld, but sweeps into it like some outside inspector checking on reports of misdoing.

Like an inspector, Mary encounters resistance from functionaries who try to hide things, but she will not be deflected. Early on, when she asks to see a certain group of sinners, the angels in charge protest they are

---

[19] Paul Strohm, 'Queens as Intercessors', in his *Hochon's Arrow: the Social Imagination of Fourteenth-Century Texts* (Princeton, 1992), 95–119 at 96.

[20] Strohm, 104.

[21] Strohm, 9.

[22] *Theotokos* §1; 115.3–6.

under orders from God to maintain eternal darkness at this site.[23] They are overruled: at her invocation of the Trinity, the area is flooded with light. The sinners, overwhelmed, exclaim that of all the visitors to the punishments – Christ, Abraham, John the Baptist, Moses, and Paul are named – she alone has condescended to speak to them.[24]

Mary is clearly in control. Most tours of hell, even Paul's, are formally more passive; the visitors are shown various scenes first, and ask the angel for an explanation second, but Mary takes active charge of what the angel shows her. She wants to know exactly how many punishments there are, and what each group has done; Michael asks at each turning where she would like to go next. Like a royal visitor passing through the wards, Mary pauses at most venues to enquire kindly about the group, and her presence occasionally causes a brief respite from torment. Throughout, she weeps freely, and sighs, like Peter, Paul and the prophets before her, that it were well for these men had they never been born. The earlier texts had taken pains to refute that idea, but this text's author seems to endorse it. Instead of contradicting her, Michael merely warns that the worst is yet to come.[25]

As the punishments grow more and more gruesome, Mary becomes ever more determined, agitated and argumentative. Finally she offers a shocking proposition, challenging God to treat her the way he is treating mankind: 'Let me too be punished with the Christian sinners, for they are the children of my Son.'[26] With this explicit statement of kinship, the hearer is reminded of Mary's double maternity: she is the Mother of God, but she is also, spiritually, the mother of all humanity. God, however, does not seem moved by the pleas of his mother. While the Archangel tries to calm Mary with soothing words, we wait in vain for a response to her challenge.

But this indignant grandmother has had enough. Summoning the chariot of the cherubim and seraphim, she demands to be taken up to the throne itself, there to marshall all the heavenly hosts in her cause.[27] Her entreaty does get results: first, 'the Lord' agrees to spare any sinner who calls upon her name at the moment of death; and in the end, like Paul before her, Mary secures for the sinners a respite from punishment, this

---

[23]   *Theotokos* §4; 116.18–117.24.
[24]   *Theotokos* §4; 117.7–14.
[25]   *Theotokos* §11; 119.5–8.
[26]   *Theotokos* §25; 124.1–12.
[27]   *Theotokos* §26; 124–126.

one for the fifty days of Easter.[28] The text leaves the distinct impression, however, that Mary has had to wrest these concessions from the men on thrones, and has had to wield extraordinary means to persuade them to show their greatness through mercy rather than retribution.

It is not in the nature of the men on thrones in either 'female' apocalypse to show mercy. Both Christ and his Father are distant, stern monarchs. Neither woman actually sees or speaks directly to 'the invisible Father' (aoratos pater), not even the Theotokos, who in both texts addresses her requests to 'the undefiled *throne* of the Father', and is answered by a 'Voice', the source of which she cannot see.[29] Christ, in the theological imagination of both 'female' apocalypses, is a poorly defined, remote divinity whose humanity is not emphasized. Both apocalypses (especially *Anastasia*) are puzzlingly imprecise when it comes to the Son's relationship to the Father and his role in the heavenly economy. The Theotokian apocalypse *is* sure of one thing – patriarchy; and this certainty leads its author on occasion into an almost subordinationist presentation of Christ. Heaven is modelled as being so thoroughly patriarchal that only at the direction of the Father does the Son climb down from his throne to talk to the sinners.[30]

The viewpoint of those awed and alienated by grand structures of power also influences the physical appearance of the otherworld in the medieval texts. For Paul, the city of God is a warm, glowing place of golden walls and thrones, comely gates, and rivers of honey, milk, oil and wine.[31] For Anastasia, separated from Paul by gender, status and seven centuries, God dwells in a frightening domain of blinding light, of ice and fire, and of massive, limitless gates, beyond which stretch alien vistas containing immense pools.[32] The chronological gap between Paul and Anastasia is probably less significant here than their divergent status and gender: another tenth-century vision, that of Kosmas the Monk, provides an instructive foil for *Anastasia*.[33] For Kosmas, a former palace official, the otherworld is but a pleasant continuation of the cultured ease, learned discourse, and access to power that he enjoyed as a favoured courtier at the imperial palace. Reflected in the two 'female' apocalypses is a

---

[28] *Theotokos* §26, 124.35–37; §29, 124–126.

[29] *Theotokos* §26; 124–126; *Anastasia* 14.10–16.2.

[30] *Theotokos* §29, 126–127.

[31] Elliott, *ANT*, 630–632; §21–29.

[32] *Anastasia*, 4–12.

[33] Christine Angelidi, ed., 'La Version longue de la vision du moine Cosmas', *AnalBoll* 101 (1983), 73–99.

different world altogether from that of Paul and Kosmas, redolent instead of exclusion from distant centres of power, and of suffering at their hands.

As medieval Byzantium constructed the celestial court in the image of its own terrestrial imperial court, so the otherworld punishment areas in the apocryphal texts correspond to earthly realities of crime and punishment. Prison imagery is developed most fully in the *Life* of Andrew the Fool, yet another Middle Byzantine apocryphon infused with 'outsider' sentiments.[34] A visionary interlude describes the visit of Andrew's disciple Epiphanios to Hades, which is depicted as a huge, dark, ugly, noisy prison of cells, iron bars, and unpleasant animals that represent the souls of specific sinners, according to type of sin. The otherworld punishment areas in the apocalypses are also full of prisoners, held captive by terrible angels carrying out God's commands – most often, punishments that entail mutilation of the specific body parts involved in the sin.

Such symbolic transformation of the body according to the type of crime would have been a literal reality for many living under Byzantine rule, especially after the mid-eighth century. The *Ecloga*, a selection of laws issued by Leo III and Constantine V, gave mutilation special prominence in the Byzantine penal code.[35] In addition to flogging and fines, its seventeenth title provided for amputation of the hand (theft), tongue (perjury), or private parts (sodomy); blinding (sacrilege); and, most commonly, nose-slitting (sexual sins). Mutilation was considered more merciful than capital punishment, more in keeping with the Christian values that the imperial father and son championed in the prologue to their revision of Roman law.

Evelyne Patlagean has traced the development of Byzantine penal mutilations, in law codes as well as in hagiographic, visionary and dream-interpretation texts, primarily between the sixth and ninth centuries.[36] The Theotokian and Anastasian apocalypses, which fall outside the chronological scope of her study, represent a culmination of the trends she noted. This is not surprising, given the probable date of composition for the Theotokian apocalypse around the ninth century,

---

[34] Lennart Rydén, ed., *The Life of St. Andrew the Fool*, Studia Byzantina Upsaliensia, 4:1,2 (Uppsala, 1995), lines 2323–2380.

[35] L. Burgmann, ed., *Ecloga* (Frankfurt-am-Main, 1983), 226–243; English translation in E.H. Freshfield, *A Manual of Roman Law: the Ecloga* (Cambridge, 1926), 104–105.

[36] E. Patlagean, 'Byzance et le blason pénal du corps', in *Du châtiment dans la cité. Supplices corporels et peine de mort dans le monde antique* (Rome, 1984), 405–426.

when the 'Eclogic' vogue for mutilation, confirmed and further developed in the laws of Basil I, was well under way. Can it be merely coincidence that Mary's apocalypse registers the strongest protest of all the apocryphal texts against symbolic 'made-to-measure' mutilations and tortures in hell? Leo III and Constantine V may have felt the new measures were more merciful, but several centuries later, once the system was entrenched, the two medieval 'female' apocalypses, and especially that of the Theotokos, begged to differ.

Most 'tours of hell', whether Jewish or Christian, Byzantine or Western, explore the tension between justice and mercy; most also contain 'made-to-measure' punishments.[37] But the issue is treated with special intensity in the two post-*Ecloga* Byzantine texts. Mary weeps more bitterly, and questions more insistently, than do her apostolic predecessors. Anastasia herself does not comment on what she sees, but the courtroom drama with which this paper opened, and later scenes with sinners, leave no doubt as to the compiler's concern regarding the state of justice in heaven and, by extension, on earth.

Both 'female' apocalypses contain implicit critiques of the structures and operating principles of the otherworld. Are they subversive? Writing in a time and place not far removed in spirit from medieval Byzantium, Dostoevsky thought so. In book five of *The Brothers Karamazov* (1880), a Slavonic version of the Theotokian apocalypse furnishes the rebellious Ivan Karamazov with inspiration for his 'Grand Inquisitor' tale, which struggles to reconcile similar questions of divine justice and mercy, but finally rejects a Creation – and a Creator – that allows human suffering.

The *Apocalypse of Anastasia*, with whose courtroom scene this paper began, is seemingly the final composition in the family of Greek texts spawned by the *Apocalypse of Paul*. Structurally, it is heavily indebted to Paul's apocalypse; spiritually, to Mary's. The basic features of its Greek and Slavonic text types were set sometime after the murder of Nikephoros II Phokas in 969, around seven centuries after the probable composition of *Paul*. It is the most eclectic of the three texts, and the most socially ambivalent.

Anastasia's attitude towards otherworld punishment and retribution is tantalizingly mixed. Here, I submit, outsider concerns and imagery have not just influenced the 'tour of hell' genre, but seem to have taken it over completely. Three themes in particular illustrate this phenomenon.

---

[37] See Eileen Gardiner, *Medieval Visions of Heaven and Hell* (New York, 1993), for the Western material.

1) The Mother of God. Mary's development through the Paul–
Theotokos–Anastasia sequence is striking. In the third-century *Paul*, she
plays a gracious but mostly decorative role in the otherworld, while the
Archangel Michael bears the terrible burden of intercession.[38] By the ninth
century, she has been transformed, in her own apocalypse, into a majestic
activist grandmother who storms the gates of heaven. By the turn of the
tenth century, as recorded in *Anastasia*, Mary is a permanent fixture
before the throne. No longer an occasional tourist in the otherworld, she
has come to stay. In her own apocalypse, Mary is a normal human being
who lives on earth, and needs Michael's help as *psychopomp* to enter the
otherworld, but in the later *Anastasia*, she is firmly entrenched as an
inhabitant of heaven. Multiple epithets affirm her as the only hope of
sinners, a sentiment we have seen mirrored in the visual culture of
Anastasia's time as well. The text does not place much hope in Christ, who
appears consistently as the stern judgmental figure of a myriad frescoed
domes.

2) From sanctuary to bureaucracy. The contrast between the Late
Antique and insider consciousness of *Paul* and the thought world of
Anastasia is especially marked in the two texts' treatment of the reports of
the guardian angels. Paul sees the angels report directly to God at the end
of the day, in an open-air assembly, as part of the preparation for the
celestial vespers service.[39] They deliver an oral report of sins and good
deeds, and receive a direct oral response. The context is liturgical, and at
the highest point of heaven stands the sanctuary. Anastasia sees the
angels come to report not to God, but to two clerk angels who sit toiling
over large ledgers, constantly updating the records of sins and good
deeds according to the latest reports.[40] At the highest point of heaven we
find not worship, but paperwork. Even the angels have lost direct access
to the throne, and everything you have ever done is written down
somewhere in those books. It is a scene worthy of Kafka.

3) Corrupt officials. Continuing the theme of bureaucratic alienation,
Anastasia develops with special passion the despair of suppliants faced
with corrupt local government officials and authority figures of all kinds.
The apocalypses of Peter, Paul and the Theotokos do not sort their sinners
by class, and by and large, the worst sins in the earlier texts are
theological and sexual, not social or economic. Officials are wholly absent

---

[38]   Elliott, *ANT*, 638, 640; §43, 46.
[39]   Elliott, *ANT*, 528–529; §8–10.
[40]   *Anastasia*, 24–26.

from the three earlier texts, but Anastasia's vision reserves a separate, purpose-built punishment zone solely for civil and ecclesiastical officials who embezzled, lied, stole, confiscated property, and cheated widows and orphans.[41] Some of the most spirited moments in the text occur in this zone, which opens with a tableau of the empty thrones, imperial and ecclesiastical, from which the mighty have been put down.

The most vivid single personality in *Anastasia* is Peter the Protospatharios, who describes with bitter remorse his official career – its murders, property confiscations, unjust judgements, accumulation of wealth and failures in almsgiving – and his present state of relentless torment.[42] He addresses a desperate plea to Anastasia to warn his wife and children, lest they suffer the same fate, and to beg them to offer alms (from the ill-gotten wealth they inherited) for the mitigation of his agony.

A disproportionately large number of the sinners in *Anastasia* are governmental and ecclesiastical authority figures, and they endure the text's most gruesome and creative punishments. In this section only, the heat is turned up, and the sound is turned on; we hear their groaning and feel the flames consuming their flesh. The vision revels in the symbolic inversion of these people's experience on earth. Patlagean has documented how it was usually the poor who suffered penal mutilations, while wealthy offenders – if tried at all – were most often let off with fines.[43] *Anastasia*'s otherworld reverses such terrestrial realities, declaring unambiguously that punishment – the more horrible the better – for the formerly powerful is just, and richly deserved. The theme of course harks back to the parable of Dives and Lazarus (Luke 16:19–31), but its presence here is an innovation for the 'tour of hell' genre.

The text also insinuates a further modification (admittedly quite subtle) which could signify the transformation of hell by the alienated. In the 'élite' punishment zone, reserved for emperors, bishops and high officials, we see and hear torture, lamentation, gnashing of teeth. But when we listen closely to the first punishment zone, inhabited largely by lay people of no special rank or station, guilty of commonplace sins of the home, the marketplace and the parish church, we will hear nothing. Someone has turned down both the sound and the heat for the ordinary people. In the Greek versions of *Anastasia*, the horrible stenches, lamentations, sizzling flesh, and torture by avenging angels with iron

---

[41] *Anastasia*, 26–30.
[42] *Anastasia*, 29–30.
[43] Patlagean, 'Blason pénal', 407.

hooks characteristic of earlier tours of hell – and preserved in *Anastasia's* Slavonic versions – have clearly been edited out.[44]

Location is also significant. We notice that these hapless lay sinners – whose babies died before they could be baptized, who slept in or baked bread on Sunday, who came to church with alcohol on their breath, who ate meat or cheese on Wednesdays or Fridays, who aborted their babies, gave false weight in the market, or tampered with sealings – unlike most of the élite sinners, are not actually boiling in the lakes and rivers of fire, but sit on the banks, as if waiting. Reading more closely still, we see that many of the verbs here are not past tense – 'they did this; now they burn' – but present tense: these are the people who *do* this kind of thing.

Could it be that what appeared as scenes of 'hell' in the other texts, visions of specific sinners who committed specific crimes and now pay the penalty for eternity, have been transmogrified in the lay punishment zone into a present-tense vision of the 'hell' created on earth by human sin? This would be sin as known in the mind of God, which sees simultaneously both the commission of a sin and its effect. Another possibility is that the fiery lakes and rivers represent the refining fires of conscience and compunction – and that we are on the path to a kind of purgatory. Eastern Orthodox church teaching has always discouraged belief in a purgatorial zone of the kind developed in the West, but it is undeniably a useful unofficial concept if one seeks to reconcile questions of justice and mercy, since it allows for both judgement and the granting of a second chance.

Whatever the theological ramifications of the silent, waiting sinners in the lay punishment zone of *Anastasia*, it is clear that the text cheerfully articulates a double standard with respect to punishment: (temporary) purgatory for outsiders, (eternal) hell for insiders. The prevailing earthly double standard, whereby the rich literally get away with murder time after time, while the poor are punished severely for even minor infractions, is thus inverted. On earth, the poor are kept in their place, but in *Anastasia's* otherworld, the rich are finally put in theirs, into the places of torment they are laying up for themselves with their treasures on earth. *Anastasia* turns the earthly standard on its head – and the 'tour of hell' genre along with it.

---

[44] For the Slavonic version see M. Speranskii, ed., 'Maloe Izvestnoe Vizantiiskoe "Videnie" i ego Slavianskie Teksty', *BSl* 3 (1931), 110–133.

5. John of Phoberou:
a Voice Crying in the Wilderness[*]

Robert H. Jordan

In the opening chapter of St John's gospel, the envoys of the Pharisees approach John the Baptist and ask him 'Who are you?' John replies 'I am the voice of one crying in the wilderness "Make straight the way of the Lord," as the prophet Isaiah said.'[1] Other accounts of John's relations with the Pharisees and Sadducees emphasize his alienation from the religious establishment of his day. 'You brood of vipers,' he said, 'God is able from these stones to raise up children to Abraham.'[2] John's adoption of the wilderness as his base of operation was highly significant for one who saw himself as an outsider. As we shall see, John the Baptist's invocation of past authority and his call for a return to the traditional path of holiness find a strong echo in the writing of another outsider who took himself off to the wilderness, the twelfth-century monk, John of Phoberou.

This John was a monk who with the aid of some important benefactors refounded and rebuilt the monastery of Phoberou dedicated to the Prodromos and became its *hegoumenos*. The only source of information on this shadowy figure and his monastery is the *Typikon* which he wrote for his restored community.[3] If we are to believe John's description of the site, it was set in a wild and rugged landscape composed of ravines, wooded hillsides, seaside promontories and high peaks.[4] Of course such a setting was part and parcel of the monastic tradition, but since no ruins have as

---

[*] This paper is dedicated to the memory of a close friend and colleague, Dr W.J. McAllister, who died on 13 March 1998.

[1] John 1:22–23; Is. 40:3.

[2] Matt. 3:7–9.

[3] A.I. Papadopoulos-Kerameus, ed., *Noctes Petropolitanae* (Petrograd, 1913), 1–88 (hereafter, *Phoberou Typikon*); on the refounder see 1.4.

[4] *Phoberou Typikon*, 6.9–17.

From *Strangers to Themselves: The Byzantine Outsider*, ed. Dion C. Smythe. Copyright © 2000 by the Society for the Promotion of Byzantine Studies. Published by Ashgate Publishing Ltd, Gower House, Croft Road, Aldershot, Hampshire, GU11 3HR, Great Britain.

yet been identified as those of the Phoberou monastery, we have no way of verifying John's description.[5]

John says very little indeed about his own background. We do know the names of his grandparents and parents, for they are listed among the people to be commemorated annually on 24th September;[6] both his grandmother and mother ended their lives as nuns. But where he was brought up and other aspects of his early life are a complete mystery. However, he had some illustrious benefactors; chief among these were Nikephoros Botaneiates and Eudokia Komnene, the daughter of the sebastocrator Isaac.[7] He also lists among those to be commemorated the patriarch Nicholas III Grammatikos.[8] From what he says about the benefactions he received, it is clear that Eudokia Komnene was especially generous, making a number of donations.[9] I get the impression also from short comments buried in his document that he had practised the ascetic life before he came to Phoberou, either in another community or possibly at home.[10]

The convictions that took him off to the wilderness are found in the long rambling first chapter of his *Typikon*.[11] There he sets out for the reader and listener, with plenty of quotations from scripture to back him up, two familiar themes: first, that man was created by God to have a citizenship in heaven,[12] to reach up to that place and contemplate the beauties there; and secondly, that all the things which confer distinction on a man in this life quickly fade and pass away. In a summary sentence he tells us that he went to the monastery of Phoberou in order to turn his back on the world and live on his own for God – a very traditional reason.[13]

Much later, when he decided to write down the *Typikon* for his community, he did what a number of other founders and refounders were doing at this period and based his document on the *Hypotyposis* written by Timothy for the monastery of the Evergetis just outside

---

[5]   R. Janin, *La géographie ecclésiastique de l'empire byzantin*, I, *Les églises et les monastères des grands centres byzantins* (Paris, 1975), 7f. For the identification of the site, see 8.

[6]   *Phoberou Typikon*, 62.22–27.

[7]   *Phoberou Typikon*, 62.12–16.

[8]   *Phoberou Typikon*, 62.18–19.

[9]   *Phoberou Typikon*, 62.30.

[10]   *Phoberou Typikon*, 14.16–23; 75.20–24.

[11]   *Phoberou Typikon*, 1.10–5.33.

[12]   Cf. Phil. 3:20.

[13]   *Phoberou Typikon*, 5.11–13.

Constantinople.[14] John does not acknowledge Timothy's *Hypotyposis* anywhere as the source for much of his document; this is in complete contrast to those portions which he added, for in these he gives us the sources of many of his quotations. It is almost as if the Evergetis *Typikon* was the acknowledged pattern for *typika* at this time. And there may be some truth in such a view, if we are to go by a sentence in Isaac's *Typikon* for the monastery of Kosmosoteira which was founded in 1152. In Isaac's *Typikon* we find the following:

> Since many of the wise people, who have renewed holy places of meditation and have attached monks to them for the praise of God, have preferred the *Typikon* of the Evergetis to the *typika* that exist in other places of meditation, we also, following them, prefer this one and we wish the monks to use it in all its arrangements.[15]

Of all the earlier *typika* referred to by Isaac, John's *Typikon* for the monastery of Phoberou is the earliest surviving copy of Timothy's *Hypotyposis*; another using the same source is the *Typikon* written for the empress Eirene Doukaina's foundation dedicated to the Theotokos Kecharitomene.[16] In the case of John, I use the word 'copy' deliberately. For when John was making use of Timothy's *Hypotyposis*, he copied it virtually word for word with the result that it has become an important check on the text of its source.

Despite this, John clearly had a somewhat different view of monastic life and practice to that encapsulated by Timothy. For different founders to have different attitudes to such matters as access to the monastery for people of the opposite gender, or monks coming from another community is not surprising and the Evergetis 'family' of *typika* provides us with plenty of evidence for such differences and the modifications that were made to accommodate them.[17] However, what is remarkable in John's case is the strident way in which he set out the modifications that *he* wished to make. He did not cut out much of what he found in his source; instead he laced the whole document with passages of ascetic

---

[14]   P. Gautier, 'Le *typikon* de la Théotokos Évergétis', *REB*, 40 (1982), 5–101.

[15]   G.K. Papazoglou, *Typikon Isaakiou Alexiou Komnenou tes mones Theotokou tes Kosmosoteiras* (Komotene, 1994), 43.137–139.

[16]   P. Gautier, 'Le *typikon* de la Théotokos Kécharitôménè', *REB*, 43 (1985), 5–165.

[17]   On this group of *typika* see R.H. Jordan, 'The monastery of the Theotokos Evergetis, its children and grandchildren', in M. Mullett and A. Kirby, eds, *The Theotokos Evergetis and Eleventh-Century Monasticism* (Belfast, 1994), 215–245. For the relationship between the *Hypotyposis* of Timothy and John's *Typikon*, see 218–225.

teaching. The impression he gives is that he considered the monastic life
as practised in communities like the Evergetis far too lax, far too soft and
did not follow the teachings of the early fathers of the church in a number
of ways.

One of the two chief criticisms of current monastic practice
highlighted by John in his *Typikon* concerns fasting. He devoted no less
than six new sections to it, some of which were written at great length.[18]
His primary aim seems to have been to re-establish the traditional
practice of fasting on every Wednesday and Friday throughout the year
to the same degree as that laid down for the holy period of Lent.

> We must genuflect as for the holy period of Lent and the diet will
> be similar, made up of steeped pulses or fruits and fresh
> vegetables, and for our drink, water or hot water flavoured with
> cumin, taken at the beginning of the ninth hour. For the most wise
> and divine teachers speak as follows in their rules setting it out in
> detail, 'If any bishop or priest or deacon or reader or choir member
> does not fast during the holy period of Lent or on Wednesday or
> Friday, unless he is prevented from doing so by some bodily
> weakness, he should be deposed; but if he is a lay person, he
> should be excommunicated'.[19]

John was not content with setting down that strong statement; he added
quotation after quotation drawn from such varied sources as the Lausiac
History, the twelfth canon of the Council of Gangra, the Panaria of St
Epiphanios, St Athanasios and St Symeon.[20] This was something he felt
very strongly about and he was utterly convinced that what he was
advocating was central to true *askesis*. When he reached the end of his
quotations on this topic he added the following:

> For I did not write things of my own choice or wish or devising,
> but what we have received in writing from our holy fathers and
> what we have learned from experience itself to be true and
> immutable and unchangeable and without which it is impossible to
> follow the path of the monastic life.[21]

---

[18]   *Phoberou Typikon*, 13.3–14.26; 27.9–28.18; 28.19–28.28; 28.29–33.16; 33.17–38.3; 47.12–49.27.

[19]   *Phoberou Typikon*, 27.12–19.

[20]   *Phoberou Typikon*: for Lausiac History 27.23–26; for the Panaria 27.30–34; for canon of the Council of Gangra 27.27–30; for St Athanasios 27.34–28.6; for St Symeon 28.9–10.

[21]   *Phoberou Typikon*, 28.14–18.

So much for the general principle. As John knew, an exception could legitimately be made when an important feast fell on a Wednesday or Friday, and of course this was the way that the tradition of fasting on these days could be easily undermined. It is possibly the result of his experience in one or more communities that he was so strict in laying down the procedures for his own. To begin with, he strictly forbade cheese, fish or eggs to be eaten on any Wednesday or Friday, whether an important feast fell on that day or not. But then as a concession he allowed one dish cooked with olive oil to be eaten to celebrate an important feast that fell on either fast day. To show that this was no light thing to have conceded he wrote:

> But I have judged myself in advance to be condemned by God because of your weakness and suggest to you that you break the fast with a cooked dish when it is the day of a great feast.[22]

In case there might be arguments about whether such and such a feast was important enough to warrant the one cooked dish, John set out a list of feasts for the year and marked which ones were important enough to merit this concession.[23] The only other way to avoid fasting on these two days at the monastery of Phoberou was to be sick. For the *hegoumenos* was instructed in the *Typikon*:

> to care especially for such [brothers] with all his heart and assist the sick on fast days with both wine and cooked food and with all his heart be anxious about their comfort and the recovery of their strength.[24]

Whether this led to increased numbers of brothers falling sick I would not like to say.

This regime evidently did not meet with wholehearted agreement right across the community. John does not talk of outright opposition or even of different factions among the monks; rather, he alludes to some who, perhaps as a cover for their own less than wholehearted support, expressed a cynical conviction that others were just going along with his

---

[22] *Phoberou Typikon*, 34.10–12.
[23] *Phoberou Typikon*, 36.13–37.2.
[24] *Phoberou Typikon*, 28.23–26.

instructions. In the midst of a section setting out the proper way to fast, we find the following:

> I know for certain that many of you, and especially the careless, receive such instructions with disgust saying, 'You labour for nothing and to no purpose, no one will carry out these instructions when you have died'.[25]

Again a little later in the same passage he wrote:

> But since there are some people who make the hands of the many feeble, and in addition to bringing nothing useful into our lives weaken the zeal of others and deride and ridicule saying, 'Cease your advice, stop exhorting; they do not wish to heed you; have nothing to do with them' ... For I know that many have said those words, since I have seen some of you not receiving my teaching with enthusiasm, but laughing and deriding it, saying to me, 'They were completely persuaded, no one scorns your instructions; all were chastened'.[26]

It is surely very unusual for the writer of a *typikon* to acknowledge that the instructions within it are not popular with some of those who are supposed to carry them out. In the case of other *typika* the suspicion has been that these documents set out what the founder or *hegoumenos* wished ideally to happen, and that some of the instructions were possibly not put into practice or were modified and watered down. Here in the case of Phoberou reluctance on the part of some at least of the community to accept the teaching of the *hegoumenos* is plainly stated. In the face of this opposition John began by calling on the backing of the apostle Paul: 'Obey your leaders and submit to them for they are keeping watch over your souls, as men who will have to give account.'[27] Then using other biblical quotations he justified his stand by saying that he as *hegoumenos* could not hide behind a plea of ignorance in these matters as perhaps some of his flock could, and furthermore 'he had been appointed to correct the ignorance of other people and forewarn them of the approach of danger from the devil'.[28] In a final flourish on this point he bluntly states:

---

[25] *Phoberou Typikon*, 29.15–18.
[26] *Phoberou Typikon*, 30.31–31.1, 31.3–7.
[27] Heb. 13:17; *Phoberou Typikon*, 29.19–21.
[28] *Phoberou Typikon*, 29.27–33.

If I scatter the seed and you do not accept it or bear the fruit of obedience, I will gain from God the reward of my advice and will receive as much of a recompense as I would have received if you had listened.[29]

The other important issue which John addressed and on which he inserted considerable material into that which he copied from Timothy's *Hypotyposis* is sexual temptation. The introduction to this topic is serious and yet mysterious:

When I have mentioned one thing, I will bring my discourse to an end. What is this thing? It is something which is greater than all evils and their chief, and one which causes great harm to our souls, or to put it more strongly, to our bodies also, and throws the whole brotherhood into confusion both as regards our wonderful way of life and the tranquillity of our souls' dwelling on this mountain.[30]

John began with the instruction that the community should never possess female animals inside or outside the monastery. To back up this severe restriction John did not invoke supporting statements or admonitions from the early fathers as elsewhere in his *Typikon*. He says:

For since I have had experience of the harm and damage, both spiritual and physical, that come from them, I am arranging for you to escape from their error and deceit, so that you may not be grieved as I was, and incur great damage and no benefit because of them.[31]

A very interesting personal reference and one which might provoke wild speculation. At the very least it raises the possibility that John had been at one time in another monastery where the presence of female animals had caused him spiritual unease and even contributed to his departure.

Next, on the question of boys and beardless youths John was not so uncompromising. He tempered his instruction that beardless youths should not be accepted, which I am sure was his personal conviction, with the possibility that the *hegoumenos* might be obliged from time to time to accept such a person either for some specific task or to look after

---

[29]   *Phoberou Typikon*, 32.19–21.
[30]   *Phoberou Typikon*, 75.9–13.
[31]   *Phoberou Typikon*, 75.20–24.

elderly monks. However, he stipulated that any such beardless youth, while ministering to members of the community, must reside on a particular estate belonging to the monastery until he had grown a beard. At that point any such young person might be admitted to the monastery.[32] John reinforced his position on the matter of boys and beardless youths by inserting, without any acknowledgement of its source, the greater part of a letter of *abba* Paul Helladikos, who is thought to have been an ascetic of the sixth century, who came to Palestine from Greece, became the disciple of Theognius and later wrote his *Life*.[33] The passage inserted by John is not short. It stretches to more than one hundred and twenty lines of the printed text and is very hard-hitting.[34] It begins with an introductory stretch of teaching on the topic of sexual temptations and pulls no punches:

> Those who say that they associate with women and children and are not harmed in their souls by this pleasure, but are greatly strengthened and face with resistance the temptations of fornication and the titillations of the flesh, are entirely possessed by the deceit of demons.[35]

I am sure that John agreed with this assessment. Paul continues his teaching by analysing the deceits of the demons and the foolishness of the men who put themselves in such a dangerous situation. He continues:

> For if he who has looked on a woman to desire her has committed adultery already with her in his heart,[36] it is much more the case with the one who associates with younger males, whether he is an old man, or a younger man in the prime of life and at the height of his powers and seething with fleshly passion.[37]

After alluding to various warriors of the faith, whom he had known, and the way that they were tempted regarding their own mothers, sisters,

---

[32] *Phoberou Typikon*, 77.12–23.

[33] On Paul Helladikos, see 'Acta Sancti Theognii episcopi Beteliae', *AnalBoll* X (1891), 75–78, and additionally, *AnalBoll* XI (1892), 476f.

[34] *Phoberou Typikon*, 77.31–82.8; for the full text of the letter see *Anecdota Byzantina e codicibus Upsaliensibus*, ed. V. Lundström (Uppsala, 1902), 17–23.

[35] *Phoberou Typikon*, 77.31–78.4.

[36] Matt. 5:28.

[37] *Phoberou Typikon*, 78.12–15.

brothers and young sons, Paul describes the clever methods employed by the demon of fornication. To counter them his advice is as follows:

> Let us instruct ourselves that whenever we meet a handsome face, whether they are our brothers or members of our own family, we do not look clearly at the handsome face, but speak looking down at the ground and in that way answer those who speak with us. For the eye of a man is like a shameless dog running in a frenzy over the faces it sees, and always the demons use this weapon against us as they also use the hand.[38]

Paul continues by reminding his readers that it was through the eye that Eve was tempted by the beauty of the tree in the garden of Eden. To bring his message home in a striking way Paul then relates the story of the eunuch Eutropios who renounced the world and became a monk, taking up residence in a monastery of eunuchs close to the city of Jericho. Some unnamed wealthy citizen of Jericho came with gifts to the monastery from time to time and a friendship grew up between him and Eutropios. When a son was born to the wealthy citizen, he asked Eutropios to act as the boy's sponsor. After the baptism the wealthy man continued to bring his son to visit Eutropios, who became exceedingly fond of the boy. When the boy reached the age of ten years, Eutropios began to entertain loathsome desires for the boy even to the extent that he wished to have intercourse with him. In his frantic state of temptation Eutropios had the good sense to tell the father of the child to take him home and never bring him to the monastery again. The result for Eutropios was that he was tempted by the demon with renewed ferocity. Despite inflicting physical harm on his own body, the evil passion did not go away and Eutropios experienced erotic dreams and seminal emissions. This lasted for quite a long time before eventually the dark cloud, as Eutropios described it, was taken away by God and he gained peace from the pernicious temptation.[39] Within this story about Eutropios is a short section dealing with the sexuality of eunuchs and containing a very brief reference to the problem of lesbian relationships in convents.[40] Paul Helladikos rounds off his story of the monk Eutropios by saying:

---

[38] *Phoberou Typikon*, 80.8–14.

[39] For the story of Eutropios, see *Phoberou Typikon*, 80.18–82.8.

[40] *Phoberou Typikon*: on the sexuality of eunuchs, see 81.2–6; on lesbian relationships in convents, see 81.6–11.

> Therefore let what happened to Eutropios the eunuch, the priest
> and *hegoumenos*, be instruction for those who say, 'We sleep with
> women and live with children and are not harmed'.[41]

At this point John dispensed with the final exhortation in Paul's letter and
continued with his own addition to Timothy's *Hypotyposis*. And what a
surprise this final section on sexual temptation is! We can almost hear
John's voice as it rises to a crescendo. To gain the full effect of his writing
I must first repeat the end of his extract from Paul Helladikos:

> Therefore let what happened to Eutropios the eunuch, the priest
> and *hegoumenos*, be instruction for those who say, 'We sleep with
> women and live with children and are not harmed'. With women
> and children! What am I saying? Sometimes we are even tempted
> with regard to irrational animals themselves, and this we know
> from many who have made confession to us and from the story
> which will now be told.[42]

This story concerns a monk who had gone on a journey with a priest from
the monastery of Ta Kellia and had then been instructed by the priest to
return with the female donkey on which the priest had ridden. On the
way back the monk was tempted by the devil seven times to commit sin
with the donkey, but he resisted. When he arrived, his *geron* praised him
and, since he had the gift of second sight, told him that he had seen seven
crowns on the monk's head as he arrived. Once this story is finished John
concluded this section on sexual temptation with a short homiletic
passage of his own.

In view of this very unusual collection of material I think we have to
ask ourselves why John felt it was necessary to discuss this topic in so
much graphic detail. Had some monasteries grown notoriously lax about
such things? Or was this the result of an unfortunate experience John had
had in another community? Incidentally, it hardly comes as a surprise to
learn that, when copying out the section from Timothy's *Hypotyposis* on
the numbers of brothers that were to occupy a cell, John changed
Timothy's stipulation of two to a cell to three to a cell.[43]

John's arrival at the monastery of Phoberou in October 1112 came
soon after the death of the patriarch Nicholas. In his *Typikon* John

[41] *Phoberou Typikon*, 82.6–8.
[42] *Phoberou Typikon*, 82.6–11.
[43] On this, compare *Evergetis Typikon*, ed. Gautier, 67.917 with *Phoberou Typikon*, 58.7.

acknowledged that it was Nicholas who had confirmed the independence of the monastery.[44] The final years of Nicholas's patriarchate had seen the upheavals on Mount Athos caused in part by the presence of Vlach shepherds with their families and flocks, but encompassing some other issues as well. This tangled episode, with the bitter recriminations of opposing factions amongst the monks, the appeals to the emperors Alexios I and John II and the mysterious *entole* which caused so much resentment, is to be found in the notorious compilation entitled the *Diegesis Merike*.[45] One of the issues dealt with there and one which provoked a deputation to go and lobby the emperor Alexios I is precisely one of those about which John felt so strongly, namely: whether boys or beardless youths were to be accepted into monasteries. Nor was this matter easily settled; for we find that after the reign of Alexios I when John II was emperor, again an accusation was made by the metropolitans that the monks on Mount Athos were receiving beardless youths and eunuchs. On this topic the patriarch Nicholas was uncompromising, as we gather from the *pittakion* allegedly issued by him:

> We have heard that there are beardless youths and boys on the Holy Mountain, and seemingly the dogmas of our fathers have been overturned backwards ... What did the fathers say? 'Do not approach a boy, do not converse with him when you are sated, and do not kiss him in church.' Are we to do the deeds of the Ninevites and not suffer the fate of the Sodomites?[46]

According to the *lysis* of the later patriarch Chariton, excommunication was pronounced on monks of Mount Athos by Nicholas when he was patriarch because of eunuchs, beardless youths and animals.[47]

---

[44]   *Phoberou Typikon*, 51.32–34.

[45]   For the text of this, see P. Meyer, *Haupturkunden für die Geschichte der Athoskloster* (Leipzig, 1894), 163–184; a new text, English translation and commentary is currently being prepared in Belfast which will be included in M. Mullett et al., eds, *Alexios I Komnenos: Texts* (Belfast, forthcoming). For recent studies of this document see R. Morris, *Monks and Laymen in Byzantium, 843–1118* (Cambridge, 1995), 275, 277–278, 280, 287; M. Angold, *Church and Society in Byzantium under the Comneni, 1081–1261* (Cambridge, 1995), 280–283; D. Krausmüller, 'The Athonite monastic tradition during the eleventh and early twelfth centuries', in A. Bryer and M. Cunningham, eds, *Mount Athos and Byzantine Monasticism* (Aldershot, 1996), 57–65.

[46]   Meyer, *Haupturkunden*, 175.10–21, translation by M. Mullett and M. McGann.

[47]   Meyer, *Haupturkunden*, 183.2–5; 183.29–30.

John's other main preoccupation, the requirement to fast on Wednesdays and Fridays, is also found in the *Diegesis Merike*, even though it only merits a short remark in passing. In the description of the gathering around the deathbed of the patriarch Nicholas, on the matter of fasting during Lent and on Wednesdays and Fridays the patriarch is reported to have said the following:

> Is fasting found in priests or emperors? All of them, both the *nomothetai* themselves and the rhetors of the churches, have taken refuge in illness and in no way is it to be found unless there is somewhere an *enkleistos* or a hermit, but even these sparsely.[48]

Note the comment that leading legal and ecclesiastical figures were avoiding the obligation to fast by resorting to illness.

It is time now to pull these strands together and see what can realistically be said about this mysterious figure. To begin with, he was brought up by a devout mother and no doubt influenced by his grandmother too. Then, from what he says in the *Typikon* for his monastery, it is likely that before he came to Phoberou he had been practising the ascetic life, possibly in some other community. To judge by the similarity of his concerns to those which surfaced in the disputes on Mount Athos at the beginning of the twelfth century, John supported those who thought that monastic communities should follow a much stricter ascetic regime than was generally current. We are on firmer ground with his powerful friends in Constantinople and elsewhere, both those on the fringes of the imperial family and those in ecclesiastical circles. In one revealing sentence in his *Typikon* we learn that John's own spiritual father and sponsor, Kyr Luke, the metropolitan of Mesembria, had been *hegoumenos* of Phoberou at one time.[49] It was probably through the influence of this man that John was made *hegoumenos* and was able to obtain confirmation of the independence of the monastery from the patriarch Nicholas. Apart from having his own spiritual father as an ally, John also managed to obtain the financial support of the sebastos Nikephoros Botaneiates and more particularly that of his wife Eudokia Komnene. A continuing connection with this imperial family was ensured over this period by the fact that one of the monks in Phoberou was the son of Nikephoros and Eudokia. The latter's benevolence towards this monastery continued even after John had died, for in October 1143 it is

---

[48] Meyer, *Haupturkunden*, 179.34–180.2, translation by M. Mullett and M. McGann.
[49] *Phoberou Typikon*, 62.3–5.

recorded in the *Typikon* that she had just given four *litrai* of gold *nomismata* for the purchase of landed property. The paragraph recording the donation is a late insertion into the *Typikon* in a hand other than that of its author. This enables us to be sure that *hegoumenos* John was dead by October 1143. The year of his death is not known; all we know is that he was to be commemorated on the 16th of December. From the construction and content of his *Typikon*, John clearly considered himself an outsider in the monastic practice then current; and he was not the only one.

From the wilderness of Palestine John the Baptist had issued a call to repentance and traditional holiness. John of Phoberou, too, from his wilderness issued a call to fasting, sexual purity and traditional monastic practice. How many heard his message we shall never know; but I feel sure that it was not the crowds that we are told flocked to hear his great namesake.[50]

---

[50] Cf. Matt. 3.5; Mark 1:5; Luke 3:7.

6. The Hermit as Stranger in the Desert

Nancy Ševčenko

As Cyril of Scythopolis relates the story, Saints Euthymios and Theoktistos were wandering in the Judean wilderness northwest of the Dead Sea in the early years of the fifth century, when they spotted the perfect place to live, a huge and marvellous cave high in the cliffs of a perilous gorge. Together they undertook the steep ascent.

> Overjoyed as if the cave had been prepared for them by God, they made it their home, feeding on the plants that happened to grow there. The cave had earlier been a lair of wild animals; but tamed by the holy hymns and ceaseless prayers of these pious men, it was sanctified by becoming a church of God.[1]

A traditional desert story, we might say: the hermit who leaves the civilized world to find a remote dwelling place, who depends on wild plants for his food, who sings and prays until the wildness of the site is tamed, the beasts no further threat, the cave transformed into a church, the desert a Paradise.[2] Here, to play with the themes of this collection of essays, the insider has willingly become an outsider, in order to become that ultimate insider, the man of God.

In this essay, I would like to look at some of these stories from a slightly different angle, and to see the desert father of the fourth and fifth century not as insider or outsider with respect to his own culture, but as an intruder into another coherent, if hitherto unfamiliar, world, that of the desert and its animal population. For, however much it might have

---

[1] Cyril of Scythopolis, *Life of Euthymios* 8, R.M. Price, tr., *The Lives of the Monks of Palestine* (Kalamazoo, 1991), 11.

[2] A. Guillaumont, 'La conception du désert chez le moines d'Egypte', *Revue de l'histoire des religions* 188 (1975), 3–21; B. Flusin, *Miracles et histoire dans l'oeuvre de Cyrille de Scythopolis* (Paris, 1983).

From *Strangers to Themselves: The Byzantine Outsider*, ed. Dion C. Smythe. Copyright © 2000 by the Society for the Promotion of Byzantine Studies. Published by Ashgate Publishing Ltd, Gower House, Croft Road, Aldershot, Hampshire, GU11 3HR, Great Britain.

seemed the case to others, the saint was not going into a wasteland, into a valley of death, but into a region that was indeed inhabited – just not inhabited by human beings. His ability to deal with the creatures of the desert, so praised by his biographers as a sign of sanctity, was, I would argue, the inevitable consequence of this choice of habitat and of long years of living amongst them.

Many of the stories about the saint in the desert strain credulity, either because of the fauna, or because of the type of actions, involved.[3] Many, however, involve encounters with animals that are native to this landscape – serpents, hippos, crocodiles, hoofed creatures such as gazelles and wild goats, hyenas, and lions[4] – and the narratives bear plausible witness to the daily challenges faced by man and beast alike when co-existing in such an environment.

Take, for example, Antony's attempt to plant a garden so that he could make his own bread and grow vegetables to offer his visitors. To his dismay, the 'beasts of the wilderness' – probably flocks of wild goats or gazelle – kept damaging his crop.[5] This experience, familiar to any rural gardener, may have been little more than an irritant, but other encounters could be considerably more hazardous for the aspiring desert hermit.[6]

---

[3] One of the earliest, and most popular of these texts, Athanasios's *Life of Antony*, resounds with the noisy and incessant clamour of demonic creatures who torment the saint with their cries, filth and temptations. But the species that bombard him are animals that in reality could never have survived on their own in the desert for more than a day, such as bulls, bears and horses: Athanasios, *Life of Antony* 9, 39, R.C. Gregg, tr., *Athanasius: The Life of Anthony and the Letter to Marcellinus* (New York and Toronto, 1980), 38, 60. In the *Historia Monachorum*, there are plenty of tall tales: holy men are said to rip open snakes with their bare hands, walk over rivers on the backs of crocodiles, or even ride them across, as did Abbot Helle to bring back a lazy and fearful priest needed to serve Helle's community of monks. *Historia Monachorum in Aegypto*, XII.6–7, N. Russell, tr., *The Lives of the Desert Fathers* (Oxford and Kalamazoo, 1981), 91. See also the *Life of Antony* 15, Gregg, 43; Palladius, *Historia Lausiaca* 18, R.T. Meyer, tr., *The Lausiac History* (New York 1965), 61, and the *Life of Pachomios*, Flusin, *Miracles*, 167.

[4] On the fauna of the region see F.S. Bodenheimer, *Prodromus faunae Palestinae. Essai sur les éléments zoographiques et historiques du sud-ouest du sous-règne paléarctique.* [= Mémoires presentés à l'institut d'Egypte ... 23] (Cairo, 1937), esp. 6, 48, 51. Bodenheimer's zone III, 'saharo-sindienne' comprises Egypt, Southeast Palestine and Syria.

[5] *Life of Antony* 50, Gregg, 69. Antony responds by taking hold of one of the animals and saying to all of them, '"Why do you hurt me when I do you no injury? Leave, and in the name of the Lord, do not come near here any longer." From then on, as if being afraid of the command, they did not come near the place.'

[6] I exclude here episodes that involve 'rogue' animals (such as the marauding hippo in *Historia Monachorum* IV, Russell, 66), which the saint, very much like a game warden in Africa today, was summoned by villagers to destroy. For a modern experience with rogue

There were vipers dozing on the night path, ready to strike if disturbed, or scorpions underfoot at prayers.[7] But the chief danger was lions.

The number and variety of stories involving lions in these early texts confirms what we know from other sources, that lions were no rarity in the landscapes of Egypt, Palestine and Syria in this period.[8] Encounters were especially likely in open country when their respective routes led man and beast to cross trails. *Abba* Aaron, for example, had been a soldier. 'An order came to *Abba* Aaron to take the troops and go with them (to another city). When he left the city, a lion met him on the road that evening and wished to seize him.' Aaron struck a quick personal bargain with Christ, promising that he would abandon everything and become a monk, if he could only come out alive. Then 'I made ready the spear in my hand. I drove it through the lion and he died.'[9]

The search for living quarters could also lead to an encounter with a lion, for the cave eyed with favour by a saint could well turn out to be already occupied. St Sabas, says Cyril of Scythopolis,

> settled in a desert spot by the river called Gadaron, and stayed there for a short time in a cave where an enormous lion was wont to withdraw. Around midnight this lion returned and found the blessed one sleeping. Taking hold of his patchwork habit with his mouth, it began to pull at him, striving to remove him from the cave. When he got up and began the night psalmody, the lion went

---

lions, see G. Adamson, *A Lifetime with Lions* (as in note 15 below), esp. 93–105, 119–128, 201–210.

[7] Theodoret of Cyrrhus, *Historia religiosa* XXII.5, R.M. Price, tr., *A History of the Monks of Syria* (Kalamazoo, 1985), 151 (Thalassios); Palladius, *Historia Lausiaca* 48, tr. Meyer, 131.

[8] See Bodenheimer, note 4 above. For maps showing the range of lions in antiquity, see J. Rudnai, *The Social Life of the Lion* (Wallingford, PA, 1973), 8, based on C.A. Guggisberg, *Simba* (Cape Town, 1961), unavailable to me. There were lions in North Africa and the Middle East until well into the nineteenth century. For additional sources involving rather routine encounters with lions, see Palladius, *Historia Lausiaca* 52, Meyer, 133; Theodoret, *Historia religiosa* VI.10, Price, 66; John Moschos, *Pratum spirituale* 92, 125, J. Wortley, tr., *The Spiritual Meadow of John Moschos* (Kalamazoo, 1992), 74, 102; Cyril of Scythopolis, *Life of Sabas* 23, Price, 116; and the story of the elder with the lion cubs, 84–85 below. See also J. Wortley, 'Two Unpublished Psychophelitic Tales', *GRBS* 37 (1996), 281–300, esp. 288–300. The very flatness with which some of the stories are related adds to their credibility, e.g. Moschos 92: 'One day he (brother George, a field labourer) was pasturing swine in Phasaelis when two lions came to seize a pig. He took up his staff and chased them as far as the Jordan.'

[9] *Histories of the Monks of Upper Egypt by Paphnutius*, 87, T. Vivian, tr., 115. Aaron kept his promise, and immediately began a career as a monk.

out and waited outside the cave; when the old man had completed the office, it came in and began to pull at him again. So, with the lion pressing him to leave the cave, the old man said to it in confidence of spirit, 'The cave is spacious enough to provide lodging for both of us, for we both have the one Creator. If you want, stay here; if not, get out.' Then he adds: 'I myself was fashioned by the hand of God and privileged to receive his image.' On hearing this, the lion felt some kind of shame and withdrew.[10]

The situation was defused: Cyril credits the saint's holy routine and the force of his argument, although we might prefer to stress the saint's acquired experience and confidence in the handling of desert creatures. Whatever the interpretation, the encounter itself is perfectly plausible. The occasional disaster even lends credence to the stories as a whole. One saint, despite long years in the desert, is reported to have been devoured by wild beasts; a long-past sin had to be unearthed to justify this untoward end.[11]

The saint ate no meat, and so did not compete with the predators; often he 'grazed', eating nothing but raw vegetables. He lived in caves, as they did; his hair grew long and covered his body, and he began to resemble physically the animal he had displaced.[12] His ascetic practices enabled him to overlook or even welcome any pain that an animal may have caused him.[13] His confidence was surely bolstered by his faith: his faith in God, in his own sense of superiority over creatures not made, as he was, in the image of God, and in his own ascetic practices in which bodily harm was often something actually sought. But it derived too from his long experience in the wild. With his insight into animal behaviour, and the confidence that gave him, the saint could stare down even lions, and compel them to step aside, as did John the anchorite when meeting a

---

[10] *Life of Sabas* 33, Price, 128.

[11] Moschos, *Pratum spirituale* 167, Wortley, 137.

[12] See P. Brown, *The Body and Society. Men, Women and Sexual Renunciation in Early Christianity* (New York, 1988), esp. 213–240; Flusin, *Miracles*, esp. 124–125, 176f, and the study cited in note 2 above. Macarius, says Palladius, was so bitten by mosquitoes that when he returned from his self-enforced stay in a marsh his flesh was so swollen 'he was recognized as Macarius only by his voice', *Historia Lausiaca* 18, Meyer, 59. See also C. Williams, 'Oriental Affinities of the Legend of the Hairy Anchorite', *Illinois Studies in Language and Literature* 10:2 (1925), 11:4 (1926).

[13] For example, Theodoret of Cyrrhus on Thalassios, as in note 7 above.

lion on a track too narrow to allow both to pass.[14] Such 'charisma', such confidence in the face of wild animals, is something remarked of special individuals by African game wardens, big game hunters, wildlife photographers and zoo-keepers, and reported with comparable awe.[15]

The saint's fearless behaviour could inspire others to surprising acts of courage even when he was not himself around: according to Cyril of Scythopolis, some thieves met a lion on the road, and managed to drive it away by crying out the name of St Sabas; some disciples of John the Hesychast in the same predicament called John's name, and feeling the presence of the saint between them, had the assurance to stand their ground, and the lion fled.[16]

The animals seem in their turn to have accepted the hermit intruder so well that when occasionally a deeply penitent or suicidal saint actually hoped they would be wild and vicious, these creatures foiled him by their gentleness or indifference. According to Palladius, a demon kept attacking Pachon so hard and long that he wanted to die:

> I went out then, and while going about the desert, I came across a hyena's cave. Here I placed myself naked one day in hopes that the

---

[14] Moschos, *Pratum spirituale* 181, Wortley, 150–151. 'Stepping aside' is considered a form of submission in modern analyses of lion behaviour; see Rudnai, *Social Life* (as in note 8 above), 48.

[15] See especially the memoirs of M. Cowie, the founder of the Kenyan park system, *I Walk with Lions* (New York, 1961) and those of G. Adamson, a game warden in Kenya, *A Lifetime with Lions* (New York 1968). George Adams and his wife adopted and reared lion cubs which lived with them in their camp in the bush: see J. Adamson, *Born Free. A Lioness of Two Worlds* (New York, 1960), and *Living Free. The Story of Elsa and her Cubs* (New York, 1961). On staring down a lion, see M. Johnson, *Lion. African Adventure with the King of Beasts* (New York and London, 1929), esp. 157, and Cowie, *I walk*, 44–45. For other stories, see C. Kearton, *In the Land of the Lion* (New York, 1930), esp. 21–47. The author of a technical handbook for zoo-keepers states, 'Self-confidence is perhaps the single most important attribute that can be developed by the restrainer. This confidence can be acquired by experience, though some individuals seem to possess such ability almost innately'; M. Fowler, *Restraint and Handling of Wild and Domestic Animals*, second edition (Ames, IA, 1978), 8. Fowler cites the case of a man who could enter an enclosure of 'large adult, untrained wild cats, including tigers and lions. These cats would wait in line to place their forepaw upon his shoulders and lick his face ... This man has absolute confidence in his ability to work with these cats. There is no evidence of fear-mastery or dominance over the cats ... Certainly it would be foolhardy for a person lacking the great confidence and behavioural skills of this individual to enter such an enclosure. Nonetheless it vividly illustrates what can be accomplished by someone with confidence and skill.'

[16] *Life of Sabas* 34 and *Life of John the Hesychast* 17; Price, 129 and 234.

wild beasts would devour me. Evening came and ... the beasts,
male and female, came out. They smelled me and licked me all
over from head to foot. Just when I was expecting to be eaten, they
left me.[17]

And Moschos tells of *Abba* Paul whose mules years before had trampled
and killed a child, a tragic event that led Paul to flee into the wilderness
and become an anchorite:

There was a lion nearby, and each day, *Abba* Paul would go into its
den, teasing and provoking it to jump up and devour him – but the
lion did him no harm whatsoever. When he realized that he was
not succeeding, *Abba* Paul said to himself: 'I will lie down on the
lion's path; then, when he comes on his way down to drink at the
river, he will devour me.' He lay there and after a little while, the
lion came by. And as though it were a human, it very carefully
stepped over the elder without even touching him.[18]

As time passed, the solitary hermit came to welcome animal companions.
In the text of the *Historia Monachorum* we hear of *Abba* Theon:

They say that he used to go out of his cell at night and keep
company with wild animals, giving them to drink from the water
which he had. Certainly one could see the tracks of antelope and
wild asses and gazelle and other animals near his hermitage. These
creatures delighted him always.[19]

Jerome in his *Vita Pauli* describes how Antony headed into the farthest
desert in search of the hermit Paul of Thebes.[20] Having spotted a wolf
disappearing into an opening in a rock, Antony follows and discovers

---

[17] Palladius, *Historia Lausiaca* 23, Meyer, 82. Pachon tries again, picking up an asp and
putting it to himself, but again to no avail. The actions could be seen as suicidal, otherwise
rather rarely reported: see Wortley, 'Psychophelitic Tales', 284–288.

[18] *Pratum spirituale* 101, Wortley, 81. Moschos concludes, 'Then the elder knew that
God had forgiven him his sin.'

[19] *Historia Monachorum* VI.4, Russell, 68.

[20] *Life of Paul of Thebes by Jerome*, in C. White, tr., *Early Christian Lives* (Harmondsworth,
1998), 75–84. Antony met much earlier a centaur and then a satyr, traditional denizens of
the desert. On Jerome's literary use of these pagan creatures, see P.C. Miller, 'Jerome's
Centaur: A Hyper-Icon of the Desert', *Journal of Early Christian Studies* 4 (1996), 209–233. I
thank Georgia Frank for calling my attention to this article.

Paul's cave and meets his desert companions.[21] As the two men dine together, Paul's raven brings a loaf of bread (a patent reference to Elijah, though the raven here is smart enough to double the usual portion since Antony has arrived). Later, after Paul has died and Antony has returned to find the body, two lions suddenly emerge out of nowhere and roar their grief over Paul's corpse. They then scratch up the earth just enough to enable Antony, who came without a shovel, to be able to bury the body properly. Finally the lions come over to Antony with 'their necks bent and their ears laid back, and licked his hands and feet'. He interprets this as their asking for his blessing, and so, praising Christ 'because dumb animals, too, were able to understand that there was a God', he asks Christ to bless them. He dismisses them with a wave of his hand, at which point they return to the desert.[22]

The animals were even put to use. Hermits, and monastic communities as well, had lions, probably raised as cubs, to protect their gardens, flocks and even the monks themselves from human marauders. Cyril of Scythopolis tells of his own visit to St Cyriacus at Sousakim. As he drew near the saint's cave, Cyril was terrified to find a lion there, though he says it let him pass when it saw where he was heading. Cyriacus greeted Cyril warmly and reassured him: 'Have no fear, my child. This lion is my faithful servant here, guarding my herbs from the wild goats.' The men settle down to a meal.

> While we were eating, the lion came and stood in front of us; rising, the elder gave it a piece of bread and sent it to guard the herbs. The elder said to me, 'It not only guards the herbs but also wards off brigands and barbarians.'

---

[21] *Life of Paul* 9, White, 79. Paul at first rebuffs Antony, who responds sharply, 'Why do you, who welcome animals, drive a person away?'

[22] *Life of Paul* 16, White, 83. See also Wortley, 'Psychophelitic Tales', 289–292. The story evidently influenced Sophronios's account of the burial of Mary of Egypt (39), in M. Kouli, translator, in Alice-Mary Talbot, ed., *Holy Women of Byzantium. Ten Saints' Lives in English Translation* (Washington, DC, 1996), 91–92. In connection with the lions' actions here, it is amusing to read modern specialists on lion behaviour analysing 'headrubbing', 'bending of head', 'scraping' (the latter often takes place after an encounter with another creature) and 'digging': see Rudnai, *Social Life* (as in note 8 above), 48; G. Schaller, *The Serengeti Lion. A Study of Predator–Prey Relations* (Chicago, 1972), 85–92, 116–118, 245. To have known that bending of the head is 'performed by a lower ranking animal when meeting a higher ranking one' (Rudnai, 48) would doubtless have pleased Antony and his successors.

Cyril stays a bit longer, and then departs. 'After leaving him, we found the lion sitting on the road and eating a wild goat. When the lion saw us standing there and not daring to advance, it left its prey and withdrew until we had passed.'[23]

One of these early lion stories was taken over with relatively few alterations into the life of St Jerome.[24] As Moschos first tells it, a lion suffering great pain with a reed stuck in his paw approached St Gerasimos, a fifth-century Palestinian father who had founded a *lavra* near the Jordan.[25] Gerasimos removed the reed, and won the loyalty of the lion. It then hung around the *lavra*, where it was fed and given the job of escorting to pasture the monastery's donkey which, when on duty, carried jugs of water up from the river. One day the lion fell asleep on the job, and Arab merchants riding by on camels stole the donkey. When the lion returned to the monastery without his charge, Gerasimos accused him of having devoured it. The story had a happy ending, though, for the Arab merchants chanced to pass by again, and the lion, recognizing his donkey, ravaged the camel train and brought back to the monastery not only the donkey but three of the camels as well. When Gerasimos died, the lion was inconsolable, and throwing itself down near the tomb, expired.[26] A comparable lion story is told of St Sabas, though here the lion actually does devour the donkey.[27]

---

[23] *Life of Cyriacus*, 15–16, Price, 255–256. John the Hesychast had a lion to protect him from Saracens: *Life of John the Hesychast* 13, Price, 231. *Abba* Stephen had a leopard for the same purpose, to guard his garden from choirogrylloi (rock hyraxes, little herbivorous African mammals looking rather like guinea-pigs), Wortley, 'Psychophelitic Tales', 295–296 (who calls them rock-rabbits).

[24] G. Ring, 'St Jerome extracting the thorn from the lion's foot', *Art Bulletin* 27 (1945), 188–194.

[25] Moschos, *Pratum spirituale* 107, Wortley, 86–88. Gerasimos is mentioned briefly in several of Cyril of Scythopolis's *Lives*, though never in connection with a lion.

[26] Moschos's story of Gerasimos and the lion was later incorporated into the life of Gerasimos written by a monk at his *lavra* on the Jordan, in the seventh century. See H. Grégoire, 'La vie anonyme de S. Gérasime', *BZ* 13 (1904), 114–135; Flusin, *Miracles*, 35–40. The Gerasimos story was illustrated in Byzantium, though not before the fourteenth century; see E. Bakalova, 'Scenes from the Life of St. Gerasimos of Jordan in Ivanovo', and S. Tomeković, 'Note sur saint Gérasime dans l'art byzantin', both in *Zbornik za likovne umetnosti* 21 (1985), 105–121 and 277–284; E. Haustein-Bartsch, '"So gehorchten die wilden Tiere Adam." Zur Ikonographie einer Ikone des heiligen Gerasimos mit dem Löwen', *Studien zur byzantinische Kunstgeschichte. Festschrift für Horst Hallensleben* (Amsterdam, 1995), 259–278.

[27] Cyril's *Life of Sabas*, 49, Price, 148–149.

This story reminds us of the vivid report provided by the Piacenza Pilgrim, a sober gentleman who travelled from Italy to the Jordan area around 570, not long after Cyril's day.

> We discovered a monastery of women in those parts, more than sixteen or seventeen of them who were in a desert place, and given food by the Christians. They had one small ass to do their heavy work for them, and they used to give food to a lion, tame from the time it was a cub, but huge and terrifying to look at. Indeed when we drew near the cells it roared, and all our animals pissed, while some of them even fell to the ground. They also told us that the lion went with the little ass to pasture. I made this visit with a real Christian whom I helped in making the nuns an offer of a hundred shillings for the two animals, but they would not accept ...

His friend is so keen on obtaining the pair of animals for himself that for two whole days he orders all sorts of additional things be bought and presented to the nuns – cassocks, vegetables, oil, dates and baskets of roast chickpeas – all in vain. 'We were unable to soothe his disappointment and grief,' says the pilgrim of Piacenza. 'All he could say was "Devil take it, what's the use of being a Christian?" ' [28]

Despite the affectionate relationship between hermit and desert beast, the relationship could be strained by divergent conceptions as to what constituted the animal's proper diet. The lion that guarded Cyriacus's garden and ate the saint's bread was later discovered down the path by the departing Cyril of Scythopolis, supplementing its diet by devouring a wild goat. [29] Cyril himself makes no comment, but the Early Christian hermit was generally unwilling to condone such carnivorous tendencies, and required of his companion Christian renunciation on a par with his own. *Abba* Paul, says Moschos, thought he had a deal with his lion whereby he would continue to feed it if it would forego eating meat. But one day it came in, its muzzle stained with blood. Paul rebuked it, saying:

---

[28] J. Wilkinson, *Jerusalem Pilgrims before the Crusades* (Warminster, 1977), 85–87. According to A. Jeannin, lions are easiest to tame at one to one-and-one-half years of age, when they readily attach themselves to animals of other species, such as dogs, goats or sheep, and become their inseparable companions: A. Jeannin, *La faune africaine* (Paris, 1951), 78–79.

[29] See above, 82.

'Never again will I feed you the food of the fathers, carnivore! Get
away from here.' He would not go away, so I took a rope, folded it
up into three and struck it three blows with it. Then it went away.[30]

St Gerasimos too accused his lion of devouring the donkey he was set to
protect.[31]

The authors of the early texts provide various explanations for the
saint's success in the encounters described here. He is said to be able to
dispatch animals by making the sign of the cross; he may invoke the
name of Christ, basing his authority on Christ's gift to his disciples of
power over snakes and scorpions (Luke 10:19), or on God's intervention
to subdue the lions that were to devour Daniel (Dan. 6:22, 27).[32]
Sometimes the authors have the saint address the animal he wishes to
sway or evict with the argument that both are servants of the same
master, products of the same creator, and should therefore refrain from
harming one another.[33] Theodoret of Cyrrhus may be the first to suggest
that a saint has actually *earned* his charisma, his special power over
animals. Theodoret says of a certain Symeon who lived in a little cave and
ate only wild plants, 'This toil won him also the gift of rich grace from
above, even to the extent of exercising authority over the most bold and
fearsome of wild animals.'[34]

Moschos suggests that our fear of animals is rooted in our sin. There
was an

> elder living in the Lavra of Abba Peter who would often go off and
> stay on the banks of the holy Jordan. There he found a lion's den in
> which he installed himself. One day he found two lion-cubs in the

---

[30] *Pratum spirituale* 163, Wortley, 134.

[31] See above, 82. Parallels for many aspects of the affectionate, but occasionally
uneasy, relationship between hermit and desert beasts can be found in stories of modern
Africa mentioned above (note 15). The Adamsons did not share the Christian hermit's
abhorrence of carnivorous behaviour, and actively encouraged their tame lions to hunt
freely. But they did face a similar practical problem: how to prevent their lions from
attacking the pack mules and donkeys at the camp, G. Adamson, *passim*.

[32] Sign of the cross: Theodoret, *Historia religiosa* II.6, III.7, Price, 26, 40. Asks to leave:
Historia Monachorum IV.3, Russell, 66; Moschos, *Pratum spirituale* 58, Wortley 45–46. Luke:
Historia Monachorum IX, Russell, 80–81; Cyril of Scythopolis, *Life of Sabas* 12, Price, 104. Also
invoked in this context is Psalm 90 (91):13.

[33] *Life of Theodosios* by Theodore of Petra 80, A.-J. Festugière, tr., *Les moines d'Orient*
III:3 (Paris 1963), 147.

[34] This Symeon was able to provide a pair of lions to escort a couple of lost travellers
safely back to the main road; Theodoret, *Historia religiosa* VI. 2, Price, 63–64.

cave. Wrapping them up in his cloak, he took them to church. 'If we keep the commandments of our Lord Jesus Christ,' he said, 'these animals would fear us. But because of our sins we have become slaves and it is rather we who fear them.' Greatly edified, the brethren returned to their caves.[35]

Cyril of Scythopolis is apparently the first of these authors to develop to any extent the argument that God is restoring to the saint the dominion he had given to Adam over the animals in Paradise, a dominion that had been lost through the fall.

> In addition to the other charisms possessed by the godly Euthymios, he also received this one from God – the grace of living with carnivorous and poisonous animals without being harmed by them. This should be doubted by no one initiated into holy Scripture, who has precise knowledge that when God dwells in a man and rests upon him, all beings are subject to him, as they were to Adam before he transgressed God's commandment.[36]

And, after describing the lion's grief and death at the grave of Gerasimos, Moschos says, 'This did not take place because the lion had a rational soul, but because it is the will of God to glorify those who glorify him, and to show how the beasts were in subjection to Adam before he disobeyed the commandments and fell from the comfort of Paradise.'[37] In Cyril too we first meet the other argument of man's superiority, 'I myself was fashioned by the hand of God and privileged to receive his image': this was voiced by St Sabas, as we have seen, in displacing the lion from his cave.[38]

Behind the growing belief in man's right to dominion over the animals, beneath the layers of interpretation, beneath the stern verbal admonitions which these Early Christian saints are said to have addressed to the animals they met in their new milieu, there are echoes of actual encounters between man and beast. These encounters, especially those with lions, were not the inventions of hagiographers or theologians,

---

[35] *Pratum spirituale* 18, Wortley, 13.

[36] *Life of Euthymios* 14, Price, 18–19. Despite this statement, no animal stories are attributed to Euthymios: his speciality was the weather, rather a different matter. On Adam and the animals, see H. Maguire, 'Adam and the Animals: Allegory and Literal Sense in Early Christian Art', *DOP* 41 (1987), 363–373, with further references.

[37] *Pratum spirituale* 107, Wortley, 88.

[38] See above, 78.

but episodes that reflect the environment of a very particular time and place in human history: the lands of Egypt, Syria and Palestine in a period when lions still roamed and hermit saints, moving into their territory, had to find a *modus vivendi* with their animal neighbours if they were to pursue the life they had chosen. Unlike later Byzantine hermits such as Hosios Loukas or Ioannikios, who lived long after lions had vanished from their regions, and who were anyway frequently on the move, these early saints lived in lion country and in one place for a very long time, sometimes even a lifetime.[39] The long years of co-existence with these creatures led to a special familiarity with animal behaviour, and this, when joined to their faith in God's protection and in their own superiority, gave these Early Christian saints their fearless confidence, their special charisma, that so impressed their less experienced contemporaries.

Though the hermit and the desert creatures were strangers at first, they nevertheless developed over time ways to accommodate to each other's presence. In the process they, and their astonished biographers, gave us the model by which all ideal Christian encounters between man and beast came eventually to be measured and interpreted.

---

[39] The restless Hosios Loukas's main problems were keeping deer out of his garden and avoiding the occasional viper on the trail. Luke addresses the deer with the familiar line-up of arguments: we have the same master, the same creator you and I, but I, you see, bear the likeness of God, C. and W. Connor, *The Life and Miracles of St. Luke* (Brookline, MA, 1994), 31, 65.

7. Exclues et Aliénées:
les Femmes dans la Tradition Canonique Byzantine*

Joëlle Beaucamp

À Byzance, le droit impérial, fondé sur les compilations de Justinien, exclut les femmes de l'exercice de l'autorité publique et leur interdit tout rôle qui impliquerait de sortir de la sphère familiale pour assumer, publiquement, une responsabilité vis-à-vis d'autrui; cette mise à l'écart, dont la composante spatiale transparaît dans certaines lois, a tendance à s'accentuer dans la législation postérieure au VIe siècle, comme en témoigne une Novelle de Léon VI.[1] Plutôt que de revenir sur ce sujet, je voudrais analyser ici une autre composante du droit byzantin, moins étudiée de ce point de vue: les canons reconnus par l'Église et leurs commentaires.

La littérature canonique offre un double intérêt, historique et idéologique. Elle couvre l'ensemble de la période byzantine, avec

---

* Il n'existe pas d'édition satisfaisante de l'ensemble du corpus canonique byzantin. La plus communément utilisée est celle de G.A. Rallès et M. Potlès, Σύνταγμα τῶν θείων καὶ ἱερῶν κανόνων, I–VI (Athènes, 1852–1859, réimpr. 1966) (désormais RP). Le Nomocanon en XIV titres se trouve aussi dans G. Voellus et H. Iustellus, Bibliotheca iuris canonici veteris, II (Paris, 1661), 785–1140 (repris dans PG 104, 976–1217) et J.B. Pitra, Mon, II, 433–640 (la meilleure édition); l'ensemble des canons dans P.-P. Joannou, Discipline générale antique (IVe–XIe s.), I–II (Grottaferrata, 1962–1963); les canons des Apôtres dans J.B. Pitra, Mon, I, 1–44 et dans Const. App., éd. M. Metzger, III (Paris, 1987, SC 336), 274–309; ceux de Basile de Césarée dans Bas., ep. 188, 199 et 217, éd. Y. Courtonne, II (Paris 1961), 121–131, 155–164 et 209–217; les canons conciliaires dans J.D. Mansi, Sacrorum conciliorum nova et amplissima collectio (Florence, à partir de 1759); les commentaires d'Aristènos, Zonaras et Balsamon dans PG 137–138 et le traité de Blastarès dans PG 144, 960–145, 212. Sur l'histoire de ces textes, voir N. Van Der Wal et J.H.A. Lokin, Historiae iuris graeco-romani delineatio (Groningen, 1985).

[1] Nov. 48, éd. P. Noailles et A. Dain (Paris, 1944), 186–191. Voir J. Beaucamp, 'La situation juridique de la femme à Byzance', CahCivM 20 (1977), 149–150 et 166–167, Le statut de la femme à Byzance (4e–7e siècle), I (Paris, 1990), 29–45, et 'Les femmes et l'espace public à Byzance: le cas des tribunaux' DOP 52 (1998), 129–145..

From Strangers to Themselves: The Byzantine Outsider, ed. Dion C. Smythe. Copyright © 2000 by the Society for the Promotion of Byzantine Studies. Published by Ashgate Publishing Ltd, Gower House, Croft Road, Aldershot, Hampshire, GU11 3HR, Great Britain.

quelques temps forts: le IVe siècle, où sont élaborés des canons d'origines très diverses (attribués aux Apôtres ou émanant de conciles œcuméniques ou locaux, ou encore de Pères de l'Église); la fin du VIIe, quand le concile *in Trullo* formule de nombreux canons disciplinaires; le XIIe siècle, quand Aristènos, Zonaras et Balsamon rédigent des commentaires montrant comment ces normes anciennes sont comprises à leur époque et indiquant, le cas échéant, si elles sont appliquées ou tombées en désuétude; ces commentaires trouvent leur aboutissement, au XIVe siècle, dans l'ouvrage de Blastarès, où la matière canonique est organisée selon l'ordre alphabétique. L'intérêt idéologique n'est pas moindre: dans quelques canons du IVe ou du VIIe siècle, les règles édictées sont accompagnées de justifications; les développements d'ordre étiologique sont beaucoup plus nombreux chez les canonistes du XIIe siècle. C'est au travers de telles exégèses que l'on peut entrevoir des aspects plus subtils ou des formes plus complexes de la discrimination affectant les femmes. Le corpus canonique fournit, de fait, deux ensembles de données pour notre sujet. Il formule des exclusions à l'encontre des femmes. Il révèle aussi diverses formes d'aliénation: dans certaines normes et, plus clairement encore, dans les discours explicatifs qui s'y rapportent, différents processus de dépersonnalisation et de réification sont à l'œuvre. Autrement dit, les femmes ne sont pas seulement rejetées à l'extérieur de la communauté; leur raison d'être est extérieure à elles-mêmes.

Les exclusions

Premièrement, les femmes sont tenues à l'écart du sacré et du sacerdoce. Le phénomène se marque dans le canon 11 du concile de Laodicée: 'Sur le fait qu'il ne faut pas instituer à l'église celles que l'on appelle anciennes ou encore présidentes'[2]. Les termes grecs sont *presbutides* et *prokathêmenai*. Aucune explication n'est fournie; le statut exact de ces femmes et leur rôle ne sont pas davantage explicités. Mais les collections canoniques byzantines autorisent quelques remarques. Déjà le Nomocanon en XIV titres, dont la composition remonte au VIIe siècle et qui rassemble, par thèmes, des références aux canons et des citations du droit impérial, fait état du canon de Laodicée sous la rubrique suivante: 'Sur les diaconesses et le fait qu'une femme ne devient pas *presbutera*'.[3] Le terme employé est

---

[2] RP III, 181.
[3] Nomoc. I 37, RP I, 81.

presbutera, au lieu de *presbutis* dans le canon. Le rapprochement avec le masculin *presbuteros* est ainsi accentué, et la rubrique du Nomocanon me paraît signifier: il n'y a pas d'équivalent femme à *presbuteros*.[4] Au XIIe siècle, Zonaras s'attache seulement au fait qu'il s'agit d'une pratique ancienne (sous-entendu: disparue): ces *presbutides* étaient, d'après lui, 'des femmes âgées', qui prenaient la tête des femmes entrant à l'église, leur indiquaient où se placer et veillaient au bon ordre.[5] Balsamon, lui, établit une relation avec l'interdiction d'enseigner en public, et fait cette remarque révélatrice: 'qu'une femme instruise dans une église catholique, là où une foule d'hommes est rassemblée ... est tout à fait inconvenant et funeste'.[6] Aristènos marque encore mieux que la norme représente une exclusion: 'Si en effet il est interdit [aux femmes] d'exercer des fonctions civiques, comment pourront-elles, dans l'assemblée [des fidèles], tenir le premier rang du clergé?'[7] L'exclusion du pouvoir dans la cité et celle de la hiérarchie ecclésiastique se renforcent l'une l'autre,[8] et elles sont trop évidentes pour nécessiter une justification. D'autres passages du corpus canonique confirment l'évidence de l'interdit. Balsamon, quand il commente le texte du Nomocanon définissant qui est clerc,[9] critique l'opinion selon laquelle la simple tonsure conférerait aux moines le rang de lecteur et déclare: 'c'est absurde.' Or il a en réserve un argument manifestement imparable: 'Aux femmes aussi qui sont moniales ce droit sera octroyé en raison de la tonsure, ce qui est, à un degré encore plus fort, tout à fait absurde'. Nul besoin d'explication: le fait que la femme est à l'extérieur du clergé va de soi.

Dans un tel contexte, le statut des femmes diacres pose évidemment problème. Il est hors de question de revenir ici sur le problème des origines. L'évolution byzantine, elle, est claire.[10] Comme Balsamon

---

[4] De même, Joannou, I 2, 135, traduit par 'femme-prêtre'.

[5] RP III, 181.

[6] RP III, 181, repris dans Blastarès (*gamma* 21, RP VI, 196). Sur l'expression 'église catholique', voir G. Dagron, 'Le christianisme dans la ville byzantine', *DOP* 31 (1977), 9 n. 31.

[7] RP III, 181–182. Sur la notion de clergé à Byzance, voir G. Dagron, 'Remarques sur le statut des clercs', *JÖB* 44 (1994), 33–48.

[8] Le même type de rapprochement entre un interdit canonique visant les femmes (s'exprimer à l'église) et les incapacités du droit impérial est fait par Balsamon à propos du canon 70 du concile *in Trullo* (RP II, 468–469).

[9] Nomoc. I 31, RP I, 71–72.

[10] Sur le déclin du rôle public des diaconesses, voir J. Herrin, 'Public and Private Forms of Religious Commitment among Byzantine Women', dans L.J. Archer, S. Fischler, M. Wyke eds, *Women in Ancient Societies* (London, 1994), 191.

l'explique notamment, il n'y a pas, de son temps, d'ordination de diaconesse.[11] Et accorder à des diaconesses un rôle actif dans la liturgie est un trait caractéristique de l'hérésie. Une décision patriarcale de 1143 condamne les bogomiles pour 'avoir ordonné diaconesses des femmes, en leur permettant de dire les prières ecclésiastiques d'usage, de lire les saints évangiles et de concélébrer avec Clément'.[12] Nous verrons que, si la diaconesse appartient à la sphère du sacré, c'est d'une toute autre façon.

Deuxièmement, les femmes sont maintenues en dehors de l'espace le plus sacré, celui qui entoure l'autel et qui est séparé du reste de l'église par la barrière du chancel. Le texte fondamental est encore un canon de Laodicée: 'Il ne faut pas que les femmes entrent dans le sanctuaire (*thusiastêrion*).'[13] Comme dans le cas précédent, aucune explication n'est fournie. Les commentaires, eux, donnent deux justifications.[14] La première renvoie à l'exclusion précédente, qui laisse les femmes à l'écart du clergé. De fait, puisque l'accès au 'sanctuaire' est réservé aux clercs et interdit aux laïcs, il est nécessairement interdit aux femmes, qui appartiennent au groupe des laïcs. Le point intéressant réside dans la façon dont cette évidence logique est formulée. Selon Zonaras, 's'il est interdit aux hommes laïcs d'entrer à l'intérieur du sanctuaire, selon le canon 69 du VIᵉ concile,[15] cela serait bien davantage interdit aux femmes...'. Blastarès reprend le même raisonnement a fortiori: si les hommes laïcs sont écartés, les femmes le sont encore plus.[16] On décèle ainsi, en filigrane, une représentation de la société chrétienne, organisée en cercles concentriques: les clercs sont au centre et les laïcs sur le pourtour; mais, dans le cercle des laïcs, les femmes sont plus périphériques que les hommes.

La seconde raison, qui vient renforcer la première, est le risque d'impureté lié à la présence féminine: le sang menstruel est tenu pour une

---

[11]   RP II, 255–256.

[12]   *Les regestes des actes du patriarcat de Constantinople*, I 2–3, éd. V. Grumel et J. Darrouzès (Paris, 1989), n° 1012 ; J. Gouillard, 'Quatre procès de mystiques à Byzance (vers 960–1143)', *REB* 36 (1978), 74.

[13]   Canon 44, RP III, 212.

[14]   RP III, 212.

[15]   Ce canon du concile in *Trullo* ne parle pas des hommes spécifiquement, mais des laïcs d'une manière générale. Dans le commentaire correspondant (RP II, 466), Balsamon distingue aussi les hommes des femmes, à qui l'interdit s'impose encore plus: 'Chez les Latins ... non seulement des laïcs hommes, mais aussi des femmes entrent dans le saint *bêma* et s'y tiennent assis.'

[16]   RP VI, 196–197 et 306.

souillure, tout comme celui qui accompagne un accouchement. Les textes canoniques désignent les femmes qui ont leurs règles par une périphrase empruntée à la Septante: 'celles qui se tiennent à l'écart' (αἱ ἐν ἀφέδρῳ).[17] La dénomination même implique l'exclusion, et le fait n'a pas échappé aux canonistes byzantins: 'Les femmes des Hébreux', commente Zonaras, 'lorsque se produisait pour elles l'écoulement de la menstruation, demeuraient dans un lieu isolé et n'avaient de contact avec personne jusqu'à ce que sept jours se fussent écoulés; c'est de là qu'a été prise l'expression ἐν ἀφέδρῳ, qui montre qu'elles sont séparées de la résidence (*hedra*) des autres, en tant qu'impures.'[18] Or, souligne-t-il, 'l'écoulement du sang menstruel se produit inopinément'.[19] À cause de ce caractère imprévisible, une impureté temporaire entraîne une exclusion permanente.

Dans le développement du droit canonique byzantin, l'exclusion a tendance à se renforcer. Au XIIe siècle, le patriarche de Constantinople Luc Chrysobergès rappelle que l'entrée du sanctuaire est interdite à toute femme, quel que soit son âge, et condamne une pratique qui avait cours dans des villages proches de la capitale: des fillettes de sept ans servaient à l'autel.[20] Dans leur cas pourtant, l'impureté physiologique ne pouvait être évoquée. Et les canonistes byzantins sont conscients d'une évolution. Balsamon note déjà que l'interdiction n'a pas cours chez les Latins.[21] Plus clairement encore, Blastarès fait observer que cet interdit n'a pas toujours existé: entre autres indices d'un changement, il cite le discours funèbre de Grégoire le théologien pour sa sœur Gorgonia.[22] Toutefois, même à Byzance, une exception au moins[23] est prévue: d'après un canon qui est attribué au patriarche Nicéphore, mais doit dater de la fin du Xe ou du XIe siècle[24], les moniales peuvent nettoyer et décorer cette partie de l'église. Elle est certainement due à un autre impératif, qui prévaut sur

---

[17] C'est une des rubriques de Blastarès, à la lettre *alpha* (RP VI, 106).

[18] RP IV, 7. Le texte de Balsamon (8) est à peu près identique.

[19] RP III, 212. Voir aussi Blastarès, RP VI, 172.

[20] *Regestes du patriarcat* (voir n. 12), n° 1087.

[21] RP III, 212.

[22] RP VI 172. La référence est à Gr. Naz., *or.* 8, ß18, éd. M.-A. Calvet-Sebasti (Paris, 1995, SC 405), 284–286, qui dépeint Gorgonia, malade, venant en pleine nuit se jeter au pied de l'autel.

[23] La situation particulière de l'empereur est longuement commentée, notamment par Balsamon (RP II, 466–467): voir G. Dagron, *Empereur et prêtre. Étude sur le 'césaropapisme' byzantin* (Paris, 1996), 117, 126–129, 268–269; mais le cas où une femme exercerait le pouvoir impérial n'est pas envisagé.

[24] Canon 15 (RP IV, 428): *Regestes du patriarcat* (voir n. 12), n° 406.

l'exclusion féminine: les hommes doivent entrer le moins possible dans les monastères féminins.

Troisièmement, les femmes sont potentiellement à l'écart du temps du sacré, c'est-à-dire du temps liturgique. Les trois canons anciens qui statuent sur ce point sont tous d'origine alexandrine. Le canon 6 de Timothée concerne la femme catéchumène dont le baptême a été fixé (à la veillée pascale suivante). Que faut-il faire, si 'le jour du baptême, il lui arrive ce qui est habituel aux femmes'? 'Il faut différer jusqu'à ce qu'elle soit purifiée.'[25] Le canon 7 de Timothée pose le problème de la participation aux saints mystères (la communion), toujours pour ce même cas de figure. La réponse est identique: 'il ne faut pas, jusqu'à ce qu'elle soit purifiée'.[26] Quant au canon 2 remontant à Denys d'Alexandrie,[27] il estime superflu de s'informer sur ce sujet: car des femmes croyantes et pieuses n'oseront jamais avoir un tel comportement, mais prendront modèle sur l'hémorroïsse qui n'avait pas osé toucher le Christ. La remarque donne à penser que le droit canonique ne créerait pas l'exclusion, mais consacrerait plutôt des usages reconnus. Toutefois le canon élargit encore l'interdit: d'après lui, ces femmes qui ne doivent pas 's'approcher de la table sainte' ne doivent pas non plus 'entrer dans la maison de Dieu', c'est-à-dire dans l'église; prier leur est certes permis, mais 'celui qui n'est pas complètement pur de corps et d'âme se verra interdire d'approcher ce qui est saint'. Balsamon en tire la conclusion que ces femmes ne doivent même pas se tenir dans le pronaos de l'église.[28]

Semblablement, l'accouchement exclut les femmes de la communion; et, s'il a lieu pendant le Carême, elles ne peuvent s'associer à la célébration pascale qui suit. Cette règle est énoncée dans une réponse canonique de la fin du XIe siècle.[29]

Sans doute la question de la pureté est-elle au cœur de toutes ces décisions.[30] En tout cas, elles ont pour effet d'exclure les femmes, à

---

[25] RP IV, 334.

[26] RP IV, 335.

[27] RP IV, 7.

[28] RP IV, 8–9.

[29] *Regestes du patriarcat* (voir n. 12), n° 990. La Novelle 17 de Léon VI exclut l'accouchée du baptême ou de la communion pendant quarante jours, sauf en cas de danger vital.

[30] Sur la signification de cette impureté, liée au mélange entre la vie et la mort, voir I. Sorlin, 'Striges et géloudes. Histoire d'une croyance et d'une tradition', *TM* 11 (1991), 432–434.

intervalles réguliers, des célébrations de l'Église. Une temporalité qui leur est spécifique rompt pour elles le temps liturgique.

Les formes d'aliénation

Outre la demi-douzaine de canons tenant les femmes à l'écart du sacré, la littérature canonique témoigne d'une forme d'extériorité autre que la marginalité ou l'exclusion: les femmes y apparaissent non pas étrangères à une communauté où elles ne s'intègrent que partiellement, mais 'étrangères à elles-mêmes', parce qu'affectées par différentes formes d'aliénation.

En premier lieu, la femme n'est pas son propre principe. Son principe – l'homme – est extérieur à elle. Tant Zonaras que Balsamon l'affirment dans leurs commentaires au canon 17 du concile de Gangres,[31] interdisant aux femmes de raser leur chevelure. Ils rappellent que l'apôtre Paul a écrit: 'l'homme est la tête de la femme'; puis ils expliquent: 'il a dit cela parce que l'homme est sa cause (*aitios*), en tant qu'elle est née de lui'. Que l'homme soit cause de la femme entraîne que celle-ci est référée à lui. Il y a là un mécanisme d'aliénation, qui se manifeste de différentes façons.

D'abord, elle est instrumentalisée à son profit, comme le montre le commentaire de Zonaras sur le canon 21 de Basile.[32] Ce canon punit l'homme marié qui tombe dans la fornication (*porneia*) plus sévèrement que celui qui n'a pas d'épouse. Zonaras justifie ainsi la différence de traitement: le second a quelque excuse 'à cause de la nécessité naturelle'; le premier, lui, n'a aucune circonstance atténuante, lui 'qui a son épouse légitime comme calmant (*paramuthia*) à la nécessité naturelle'. L'épouse est vue comme un moyen, par lequel la sexualité peut être apaisée. Semblablement, le traité de Blastarès dit de l'homme marié qu'il dispose 'd'un calmant légitime contre la tyrannie naturelle'.[33] La même conviction semble à l'œuvre dans le canon 16 du concile d'Ancyre, relatif à la bestialité.[34] Il établit des degrés divers dans la gravité de l'acte, en fonction de deux critères: l'âge du coupable et le fait qu'il soit marié ou non. Balsamon rapporte ces différences à un principe d'explication commun: 'la nécessité naturelle', conçue comme une circonstance

---

[31] RP III, 113–114.
[32] RP IV, 449.
[33] *Gamma* 16, RP VI, 187.
[34] RP III, 53.

atténuante.[35] On s'attend donc à ce que cette nécessité diminue avec l'âge, d'une part, et à ce que l'épouse serve à l'apaiser, d'autre part.

Ensuite, la femme subit une appropriation au profit de l'homme. Les textes les plus révélateurs sont le canon 4 de Grégoire de Nysse concernant la fornication et l'adultère (*porneia* et *moicheia*) ainsi que les commentaires formulés à son propos.[36] Grégoire expose comment l'éthique chrétienne a dû s'adapter à la norme sociale, qui s'attache particulièrement à la fidélité des épouses et distingue l'adultère, défini comme une relation sexuelle impliquant la femme d'autrui, de toutes les autres formes d'inconduite. Selon les principes chrétiens, eux, les époux ont les mêmes obligations de chasteté et de fidélité: comme le développe Grégoire à partir d'un passage paulinien,[37] chaque conjoint est pour l'autre 'un ustensile propre' (τὸ ἴδιον αὐτοῦ σκεῦος), dont celui-ci peut user légitimement dans le mariage; sinon, tout ce qui n'est pas 'propre' (*idion*) est 'étranger' (*allotrion*), même s'il n'a pas de maître (τὸν κυριεύοντα) manifeste, précision qui renvoie implicitement au cas de l'épouse (en puissance de mari). Autrement dit, toute relation sexuelle hors mariage est adultère, et il n'y a pas lieu de différencier entre l'adultère (de l'épouse) et la fornication. Mais l'Église a dû composer: pour employer le langage de Grégoire, les Pères ont infléchi les principes au profit des plus faibles et introduit une distinction entre la fornication, qui se produit 'sans injustice envers autrui', et l'adultère, qui comporte une telle injustice. Ce que la traduction ne rend pas, mais qui va de soi en grec (ἀδικία ἑτέρου), c'est qu'autrui est un masculin. L'adultère redevient ainsi une atteinte aux droits d'un homme. Du même coup, l'être 'étranger' que Grégoire désignait par un neutre (*allotrion*) au début de son texte redevient une femme, et une femme 'qui appartient à un autre', conformément au sens premier de l'adjectif *allotrios*. Zonaras et Balsamon confirment cette interprétation. Pour eux, la relation charnelle sans 'injustice envers autrui' est celle qui a lieu 'envers une femme libre d'homme'; et l'injustice envers autrui consiste à 's'approprier celle d'un autre' (τὴν ἀλλοτρίαν οἰκειούμενος). Bref, l'épouse (et elle seule) est objet d'appropriation par son conjoint et sous la maîtrise de celui-ci.

Enfin, la femme est parfois privée de libre choix et de pouvoir sur elle-même. La décision aliénante remonte, cette fois, au concile in Trullo et concerne l'épouse d'un homme qui va devenir évêque: une fois séparée

---

[35] RP III, 54–55.
[36] RP IV, 308–314.
[37] 1 Thess. 4:4.

de son mari d'un commun accord, la femme est contrainte d'entrer dans un monastère après l'ordination de celui-ci.[38] La raison n'est nulle part explicitée, mais ne fait aucun doute. Il est interdit aux clercs, sous peine de déchéance, d'avoir pour épouse une femme qui ne serait pas *univira*, que ce soit une veuve, une divorcée ou une femme de mœurs légères. L'ancienne épouse de l'évêque, si elle était laissée libre, tiendrait ainsi en son pouvoir la fonction épiscopale de celui-ci: en se remariant ou même en menant une vie licencieuse, elle la mettrait en péril. Une telle dépendance ne pouvait qu'apparaître intolérable à la société et à l'Église byzantines. La solution passe par une mesure aliénante pour la femme, astreinte à devenir moniale. Cette contrainte, qui fait fi de son libre choix, n'était pas sans poser problème. Balsamon dut rappeler avec insistance que telle était la solution canonique et qu'un *sêmeiôma* d'Isaac Ange l'avait confirmée récemment.[39] Il lui fallut aussi justifier ladite norme. Certains soutenaient en effet que personne ne doit entrer contre son gré dans la vie monastique: pourquoi donc ces femmes ne seraient-elles pas enfermées dans un monastère, mais sans être tonsurées? Balsamon répond qu'elles pourraient alors chercher à sortir du monastère et à se remarier (ce qui mettrait en cause l'ordination de leur ancien mari). Son deuxième argument est qu'être enfermé dans un monastère sans être tonsuré représente un châtiment (prévu pour les femmes adultères, par exemple):[40] appliquer cette solution à l'ancienne femme de l'évêque déshonorerait l'ordination de celui-ci. On remarque, une fois de plus, que le problème est pensé en fonction de l'évêque (de l'homme), et non pas par rapport à la femme. Enfin, en ce qui concerne la contrainte exercée sur la femme, Balsamon explique que celle-ci pouvait refuser le divorce, empêchant ainsi l'ordination de son mari et sa propre tonsure; mais à partir du moment où elle l'a accepté, la conséquence (à savoir sa propre tonsure) est inévitable. Le premier choix est donc censé englober le second, et la tonsure est considérée comme choisie et non imposée. On peut se demander si le choix initial était vraiment libre. On notera de toute façon que ces normes sont élaborées par rapport à un homme et à son profit.

---

[38]   Canon 48, RP II, 419. Voir Herrin, 'Public and Private Forms', 194–195.

[39]   RP II, 420–423. Sur le *sêmeiôma* de 1186, précisant que la règle canonique a dû être rappelée parce qu'elle n'était pas toujours respectée, voir J. et P. Zepos, *Ius graecoromanum*, I (Athènes, 1931), 435–436; *Regestes du patriarcat* (voir n. 12), n° 1171; *Regesten der Kaiserurkunden des oströmischen Reiches*, II 2, éd. F. Dölger et P. Wirth (Munich, 1995), n° 1573.

[40]   Sur le monastère comme prison, voir Herrin, 'Public and Private Forms', 193–195.

Un deuxième aspect de l'aliénation féminine ne se limite pas, comme le précédent, au cas de l'épouse. Dans le droit canonique, l'homme est au cœur du dispositif normatif; la femme est envisagée en fonction de lui et peut même se retrouver objet de normes, dont il est à la fois le sujet et l'agent. Le canon 77 du concile *in Trullo* et le commentaire qu'en fait Zonaras le montrent bien.[41] Le canon interdit aux clercs et aux moines, ainsi qu'à tout chrétien laïc, de se baigner avec des femmes. Zonaras développe l'explication suivante: rencontrer des femmes dans une maison ou dans la rue peut déjà provoquer une tempête dans la raison des hommes; à plus forte raison se baigner avec elles risque de submerger leur esprit. La règle s'adresse donc à des hommes, alors que les femmes en sont l'objet. Et l'interdit est justifié par le fait que toute femme représente un danger potentiel pour l'équilibre masculin; la femme est pensée par rapport à l'homme, sans qu'il y ait réciprocité.[42]

Les observations que suscite ce canon ont-elles une portée plus générale? Ne pourrait-on objecter que le droit canonique s'adresse aussi aux femmes et les traite comme des sujets? Il y a, de fait, des règles spécifiques aux femmes ou à certaines catégories d'entre elles. Les rubriques des différents chapitres du Nomocanon suffisent à le montrer, ainsi que les titres rassemblés dans le traité alphabétique de Blastarès, à la lettre *gamma*, dont dix-sept comportent le mot *gunaikes*.[43] Apparemment, les femmes sont, elles aussi, destinataires du droit canonique. Mais il faut apprécier ce fait à sa juste valeur. Premièrement, une bonne moitié de ces dispositions prend en considération les femmes en raison de spécificités physiologiques, comme nous le reverrons. Deuxièmement, le statut des deux sexes, dans les énoncés du droit canonique, présente une dissymétrie manifeste. Dans le traité alphabétique de Blastarès, justement, si la lettre *gamma* réunit dix-sept titres avec le terme *gunaikes*, la lettre *alpha*, elle, ne comporte aucune rubrique *andres*. Autrement dit, l'homme est le genre normal; la femme est le genre marqué. Certes, le phénomène a une composante grammaticale et il ne m'échappe pas que, grammaticalement, le masculin englobe le féminin. Il en va manifestement ainsi, quand un titre du Nomocanon a pour rubrique: 'Sur les laïcs'. Néanmoins ces énoncés sont des masculins et renvoient d'abord à des hommes ou même exclusivement à eux: c'est assurément le cas, chez Blastarès, de la rubrique 'Sur ceux qui se baignent avec des

---

[41] RP II, 483–484.

[42] Toutefois, à propos du canon 30 de Laodicée qui formule la même règle, Zonaras dépeint la pulsion sexuelle comme affectant semblablement les deux sexes (RP III, 197).

[43] Dix fois, c'est le sujet grammatical.

femmes'.[44] Les hommes s'avèrent ainsi les véritables destinataires du droit canonique; les femmes ne le sont que si c'est explicitement marqué.

Il faut prendre en compte une autre objection: par nature, le droit canonique se préoccupe particulièrement des clercs, qui sont des hommes; dans un tel contexte, il n'y aurait pas à s'étonner que l'homme soit mis au centre du dispositif normatif. Certes. Les développements qui suivent se limitent donc à des exemples où ce facteur n'interfère pas et où les relations entre hommes et femmes pourraient être envisagées de façon réciproque, entraînant des normes symétriques. Or c'est loin d'être le cas.

Le phénomène se marque déjà dans la syntaxe des prescriptions. Quand elles concernent un couple, la femme n'en est pas le sujet (grammaticalement parlant), mais l'objet ou le support. Il y a, notamment, un titre du Nomocanon, formulé ainsi:[45] 'Quand faut-il s'abstenir de son épouse en raison de la communion?' La femme apparaît privée de toute autonomie. La façon dont les interdictions de mariage sont énoncées aboutit à la même constatation: ces prohibitions s'adressent le plus souvent à un homme, la femme étant l'objet de l'interdit.

Mais il y a plus que ces manifestations grammaticales, comme le montre un des commentaires au canon 51 des Apôtres.[46] L'écrit attribué aux Apôtres est un des nombreux textes du IVe siècle par lesquels l'Église condamne des comportements ascétiques où le mépris de la chair semble inspiré par des convictions dualistes. D'après lui, l'abstinence, qu'elle s'applique au mariage, à la viande ou au vin, est répréhensible si elle est due au mépris de la Création, et non pas à l'ascèse; cela vaut pour les clercs et pour les laïcs. Chez Aristènos et Balsamon, la règle est reprise sous une forme 'neutre' et rien n'interdit de penser qu'elle s'adresse aux femmes comme aux hommes; Balsamon rappelle à ce propos que Dieu a fait l'être humain mâle et femelle et que, pour cette raison, le mariage n'est pas rejeté par l'Église. Le commentaire de Zonaras a, lui, une tout autre tonalité: 'Rien de ce qui vient de Dieu n'est mauvais; mais c'est le mauvais usage qu'on en fait qui est nuisible. Si la femme était cause du mal, ainsi que le vin et le reste, ils n'auraient pas été introduits par Dieu. En conséquence, celui qui calomnie les œuvres de Dieu blasphème contre Sa création.' Ici, le choix de l'ascèse ne concerne pas tous les êtres humains, mais les seuls hommes. Le problème est pensé par rapport à un homme et du point de vue d'un homme. Dans cette perspective, il

---

[44] *Gamma* 20 (RP VI, 195). Le Nomocanon (XIII 25, RP I, 28 et 326) précise, lui: 'Sur le fait qu'il est interdit à des hommes de se baigner avec des femmes'.

[45] Nomoc. III 21, RP I, 120.

[46] RP II, 67–68.

devient superflu de dire que l'homme n'est pas source de mal, puisque créé par Dieu. En installant ainsi l'homme au centre des relations humaines, en le traitant comme seul agent et seul sujet, le texte de Zonaras en viendrait presque à le soustraire à l'œuvre créatrice de Dieu. Par ailleurs, cette exégèse réifie la femme. Zonaras la place sur le même plan que le vin et la viande, alors que le canon originel mentionnait le mariage à cet endroit; elle devient ainsi un produit créé par Dieu et mis à la disposition de l'homme, qui en use, selon les cas, bien ou mal.

Ce processus de réification représente un troisième aspect de l'aliénation féminine: la femme est réifiée, en ce qu'elle est réduite à son corps. La réflexion peut partir du canon 44 de Basile de Césarée, qui condamne comme un sacrilège (*hierosulia*) les relations sexuelles impliquant des diaconesses et déclare: 'Nous ne permettons pas que le corps de la femme diacre, en tant qu'il est consacré, ait un usage charnel.'[47] L'affirmation suscite deux remarques. Premièrement, cette faute sexuelle n'est pas traitée comme une fornication ou une forme aggravée de fornication. C'est un sacrilège. La diaconesse ne serait-elle pas mise sur le même plan qu'un objet consacré à Dieu? L'hypothèse trouve des appuis dans le corpus canonique. Balsamon, dans son commentaire du canon, explique que la règle s'applique même à celle qui a été déchue du diaconat, en fonction du principe: 'ce qui est sacré ne devient pas pollué (*miaron*)'.[48] On relèvera le neutre. On peut également invoquer les considérations analogues relatives aux vierges consacrées. Un autre canon de Basile définit la vierge comme 'la fiancée du Christ', mais aussi comme 'un ustensile (*skeuos*) sacré dédié au Maître'.[49] Certes, dans le Nouveau Testament, *skeuos* est utilisé pour des êtres humains, dont Paul.[50] Le sens d'objet, d'ustensile demeure néanmoins présent, quand une femme est ainsi désignée. La preuve en est fournie par le commentaire de Zonaras au canon 4 du concile *in Trullo*,[51] punissant les clercs qui ont une relation sexuelle avec une femme consacrée à Dieu. Zonaras justifie la mesure en ces termes: 'De même qu'il est interdit de s'approprier n'importe quel ustensile ou tissu, qui a été dédié à Dieu et sanctifié de ce fait, et d'en faire usage ..., de même, à plus forte raison, le

---

[47]   RP IV, 191–192.
[48]   RP IV, 193.
[49]   Canon 18, RP IV, 141.
[50]   Act. 9, 15; Rom. 9, 22–23; 1 Thess. 4:4; 2 Tim. 2:21; 1 Pet. 3:7.
[51]   RP II, 315–316.

corrupteur de la femme consacrée à Dieu ne sera pas impuni.'[52] Même si le cas de la femme apparaît plus grave que celui de l'objet, la comparaison à la chose consacrée demeure. Elle est d'autant plus frappante que le texte du canon suggérait une autre justification: en parlant de corruption de 'la fiancée du Christ', il invitait à une comparaison avec l'adultère et non avec l'appropriation d'objets sacrés.[53]

La deuxième remarque permet de revenir sur les femmes et la sphère du sacré. Si elles en sont exclues, ce qui est dit de la diaconesse vient préciser la situation. D'après les textes réunis dans le corpus canonique byzantin, la femme diacre n'est pas, comme l'homme diacre, quelqu'un qui exerce un ministère sacré. C'est quelqu'un qui est consacré à Dieu, comme le serait un objet, et dont le corps est tabou. Tant le canon 44 de Basile que Zonaras, Balsamon ou Blastarès parlent catégoriquement de corps consacré à Dieu.[54] S'agissant du corps et de son usage sexuel, la différence avec leurs homonymes masculins est, de fait, patente: pour les hommes diacres comme pour les prêtres, il n'y a pas de tabou général d'ordre sexuel, autrement dit d'interdiction de toute activité sexuelle. Les commentaires sur le degré d'abstinence sexuelle exigé des clercs, à propos du canon 25 de Carthage, suffiraient à le prouver.[55] Le caractère sacré de la diaconesse est ainsi attaché au corps de celle-ci et a une définition physique. On le constate encore à un autre effet. Quand Balsamon commente le canon 49 de Basile, d'après lequel une femme qui subit une corruption par violence n'en porte pas la responsabilité, il précise que, s'il s'agit d'une diaconesse, elle ne subira pas de peine, mais cessera néanmoins d'être diacre, 'parce que Dieu a permis qu'elle tombe dans le mal'.[56] La raison est claire: la souillure, même involontaire, existe matériellement et fait perdre à la femme un caractère sacré qui se limitait à son corps.[57]

Réduite à son corps, la femme l'est encore bien plus radicalement, quand elle est ramenée à des spécificités de sa physiologie. Comme il a

---

[52] Balsamon (RP II, 316) utilise le même registre ('il souille l'ustensile dédié à Dieu'), mais sans développer la comparaison.

[53] C'est ce que fait Aristènos (RP II, 317), en renvoyant au canon 18 de Basile qui condamne l'homme comme adultère.

[54] RP IV, 192–193 et VI, 436.

[55] RP III, 369–372.

[56] RP IV, 202–203.

[57] Le même point de vue s'applique aux jeunes gens contraints à la pédérastie (Blastarès, *alpha* 14, RP VI, 104–105, à partir d'un texte de Jean le Jeûneur).

été dit plus haut, certains aspects de son statut sont déterminés par le phénomène de la menstruation, ou plutôt par l'impureté affectant le sang menstruel ou celui de l'accouchement. Cette impureté spéciale aux femmes est une des raisons avancées pour les exclure de l'espace sacré; elle les écarte aussi des célébrations liturgiques, le baptême comme la communion. Elle peut également avoir pour effet de séparer la mère de l'enfant qu'elle vient de mettre au monde. Un canon attribué au patriarche Nicéphore envisage le cas du nouveau-né qu'il a fallu baptiser, parce qu'il était en danger de mort: il doit être allaité par une femme baptisée et pure, ce qui veut dire par une femme autre que sa mère, impure pendant quarante jours après l'accouchement; sa mère ne peut ni le toucher ni même entrer dans la pièce où il est, et cela jusqu'au moment de sa purification, au quarantième jour.[58]

Ce qu'il faut ajouter, c'est que ces spécificités physiologiques déterminent le statut des femmes dans un sens uniquement négatif. Elles aboutissent, d'une part, à toute une série d'exclusions. D'autre part, la possibilité d'une identification positive, qui ne serait pas aliénante, est expressément refusée. Ici, c'est le canon 79 du concile *in Trullo* et ses commentaires qui entrent en ligne de compte.[59] Le canon condamne une pratique apparemment répandue à la fin du VIIe siècle: au lendemain de la fête de la Nativité, on confectionnait une bouillie de semoule, que l'on partageait en l'honneur de l'accouchement de la Mère de Dieu.[60] Il rappelle que Marie a enfanté sans accouchement et déclare que ce n'est pas à son honneur que de penser cet enfantement à partir de notre expérience. Certes, il ne présente nullement cette coutume comme une pratique féminine, et elle ne l'était pas exclusivement, puisqu'il prévoit une peine pour les clercs qui s'en rendent coupables. Néanmoins son aspect culinaire devait impliquer la participation des femmes et on peut supposer qu'elle était particulièrement en faveur chez elles.

Or les commentaires explicitent ce qui, dans cette pratique, choquait l'Église: c'est le rapprochement qu'elle instaurait entre la Vierge et des femmes, dans un vécu spécifiquement féminin, dont les hommes sont

---

[58]   Canon 38, RP IV, 431. Mais, au XIIe siècle, une réponse canonique bien différente est faite (RP V, 372): voir M.-H. Congourdeau, 'Regards sur l'enfant nouveau-né à Byzance', *REB* 51 (1993), 169.

[59]   RP II, 486–489; Blastarès, *kappa* 8, RP VI, 322.

[60]   Voir Congourdeau, 'Regards', 156, J. Herrin, '"Femina byzantina": The Council *in Trullo* on Women', *DOP* 46 (1992), 104–105 et 'Public and Private Forms', 196–197, qui l'interprète comme un rituel public, dans l'église. Sur ce mets, voir Ph. Koukoulès, Βυζαντινῶν βίος καὶ πολιτισμός, IV (Athènes, 1951), 31–32.

exclus. Voici ce que dit Zonaras: 'Certains faisaient [pour la Mère de Dieu] ce que l'on fait dans le cas des femmes qui accouchent'; or elle n'a pas fait l'expérience de l'accouchement; dans son cas, l'enfantement, tout comme la conception, est au-dessus des caractéristiques naturelles, et 'c'est un outrage envers [elle] et non pas un honneur qu'ait lieu à propos de son enfantement indicible la même chose que pour les autres femmes qui enfantent'. Ce qui est ainsi refusé, c'est une identification entre Marie et les autres femmes, dans ce que la féminité a de spécifique: au lieu que l'enfantement les rapproche, la réalité physique de l'accouchement les sépare. Le commentaire de Balsamon développe les mêmes thèmes, avec une notation supplémentaire qui confirme l'interprétation: il remarque qu'il existe bel et bien une fête des *epilochia* de Marie, célébrée avec des psaumes et des hymnes. Et il suffit de penser que la fête de l'Hypapantè, au 2 février, marque aussi la purification de Marie, quarante jours après la naissance du Christ, comme pour les femmes qui ont accouché, conformément aux prescriptions du Lévitique. Ce que refuse l'Église n'est donc pas vraiment de célébrer l'accouchement et les relevailles de Marie, mais de les célébrer avec une pratique qui caractérise les femmes accouchées. L'intolérable, en définitive, est l'assimilation de Marie et des autres femmes, dans leur spécificité physique. La possibilité d'une identification positive est ainsi refusée aux femmes. Leur spécificité physique les détermine de façon uniquement négative, par l'impureté qui en reste inséparable. Facteur d'exclusion, elle est aussi facteur d'aliénation.

Je terminerai par quelques textes relatifs au baptême de la femme enceinte. Le canon 6 de Néocésarée affirme qu'elle doit être baptisée quand elle le veut et justifie ainsi sa décision: 'Celle qui enfante n'a sous ce rapport rien de commun avec l'enfant, car la volonté concernant la profession [de foi] est manifestement propre à chacun.'[61] À première vue, ce texte témoigne d'une parfaite autonomie de la femme: le fait de porter en elle un être qui sera un autre ne la rend pas étrangère à elle-même, ne l'aliène pas. Mais les commentaires montrent que la menace d'aliénation est en réalité toute proche.[62] Balsamon explique bien la nature du problème. Il y avait une incertitude sur l'effet du baptême de la mère: le fœtus était-il, oui ou non, baptisé simultanément? Aussi courait-on inévitablement un risque: ou bien on baptisait l'enfant après la naissance

---

[61] RP III, 79.
[62] RP III, 79–80.

et on risquait de perpétrer un second baptême; ou bien on ne faisait rien et on risquait de laisser l'enfant non baptisé. En fait, l'incertitude n'a pas lieu d'être. Car, comme Zonaras le souligne de son côté, 'l'embryon est privé de volonté' et n'est donc pas baptisé avec sa mère. Au total, si le baptême de la femme enceinte est possible, c'est parce que l'enfant ne reçoit pas le baptême en même temps, du fait de ses caractéristiques propres. Le sort de la femme est déterminé non par ses caractères à elle, mais par les spécifications attachées à l'embryon: l'absence de volonté de l'enfant à naître est déterminante pour faire obstacle à son baptême et permettre, du même coup, celui de sa mère.

Un autre texte de Balsamon sur la question est encore plus révélateur. Il s'agit de son commentaire au Nomocanon, à la rubrique 'Sur le baptême de la femme enceinte'.[63] Balsamon y reprend l'affirmation du canon, comme quoi le baptême de la femme enceinte est possible 'parce que la femme qui porte un enfant n'a [rien] en commun avec lui (*epikoinônein*)', et il l'explique ainsi: 'on ne la conjecture pas, elle aussi, inapte au baptême du fait que le fœtus ne peut s'engager dans la profession du baptême'. Autrement dit, la décision prise à propos de la mère dépend de son rapport à l'enfant et est pensée, avant tout, par rapport à lui. L'impossibilité de baptiser l'enfant aurait pu entraîner l'impossibilité de baptiser la mère. C'est bien l'autonomie de la femme qui était mise en cause, même si la décision finale la conforte. Il y a plus. Comme toujours, le Nomocanon donne d'abord les renvois nécessaires aux textes canoniques (en l'occurrence, le canon 6 de Néocésarée); puis il cite les dispositions du droit impérial relatives au même sujet. Ce sont, ici, trois passages du Digeste: d'après l'un, 'le fœtus est une partie (*meros*) de la femme enceinte';[64] d'après les deux autres, 'le fœtus n'est pas une partie de la mère'.[65] Balsamon veut expliquer pourquoi ces textes sont évoqués à propos du baptême de la femme enceinte. Selon certains, écrit-il, 'le fœtus ... est complètement uni à sa mère en tant que partie d'elle; et il ne peut pas être baptisé avec sa mère parce qu'il n'est pas encore venu à la lumière et n'a pas la volonté pour accomplir la profession du saint baptême. Par conséquent, la femme enceinte elle non plus ne doit pas être baptisée, mais doit attendre la sortie du fœtus à la lumière, afin d'éviter que l'une de ses parties soit baptisée, alors que l'autre reste privée de l'illumination du baptême.' L'une de ses parties: τὸ μὲν ἐκ τῶν μερῶν

---

[63]   Nomoc. IV 10, RP I, 124–126.

[64]   D 25, 4, 1, 1.

[65]   D 41, 3, 10, 2 et D 50, 16, 26. Balsamon renvoie aux passages correspondants des Basiliques.

αὐτῆς. Donc ce n'est plus le fœtus qui est considéré comme partie de la mère, mais la femme elle-même qui est réduite à l'état de partie d'un tout qui la dépasse. De totalité, elle devient fragment: l'accomplissement lui fait défaut et elle cesse en quelque sorte d'être une personne. Il serait difficile de trouver plus bel exemple de perspective aliénante.

8. Hebrews, Greeks or Romans?
Jewish Culture and Identity in Byzantium

Nicholas de Lange

The presence of Jews in Byzantium is generally overlooked, or mentioned in the most cursory fashion. And yet, while not numerous, they were a definite presence in the population of the major towns, and in the literature of the Orthodox Christian majority they receive an attention that verges on the obsessive, for obscure theological reasons. They also receive attention in the legislation both of the state and of the church, and so in speaking of Jewish identity we are considering something that had a formal and publicly recognized aspect. However, in what follows I shall be mostly concerned with the Jews' own sense of their minority identity, rather than the identity that was inflicted on them by others, which is in some respects a different story.

In speaking of the Jewish minority in Byzantium, I have in mind mainly the period from 1000 to 1200. This is a period that is relatively well documented from the Jewish side, and it is the availability of this documentary evidence that makes the subject particularly interesting. There are not many minorities that have left us such abundant writings, from which, although it is not a constant preoccupation in the sources themselves, we can glean a certain impression of how the minority saw itself *vis-à-vis* the majority. The documents are mainly written in Hebrew, and very few of them have been translated; indeed most of them are only accessible in manuscript. It is to be hoped that they will be made available to Byzantinists, because they are of more than passing interest.

The Jews can be considered either as an *ethnic* or as a *religious* minority. In fact they were both, and I do not think it makes much difference which term we use. The Jewish religion belonged exclusively

From *Strangers to Themselves: The Byzantine Outsider*, ed. Dion C. Smythe, for the Society for the Promotion of Byzantine Studies. Published by Ashgate Publishing Ltd, Gower House, Croft Road, Aldershot, Hampshire, GU11 3HR, Great Britain. Copyright © 2000 Nicholas de Lange. The right of Nicholas de Lange to be identified as the author of the article 'Hebrews, Greeks or Romans? Jewish culture and identity in Byzantium' has been asserted by him in accordance with the Copyright, Designs and Patents Act, 1988.

to the Jewish *ethnos*, and a Jew converting to another religion ceased to belong to the *ethnos*. The cultural manifestations of ethnic Jewish identity are features which are often categorized as religious, but in many cases there is nothing specifically religious about them.

Every ethnic minority needs to develop a sense of belonging, of self-perception as a group, of common identity and of difference from other groups. The boundaries of Jewish ethnic identity were laid down long before the period I am looking at. They have very ancient roots, and were established for Jews in general within the Roman empire in the early days of that empire. The Jewish self-perception was linked to an established theology in which the Jews were in a state of conflict with other ethnic groups (called collectively 'the nations', τὰ ἔθνη) which would at some future time be resolved by the triumphal return of the Jews to their own land. This belief seems to have helped the Jews to accept passively their state of legal and social subjection and occasional oppression. It receives regular, frequent and explicit articulation in the Hebrew liturgy of the synagogue, and is taken for granted in hymns and homilies.[1]

How numerous were the Jews in the Byzantine empire? According to Benjamin of Tudela, visiting the empire *c*.1165, there were 2,500 Jews in Constantinople, 2,000 in Thebes, 500 in Thessalonike, and a scattering of smaller communities or small groups elsewhere, totalling well under 10,000 in all.[2] Are these numbers to be taken at their face value? David Jacoby[3] has argued that the figure of 2,500 for Constantinople is close to what is reasonable for a piece of land of the size of the Pera Jewry, and that consequently Benjamin's other figures, too, should be accepted as referring to individuals, and not to households as some have maintained.[4]

---

[1]   For some illustrations of this outlook see below, and N.R.M. de Lange, 'A Fragment of Byzantine Anti-Christian Polemic', *JJS* 41 (1990), 92–100. Its foundations lie in the pre-Christian empire: see Nicholas de Lange, 'Jewish Attitudes to the Roman Empire', in P.D.A. Garnsey and C.R. Whittaker, eds, *Imperialism in the Ancient World* (Cambridge, 1978), 255–281, 354–357.

[2]   Sandra Benjamin, *The World of Benjamin of Tudela. A Mediterranean Medieval Travelogue* (Madison, WI, 1995). Extracts are translated in Joshua Starr, *The Jews in the Byzantine Empire 641–1204* (Athens, 1939), 228ff. and in Andrew Sharf, *Byzantine Jewry from Justinian to the Fourth Crusade* (London/New York, 1971). See also José A. Ochoa, 'El imperio bizantino en el viaje de Benjamín de Tudela', in G. Busi, ed., *Viaggiatori Ebrei* (Atti del Congresso europeo dell' AISG) (Bologna, 1992), 81–98.

[3]   D. Jacoby, 'Les Quartiers juifs de Constantinople', *B* 37 (1967), 167–227, reprinted in his *Société et démographie à Byzance et en Romanie latine* (London, 1975), 185ff.

[4]   E.g. Sharf, *Byzantine Jewry*, 3: 'The final figure [of Jews in the empire] may be close to 100,000 of whom ... not less than ten thousand ... lived in Constantinople.' On this

So they were a small minority, not exceeding perhaps one per cent of the population of Constantinople.[5]

The Jews were mainly an urban minority, and at least in some cities they had quarters of their own. There is some evidence that the Jews of the capital were concentrated by edict in a part of Pera, and were not permitted to dwell elsewhere in Constantinople. So Benjamin of Tudela notes:

> The Jews are not amongst them [the Greeks] within the city, for they have transferred them behind an arm of the sea: an arm of the Sea of Russia surrounds them on one side so that they cannot leave except by sea in order to trade with the inhabitants of the city.[6]

Even if the law required them to live in their own quarter, however, we cannot be certain that they did so in all times and places, and indeed a few years later we find Eustathius of Thessalonike writing to the Patriarch of Constantinople complaining that the Jews have begun to spread all over that city, even living in Christian houses that are decorated with holy images.[7]

How visible were the Jews? I do not know of any discussion of this question in medieval or modern sources. In Byzantium Jews were not forced to wear distinctive clothing, or a badge such as that imposed in the Latin West by the 4th Lateran Council (1215). Does that suggest that they could be sufficiently distinguished without such measures? I simply do not know the answer to this question. Elisabeth Revel-Neher has drawn attention to representations of Jewish men in Byzantine art wearing phylacteries:

> How striking the Jew-in-the-street must have looked, his forehead bound with leather thongs which ended in a totally closed and undecorated square box, and his left arm surrounded with circles formed by these same thongs wrapped around it from the elbows

---

reckoning the Jews would have constituted some 2% of the population of the capital, and perhaps more in the empire as a whole.

[5] On the population of Constantinople see D. Jacoby, 'La population de Constantinople à l'époque byzantine: un problème de démographie urbaine', *B* 31 (1961), 81–109, reprinted in his *Société et démographie à Byzance et en Romanie latine* (London, 1975). See also Jacoby's more recent study, 'Les Juifs de Byzance: une communauté marginalisée', in *I Perithoriaki sto Vizantio* (Athens, 1993), 103–154, esp. 129ff.

[6] See Jacoby, 'Quartiers', 178ff.

[7] Jacoby, 182. Cf. Sharf, *Byzantine Jewry*, 147f.

to the fingers in such a way as to form the first letter of one of the names of the Ineffable God.[8]

Revel-Neher supposes that Jews ceased to dress like this in public, although she presents no evidence for this supposition. Nor do I know of any concrete evidence that Jewish men regularly wore striped shawls such as we see in some Christian icons. The silence of the sources seems to be the most telling indication that there was nothing distinctive about the dress, habits or speech of the Jews, unless there was something that was so taken for granted that it is not mentioned.

We may wonder whether, clothing or customs apart, there was anything in the physical appearance or physiognomy of Jews that distinguished them from gentiles. *Prima facie* I do not think it at all probable. Many if not most of the original Jewish inhabitants of Byzantine lands had ended up being absorbed into the Christian majority by conversion, and the much smaller Jewish community in turn had absorbed a certain number of converts. The general Byzantine population was racially very mixed, and the Jewish community too had received immigrants from all over the world. No distinctive physical characteristics are attributed to Jews by gentile or Jewish writers, and so I conclude that they were physically indistinguishable from non-Jews.

The Jews practised fairly strict endogamy, that was simultaneously an expression and a buttress of their separateness. Christians, too, were prohibited from marrying Jews by both state and church law. Both Jewish and Christian law, however, permitted marriage with converts. Not much is known about how this worked out in practice.[9]

Christian sources refer to Jews in a casual manner that does not suggest any difficulty in identifying or distinguishing them. Their presence is taken for granted. No particular characteristics are attributed to them. There is some doubt as to whether Jews were subjected to a special tax as Jews. They suffered some legal disabilities, for example

---

[8]   Elisabeth Revel-Neher, *The Image of the Jew in Byzantine Art* (Oxford, 1992), 57.

[9]   The Karaite Tobias ben Moses writes to his daughter in 1040: 'My daughter, I do not know who you are with, whether you are among Jews, who are your father's people, or with your mother's race, the Gentiles.' See Moshe Gil, *A History of Palestine, 634–1099*, translated by E. Broido (Cambridge, 1992), 816. In the twelfth-century pamphlet *Anacharsis or Ananias*, the unfortunate John befriends a leader of the synagogue with a view to converting him to Christianity, but is persuaded instead to marry a Jewess. As the newlyweds emerge from church they are greeted by a throng of 'Pharisees, Sadducees and rabbis' (ed. D.A. Chrestides (Thessalonike, 1984), 260–261. I am grateful to Elizabeth Jeffreys for this reference).

they could not serve in the armed forces or in any government position, so that they could not exercise any power or influence over Christians, nor could they own Christian slaves. In law-courts they could not give evidence in cases involving Christians, and we know of special forms of oath to be taken by Jews.[10]

The Jews were clearly distinguished from the Orthodox Christian majority and from other minorities by their religious practices and rituals as well as by their theological beliefs. Their religious adherence entailed the use of a distinct calendar, and it was also connected to the use of a distinctive language, Hebrew (and to a much lesser extent also Aramaic), at least for certain religious and cultural purposes.

I have mentioned the enforcement of separate quarters for Jews. Christian legislation also limited contact with Jews, at least in theory. For example the Council *in Trullo* forbade mixed bathing, yet a visiting Italian rabbi in the late-twelfth to early-thirteenth century, Isaiah of Trani, castigates Byzantine Jews for bathing in public baths,[11] so it is quite possible that this kind of restriction too was honoured in the breach.

Benjamin of Tudela has left us the following vignette of the Jewish quarter of Constantinople:

> They live under heavy oppression, and there is much hatred against them which is engendered by the tanners, the workers in leather, who pour out their dirty water in the streets before the doors of their houses and defile the Jewish quarter. So the Greeks hate the Jews, good and bad alike, and subject them to severe restrictions and beat them in the streets and force them to hard labor. Yet the Jews are rich and good, kindly and charitable, and cheerfully bear the burden of their oppression. The place in which the Jews live is called Pera.[12]

Although the Jewish minority is treated in the sources as a unity, it was a divided unity. The most important division was a religious one, between

---

[10]   E. Patlagean, 'Contribution juridique à l'histoire des Juifs dans la Méditerranée médiévale: les formules grecques de serment', *REJ* 124 (1965), 137–156, reprinted in her *Structure sociale, famille, chrétienté à Byzance* (London, 1981). Cf. Nicholas de Lange, 'Jews and Christians in the Byzantine Empire: Problems and Prospects', in Diana Wood, ed., *Christianity and Judaism* (Oxford, 1992), 24. Generally on the status of the Jews, see Sharf, *Byzantine Jewry*.

[11]   Translation in Steven B. Bowman, *The Jews of Byzantium 1204–1453* (Alabama, 1985), 213.

[12]   Translation from Bowman, *Jews*, 335.

Karaites and Rabbanites. A disturbance between the two groups resulting in the imposition of a heavy fine is recorded in the 1060s, and Benjamin of Tudela states that in Constantinople a fence or wall divides Rabbanites from Karaites.[13] In Cyprus, again according to Benjamin, there are three groups of Jews, Rabbanites and Karaites, and also 'Epicureans', who have their own calendar, observing the Sabbath for the whole of Saturday instead of from Friday evening to sunset on Saturday.[14]

The origin of Byzantine Karaism is generally associated with a wave of immigration from the east in the course of the late tenth and early eleventh centuries. This is the view of the foremost modern specialist on the subject, Zvi Ankori.[15] A rival view has been strenuously advanced by the Karaite scholar S. Szyszman, who observes that the Byzantine Karaites preserve traces of the ancient Hellenistic Jewish religious culture, and insists that Karaism spread in the empire mainly through missionary activity among Jews.[16]

While it is true that we have some evidence of immigration, due to a propitious economic and political climate and to troubles elsewhere, the precise contribution of the newcomers to the Hebrew culture of the empire remains to be determined. There are indications that academically minded Jews elsewhere were attracted to Byzantium precisely because of the scholarly opportunities that were available there.[17]

Whatever the truth about the spread of Karaism, Szyszman is correct in drawing attention to the traces of Hellenistic Judaism to be found in Byzantine Karaite texts. The phenomenon is not confined, however, to Karaism. The whole of Byzantine Jewish culture rests on foundations laid down by Greek-speaking Jews in antiquity, just as the roots of Byzantine Christianity are in the early Greek-speaking church. The (sadly very fragmentary) Byzantine Jewish remains in the Cairo Genizah preserve distinctive renderings associated with Greek Bible translations that

---

[13]   Jacoby, 'Quartiers', 179.

[14]   Bowman, *Jews*, 336.

[15]   In Zvi Ankori, *Karaites in Byzantium* (New York and Jerusalem, 1959), followed e.g. by Andrew Sharf, *Byzantine Jewry*, 120, and by David Jacoby, 'The Jews of Constantinople and their demographic hinterland', in C. Mango and G. Dagron, eds, *Constantinople and its Hinterland* (Aldershot, 1995), 225.

[16]   S. Szyszman, 'Les karaïtes de Byzance', *Bulletin des Etudes Karaïtes* 3 (1993), 55–75.

[17]   See Nicholas de Lange, 'Jewish Education in the Byzantine Empire in the Twelfth Century', in Glenda Abramson and Tudor Parfitt, eds, *Jewish Education and Learning* (Chur, CH, 1994), 115–128, esp. 116–117.

originated among Jews in the early Roman empire.[18] It seems that these translations – Aquila and the rest – were still used in our period, perhaps in a mainly oral tradition, since they have left hardly any written traces. This discovery raises the question, not yet addressed, of whether other ancient Greek Jewish writings, such as Philo, Josephus, or the pseudepigraphic apocalypses, were also preserved orally.

Yet despite such traces of loyalty to a living tradition going back to antiquity, by the period that concerns us the written culture of the Byzantine Jews, Karaites and Rabbanites alike, was based on the Hebrew language. Hebrew became the foundation of Byzantine Jewish culture. All its written texts are inscribed in the Hebrew alphabet, even if, as sometimes happens, the language is Greek. The reason for this is that the Jews had their own schools. Both Karaites and Rabbanites invested heavily in Hebrew education. Its aim was to ensure that Jewish boys (at least) could follow the Hebrew prayers and understand the Bible.[19] At its best its results were impressive, to judge by the technically very competent and linguistically accomplished Hebrew hymns (called *piyyutim*, a word derived from the Greek word for poet), of which large numbers have come down to us.

We can witness in the texts of our period the end result of a long and fundamental process of cultural change, but we cannot observe the process of change itself, for want of evidence. All we have are tantalizing glimpses. The change from Greek to Hebrew culture was, in the long term, the salvation of the Greek-speaking Jews, even if it involved making enormous sacrifices, involving the jettisoning of their sacred scriptures and the old texts (such as the writings of Philo) that expounded them, as well as the traditional liturgy of the synagogue and much secular literature.

In earlier times Greek was the common language of Jews in Europe, as well as in Egypt and parts of Palestine. It was the cement of a common religious culture. By the year 1000 the Greek-speaking world had shrunk to a relatively tiny area. Their Greek tradition, had they clung to it doggedly, would have served to isolate the Byzantine Jews from other Jews, whether in Romance- and German-speaking Europe, in the Arab

---

[18] N. de Lange, 'La tradition des «révisions juives» au moyen âge: les fragments hébraïques de la Geniza du Caire', in G. Dorival and O. Munnich, eds, *'Selon les Septante'*, *Hommage à Marguerite Harl* (Paris, 1995), 133–143. On Byzantium and Cairo Genizah see the remarks of David Jacoby in *BZ* 91 (1998), 110–112, and Nicholas de Lange, 'Byzantium in the Cairo Genizah', *BMGS* 16 (1992), 34–47.

[19] See de Lange, 'Jewish Education'.

world, or elsewhere. Hebrew, the universal language of the Jews by our period, was far more than a useful means of communication for a society busily involved in international trade.

For more academically minded students the study of Hebrew opened up the whole world of traditional Jewish scholarship (although it should not be forgotten that Arabic, also written in Hebrew characters, was establishing itself as a vehicle of culture as well as a means of communication for many Jews in the Mediterranean region and further afield). It also enabled Jews to participate in a rich contemporary written culture that knew no geographical or political boundaries. Jewish students from Byzantium sat at the feet of great teachers such as Rashi (d. c.1105) in the West and of Hai Gaon (d. c.1038) in the East, and we have many indications that works by Byzantine Jews were read abroad, while writings by foreign Jews were studied in Byzantium.[20] Byzantine scholars can turn an elegant Hebrew letter when the occasion demands it, as we can see from the three Hebrew letters of a leading Karaite figure, Tobias ben Moses, preserved in the Genizah. Their style is accomplished and they are written partly or entirely in rhyme.[21]

The ability to write was also a useful tool for a society based to a large extent on long-distance trade, and writing Hebrew allowed Byzantine Jews to communicate with each other without gentiles (who might be the bearers of letters) being able to understand what was written, as well as facilitating contact with foreign Jews who did not speak Greek. Among the Cairo Genizah documents are a number of Hebrew letters from Byzantium showing that the language could be used as a medium of communication even among businessmen: the level of fluency is not particularly high, but the writers do not seem to experience any particular difficulty.[22] Indeed there is scarcely any evidence of Byzantine Jews being able to write in any script except the Hebrew, and on the rare occasions when they use Greek characters to write Greek it is always clear that they have a Hebrew education as well.

---

[20] See for example Nicholas de Lange, 'Abraham Ibn Ezra and Byzantium', in F. Díaz Esteban, ed., *Abraham Ibn Ezra y su Tiempo* (Madrid, 1990), 181–192, and supplementary remarks in *Bulletin of Judaeo-Greek Studies* 17 (Winter, 1995), 20.

[21] See de Lange, 'Byzantium in the Cairo Genizah', 39–40; Gil, *History of Palestine*, 815–818; Z. Ankori, 'The Correspondence of Tobias ben Moses the Karaite of Constantinople', in J.L. Blau et al., eds, *Essays on Jewish Life and Thought presented in honor of Salo Wittmayer Baron* (New York, 1959), 1–38.

[22] See de Lange, 'Byzantium in the Cairo Genizah'.

Besides these practical uses for Hebrew literacy, we should bear in mind that the Hebrew language also functioned as a factor in the expression of distinctive Jewish identity. This aspect comes across very clearly in the polemic of the twelfth-century author Judah Hadassi, addressing himself to his fellow Karaites:

> It is not proper for legal documents to be written in any other language than your own. The Rabbanites, in expressing themselves partly in the vernacular [i.e. Greek] language in their documents, behave like gentiles ... This is not the way of your Torah, for our language is the language spoken by our God at Mount Sinai before the whole of his people Israel through his Prophet ... Hence this is the way our deeds and contracts are to be written.[23]

This statement embodies a polemic against Christianity as well as against the Rabbanites, who are the main opponents of Karaism. And Hadassi is making a double point: Hebrew is the language of the Jewish religion, to be used in marriage and divorce deeds and other documents, because it is the language in which God himself chose to speak to Moses; by the same token, its use asserts the unity of the Jewish people. Jews, by using their ancestral sacred tongue in preference to the local vernacular, were reasserting their links with their own classical tradition, as well as their horizontal links with other Jews worldwide, and clearly differentiating themselves from non-Jews. While the relationship of Greek Christians to the Greek language is not identical, it is analogous in some respects, and in particular the tendecy to Atticism is somewhat reminiscent of the Jewish attitude to biblical Hebrew. It may be speculated that Atticism may have been one of the factors that determined the Jewish return to Hebrew: even if some earlier Jewish authors, like Philo and Josephus, had themselves cultivated a high Greek style, in the Middle Ages Jews do not seem to have felt much attraction to Greek antiquity or seen it as part of the foundation of their own culture.[24]

The linguistic change from Greek to Hebrew, however gradual, must have had profound effects on the way the Jewish communities related to the Christian majority. In earlier times, in Asia Minor and Europe, language had never been a barrier between Jews and Christians. By the tenth century this was no longer true. At the most everyday level Jews

---

[23] *Eshkol ha-Kopher* (ed. Yevpatoria, 1836), fol. 13a.
[24] See Nicholas de Lange, 'The Classical Tradition in Byzantium', in D. Cohn-Sherbok, ed., *A Traditional Quest. Essays in Honour of Louis Jacobs* (Sheffield, 1991), 86–101.

continued to communicate with Christians in Greek, but their education and their religious ceremonies were marked by an allegiance to a distinctive language. Did this matter? It is true that among the Christians there were communities that were identified by distinctive languages, such as Syriac, Armenian or Georgian. But the ethos of the empire had changed considerably since the time of Justinian, when someone like John of Ephesus, who lived for a long time in Constantinople and was close to the emperor, chose to write in Syriac.[25] The dominant culture of the state was Greek, and as time went on this became truer than ever, despite the very varied ethnic composition of the population. The Jews' use of Hebrew was a strong statement of difference that was perhaps deliberately provocative. Was not Hebrew the original language of the world, that would be restored to its rightful place in the end of days, when Greek would finally disappear? A fourteenth-century Hebrew hymn couples a prayer for the end of subjection to foreigners with a plea for the eradication of Greek:

> On the day you exalt your choice possession above all,
> Humbling and laying low mighty foes,
> Eradicate the Greek tongue by the power of your spirit ...[26]

The Jews of Byzantium knew themselves to be the people of Israel, part of a worldwide diaspora that would one day be gathered in to the Land of Israel at the coming of the Messiah. They shared with other Jews a keen sense of the pain of exile, and they resented the heavy yoke of Christian oppression. Their hymns frequently express astonishment or impatience at the endurance of Christian rule. Here is a typical example, an alphabetical acrostic by Abraham ben Isaac ben Moses (twelfth century):

> Antagonist placidly quaffing and trampling,
> Babbling, stabbing, brandishing swords,
> Chiding, chastising, menacing, cursing,
> Despotically dominating, dancing, reviling,

---

[25] See Robert Browning, 'The Continuity of Hellenism in the Byzantine World: Appearance or Reality?', in Tom Winnifrith and Penelope Murray, eds, *Greece Old and New* (London, 1983), 111–128, here 118.

[26] Isaac ben Kalo, Passover hymn. Hebrew text in J.L. Weinberger, *Rabbanite and Karaite Liturgical Poetry in South-Eastern Europe* (Cincinnati, 1991), Hebrew section 242.

Exploding murderously, burning synagogues,
Forging and smelting, consuming and crushing ...[27]

And another, written for the joyful festival of Hanukkah, commemorating
the victory of the Jews over the Syrian Greeks:

Remember the nation that trusts in thee
And rescue them from the viper's clasp,
Performing wonders at this time.
Spare, O Lord, the myriad folk,
Consign my tormentors to the flames,
As thou didst through the Hasmoneans.
Redeemer, hasten our salvation
That we may delight in thee
When thou destroyest the evil Greek empire.[28]

Manuscript fragments recovered from the Cairo Genizah preserve several
different wordings of a prayer that formed a central part of the thrice-
daily liturgy:

For the apostates let there be no hope; speedily uproot, smash and
humble the arrogant empire in our days; may the Christians and
the heretics perish in an instant, and may all the enemies of thy
people be speedily cut off; break the yoke of the gentiles off our
necks: Blessed art thou, Lord, Destroyer of the wicked and
Humiliator of the arrogant.[29]

This explicit prayer for the overthrow of the empire is accompanied by a
string of prayers for the coming of the Messiah and the establishment of
God's rule on earth.

The diglossic culture of the Byzantine Jews was not unique, either in
their own day or at other times. Most Jews in the Middle Ages used
Hebrew as their written language and as the language of prayer and
Bible study, while speaking one or more of the local vernaculars. The use
of Greek by the Byzantine Jews, however, was unique in two ways. In the
first place, it was the language of their own ancient religious culture,

---

[27] Hebrew text in Weinberger, *Rabbanite and Karaite*, Hebrew section 26; for further examples see English section, 12–13.

[28] Avmelech ben Yeshua; Hebrew text in Weinberger, *Rabbanite and Karaite*, Hebrew section 123.

[29] This particular text is taken from ms Cambridge UL T-S 8H10.12(2).

which they had abandoned in the change to Hebrew but had never entirely lost sight of, as evinced by the continuing use of the old Greek Bible translations. Secondly, it was not only the spoken language of their Christian neighbours but also the language of their church and their written literature. This situation stands in stark contrast to that of the Jewish communities of the Latin West. The French-speaking Jews of Northern France and England, for example, were creating something new in translating the Bible into French; their versions appear to antedate the oldest local Christian vernacular versions. It appears that they had long since abandoned their Latin liturgy and Latin Bible (which had themselves in their turn replaced the ancient Greek liturgy and Bible), and so were cut off both from their own past and from the religious culture of their environment. The case of the Byzantine Jews was different in some crucial respects. True, they were not educated in Greek grammar, and did not read Greek literature. But when they used the unique and astonishing Greek of the ancient Bible translator Aquila they must surely have been aware, however dimly, that they were handling a precious ancient heirloom, something that went back to the dawn of Christianity, to a time when the Jews were more numerous than the Christians in Greek lands. Their Greek language was not only a vehicle of communication with their Christian neighbours on a mundane level but could also serve for religious debate, in which, if we can believe Christian sources from as late as the thirteenth century, the Jews continued to quote from Aquila's Bible while the Christian disputants preferred the Septuagint.[30]

At the same time, their attitude to Greek was not without ambiguity. As we have seen, they could express hatred for Greek (their own mother tongue) as the language of the oppressor, and pray for its disappearance. The place of the Greek language within the nexus of factors making up the cultural identity of the Byzantine Jews was evidently far from straightforward.

A study of the ways in which these Jews named their language underlines this complexity. An old Hebrew name for Greece, going back to the Bible, was *Yavan*, a cognate of 'Ionia'. Hence the Mishnah and other early rabbinic writings refer to Greek as *yevanit*, 'Yavanic'. Hebrew writers in the Middle Ages also sometimes refer to Greece as *Yavan*, and a

---

[30] E. Patlagean, 'La "Dispute avec les Juifs" de Nicolas d'Otrante (vers 1220) et la question du Messie', in M.G. Muzzarelli and G. Todeschini, eds, *La storia degli ebrei nell'Italia medievale: tra filologia e metodologia* (Bologna, n.d.), 19–27.

Jew from Greece can be surnamed *hayevani*, 'the Yavanite' (for example we know of a grammarian named Joseph ben David the Yavanite). In the hymn of Isaac ben Kalo quoted above in which the poet prays for the destruction of the Greek language it is termed *Lashon yevanit* ('Yavanic tongue'). The oldest Bible translations render *Yavan* by *Hellas*, but the medieval sources do not use this name, nor do they refer to the language as 'Hellenic'.

The Hebrew sources sometimes name the Byzantine empire *Edom*, in acknowledgement of its status as heir to ancient Rome.[31] This reflects the view that the biblical story of Jacob and Esau/Edom is really about the relations between Jews and Christians. So the commentator Tobias of Yavan (Tobiah ben Eliezer of Kastoria) explains Genesis 25:22, in the story of the birth of Jacob and Esau, to mean that even in their mother's womb the twin sons issued conflicting laws: one said that the day of rest should be Saturday, the other said it should be Sunday; one said it was forbidden to eat pork, the other said it was permitted. So far as I am aware, however, the Greek language is never called 'Edomite'.

Probably the most usual name for the Greek language in our period is *lšwn rwmi*, 'the Roman tongue'. This name reflects the most typical and distinctive designation for the empire in the documents of the period, namely *Romania*. The Jews of the empire are collectively designated 'the communities of Romania';[32] the prayer book of the Byzantine Jews is generally termed 'the ritual of Romania' (*Maḥzor Romania*), and the descendants of the Byzantine Jews continued to be called Romaniotes until modern times.

In calling their language 'Roman' the Byzantine Jews were following the usage of their Greek Christian and Arab Muslim neighbours, and there is nothing remarkable about that. When seen in the wider context I have tried to sketch out, it appears as one more ambivalent element in a very complex picture, in which the Jews seem to have felt drawn in different directions at once. As Romaniotes they were part of a Roman empire embracing a multiplicity of ethnic groups. Their roots within that empire were as old as anyone's, and their Romaniote identity distinguished them from foreign Jews. At the same time, as Israelites they

---

[31] See de Lange, 'Jewish Attitudes to the Roman Empire', and M. Hadas-Lebel, 'Jacob et Esaü ou Israël et Rome dans le Talmud et le Midrash', *Revue de l'Histoire des Religions* 201 (1984), 369–392.

[32] For examples see Starr, *Jews of the Byzantine Empire*, 214, 227, 228, 241; Bowman, *Jews*, 211–216. See also J. Starr, *Romania: The Jewries of the Levant after the Fourth Crusade* (Paris, 1949).

knew that there was enmity between them and Rome/Edom for all time, and they were taught that at the end of time God would shatter the Romans and establish the triumphant rule of his own people.

9. The Enigma of the Romaniote Tombs[*]

Hanna Jacobsohn

There is only one extant description of an old Jewish cemetery on Greek soil. In 1675 two travellers through Greece, George Wheler and Dr Spon, visited the city of Patras, the capital of the Morea. Wheler noted the Jewish cemetery and its gravestones which he described as follows:

> Thence passing the River, and the Hill near the Town [Patras], we came to the Jewish Burying-place; where I observed their Sepulchres to be made in the fashion of little Houses of stone-building; having at each end a Marble-Stone whereon is engraved an inscription of their Name and Family; which looking like the doors of the little House of Death, make the Burying-place like a great Town when it is viewed at a distance from the wrong end of a Microscope.[1]

In 1994 the Jewish Community of Chalkis, capital of the island of Euboea, decided to renovate and restore the old part of their cemetery which had been neglected for centuries. After clearing all the debris, there came to light a Jewish cemetery similar to the one seen by George Wheler and Dr Spon three hundred years ago.

Most of the tombs were in a state of disintegration. Even so, it is absolutely clear that all the tombs were originally identical in

---

[*] This paper is dedicated to Prof. Z. Ankori, my teacher and mentor, with gratitude for his guidance and support for many years; to Marios Maissis, President of the Jewish Community, whose ingenuity and tenacity made it all possible; and to all members of the Jewish Community of Chalkis for their support, generosity, hospitality and kindness.
[1] George Wheler, *A Journey into Greece by George Wheler Esq; in Company of Dr Spon of Lyons* (London, 1678), Book IV 297; S. Bowman, 'A Corpus of Hebrew Epitaphs in Patras', *Anthypon*, Athens, (1980), 49–75 and 14–19.

construction, being of the type known technically as 'graduated sarcophagus'.

The 'graduated sarcophagus' type consists of two 'stories': the lower one is about 30 to 40 centimetres high and the upper one about 10 centimetres. The upper 'story' forms a narrow ledge, upon which rests a half-cylinder, as a kind of 'roof'. The average length of the tombs is about 180 centimetres (tombs of children are, of course, smaller). All three elements of the structure are built of local undressed chalk-stone held together with loam. After the structure was erected, it was coated with plaster and probably whitewashed.

This rather common grave type has one unusual feature: in the rectangular base on its short end facing west there is a rectangular recess of about 30 x 40 x 35 (or sometimes 40) centimetres, so the structure truly does look like 'a small house with a recess resembling a door'.[2]

The epitaphs bearing the name, date of demise and sometimes some other details concerning the deceased are placed at the back of the recess. This means that the epitaph is hidden from view and cannot be seen from the outside. All epitaphs are in Hebrew. The stone slabs bearing the epitaphs as well as the inscription itself vary greatly: some are marble and the epitaph is well carved in elegant letters of good workmanship; others are done on shell or limestone and the epitaph is just scratched into the soft stone with a sharp instrument. This difference most probably is an indication of a difference in social status.

But what difference does it make when the inscriptions were obscured from sight and the casual passer-by would not have been able to see it anyway? The stone slabs by necessity are small and therefore the inscriptions are short and nearly always unadorned. All the epitaphs in the graveyard of Chalkis (as well as the slabs bearing inscriptions inserted in the walls of the synagogue or just stored there[3]) are of exactly the same type: small in size with a short inscription of limited information. All the inscribed epitaphs – *in situ* or removed to the

---

[2]   See photographs, 125–126. Wheler says that there was an opening at each end; in Chalkis there was only one opening, always on the end facing west.

[3]   It is a Jewish custom that inscriptions in Hebrew of any kind (tombs or memorials etc.), found not in their original setting, are collected and, if possible, inserted in the walls of the Synagogue, or stored there until an opportunity (such as a renovation) makes it possible to insert them into the walls.

synagogue – date from the Ottoman period: the oldest is dated May 1539 and the most recent is dated 26th May 1849.[4]

In 1907 M. Schwab published the text and photograph of an epitaph of this same type, dated to 1326 from Chalkis. In 1933, the same author published seven epitaphs, one of which from Thebes, dated to 1330. In 1933, N.I. Tiannopoulou published one epitaph dated 1348.[5] The dates of these published epitaphs means that they are all from the Byzantine period.[6] In 1982 Steven Bowman published the text and photographs of seven Jewish epitaphs from Thebes, which also conform to the same descriptive type.[7] In 1981, Daniel Spiegel and Steven Bowman published a corpus of Hebrew epitaphs of Mistra. These two writers state that 'The stones are generally small, paralleling the usage of Patras, Naupaktos, Thebes, and Chalkis.' In this corpus, one is from the late fourteenth century and three from the fifteenth century (1455, 1460 and 1481).[8] Indeed, these dates take us into the Ottoman period, but their significance lies in that they all date from before the Jews' expulsion from Spain in 1492 and the influx of the expelled Jews from Spain into the Ottoman Empire.

These Jews from the Iberian peninsula brought with them a totally different burial tradition. Their tombs are mostly of the 'box' type with a large horizontal stone bearing the inscription on top, which is often rather elaborate. In later centuries there are other variations but never anything similar to the 'graduated sarcophagus' described above. The Spanish–Jewish tombs are also notable for their individuality in decoration and their undisguised insistence on the strict separation of social classes.[9]

It should be stressed at this point that all the places at which tombs of the 'graduated sarcophagus' type were found are well known old Jewish

---

[4]   The dates are always in the Jewish calendar calculated from the creation so that May 1539 = Sivan 5239 and 26 May 1849 = 5 Sivan 5609.

[5]   M. Schwab, 'Une inscription Hebraique à Chalcis', *Revue des Etudes Juives* 53 (1907), 283: M. Schwab, 'Sept Epitaphes Hebraiques de Grèce', *Revue des Etudes Juives* 57 (1909), 106; N.I. Tiannopoulou, *SYMBOLAI*, 'Eis tin istorian ton Iodaikon paroikion en th Anatolikh hipirotikih Elladi' (Athens, 1933) 190, photograph 2 [in that text].

[6]   Chalkis was conquered in 1470.

[7]   Two are from the year 1330, and one dated to 1380; of the other three, two are dated 1555, one 1538.

[8]   S. Bowman, 'Jewish Epitaphs in Thebes', *Revue des Etudes Juives* 141 (1982), 317–370; D. Spiegel and S. Bowman, 'Hebrew Epitaphs in Mistra', in , *Michael VII*, eds Z. Ankori and S. Simonsohn (Tel Aviv, 1981), 201–247.

[9]   See Mina Rosen, *Haskoy Cemetery, Typology of Stones* (University of Pennsylvania, 1994).

settlements, which have been in fairly continuous occupation throughout the pre-Ottoman period, and which are well documented both in Jewish and non-Jewish sources. The classic and well-known source from the Byzantine period, of course, is the Spanish–Jewish traveller, Benjamin of Tudela, who visited all these settlements in the mid-twelfth century.[10]

One striking aspect of the inscriptions is the names of the deceased. Out of seventy-two tombs, only forty-nine names are preserved. Of these forty-nine names, only thirty-three are full names; one is only a family name and eleven are first names only. If the names are analysed by origin, fifteen of the family names are Romaniote (Greek) names; ten are common Jewish names (Cohen or Levy); the remaining sixteen are from all around the Mediterranean.

If we turn to the first names, all males bear biblical names. This is not surprising, since every Jewish male, even if he uses a non-Jewish name in daily life, will be known only by his Hebrew name in any religious function, as well as in death. Turning to the first names of women, out of thirteen first names, three are Greek names, two Italian and eight are Hebrew names. Even in women's names, therefore, there was a preference for Hebrew names, which points to the Romaniote (Greek–Jewish) origin of the deceased, rather than Spanish–Jewish.

Even though the material evidence is scanty, it may be safely concluded that what we have before us is a unique custom practised by Jews of Greek–Byzantine origin, a custom those Jews kept for hundreds of years. This leads to the two questions of the enigma: why are the tombs absolutely uniform? And why were the epitaphs hidden?

So far, all my attempts at complete explanation have been less than fully convincing. I can only make two suggestions. Hiding the inscription might have been an attempt to prevent too much attention being drawn to the tombs, thus guarding them from vandalism and desecration. This practical reason appeals to the modern rational mind; but the desire for modesty in death may have had a religious reason. Such a religious reason might explain both curiosities about the tombs: namely their uniformity in construction, their 'monumental display' if you will, and the concealed epitaphs. In death all are equal, as is expressed in Psalm 49:1:'For he seeth that wise men die, the fool and the brutish together perish ...'. In their burial practice the Romaniote Jews of Chalkis leave us perhaps with an impression of their piety.

---

[10]   M.N. Adler, ed., *The Itinerary of Benjamin of Tudela* (London, 1907); S. Bowman, *The Jews of Byzantium*, 49–96.

By way of an appendix to this treatment of the 'problem' of Romaniote tombs of Chalkis, I present this selection of seven epitaphs.

The grave quarried / for the patron in the year [5]356
of the creation the eminent / pleasant to all the sage Rabbi Absalom
is his name our Rabbi / Galimidi[11] is his name in every
plain language / the Most On-High shall be his salvation Amen.

This is the burial stone / of the eminent the Rabbi Joseph Malti
May his soul be bound up in the bond / of eternal life who was stricken to
death by a blow of judgment[12] on / Sunday nineteenth of Tamuz in the
year of the breast plate of judgment (Exodus, 28:15–31) [5358 (23 vii 1598)]
may his soul rest in paradise / and his three sons who are buried at his
feet the King the Most on High shall be his salvation.

This / is the burial stone / of the virtuous lady
Malka daughter of / the sage Rabbi Avraham Saloni[ko]
shall she rest in peace died on Monday
first of Adar in the year 5363 of the creation [12 ii 1603][13]

This is the marking / of the burial stone which was inscribed
for the man who never committed a sin
the wise and exalted the Sage Rabbi / Elya[14] son of our honourable teacher
Rabbi Abraham Saloniko his memory / be of blessing who departed
on Friday of second Adar / 5373 of the creation [27 ii 1613]
May his soul be bound up in the bond

---

[11]   This family has been known in Chalkis from the thirteenth century; see S. Bowman, *The Jews of Byzantium (1204–1453)*, (Alabama, 1985), 234–240; J. Starr, *Romania* (Paris, 1949), III, 37–61.

[12]   The wording suggests that R. Joseph Malti and his sons had died of the plague, cf.: Isaiah 6:1. The name suggests the family came from the island of Malta.

[13]   Mentioning the name of the lady's father and not her husband means that her father was of higher rank than her husband: in this case the eminence was his erudition. The name Malka means Queen. The family originated in Thessalonike. The Jewish settlement in Thessalonike was very old, as attested by the New Testament. In 1453, after the conquest of Constantinople by the Ottomans, the Jewish community was transferred to the new capital where they established a community called Selanik (Salonika). See M.A. Epstein, *The Ottoman Jewish Communities and their Role in the Fifteenth and Sixteenth Centuries* (Freiburg, 1980), 178–179. No Romaniote Jews ever settled again in Thessalonike.

[14]   Writing the name in Hebrew with the letter alef instead of the usual heh is a typical Romaniote custom to avoid using the Tetragrammaton (the four-letter Name of God), a 'fence around the Law' to avoid taking the Lord's name in vain.

of eternal life and God will guard him / in the king's dale. (2 Samuel,
18:18)
This / is the burial stone of the / physician the honourable Rabbi
Elya Halevi his memory of blessing
who departed in peace to his house of
eternal life in the month of Kislev in the
year of 5426 [December 1665] and life to
all Israel he passed away may his soul
be bound up in the bond of eternal life.

The tombstone / [marking] the burial of the sage Rabbi
Asher Halevi may he rest in paradise
who was taken to the house of eternal
life within the year of his marriage the
fifteenth of the month Elul in the year
'Thy dead shall live ... ' (Isaiah 26:19) [31 viii 1670]
may his soul be bound up in the bond / of eternal life

The burial stone / of Mrs. Miriam[15] may her soul be
bound up in the bond of eternal life / deceased on the [Holy] Shabbat
twenty-ninth of Shwat in the year
'He kisseth the lips ... ' (Prov. 24:26) [5410 (24 ii 1656)]
her soul shall abide in prosperity (Ps. 25:13)[16]

A detailed analysis of these epitaphs, presented here in my own
translation, would be out of place. Written in Hebrew, the language
understood by their co-religionists and which marked them off to a
degree as outsiders to the surrounding Christian Orthodox population,
they provide a tantalizing glimpse into a very different world of
Byzantium.

Of the seven, two are women (one is the daughter of a rabbi, the other
a wife blessed in death); the five men are all rabbis with one described as
a physician as well. All are connected in their epitaphs to learning or
virtue or both. As such they may have been outside the 'normal' of their
own society, being members of the élite.

This paper has presented questions and problems rather than
solutions; its aim was largely to draw inside the orbit of the Byzantine
studies the vanished world of the Romaniot Jews.

---

[15]   For this lady, neither family, husband's nor father's name is given.

[16]   In Jewish tradition, it is believed that only the righteous die on the Holy Sabbath,
and therefore it is considered as a great honour.

Plate 9.1: General View of the Romaniote Tombs at Chalkis (photo: Hanna Jacobsohn)

Plate 9.2: Detail of one of the Romaniote Tombs at Chalkis
(photo: Hanna Jacobsohn)

Plate 9.3: Detail of Hebrew Inscription of one of the Romaniote Tombs at Chalkis
(photo: Hanna Jacobsohn)

Plate 9.4: Detail of Hebrew Inscription of one of the Romaniote Tombs at Chalkis
(photo: Hanna Jacobsohn)

10. The Byzantine Outsider in Trade (c.900–c.1350)

David Jacoby

Byzantine traders travelling or residing in foreign countries were for obvious reasons outsiders. Surprisingly, however, at times we also find them as outsiders in the empire itself, whether individually or collectively. This seemingly paradoxical situation raises a series of questions, only some of which can be addressed here. First, who in fact were the Byzantine traders we are dealing with? Under what circumstances did they become outsiders, and exactly in what sense? How did they react as outsiders? Did their individual attitudes and responses generate collective ones, and to what extent did the former and the latter coincide? And, finally, what were the official, learned and popular expressions of 'outsiderness' in trade and in what way did they differ?

Traders are individuals acting as middlemen in the economic diffusion of goods, distinct from those selling only their own surpluses or products. It is impossible to arrive at a collective profile of Byzantine traders in the period covered by this study. There was much social and economic diversity among them, and they covered a wide spectrum of activities. Though most of them were city-dwellers, they ranged from urban peddlers and those travelling along the roads to retailers and wholesalers at fairs, at markets and in cities, and to merchants conveying goods over varying distances to these locations, whether by land, river or sea.[1] Although ubiquitous, Byzantine traders remain rather elusive

---

[1] See John Tzetzes, *Epistulae*, ed. P.M. Leone (Leipzig, 1972), 79–84, no. 57; A.E. Laiou, 'Händler und Kaufleute auf dem Jahrmarkt', in G. Prinzing and D. Simon, eds, *Fest und Alltag in Byzanz* (Munich, 1990), 53–70, 189–194 (notes), reprinted in A.E. Laiou, *Gender, Society and Economic Life in Byzantium* (Aldershot, Hampshire, 1992), no. XI; A. Kazhdan, 'Byzantine Town and Trade as seen by Niketas Choniates', *BSl* 56 (1995), (= *ΣΤΕΦΑΝΟΣ. Studia byzantina ac slavica Vladimíro Vavrínek ad annum sexagesimum quintum dedicata*), 214–

characters. They are hidden behind a thick wall of rhetoric, social prejudices and cultural stereotypes, and they lack a voice of their own to express their attitudes, perceptions and frustrations. There are no Byzantine business letters similar to those of Jewish merchants discovered in the Cairo Genizah, nor to those written by Italian merchants in the late Middle Ages.[2] Neither do the few Byzantine notarial deeds and wills that have survived reflect Byzantine traders. While Byzantine court proceedings or legal treatises occasionally shed some light on them, it is mainly on official documents and Byzantine authors, with all the limitations imposed by their writings, as well as on Western notarial sources and circumstantial evidence that we have to rely.

To be sure, some Byzantine writers stress the audacity of traders and sailors engaging in maritime trade in their quest for profit. Such is the case of the eleventh-century John Mauropous in one of his letters, Constantine Manasses in a romance in the twelfth, and the historian George Pachymeres in the early fourteenth century with respect to the Genoese.[3] However, regardless of their social origin, most Byzantine authors identified with the values and attitudes of the Empire's élite, especially that of Constantinople, and presented a negative view of Byzantine traders. Their references to them or, for that matter, to any traders, are clouded by bias and literary conventions and tainted by social and cultural arrogance.[4] Trade, they claim, is a lowly occupation involving lying and cheating, which does not befit respectable men.[5] On the whole, these views were supported by the normative statements of ecclesiastical sources.[6]

216; E. Patlagean, 'Byzance et les marchés du grand commerce, vers 830–vers 1030. Entre Pirenne et Polanyi', in *Mercati e mercanti nell'alto medioevo: l'area euroasiatica e l'area mediterranea* (Settimane di studio del Centro italiano di studi sull'alto medioevo, 40) (Spoleto, 1993), 587–629, esp. 612–614; N. Oikonomidès, 'Le marchand byzantin des provinces (IXe–XIe s.)', in ibid., 633–660.

[2]   The Genizah letters have been extensively exploited by S.D. Goitein, *A Mediterranean Society. The Jewish Communities of the Arab World as Portrayed in the Documents of the Cairo Geniza* (Berkeley and Los Angeles, 1967–1988).

[3]   References and discussion in A.E. Laiou, 'Byzantine Traders and Seafearers', in Sp. Vryonis, Jr, ed., *The Greeks and the Sea* (New Rochelle, NY, 1993), 79.

[4]   On snobbery and its literary expressions, see P. Magdalino, 'Byzantine Snobbery', in M. Angold, ed., *The Byzantine Aristocracy, IX to XIII Centuries* (B.A.R., S221) (Oxford, 1984), 58–78.

[5]   See A. Kazhdan, 'Byzantine Town', 214–216, 218.

[6]   See A. Laiou, 'God and Mammon: Credit, Trade and Profit and the Canonists', in N. Oikonomides, ed., *Το Βυζάντιο κατά τον 12ο αιώνα. Κανονικό Δίκαιο, κράτος και κοινωνία* [=Byzantium in the 12th Century. Canon Law, State and Society], (Athens, 1991), 261–300.

It is still widely believed among Byzantinists that until the fourteenth century the social élite professed and practised self-sufficiency as a virtue, abstained from trade, and was contemptuous of profit.[7] Yet a growing body of evidence implies that since the eleventh century some of its members fulfilled a far more active role than hitherto ascribed to them in the Byzantine economy, trade included. They as well as various monasteries were involved in the commercialization and transportation of rural products other than their own.[8] Agents and employees acting on behalf of the fisc or great landlords had the means to operate trade networks to their own profit.[9] In addition, some *archontes* acting as entrepreneurs who had invested capital in the silk industry of Thebes also engaged in the diffusion of the latter's finished products.[10] Until the fourteenth century, however, Byzantine authors on the whole wilfully overlooked the activity of traders belonging to the higher ranks of society.

More generally, the actual Byzantine trader remains beyond the social horizon of these authors. He becomes conspicuous only when intruding upon the political stage or when his actions interfere with the affairs of government, especially in Constantinople. Such was the case of Kalomodios, a banker of that city who had amassed a fortune in long-distance trade operations. His arrest and the confiscation of his property in 1200 created serious turmoil in the capital among the 'people of the marketplace', which ended only after his release and the restoration of his assets.[11] Kalomodios reminds us of the rich traders and craftsmen of Constantinople who in the eleventh century gained access to the Senate.[12] Since the activity of Italian traders was tightly connected with the empire's external relations and had an impact on its government, it also entered into the sphere of interest of Byzantine authors. Paradoxically, precisely thanks to the latter's concern with Italian traders we are

---

[7] N. Oikonomidès, *Hommes d'affaires grecs et latins à Constantinople (XIIIe–XVe siècles)* (Montréal and Paris, 1979), 86, 119–123, argues that the members of the Byzantine élite turned to trade only after losing their landed property in Asia Minor and in the Balkans in the fourteenth century. This is still the prevailing view.

[8] I shall deal with this subject in a forthcoming study.

[9] See P. Magdalino, *The Empire of Manuel I Komnenos, 1143–1180* (Cambridge, 1993), 139 and n. 128, 144, 149–150, 156–159, 170 and n. 243.

[10] See D. Jacoby, 'Silk in Western Byzantium before the Fourth Crusade', *BZ* 84/85 (1991–1992), 470–488, reprinted in D. Jacoby, *Trade, Commodities and Shipping in the Medieval Mediterranean* (Aldershot, 1997), no. VII.

[11] Niketas Choniates, *Historia*, ed. J.L. van Dieten (Berlin and New York, 1975) (CFHB, XI/1), 523–524.

[12] See P. Lemerle, *Cinq études sur le XIe siècle byzantin* (Paris, 1977), 287–293.

sometimes able to gain a better knowledge of Byzantine outsiders in trade.

It is primarily in Constantinople that these can be traced. Until the Latin conquest of 1204 the imperial capital was the focus of the Byzantine economic system, and the preservation of this function was considered by the imperial government a matter of vital importance. While Constantinople's economy was tightly supervised precisely for that reason, no such effective control could be exercised in the provinces or at the borders of the empire. Therefore, traders residing outside the capital were viewed with mistrust, regardless of their origin. Ἐθνικοί or foreigners such as Muslims, Syrians, Bulgarians and Rus reaching Constantinople were subject to residential segregation in *mitata*, special lodgings where they and their transactions could be easily supervised. The period of their sojourn was limited, and their trade was restricted in various ways.[13] Restrictions also applied in various circumstances to the ἐξωτικοί or ἔξωθεν ἐρχομενοί, terms referring to those residing outside Constantinople, in particular the inhabitants of the provinces. As a result, they too became outsiders when trading in the capital. Incidentally, in accordance with Byzantine political ideology and terminology, Venice was considered part of the empire and, therefore, its inhabitants appear as *extranei*, the equivalent of Greek *exotikoi*, in the Latin version of the *sigillion* of 992 which Basil II and Constantine VIII issued in their favour.[14] This fiction was still maintained in 1198 in the chrysobull of Alexios III Angelos.[15] While the Jews of the empire were considered a distinct ethnic and religious group and subject to residential segregation and special

---

[13] See R.S. Lopez, 'Silk Industry in the Byzantine Empire', *Speculum* 20 (1945), 25–35, reprinted in R.S. Lopez, *Byzantium and the World around it: Economic and Institutional Relations* (London, 1978), no. III.

[14] G.L.Fr. Tafel and G.M. Thomas, eds, *Urkunden zur älteren Handels- und Staatsgeschichte der Republik Venedig* (Vienna, 1856–1857) (hereafter: TTh), I, 36–39, with wrong dating. All previous editions are superseded now by that of M. Pozza and G. Ravegnani, *I trattati con Bisanzio, 992–1198* (Pacta veneta, 4) (Venice, 1993), 21–25, yet this one too requires emendations, suggested in my review in *Mediterranean Historical Review* 9 (1994), 139–143. On the terms used in this document, the Greek version of which has not survived, see J. Koder, 'Das Sigillion von 992 – eine "aussenpolitische" Urkunde?', *BSl* 52 (1991), 40–44.

[15] TTh, I, 276, with wrong dating; new ed. Pozza-Ravegnani, *Trattati*, 136, §17: 'inter extraneos et indigenas cives'.

taxation,[16] there is no evidence that the status of Jewish traders differed from that of their Christian counterparts.

The position of Byzantine provincial traders as outsiders in Constantinople is well illustrated in the tenth century. Their sojourn was limited to three months and their goods strictly controlled at arrival and departure.[17] Those importing silk were obliged to reside in *mitata*, where the fibre was sold.[18] They were not allowed to export silk from the city.[19] The sale of specific types of silk textiles to provincial traders was either forbidden or in any event strictly supervised.[20] The government also prohibited and severely punished the transfer of highly skilled craftsmen engaged in the manufacturing of silk textiles to both *ethnikoi* and *exotikoi*. Like the aliens, provincial traders were considered potential smugglers liable to serve as intermediaries in the illegal export of goods and technical expertise to foreign countries, harmful to the empire.[21] For that same reason the *sigillion* of 992 forbade Venetian ships leaving Constantinople for the Byzantine provinces of Southern Italy to take on board Latin traders from Amalfi, Bari and elsewhere, as well as Jews from that region. Strangely, that document does not refer to Greeks, and one may wonder whether they enjoyed a favoured treatment in this respect.[22] It is unclear how long the stringent regulations of the tenth century were enforced. Whatever the case, the 'outsiderness' of provincial traders was not limited to the capital, nor by legal and administrative impediments, more examples of which could be easily adduced. The residents of Constantinople also considered them outsiders, distrusted them collectively, and viewed them with contempt in the same way as they did foreigners. According to the twelfth-century John Tzetzes, 'Cretans and Turks, Alans, Rhodians and Chiots' were 'notorious

---

[16] See D. Jacoby, 'Les quartiers juifs de Constantinople à l'époque byzantine', B 37 (1967), 168–196, reprinted in D. Jacoby, *Société et démographie à Byzance et en Romanie latine* (London, 1975), no. II.

[17] J. Koder, ed. and tr., *Das Eparchenbuch Leons des Weisen. Einführung, Edition, Übersetzung und Indices* (CFHB, XXXIII) (Vienna, 1991) (hereafter: *EB*), 20.1–2.

[18] *EB*, 6.5. My interpretation differs here from that of Koder, who considers these to be foreigners. I shall fully discuss all issues regarding the terms *exotikoi* and *ethnikoi*, as well as silk in *EB*, in my forthcoming book on the Byzantine silk industry.

[19] *EB*, 6.16.

[20] *EB*, 4.1, 8.3.

[21] *EB*, 8.7. This role is clearly stated with respect to textiles in *EB*, 4.1.

[22] My reading, translation and interpretation of this provision appear in the review cited above, note 14.

thieves'.[23] This capital-centred attitude toward the inhabitants of the provinces was a recurrent theme of Byzantine snobbery.[24]

In the political and social context of the empire, relatives of the emperors, high-ranking imperial officials and military commanders as well as great landowners were likely to benefit from imperial privileges, including tax exemptions on trade and transportation. The same applied to ecclesiastical institutions because of their spiritual functions.[25] The Venetians did not belong to either category, yet nevertheless were granted such privileges. It is generally believed that this already occurred in 992. In fact, however, the Venetians obtained then no more than a return to the customary lump sum previously paid by Venetian ships sailing past Abydos, at the mouth of the Dardanelles, and the prevention of its increase by unlawful exactions.[26] The trade and maritime privileges bestowed by Alexios I Komnenos upon Venice in 1082 were clearly of a completely different order.[27] First, fiscal privileges enjoyed by Byzantine individuals or institutions were limited in extent, and both their geographic range and their practical effects on Byzantine trade were fairly restricted. By contrast, the Venetians benefited from sweeping collective exemptions. Once they were granted freedom of movement and residence without any time limitation,[28] their activity became of constant relevance to all Byzantine traders and carriers, though in practice its impact was felt mainly in the cities and areas they visited, Constantinople in particular. As a result, paradoxically all Byzantine traders and carriers with few exceptions only became outsiders in 1082, although they constituted the majority among those active in the empire, and that status persisted until the fall of Byzantium. The Venetian privileges of 1082 created a precedent, followed by the grant of others to Pisa from 1111 and to Genoa from 1155, although these were less extensive and their

---

[23] John Tzetzes, *Historiae*, XIII, vv. 354–362, ed. P.A.M. Leone (Naples, 1968), 528.

[24] See, for example, Nicholas Mesarites, *Die Palastrevolution des Johannes Komnenos*, ed. A. Heisenberg (Würzburg, 1907), 39.

[25] See A. Harvey, *Economic Expansion in the Byzantine Empire 900–1200* (Cambridge, 1989), 69–70, 238–241.

[26] See S. Borsari, *Venezia e Bisanzio nel XII secolo. I rapporti economici* (Venice, 1988), 16–17.

[27] TTh, I, 43–49; new edition by Pozza-Ravegnani, *Trattati*, 35–45.

[28] Amalfitans already enjoyed earlier in the eleventh century the lifting of this limitation: see Lopez, 'Silk Industry', 40.

geographic range more limited until 1192.[29] The cumulative effect of the process set in motion in 1082 upon Byzantine traders was compounded by the growing role of Italian middlemen within the empire's inter-regional trade and shipping networks.[30] The position of Venetian traders was further boosted in 1198, when Alexios III Angelos agreed that in Constantinople Venetian judges should be empowered to try pecuniary suits when Greek plaintiffs opposed Venetians.[31] For the first time ever a Byzantine emperor was compelled to admit the exercise of foreign jurisdiction over his own subjects on imperial soil.

The establishment of the Venetian quarter in Constantinople in 1082 was initially intended to supply temporary lodgings and storage to visiting merchants between two shipping seasons. Yet shortly afterwards some Venetians began to prolong their residence in the city and over time a growing number of them, both visiting and settled traders, resided outside the original quarter. Venice requested the latter's enlargement, which was bound to enhance its revenue from property, taxation and fines. Manuel I Komnenos agreed in 1148, since it suited the traditional Byzantine policy aimed at the residential concentration of Latins in the capital,[32] different from the segregation implemented with respect to other aliens.[33] After 1148 some Venetians intending to remain permanently in the city nevertheless continued to reside or settle outside the enlarged quarter. A number of them wedded Greek women and acquired houses beyond its boundaries, transactions apparently prohibited to aliens in Constantinople. These Venetians combined the privileges and exemptions of Venetian citizens with the rights of Byzantine subjects, a situation causing losses to the imperial treasury, affecting the activity of Byzantine outsiders in trade, and deeply resented

---

[29] See D. Jacoby, 'Italian Privileges and Trade in Byzantium before the Fourth Crusade: A Reconsideration', *Anuario de estudios medievales* 24 (1994), 349–368, repinted in Jacoby, *Trade*, no. II.

[30] On this role, see Laiou, 'Byzantine Traders', 83–87, 90–91.

[31] TTh, I, 273–276, with wrong dating; new edition, Pozza-Ravegnani, *Trattati*, 132–135, §16.

[32] TTh, I, 109–113; new edition, Pozza-Ravegnani, *Trattati*, 70–75.

[33] In 1082 Alexios I granted houses '*in quibus Venetici manent et Greci*': TTh, I, 52, and new edition Pozza-Ravegnani, *Trattati*, 39, §5; Greeks also resided in the Venetian quarter in 1189 and 1195: L. Lanfranchi, ed., *S. Giorgio Maggiore* (Fonti per la Storia di Venezia, Sez. II: Archivi ecclesiastici) (Venice, 1967–1974), II, nos 500, 581. Such was also the case in the Genoese quarter in 1202: G. Bertolotto, ed., 'Nuova serie di documenti sulle relazioni di Genova con l'Impero bizantino', *Atti della Società Ligure di Storia Patria* 28 (1897), 475–476 (Greek), 483–484 (Latin).

among the population of the capital. However, some time before 1171 Manuel I compelled these Venetians to choose between Venetian and Byzantine status, with all the relevant rights, restrictions and obligations deriving therefrom.[34] It should be noted that the presence of Italian traders in provincial cities did not raise the same problems. From developments occurring in Halmyros we may gather that these cities witnessed a spontaneous concentration of Italians along national lines, yet there was no establishment of privileged quarters with well-defined boundaries by imperial order. Nor were there, it seems, any legal or administrative impediments to Venetian and Pisan purchases of real estate from Greeks.[35]

The developments particular to Constantinople described above were not restricted to Venetian traders. Some Pisans also became imperial subjects and resided outside their city's quarter. Such was the case of Signoretto, apparently a trader judging by the large fortune he left at his death in 1165. In addition, Pisan sailors who had opted for Byzantine citizenship are attested in 1174.[36] William of Tyre's account of the attack on the Latin quarters in April 1182 reveals that Pisans and Genoese too occasionally married Greek women, although it is unclear where they were residing and whether they had become Byzantine citizens.[37] Some of

---

[34] John Kinnamos, *Epitome*, VI, 10, 281–282. On the whole issue, see D. Jacoby, 'La dimensione demografica e sociale', in G. Cracco and G. Ortalli, eds, *Storia di Venezia*, II, *L'età del Comune* (Rome, 1995), 691–692. Kinnamos's complex formulation seems to suggest that those who opted for Byzantine status became *bourgesioi* of the emperor, yet this common interpretation is mistaken. The term stands for permanent residents, as opposed to visiting traders, in conformity with *burgenses* in Italian contemporary usage, to which Kinnamos alludes: see D. Jacoby, 'Les Vénitiens naturalisés dans l'Empire byzantin: un aspect de l'expansion de Venise en Romanie du XIIIe au milieu du XVe siècle', *TM* 8 (1981), 219, reprinted in D. Jacoby, *Studies on the Crusader States and on Venetian Expansion* (Northampton, 1989), no. IX.

[35] On these Italian purchases and quarters, see Borsari, *Venezia*, 34–35; Borsari, 'Pisani a Bisanzio nel XII secolo', *Bollettino Storico Pisano* 60 (1991), 65–66. One should note that until 1192 the Pisans did not enjoy any tax exemptions on the sale of goods purchased in the empire itself, nor on exports: see Jacoby, 'Italian Privileges', 357–359.

[36] G. Müller, ed., *Documenti sulle relazioni delle città toscane coll'Oriente cristiano e coi Turchi fino all'anno MDXXXI* (Florence, 1879), 11–13, no. 10; see Borsari, *Venezia*, 50. On the location of Signoretto's house, see R.-J. Lilie, *Handel und Politik zwischen dem byzantinischen Reich und den italienischen Kommunen Venedig, Pisa und Genua in der Epoche der Komnenen und der Angeloi (1081–1204)* (Amsterdam, 1984), 299. Despite having become a Byzantine citizen, Signoretto willed his fortune to Pisan churches. I am not dealing here with Italians who were not traders and entered imperial service in various capacities.

[37] Guillaume de Tyr, *Chronique*, 22.13, ed. R.B.C. Huygens (*Corpus Christianorum, Continuatio Mediaevalis*, LIII–LIII A) (Turnhout, 1986), 1024. On the circumstances, see C.M.

them sought shelter with members of the Byzantine élite, with whom they obviously entertained friendly relations, whether as a result of intermarriage, business, or both.[38] Yet other Pisans living for many years or born in Constantinople retained their original status. A number of these testified in 1200 about the ecclesiastical rights previously exercised by the prior of the Pisan churches in Constantinople.[39] At the time of the Fourth Crusade we find once more Venetians residing outside their national quarter. Soon after the Latin conquest of 13 April 1204 one of them, a trader on particularly good terms with Niketas Choniates, joined him with family and belongings. A few days later all of them moved to a house inhabited by other Venetians which, however, had to be evacuated since it was situated within the portion of the city allotted to the Frankish knights. It was thus located at a substantial distance from the Venetian quarter existing before the conquest.[40] We do not know whether the regulation issued by Manuel I was still applied and, therefore, whether these Venetians, some possibly wedded to Greek women, had retained their citizenship or had become imperial subjects.

In the late eleventh century the Byzantines paid little attention to the Venetians active in the empire.[41] Yet their perceptions and attitudes with respect to Italians changed drastically in the course of the twelfth century, when the latter expanded their trading and became more visible in the empire and especially in Constantinople. In various ways Anna Komnene, John Kinnamos and Niketas Choniates in the twelfth, Patriarch Gregory of Cyprus in the thirteenth, Patriarch Athanasius I, Alexios Makrembolitis and Nikephoros Gregoras in the fourteenth century, among others, point to specific collective characteristics and patterns of behaviour of the Italians. They accuse them of being rude, corrupt, malicious, disloyal, haughty and aggressive, and depict them as

---

Brand, *Byzantium confronts the West, 1180–1204* (Cambridge, MA, 1968), 39–42. There were no Venetian residents in the city from 1171 to 1183: see D. Jacoby, 'Conrad, Marquis of Montferrat, and the Kingdom of Jerusalem (1187–1192)', in L. Balletto, ed., *Atti del Congresso Internazionale 'Dai feudi monferrini e dal Piemonte ai nuovi mondi oltre gli Oceani', Alessandria, 2–6 Aprile 1990* (Alessandria, 1993), 221, reprinted in Jacoby, *Trade*, no. IV.

[38] Niketas Choniates, *Historia*, 251.

[39] Müller, *Documenti*, 81, no. 51. See Borsari, 'Pisani a Bisanzio', 67, n. 49, and Lilie, *Handel*, 296–300.

[40] Niketas Choniates, *Historia*, 588. See also D. Jacoby, 'The Venetian Quarter of Constantinople from 1082 to 1261: Topographical Considerations', in C. Sode and S.A. Takács, eds, *Novum Millennium* (Aldershot, 2000), 171–192, and map.

[41] See M. Angold, *The Byzantine Empire, 1025–1204. A Political History* (London and New York, 1984), 202.

contemptuous of Byzantine subjects of high rank, challenging imperial power and the Byzantine church, ungrateful for the imperial benefits bestowed upon them, and enriching themselves at the expense of the empire.[42] With respect to Italians, then, regardless of whether they were traders, Byzantine authors shared some basic views deeply imbued with social stereotypes regarding traders in general, mingled with ethnic and cultural stereotypes about aliens.[43] These were amplified by the frustration deriving from the recurrent need of the empire to rely on the naval power of the Italian maritime cities, the growing presence of the Italians in imperial service, especially in the reign of Manuel I,[44] and the seemingly unstoppable Italian economic expansion, even more obvious after 1261. Yet animosity was not the only feeling expressed by these authors. While critical of the Latins and blaming them collectively for all kinds of evil, Niketas Choniates could not conceal his admiration for Venetian trading and maritime skills,[45] and entertained good relations with some Venetians, as noted earlier. It remains to be seen to what extent this ambivalent approach was shared at various levels of Byzantine society and particularly among Byzantine outsiders in trade.

The latter's attitudes were moulded by immediate and concrete concerns, rather than by matters of imperial prestige, political power, ethnic diversity or religious identity. The Byzantine outsider in trade had a choice between four alternatives: he could resign himself to his fate, with all the disadvantages it implied; vent his frustrations in word and deed, to the point of acting aggressively toward insiders; find ways to improve his economic condition by co-operating with them; or attempt to proceed beyond that stage, the ultimate achievement being the crossing of the divide between outsider and insider. These four alternatives were reflected throughout the period following 1082 in some recurrent behavioural patterns which, however, varied according to the trader's

---

[42] References and discussion in A.E. Laiou, 'Monopoly and Privilege: the Byzantine Reaction to the Genoese Presence in the Black Sea', in L. Balletto, ed., *Oriente e Occidente tra medioevo ed età moderna. Studi in onore di Geo Pistarino* (Genoa, 1997), 676–686; A. Laiou, 'L'interprétation byzantine de l'expansion occidentale (XIe–XIIe siècles)' in M. Balard and A. Ducellier, eds, *Le partage du monde. Echanges et colonisation dans la Méditerranée médiévale* (Paris, 1998), 173–178. I am not dealing here with ecclesiastical literature.

[43] M. Angold, *Church and Society in Byzantium under the Comneni, 1081–1261*, (Cambridge, 1995), 506–514, overestimates the importance of theological matters in the shaping of anti-Latin attitudes in Byzantine society at large.

[44] See Angold, *Byzantine Empire*, 203–206; Magdalino, *Manuel I*, 221–226.

[45] Niketas Choniates, *Historia*, 171.

social and economic standing, his specific role in trade, and the particular circumstances in which he operated.

To be sure, Byzantine traders resented their position as outsiders with respect to the privileged Italians, especially since these were foreigners, yet had no choice but to conduct business with them. These deals may have even alleviated somewhat their animosity, since they were generally more advantageous than with Byzantine subjects. Indeed, as a result of their tax exemptions, especially the Venetians could afford to pay more for the goods they acquired and to sell at lower prices than the Byzantine trader, while still remaining competitive. These conditions may explain why some *archontes* of the Peloponnese acting as middlemen sold large quantities of oil to Italian wholesale traders, while others in Thebes sold silk textiles to Venetian merchants.[46] In addition to *archontes*, Byzantine wholesalers in some important commercial centres such as Halmyros also appear among the main trading partners of the Italians in the twelfth century.[47] On the other hand, there must have been Byzantine traders and carriers who strongly objected to the expansion of Italian involvement in domestic Byzantine trade and transportation. As noted earlier, John Tzetzes mentions Cretans, Rhodians and others coming to Constantinople on business, to which we may add the monks or agents of monasteries such as St John of Patmos.[48] Animosity must have been particularly strong among Byzantine retailers in the capital, exposed to the competition of Italian traders whose operations in their respective quarters were controlled neither by the city's Prefect nor by the gilds. Cretan cheese, as well as oil and wine were sold in the Venetian quarter from the first half of the twelfth century,[49] and wine presumably also in the other Italian quarters.[50]

The intermarriage of Italian traders with Greeks was decried by Byzantine authors as a device used by the former to exploit maliciously

---

[46] See above, note 30, and Jacoby, 'Silk in Western Byzantium', 466–467, 479, 490–497, 500.

[47] In Halmyros two members of the Greek family Pillari sold contiguous plots of land to Venetians, respectively, before 1150 and 1156: see Borsari, *Venezia*, 35. One piece was located on the sea shore, which suggests that these Greeks were traders: Lanfranchi, *S. Giorgio Maggiore*, II, no. 232.

[48] See above, note 23.

[49] See Jacoby, 'Silk in Western Byzantium', 494 and n. 239; TTh, I, 67–74, and new edition in Lanfranchi, *S. Giorgio Maggiore*, II, no. 224: Constantinople in 1107; TTh, I, 107–108: use of Venetian weights and measures in Rhaidestos before 1147.

[50] As suggested for the Pisan quarter: Müller, *Documenti*, 10, no. 8.

the privileges bestowed upon them,[51] and modern historians have followed their lead in this respect. It is obvious, though, that these marriages took place because they suited the interests of both parties. For a Greek offering his daughter in marriage to a Venetian trader must have often, if not always, been coupled with business association. Undoubtedly, such a co-operation also took place without marital bonds. While remaining an outsider, the Byzantine trader could benefit to some extent from the advantages enjoyed by his Italian partner, though presumably under the terms imposed by the latter. It was common practice among privileged Italian merchants to enlarge the volume of their business by handling capital and goods belonging to outsiders. At the imperial customs they declared these goods as their own so as to exempt them totally or partially from Byzantine taxation, in accordance with their respective privileges.[52] In all likelihood they acted similarly within their respective national quarter in Constantinople or national community in provincial cities,[53] paying the lower tariff applied to fellow-citizens for the weighing and measuring of merchandise, as attested in 1147 for the Venetians in Rhaidestos and in 1162 for the Pisans in the capital.[54] The first practice was strongly opposed by the Byzantine authorities, as attested explicitly by the Byzantine Venetian treaty of 1265, and may have occasionally led to the confiscation of goods handled by Italian traders accused of fraud.[55] As for the Italian maritime cities, they attempted to prevent deception in their own quarters.[56]

The attitude of Byzantine officials toward Italian traders warrants some attention, especially that of *kommerkiarioi* who were in direct contact

---

[51] See above, 135–136. Such unions generated conflicting demands of the Byzantine and Latin clergy regarding the marriage ceremonial and the religious allegiance of the Italian partners: see P. Schreiner, 'Untersuchungen zu den Niederlassungen westlicher Kaufleute im Byzantinischen Reich des 11. und 12. Jahrhunderts', *ByzForsch* 7 (1979), 186–188, and Angold, *Byzantine Empire*, 208. Yet these were not impediments to intermarriage.

[52] On differences in exemptions until the Fourth Crusade, see above, note 29.

[53] On the latter, see above, 136.

[54] See above, notes 49 and 50.

[55] TTh, III, 73 (Greek), 84 (Latin). The practice was certainly also common before 1204. On confiscation, see G. Makris, *Studien zur spätbyzantinischen Schiffahrt* (Collana storica di fonti e studi, diretta da Geo Pistarino, 52) (Genova, 1988), 258.

[56] There is no direct evidence for the empire, yet the Venetian authorities took measures to counter similar practices in thirteenth-century Acre: see D. Jacoby, 'L'expansion occidentale dans le Levant: les Vénitiens à Acre dans la seconde moitié du treizième siècle', *Journal of Medieval History* 3 (1977), 234–236, reprinted in D. Jacoby, *Recherches sur la Méditerranée orientale du XIIe au XVe siècle. Peuples, sociétés, économies* (London, 1979), no. VII.

with them. Time and again the Italian maritime powers complained about officials disregarding the exemptions to which their respective traders were entitled. Venice complained about illegal exactions of the *kommerkion* or sales and customs tax in 1126 and 1136 and, more generally, about the infringement of Venetian privileges throughout the empire in 1278, while Genoa demanded compensations for its traders in 1174, 1290 and 1294.[57] Even if we believe that these incidents, which appear to have been rather common, were due to overzealous imperial officials, the personal interests of customs officials should not be excluded. They were particularly well placed for the pursuit of private profit by the exertion of pressure and the extortion of bribes.[58] To be sure, they spared neither Byzantine nor foreign traders, yet one may wonder whether they did not target particularly the Italian insider. There is good reason to believe that various officials were personally involved in business, viewed the Italian trader as a competitor, and had a vested interest in curtailing his activity and his profits.[59] Yet the actions of customs officials may have also reflected collective attitudes of the Byzantine traders, resentful of the privileged foreigner. A similar attitude of resentment was apparently common among Byzantine corsairs and pirates, although profit was clearly their primary motive. It may well explain a colourful incident that took place in 1274. A Venetian ship was caught in the Aegean by Bulgarino of Ania, a Latin sea-captain operating as Byzantine corsair. When the Venetians on board presented him documents stating their national identity, he threw them to the ground and trampled them, shouting that he was precisely looking for Venetians.[60]

---

[57] See Jacoby, 'Italian Privileges and Trade', 354–356; G. Morgan, 'The Venetian Claims Commission of 1278', *BZ* 69 (1976), 411–438; C. Imperiale di Sant'Angelo, ed., *Codice diplomatico della Repubblica di Genova* (Rome, 1936–1942), II, 206–222; A.E. Laiou, *Constantinople and the Latins. The Foreign Policy of Andronicus II, 1282–1328* (Cambridge, MA, 1972), 72–73.

[58] See the fourteenth-century Francesco Balducci Pegolotti, *La pratica della mercatura*, ed. A. Evans (Cambridge, MA, 1936), 42, on bribes to *kommerkiarioi*, their scribes and their interpreters; also Kl.-P. Matschke, 'Tore, Torwächter und Torzöllner von Konstantinopel in spätbyzantinischer Zeit', *Jahrbuch für Regionalgeschichte*, 16/II (1989), 41–57. The information is also relevant for earlier periods.

[59] For evidence from the Palaeologan era, see Makris, *Studien*, 252–256.

[60] TTh, III, 219; see also Morgan, 'The Venetian Claims Commission', 424, and for the dating, 431.

There has been much speculation about the number of Latins staying in Constantinople at any given time in the twelfth century.[61] Whatever the actual figure, it is the collective image of the Italians as perceived by the city's inhabitants that counted when it came to popular reaction. We have already noted the friendly relations of some Pisan and Genoese traders with members of the Byzantine élite, as illustrated in 1182, and this was presumably also the case of Venetians. It is rather unlikely that Byzantine wholesalers conducting business with Italians should have been among the Greeks and other residents of Constantinople taking part in the second assault on the Genoese quarter in 1162,[62] or in the massacre of the Latins in 1182.[63] On the other hand, retailers facing severe Italian competition, as noted earlier, may well have joined the attacking crowds. Rather than the direct confrontation between Byzantine outsiders and Italian insiders in trade, the aggressiveness of the population appears to have been fuelled by the rapidly expanding market economy. As nowadays in some countries, it generated deepening economic and social inequalities, more visible and more vividly perceived than before, and as often frustration found its outlet in intense xenophobia.[64] The atrocities committed in 1182 by the Constantinopolitan rabble against the Latin clergy provided an extreme manifestation of these widely shared collective attitudes.[65] Yet violence erupted also in some provincial cities. In 1197 Pisa requested the rebuilding and restitution of Pisan churches, houses, *embolon* or commercial premises, and the hospice for passing traders in Halmyros, all apparently damaged or destroyed in 1182.[66]

The divide between Latin insider and Byzantine outsider in trade in Constantinople deepened under Latin rule, which extended from 1204 to 1261. Yet the city also witnessed then some important developments, which are of particular interest for the following period. Latin rule favoured Venetian citizens, who enjoyed a privileged status in their

---

[61] See P. Schreiner, 'Untersuchungen', 182–186; Lilie, *Handel*, 290–296, 539–540.

[62] L.T. Belgrano and C. Imperiale di Sant'Angelo, eds, *Annali genovesi di Caffaro e de' suoi continuatori dal MXCIX al MCCXCIII* (Rome, 1890–1929), I, 67–68.

[63] Niketas Choniates, *Historia*, 250–251; Guillaume de Tyr, *Chronique*, 22. 13, ed. Huygens, 1022–1024.

[64] See M. Angold, 'The Shaping of the Medieval Byzantine "City"', *ByzForsch* 10 (1985), 32–34. However, I do not share the author's assessment that the Italian impact on the Byzantine economy was decisive.

[65] See above, note 63.

[66] Müller, *Documenti*, 71, no. 44.

national quarter, the urban focus of commerce.[67] Another group enjoying Venetian status and that of insiders in trade consisted of those born of the marriage or the extra-marital relations of a Venetian father and a Greek mother, known as *gasmouloi* or *basmouloi*.[68] According to Venetian law, in either case the father transmitted his Venetian status to his offspring in the same territory, though not Venetian citizenship. Since these descendants generally adopted their father's surname in order to promote their own social standing, it is almost impossible to detect them.[69]

Greeks, however, were not excluded from Constantinople's trade, although lack of direct evidence prevents any assessment of their role in its framework. Some of them obviously took advantage of their acquaintance with the resources and commercial networks of Constantinople's hinterland to ensure their continuing participation in the city's provisioning in foodstuffs. Greeks are attested as lease-holders in the section of the Venetian quarter located between the Golden Horn and the northern city wall, the urban area most involved in maritime trade in the Latin period.[70] Their residence in that quarter may have been related to their status in trade. While in Constantinople they remained outsiders with respect to Venetian citizens, being a Venetian subject in the city apparently entailed certain advantages. Indeed, later sources reveal that Venice extended diplomatic protection to the subjects of its territories overseas trading in Romania and elsewhere and insisted upon their right

---

[67] See D. Jacoby, 'Venetian Settlers in Latin Constantinople (1204–1261): Rich or Poor?', in Ch.A. Maltezou, ed., Πλούσιοι καὶ πτωχοί στὴν κοινωνία τῆς ἑλληνολατινικῆς Ἀνατολῆς [=Ricchi e poveri nella società dell'Oriente grecolatino], (Biblioteca dell'Istituto ellenico di Studi bizantini e postbizantini di Venezia, no. 19), (Venezia, 1998), 181–204.

[68] There were also *gasmouloi* born of a Latin, though non-Venetian father: see Jacoby, 'Vénitiens naturalisés', 221. G. Makris, 'Die Gasmulen', *Thesaurismata* 22 (1992), 83–84, argues that since Marco Polo's voyage account uses the French form *guasmul*, the *gasmouloi* who were subjected to the French-speaking administration of the Latin emperors must have been more numerous than Venetian *gasmouloi*. However, he overlooks the fact that Polo's account was written in French and, therefore, cannot provide any indication in this respect.

[69] Examples in Venetian Crete in D. Jacoby, 'Les états latins en Romanie: phénomènes sociaux et économiques (1204–1350 environ)', *XVe Congrès international d'études byzantines (Athènes, 1976), Rapports et co-rapports*, I/3 (Athens, 1976), 29–30, reprinted in D. Jacoby, *Recherches*, no. I. Contrary to Makris, 'Gasmulen', 69–70, there is no indication whatsoever that the status was limited to the *legal* offspring of mixed parentage.

[70] Greek names are mentioned by Ch. Maltezou, 'Il quartiere veneziano di Costantinopoli (Scali marittimi)', *Thesaurismata* 15 (1978), 40 and 57–61 (index). On the area in which they resided, see Jacoby, 'Venetian Settlers', 189–196.

to enjoy the same fiscal privileges as Venetian citizens, though not in Venice itself.[71]

It is in this general context that Philippos Vistariti, first attested in 1254, warrants our attention. Vistariti is obviously a transcription of βεστιαρίτης, a term applied in twelfth-century Byzantium to imperial wardrobe guards and members of a contingent participating in military expeditions, and in the thirteenth century to some officials levying taxes in the provinces.[72] Philippos, however, had clearly inherited the administrative term from his father or a forefather having exercised the function of *vestiarites* and used it as surname.[73] If Philippos himself had served the Latin emperors in that capacity, there would have been no apparent reason for Venice to bestow upon him Venetian citizenship in 1254.[74] Judging by his Greek name, Philippos Vistariti was not a *gasmoulos*, nor was he a Greek included among Venice's subjects in Constantinople. Considering Venice's motivations in the grant of Venetian status in that period, he must have been a subject of the Latin emperor, have closely co-operated with Venetian officials in Constantinople, and was most likely a trader who had loaned money to the Commune.[75] A provision attached to his privilege lends support to this assumption. His obligation to marry a Venetian woman, as proof of his genuine intention to integrate within the local Venetian community, suggests that he was well acquainted with the latter's members. To be sure, in 1254 his new status as Venetian citizen was restricted to Romania, yet in this region he became an insider in trade. In all likelihood Vistariti wedded a Venetian woman in Constantinople and both joined the 3,000 Latins, mostly Venetians, who abandoned the city in 1261.[76] In 1264

---

[71] On the distinction between Venetian citizenship and nationality, see Jacoby, 'Vénitiens naturalisés', 217–220.

[72] Anne Comnène, *Alexiade*, IV, 3, ed. B. Leib (Paris, 1937–1945), I, 152,1–4; R. Guilland, 'Protovestiarite', *RSBN* 4 (1967), 3–4, reprinted in R. Guilland, *Titres et fonctions de l'Empire byzantin* (London, 1976), no. XV; R. Guilland, *Recherches sur les institutions byzantines* (Amsterdam, 1967), I, 589; *ODB*, III: 2163, s. v. Vestiarites.

[73] The same surname is attested in 1348–1349: *PLP*, no. 2,755.

[74] R. Cessi, ed., *Deliberazioni del Maggior Consiglio di Venezia* (Bologna, 1931–1950), II, 143, §7.

[75] Such was apparently the case of the Jew David of Negroponte, a subject of one of the island's feudal lords, who in 1268 obtained Venetian nationality: see D. Jacoby, 'On the Status of the Jews in the Venetian Colonies in the Middle Ages', *Zion* 28 (1963), 59–64 (in Hebrew).

[76] On these Latins, see D.J. Geanakoplos, *Emperor Michael Palaeologus and the West, 1258–1282. A Study in Byzantine–Latin Relations* (Cambridge, MA, 1959), 113–114.

Vistariti obtained full and unrestricted citizenship 'in Venice and everywhere', which implies that by then he was established in Venice itself.[77] In view of the fragmentary state of thirteenth-century Venetian documentation, we do not know whether other Greeks of Constantinople similarly obtained Venetian citizenship limited to Romania in the Latin period.

The case of Philippos Vistariti has been considered here at some length, in view of its significance for later developments. While foreigners residing for some time in the Italian maritime cities occasionally obtained citizenship, his is the earliest known instance of a Greek living in the former territories of the empire being granted Venetian citizenship and thus crossing the line separating Byzantine outsiders from Venetian insiders in trade. More importantly, the privilege bestowed upon Vistariti heralds a new Venetian policy in this respect in the Palaeologan period, especially in Constantinople. Venice not only insisted upon the Venetian status of its own *gasmouloi*, their descendants, and its colonial subjects.[78] Regardless of their place of residence, it also naturalized a growing number of Byzantine subjects eager to obtain Venetian identity and staunchly defended their new status.[79] Genoa too granted naturalization to Byzantine subjects, including traders. Yet, in addition, the establishment of its quarter in Pera in the 1260s and the latter's expansion in 1303 entailed for the Greeks remaining within its boundaries the benefit of Genoese status and that of insiders in trade.[80]

To some extent Venetian and Genoese economic activity in the empire necessarily relied on local middlemen having easy access to indigenous producers, traders and carriers. In Constantinople local retailers contributed their share to the supply of goods and services to the respective local communities, travelling merchants, and passing ships of the two maritime powers. The naturalization of these Byzantine subjects integrated them more firmly within the respective trade networks of

---

[77] Cessi, *Deliberazioni*, II, 148, §27; illustration of the link between residence and citizenship in Venice: ibid., II, 145, §16.

[78] See Jacoby, 'Vénitiens naturalisés', 221–224; also Makris, 'Gasmulen', 70–71, on the descendants.

[79] See below, note 81.

[80] See D. Jacoby, 'Les Génois dans l'Empire byzantin: citoyens, sujets et protégés (1261–1453)', *La Storia dei Genovesi* 9 (1989), 245–264, reprinted in Jacoby, *Trade*, no. III. Michael VIII ordered Greeks to leave the territory he had granted to Genoa, apparently in order to prevent them from becoming Genoese subjects, yet many stayed.

these powers. The latter also benefited from the increase in the number of their nationals, which enhanced their fiscal revenues in the empire.

The repeated Byzantine assaults on the status of the so-called 'white Venetians' and 'white Genoese' were clearly attempts to reassert imperial rights upon former subjects and increase state revenues. Yet they also carried with them a reaction, fuelled by popular resentment, to the privileged status of these new insiders in trade. Thus, frustration must have grown considerably among Byzantine tavern keepers when 'white Venetians' established their own taverns outside Venice's quarter, the operation of which the imperial authorities sought to prevent.[81]

Economic co-operation between Byzantine outsiders and Italian insiders in trade generated varying degrees of social contact, which in the case of intermarriage could result in the assimilation of the latter to the Greek milieu. Naturalization did not produce any similar integration. It promoted a social rapprochement between old and new members of the national communities which, however, was limited by three factors. First, differences in religious affiliation, language and culture were not obliterated; secondly, until the mid-fourteenth century the traders who obtained naturalization belonged mostly to the middling and lower strata of Byzantine society; and, finally, Venetian and Genoese citizens were intent on preserving their social supremacy within their respective communities. They were assisted in this respect by their own governments, which maintained a strict legal distinction between citizens and other nationals.[82] On the social level, then, the naturalized Byzantine trader remained an outsider.

The second half of the fourteenth century witnessed a broader participation of members of the Byzantine élite in trade. The latter's stronger co-operation with Venice's and Genoa's traders enabled some of them to obtain naturalization from either of these powers.[83] Byzantine traders gradually absorbed the more sophisticated commercial practices common among their Italian counterparts.[84] Although this process had a practical purpose, it may also be considered a way of narrowing somewhat the gap between outsiders and insiders in Byzantine trade. The

---

[81]   See Jacoby, 'Vénitiens naturalisés', 223, n. 56, 224–235; Jacoby, 'Génois', 254–260.

[82]   See Jacoby, 'Vénitiens naturalisés', 219; Jacoby, 'Génois', 266–270.

[83]   See Jacoby, 'Génois', 264–266, 269.

[84]   See Oikonomidès, *Hommes d'affaires*, 53–83; Kl.-P. Matschke, 'Geldgeschäfte, Handel und Gewerbe in spätbyzantinischen Rechenbüchern und in der spätbyzantinischen Wirklichkeit. Ein Beitrag zu den Produktions- und Austauschverhältnissen im byzantinischen Feudalismus', *Jahrbuch für Geschichte des Feudalismus* 3 (1979), 181–204.

impact of these developments on the relations between the two groups requires another study.

11. Constantinople and the Outside World

Paul Magdalino

In a couple of rare autobiographical asides, the twelfth-century chronicler John Zonaras complains that he is having to write his history of the world 'in this place at the back of beyond' (παρὰ τῇ ἐσχατιᾷ ταύτῃ), where he suffers from an acute shortage of books.[1] According to the title of the work in some manuscripts, the author was a monk of Hagia Glykeria. The straightforward reading of this information has met with some incredulity because it means that the back of beyond was a small island, one of the Princes' Islands, in the Sea of Marmara, a short sea journey from Constantinople. Today the island is the well-appointed summer retreat of a wealthy Turkish industrialist, and in Byzantine times it was the site of a 'posh monastery', re-founded about 1100 by a high-ranking aristocrat, and served by an *hegoumenos*, Joseph, who went on to become abbot of the Pantokrator monastery.[2] Hagia Glykeria had also received a substantial endowment from one Naukratios Zonaras, possibly the father of John the chronicler; in any event, the latter was working in a suburban monastery with family connections. It was hardly the 'back of beyond'. We can explain his words as the rhetoric of exile;[3] we can also point to the reality of exile suffered by many Byzantines who were banished to the Princes' Islands in political disgrace; and we can point to modern examples of islands near big cities which are places for the isolation of undesirables. But when we have done everything to get Zonaras's notion of the 'back of beyond' in proportion, it is hard to avoid the conclusion that it is what it appears to be: a reflection of the Byzantine equivalent of

---

[1] John Zonaras, *Epitomae historiarum*, M. Pinder and Th. Büttner-Wobst, eds, 3 vols (Bonn, 1841–184, 1897), I, 3–4; II, 297–298.

[2] C. Mango, 'Twelfth-Century Notices from Cod.Christ Church Gr. 53', *JÖB*, 42 (1992), 221–228; C. Mango, 'Introduction' in C. Mango and G. Dagron, eds, *Constantinople and its Hinterland* (Aldershot, 1995), 2.

[3] Cf. M.E. Mullett, 'Originality in the Byzantine Letter: The Case of Exile', in A.R. Littlewood, ed., *Originality in Byzantine Literature Art and Music* (Oxford, 1995), 39–58.

From *Strangers to Themselves: The Byzantine Outsider*, ed. Dion C. Smythe. Copyright © 2000 by the Society for the Promotion of Byzantine Studies. Published by Ashgate Publishing Ltd, Gower House, Croft Road, Aldershot, Hampshire, GU11 3HR, Great Britain.

the attitude caricatured in the cartoon of the *New Yorker's* view of the world, where New Jersey gives way to the Mid West beyond a Hudson River that is definitely on the edge of civilization. Other writers of the period contain little that qualifies, and much that confirms, this literal reading. John Tzetzes lumps ethnic foreigners together with Greeks from the Aegean islands as undesirable aliens.[4] Bishops and government officials always want to be back in Constantinople and not where they happen to be posted. It is bad for a monastery to be rich in Thessalonike, Archbishop Eustathios tells the people of that city, but good in Constantinople, because they do things properly there.[5] Theodore Balsamon, the canonist, agrees, being, in his own words, 'a Constantinopolitan through and through' (Κωνσταντινουπολίτης ἀκραιφνέστατος).[6] In his canon law commentaries, he repeatedly distinguishes between Constantinople, where people know and keep the rules, and the 'outer territories' (ἔξω χῶραι), where anything goes, including heresy.[7] Three writers of the generation of 1204 – Michael Choniates, Niketas Choniates, and the patriarch Germanos II – have left an unforgettable picture of smug Constantinopolitans assuming that the world owes them a superior living just because Constantinople is the place to be, and to be born.[8]

Altogether, there is a fairly impressive body of twelfth-century evidence that for a powerful consensus of opinion, the Byzantine outsider was someone who did not belong in Constantinople, for whatever reasons people who did belong in Constantinople chose to name. The statements of Constantinopolitan exclusiveness are supported by the further consideration that the constitutional and ideological role of Constantinople within Byzantium far exceeded that of any capital city or

---

[4] P.A.M. Leone, ed., *Ioannis Tzetzae historiae* (Naples, 1968), Chiliad XIII, 359ff.

[5] T.L.F. Tafel, ed., *Eustathii metropolitae Thessalonicensis opuscula* (Frankfurt am Main, 1832), 230–231, 237, 262.

[6] G.A. Rallis and A. Potlis, eds, *Σύνταγμα τῶν θείων καὶ ἱερῶν κανόνων*, 6 vols (Athens, 1852–1859), II, 285–286. Hereafter, Rallis-Potlis.

[7] Rallis-Potlis, I, 246; II, 404, 450, 620, 627. On this and the sources cited in the following notes, see P. Magdalino, 'Constantinople and the ἔξω χῶραι in the time of Balsamon', in N. Oikonomides, ed., *Byzantium in the 12th Century: Canon Law, State and Society* (Athens, 1991), 179–197; P. Magdalino, *Tradition and Transformation in Medieval Byzantium* (Aldershot, 1991), nos I and VII.

[8] Michael Choniates, *Μιχαὴλ Ἀκομινάτου τοῦ Χωνιάτου τὰ σωζόμενα*, Sp. Lampros, ed., 2 vols (Athens, 1879–1880), I, 82–84; Niketas Choniates, *Nicetae Choniatae historia*, J. van Dieten, ed., 2 vols (Berlin and New York, 1975), I, 593; S. Lagopatis, ed., *Γερμανὸς ὁ Β΄ πατριάρχης* (Tripolis, 1913), 282–283.

metropolis in almost any other territorial state. It was the status of Constantinople as the New Rome which made it legitimate for Byzantines to call themselves *Romaioi* and their state *Romania*. For both these identities, Constantinople was the fixed point on the map, more fixed than any frontier, the peg from which all definitions hung[9] – at least until 1204, when Constantinople under Latin occupation became the outsider to *Romaioi* associated with the Byzantine governments in exile. The equivalence of the city with the state was further reinforced by the legal definition, transferred to Constantinople from Rome, of the capital as the 'common homeland' (κοινὴ πατρὶς) of all imperial subjects,[10] and by the designation of 'reigning city' (βασιλεύουσα πόλις/urbs regia), or 'queen of cities' (βασιλὶς τῶν πόλεων), which was commonly applied to it.[11] This expression implied not only that Constantinople was the greatest city in the world, but also that it was sovereign by virtue of its role in validating imperial power. An emperor was not emperor until he had been acclaimed in Constantinople. An eleventh-century author famously declared, 'The emperor in Constantinople always wins',[12] and twelfth-century panegyrics represent the emperor winning victories on behalf of the City, his mother, and subjecting reconquered towns in Asia Minor to her yoke.[13]

All Byzantines were *Romaioi*, but Constantinopolitans were more Byzantine than the rest. But who truly belonged inside Constantinople? Who or what was typically, quintessentially and unambiguously Constantinopolitan? For Tzetzes, it was not the fashionable holy men about town – they were all foreigners and provincials.[14] For Alexios I Komnenos, as represented by Niketas Choniates, it was not his noble, learned son-in-law, the Caesar Nikephoros Bryennios, because this fellow was a Macedonian – that is, his family were from Adrianople.[15] For the

---

[9]   See D. Olster, 'From Periphery to Center: The Transformation of Late Roman Self-Definition in the Seventh Century', in R.W. Mathisen and H.S. Sivan, eds, *Shifting Frontiers in Late Antiquity* (Aldershot, 1996), 93–101.

[10]   *Digest* 48.22.18, 27.1.6; Heraclius, Novel 2, J. Konidaris, ed., 'Die Novellen des Kaisers Herakleios', *Fontes Minores* 5 (1982), 74.

[11]   Cf. G. Dagron, *Naissance d'une capitale. Constantinople et ses institutions de 330 à 451* (Paris, 1974), 53.

[12]   Kekaumenos, *Strategikon*, B. Wassiliewsky and V. Jernstedt, eds (St Petersburg, 1896; repr. Amsterdam, 1965), 74.

[13]   Theodoros Prodromos, *Historische Gedichte*, W. Hörandner, ed. (Vienna, 1974), nos IV.157–158, V.1–10, VIII.145–172, Xb.5, XIX.196–197.

[14]   See above, note 3.

[15]   van Dieten, ed., I, 6.

detractors of the patriarch Germanos II, he was of lowly birth because he had not been born in Constantinople. Yet, as the patriarch pointed out, the natives of Constantinople included many illegitimate half-breeds, spawned by adulterous liaisons with Russian and Turkish slave girls. 'Are these persons, who resemble mules in their racial mixture, well born and respectable, and will the soil of Constantinople ennoble them?'[16]

All the people labelled as outsiders in the above remarks clearly regarded themselves, and were accepted by their friends, as insiders. Constantinople was the place to be because it was the place where outsiders became insiders. This is exactly how the author of the *Vita Basilii* describes the career début of the young Basil the Macedonian, the country boy from Adrianople who went on to found a successful imperial dynasty:

> Since a living from agriculture seemed petty and mundane to him, he decided to go to the reigning city and display his virtue, and thus to procure the necessities of life for himself and his family, and provide patronage for their great benefit. For he knew that in big cities, and especially royal capitals, talents flourish and men who stand out in any way receive recognition and advancement, whereas in undistinguished, obscure towns, as in village society, virtues fade and waste away, and, consumed by lack of opportunity for display or admiration, wither away to extinction.[17]

Michael Attaleiates explicitly presents his life as a conversion from outsider to insider status through immigration to Constantinople. He had given up his inheritance in his home town (no doubt Attaleia) in order to acquire an education 'in the metropolis of learning and queen of cities'. With learning he had acquired prosperity, in spite of everything that counted against him, 'especially the fact of being of alien race' (ἡ τοῦ γένους ἀπαλλοτρίωσις). He thanked God that he had risen 'from foreign and humble condition' (ἀπὸ ξένης καὶ ταπεινῆς τύχης) to become one of the senatorial aristocracy, a senior judge loaded with public honours. This was due to his studies in grammar, rhetoric and philosophy, and his initiation into the 'sacred mystery of the law'.[18]

Only a detailed and exhaustive series of case studies will allow us to create a profile of the typical Constantinopolitan insider, if there was such

---

[16] Lagopatis, ed. (see above, note 8).

[17] *Theophanes Continuatus*, I. Bekker, ed., CSHB (Bonn, 1838), 221.

[18] P. Gautier, ed. and tr., 'La Diataxis de Michel Attaliate', *REB* 39 (1981), 18–21, 28–31.

a thing. For this, we shall have to await the completion of the Prosopography of the Byzantine Empire. In the meantime, there are three preliminary questions which it is useful and reasonable to consider in the present context. Firstly, what distinguished those visitors to Constantinople who remained outsiders from those who became insiders, at least to their own satisfaction? What were the frontiers which some outsiders managed to cross while others did not? Secondly, was the status of insider to the city merely the construction of naturalized provincials, or did it correspond to the reality of a hard core of indigenous Constantinopolitans? What did it mean to be 'Constantinopolitan through and through', as Balsamon claimed to be? Thirdly, it is important to consider the diachronic dimension of these issues. Is it significant that so much evidence comes from the twelfth century, and that the most extreme statements of exclusiveness date from the years immediately before and after 1204? Was the role of Constantinople as the ultimate in-place a cumulative one which peaked at the moment when its *raison d'être* was temporarily destroyed and forever damaged?

The sources allow us to identify four clear categories of visitors who tended to remain outsiders to the city because of the nature of their business there: litigants and petitioners, pilgrims, diplomats, and the majority of merchants, although there were always merchants who stayed on, particularly with the growth of the Italian trading concessions in the twelfth century and the formation of a class of foreign residents, the *bourgesioi* or *burgenses*.[19] The last three categories are often noticed because of their interest for the study of urban topography, foreign relations and economic life. The litigants and petitioners receive less attention, although they are frequently mentioned, and they are worth considering here, because they, perhaps more than any others, knew what it was like to be in Constantinople but not to belong there. Lawsuits and petitions were notoriously slow to process, and put provincials and foreigners at a severe disadvantage against residents. Twelfth-century commentators on the *Rhetorica* of Aristotle noted that foreigners, 'for example Egyptians or Corinthians', were regularly cheated, because the perpetrators knew that the victims would not take them to court, 'for a

---

[19] See most recently A.E. Laiou, 'Institutional Mechanisms of Integration', in H. Ahrweiler and A.E. Laiou, eds, *Studies on the Internal Diaspora of the Byzantine Empire* (Washington, DC, 1998), 171ff.

lawsuit will often not be finished in two years'.[20] Like prostitutes, provincial plaintiffs in this plight were repeatedly targeted by philanthropic emperors: Justinian I, Basil I and Romanos I are all said to have made provision for them to be able to stay in Constantinople for the duration of their cases.[21] In the *Life of Andrew the Fool*, the devil on one occasion assumes the guise of an old woman dossing down in the Hippodrome while her case is being heard.[22] Nicholas Mesarites, in his account of the revolt of John Komnenos the Fat in 1200, describes another such unfortunate who joined the insurgents: a monk from the East, who had come to the city and spent a long time there on some necessary business of his monastery. Being of a simple nature, and having used up all the funds he had brought with him, he was wandering the streets with a pouch, begging for his daily sustenance. Lacking accommodation and money, he slept out in the churches, wrapped in a decaying cloak and a habit in complete tatters.[23]

Speeding up court cases involving provincials was one of the duties of the *quaesitor*, the magistrate appointed by Justinian in 539 to investigate and repatriate people who had no business in the city.[24] The terms of the appointment, as set out in Novel 80, show a concern to halt the drift of immigrants from the provinces, especially from the countryside. A similar concern is evident in Heraclius's novels regulating clerical appointments in the capital; Novel 2, of 617, deplores the fact the numerous churches and other pious foundations of the city are attracting many unknown men from various provinces, villages and trading centres, who had either never received holy orders or had been suspended.[25] Yet both these Novels are 'one-off' pieces of legislation, which hardly constitute evidence for a consistent policy of immigration control.[26] Does this mean there was no formal barrier to prevent outsiders

---

[20] H. Rabe, ed., *CAG* XXI, 2 (Berlin, 1896), 285; for corrective legislation issued by Manuel I in 1166, see R.J. Macrides, 'Justice under Manuel I Komnenos: Four Novels on Court Business and Murder', *Fontes Minores* 6 (1985), 122–139, 172–182.

[21] Procopius, *De aedificiis*, I, 11.23–27; *Theoph.Cont.*, 260, 430.

[22] L. Rydén, ed. and tr., *The Life of St Andrew the Fool*, 2 vols (Uppsala, 1995), II, 64–65.

[23] A. Heisenberg, ed., *Die Palastrevolution des Johannes Komnenos* [*Programm des Königlichen alten Gymnasiums zu Würzburg für das Studienjahr 1906/1907*] (Würzburg, 1907), 22.

[24] Cf. John Lydus, *De Magistratibus*, III.70.

[25] Konidaris, ed., 74.

[26] The repetition of the legislation on the *quaesitor* in the ninth-century *Eisagoge* (*Epanagoge*), 5 (where he is confused with the *quaestor*) is not, in my opinion, a reliable indicator.

from becoming insiders? Several texts represent their protagonists as simply moving to Constantinople without introduction or invitation. Basil I is again the most famous case in point; one might also mention Leontios of Jerusalem, who wandered to Constantinople from the Strymon valley, took the tonsure in a suburban monastery, then entered the city as 'a stranger among strangers and a foreigner to the city, a foreigner to the citizens and ignorant of urban ways'.[27] Yet both Basil and Leontios went on to make their way by finding patrons. In other words, the key to integration was *prostasia*, and other sources suggest that the usual access route for an ambitious young provincial was by way of a household, an *oikos*, to which he had an introduction. St Evaristos,[28] St Athanasios the Athonite,[29] and St Symeon the New Theologian[30] all followed this route. St Nikephoros of Miletos was sent, as a eunuch, by his parents from the Boukellarion theme to Constantinople, where he was taken in by the *patrikios* Moseles, to receive an education and to serve in the household.[31] This was how it worked towards the top of the social scale. We can only speculate as to how it worked lower down – how the workers and artisans of Constantinople got there if they were not born there. It was presumably possible for outsiders to turn up and find work. But I would suggest that the aristocratic *oikos*, again, was the medium by which outsiders became insiders: that a large proportion of the common people originated with household slaves. Not only did slave girls have a habit of getting pregnant, but masters commonly freed their slaves in their wills and granted them small legacies. The case of the widow Zoe Pakouriane, whose will of 1098 is preserved in the archives of Iviron, is probably not untypical. She left legacies of money, clothes and animals to nineteen freed slaves.[32] It is not clear where they lived, but the mentions of livestock do not preclude an urban location, since we know that farm animals and beasts of burden were kept inside the city.[33]

---

[27] *The Life of Leontios Patriarch of Jerusalem*, D. Tsougarakis, ed. and tr. (Leiden, 1993), 40–41.

[28] Ch. van der Vorst, ed., *AB* 41 (1923), 300.

[29] J. Noret, ed., *Vitae duae antiquae Sancti Athanasii Athonitae* (Turnhout, 1982), 5, 7–8.

[30] Niketas Stethatos, *Vie de Syméon le Nouveau Théologien*, I. Hausherr, ed. and tr. (Rome, 1928), 2–4.

[31] H. Delehaye, ed., *AB* 14 (1895), 136–137.

[32] *Actes d'Iviron*, J. Lefort, N. Oikonomidès, D. Papachryssanthou, eds, II (Paris, 1990), no. 47.

[33] E.g. Attaleiates, Gautier, ed. and tr., 'Diataxis', 28–29; John Tzetzes, P.A.M. Leone, ed., *Ioannis Tzetzae epistulae* (Leipzig, 1972), 31–34.

It is clear that for most of the people mentioned so far, a Constantinopolitan social identity was the construction of a deliberate choice on the part of upwardly and inwardly mobile outsiders for whom destinations counted more than origins. Their attitude was expressed by Stephen, a twelfth-century commentator on the *Rhetorica* of Aristotle, when he defined natives as 'those who are not migrants or colonists from another land, or those who, if they come from another land, have lived in this land long enough to be old-timers and in this respect close to the natives, like those [who are] close to the natives of Constantinople'.[34] As a teacher of rhetoric in Constantinople, the author knew whereof he spoke, especially if he is to be identified with Stephen Skylitzes.[35] The Skylitzes family were an integral part of the capital's intellectual and bureaucratic élite, but they may have come from western Asia Minor.[36] They represented the convergence and fusion of metropolitan and provincial which was typical of Constantinopolitan society. Like all urban populations, that of Constantinople had to replenish itself by immigration – perhaps more than most, since it contained large numbers of monks and eunuchs – but it never consisted entirely of immigrants. Even in 713, at the height of the 'Dark Age' crisis, when senatorial and curial élites were in full decline and an aristocracy of service in the ascendant, the emperor Philippikos Bardanes held a lunch party 'with citizens of ancient lineage' (μετὰ πολιτῶν ἀρχαιογενῶν).[37] Several family names associated with the civil bureaucracy and the clergy of the Great Church in the eleventh and twelfth centuries are to be found in Constantinople two or three centuries earlier. Of course, recurrence of names does not necessarily mean continuity of lineage. But I think it is telling that in the mid-tenth century a Zonaras served on the staff of the Prefect of Constantinople,[38] and two centuries later three Zonarades held high judicial posts.[39] It is also surely more than coincidence that the surname Xylinites recurs in 1056 with the same first name, Niketas, with which it is linked at its first occurrence in

---

[34] *CAG* XXI, 2, 270.

[35] W. Wanda-Conus, 'À propos des scolies de Stephanos à la Rhetorique d'Aristote, l'auteur, l'oeuvre, le milieu', *Actes du XIVe Congrès international des Études byzantines*, III (Bucharest, 1976), 599–606.

[36] Cf. J. Thurn, *Ioannis Scylitzae Synopsis historiarum*, CFHB 5 (Berlin and New York, 1973), vii.

[37] Theophanes, *Chronographia*, C. de Boor, ed. (Hildesheim and New York, 1980), 383.

[38] *Theoph. Cont.*, 442.

[39] Mango, 'Twelfth-century Notices'; 226–227; P. Magdalino, 'The not-so-secret functions of the mystikos', *REB* 42 (1984); reprinted in Magdalino, *Tradition and Transformation*, no. XI.

719.[40] The prosopography will allow us to correlate patterns of naming and titulature and give us some idea of numbers. I fear it will never tell us what we would most like to know: how lineages kept going over the long term – their marriage and inheritance strategies, their association with monasteries, their houses and neighbourhoods, their sources of income, their ability to survive political disgrace and loss of office.[41] Yet this information is vital to understanding what held Constantinople together as a community of insiders, the social realities that underlay the rhetoric and the rituals of civic identity. In short, what did Constantinopolitans have in common apart from their access to the imperial court and its satellites? Was there more to the city than the infrastructure of the Palace?

The most we can do at this stage is to identify the factors that made for an accumulation of shared experience and common, exclusive identity. The structural features which made Constantinople the place to be were in place very early, and can be clearly discerned at the city's first peak of prosperity in the reign of Justinian. The best known figures in Justinian's entourage, and the authors of the main sources for his reign, were all from the provinces, predominantly from Asia Minor. The influx of petitioners, litigants and would-be immigrants was probably most intense in the years before the plague of 542. The image of Constantinople as the still centre of the turning world, as a heaven on earth against which barbarism would not prevail, was already a major tool of Byzantine diplomacy. Jordanes records the reaction of Athanaric the Goth as follows:

'Lo, now I see what I have often heard of with unbelieving ears', meaning the great and famous city. Turning his eyes hither and thither, he marvelled as he beheld the situation of the city, the coming and going of the ships, the splendid walls, and the people of divers nations gathered like a flood of waters streaming from different regions into one basin. So too, when he saw the army in array, he said, 'Truly the emperor is God on earth, and whoso raises a hand against him is guilty of his own blood'.[42]

---

[40]   Theoph., 400; Skylitzes, Thurn, ed., 478, 490.

[41]   Some of these questions are discussed by the contributors to J. Beaucamp and G. Dagron, eds, *La transmission du patrimoine: Byzance et l'aire méditérranéenne* (Paris, 1998).

[42]   Jordanes, *Getica*, XXVIII: *MGH Auct.Ant.* III, 1, 95; C.C. Mierow, tr., *The Gothic History of Jordanes* (Princeton, 1915), 91.

Jordanes, like Justinian, refers to Constantinople as the 'reigning city',[43] and Justinian's legislation is almost certainly the source for Balsamon's distinction between Constantinople and the 'outer territories'.[44] Yet in Justinian's Novels, the expressions ἔξω τόποι and ἔξω πόλεις merely make a geographical distinction; they do not imply a contrast, and do not carry the weight of association with inferiority and non-conformity which Balsamon attaches to the expression ἔξω χῶραι. Behind his usage lay centuries of investment in Constantinople at the expense of the urban life of the rest of the empire. The material investment fluctuated; it began to fall off after the plague of 542, and declined in a big way after the loss of Egypt and Syria. Yet the spiritual and moral investment only increased as Constantinople stood almost alone as the city which had not been sacked or conquered by invading barbarians. A series of events in the seventh and eighth centuries enhanced the role of Constantinople as the God-guarded city which would endure until the end of time. There was the failure of Heraclius to relocate to Carthage (619), and the murder of Constans II (668) who had set up his headquarters in Sicily – though not before stripping Rome of its bronze statues for shipping to Constantinople.[45] There were the failure of the Avar siege of 626 and the failures of the Ummayad caliphs to blockade the city in 674–678 and in 717–718. These failures helped to ensure that Byzantium did not go the way of other early medieval states with their movable capitals and itinerant courts. Crucial in this respect was the decision of Constantine V to repopulate the city after the devastating plague of 747, and, in 766, to rebuild the sections of the aqueduct which the Avars had destroyed one hundred and forty years earlier. The new settlers were transplanted from Greece and the islands, the construction teams were brought in from all over the provinces, and the food supply of the repopulated city was ensured by fiscal measures which bore heavily on the peasantry.[46] This was a major investment for a ruralized, militarized state whose economic and demographic strength so clearly lay in its provinces. If we follow the chronology of Theophanes, Constantine V waited nine years before repopulating Constantinople after the plague, nine years in which the

---

[43]   Const. Deo auctore, 10.

[44]   E.g. Nov. 14, 1; 80, 9

[45]   The shipment was subsequently captured by the Arabs and taken to Alexandria: Paul the Deacon, Historia Longobardorum, V. 11–13: G. Waitz, ed., MGH SS (Hanover, 1878), 190–192.

[46]   Theoph., 429, 440; Nikephoros, Patriarch of Constantinople, Short History, C. Mango ed. and tr. (Washington, DC, 1990), 140–141, 160–161.

empire had managed to live without an oversize capital city. I have suggested elsewhere that his motive was primarily ideological – to prove himself worthy of his baptismal name, and of the epithet New Constantine with which he was acclaimed by the iconoclast council of 754, the year before his repopulation of the city.[47]

The refoundation of Constantinople by Constantine V began a period of demographic recovery and building activity which continued until 1204. The pull of the capital was perhaps more intense than ever now that the competition had been all but eliminated; the sack of Thessalonike in 904 was a major blow to the only serious competitor. The fact that Constantinople remained inviolate contributed to its allure in more than one way: it validated and demonstrated the mystical identity between the city and its supernatural patron, the Virgin Mother of God; and it meant that the city continued, on balance, to accumulate more and more of the treasures for which it was famous. A series of medieval emperors – Basil I, Leo VI, Romanos I, Constantine VII, Nikephoros II, John I, Manuel I, Isaac II – added to the store of holy relics and other trophies. Although much of the gold and silver which came into the city went out again in the form of salaries, subsidies, tributes and diplomatic gifts, much remained in the form of gifts to churches which could not, in principle, be touched. Emperors who did touch them in moments of emergency made themselves very unpopular. Visitors were told that a third or more of the world's wealth was contained in the city.[48] This sounds like an urban myth, but it made sense of what the visitors saw, and it expressed a version of the truth contained in Michael Choniates's complaint that Constantinople took all the good things of this world and gave nothing in return.[49]

The whole development of the Byzantine state from 755 increased the importance of Constantinople, in both relative and absolute terms. This was as true of the territorial contraction of the late eleventh century as it had been of the territorial expansion of the previous two hundred years. The Turkish conquest of Asia Minor obliged provincial élites to move to the Balkans. Not all settled in Constantinople – the Manasses family, for

---

[47] P. Magdalino, 'The Distance of the Past in Early Medieval Byzantium (VII–X Centuries)', *Ideologie e pratiche del reimpiego nell'alto medioevo. Settimane di studio del Centro Italiano di studi sull'Alto Medioevo* 46 (1999), 115–146, at 138–145.

[48] See K.N. Ciggaar, 'Une description de Constantinople dans le *Tarragonensis* 55', *REB* 53 (1995), 119; Robert of Clari, *La Conquête de Constantinople*, P. Lauer, ed. (Paris, 1924), §81, 80–81.

[49] See above, note 8.

instance, were moved by Romanos IV from Adramyttion to Peristasis on the Gallipoli peninsula.[50] But the senior eastern clergy, including the patriarch of Antioch, were established in Constantinople, and on the whole the relocated Eastern aristocracy were far more court and Constantinople based than they had been in their native habitat. Of the families which made up the top drawer of the aristocracy under the Komnenoi, only those from Adrianople and Trebizond clearly maintained their provincial roots. In other words, the loss of central and eastern Anatolia enabled the Komnenoi to bring the centralization of the Roman Empire to its logical conclusion. At no previous time in the empire's history had its ruling class and the ownership of its resources been so disproportionately concentrated in the capital. The political ideology of eleventh- and twelfth-century Byzantium has been aptly described in terms of 'patriotisme grec et orthodoxe et polarisation constantino-politaine'. There was both greater emphasis on *eugeneia*, and on Constantinople as the source of it, as the only place where the γένος Ῥωμαίων, with the purple-born imperial children at its core, was truly at home.[51]

So it is not accidental that the sounds of Constantinopolitan snobbery and insularity reach a crescendo around 1204, nor is it coincidence that in this year Constantinople finally lost the inviolability which had made it the exclusive place to be. Heard in the context of the Fourth Crusade, the voices of Balsamon, Eustathios, the Choniates brothers and the patriarch Germanos are telling us that Constantinople fell because it had excluded the outside world, because it had alienated all its potential sources of deliverance. Heard in the context of the sequel, they are also telling us something else: the detachment worked both ways, and made the provinces capable of standing by themselves, as the territorial bases of imperial governments in exile, two at the extremities and one near the heart of the Byzantine world. The success of these successor states lay in their ability to graft refugee elements from Constantinople on to the structures of provincial society. The most successful of the three, Nicaea, was the one which made the least effort to recreate Constantinople in exile; as is well known, its troubles began almost as soon as it recovered Constantinople from the Latins.

---

[50] See C.M. Mazzucchi, 'Longino in Giovanni di Sicilia, con un inedito di storia, epigrafia e toponomastica di Cosma Manasse dal Cod. Laurenziano LVII 5', *Aevum* 64 (1990), 193–194.

[51] H. Ahrweiler, *L'idéologie politique de l'empire byzantin* (Paris, 1975), 67; Magdalino, *Tradition and Transformation*, nos I and XIV.

The provincial successor states flourished because local resources were invested locally during the period of exile. Yet they also undoubtedly owed something to the pre-existing vitality of provincial society. The empire of Nicaea reaped the benefits of the work of repopulation that the Komnenoi, especially John and Manuel, had carried out in western Asia Minor. Alexander Kazhdan pointed out that by the end of the twelfth century, Constantinople no longer held a monopoly in the production of manufactured goods,[52] and David Jacoby has developed this thesis in his study of the silk industry in Greece.[53] Twelfth-century writers show occasional flashes of pride in their local *patrides*, as when the Choniates brothers write of Chonai, Euthymios Tornikes of Thebes, and John Apokaukos of Naupaktos.[54]

Thus the evidence for Constantinopolitan exclusivism must be heard against a backgound of ambivalent provincial attitudes towards the metropolis, in which traditional reverence was mixed with resentment at the status of this city which literally did not produce the goods. The chorus of twelfth-century voices heralds the reversal of roles in 1204, which would make Constantinople the great outsider and turn Queen City into Strumpet City. The image is suggested by Niketas Choniates, who uses it to denounce the frequent changes in imperial power before 1204, though he does not apply it directly to Constantinople.[55] Yet like the concept of Queen City, it had a long history. John Mauropous had used it in 1061, in a way which suggests that it was part of the standard repertoire of churchmen preaching repentance in moments of adversity.[56] It naturally entered into thinking about the Apocalypse; ever since the fall of Old Rome, Constantinople had been a prime candidate for the role of Babylon the Great.[57]

---

[52] A.P. Kazhdan and A. Wharton Epstein, *Change in Byzantine Culture in the Eleventh and Twelfth Centuries* (Berkeley and Los Angeles, 1985), 39ff.

[53] D. Jacoby, 'Silk in Western Byzantium before the Fourth Crusade', BZ 84–85 (1991–1992), 452–500 (reprinted with additions in D. Jacoby, *Trade, Commodities and Shipping in the Medieval Mediterranean* (Aldershot, 1997), no.VII).

[54] See Magdalino, *Tradition and Transformation*, no. XIV, 8, 15.

[55] van Dieten, ed., 498–499. In his lament on the capture of the City (576ff.) Choniates develops the image of a wronged but virtuous woman.

[56] P. de Lagarde, ed., *Iohannis Euchaitorum metropolitae quae in Vat. Gr. 676 supersunt* (Göttingen, 1882; repr. Amsterdam, 1979), 169.

[57] Andreas of Caesarea, J. Schmid, ed., *Studien zur Geschichte des griechischen Apokalypse-Textes*, I (Munich, 1955), 201–202; *Life of Andrew the Fool*, Rydén, ed. and tr., I, 278–279 and n. 79; cf. G. Podskalsky, *Byzantinische Reichseschatologie* (Munich, 1972), 86–90.

I began this paper by alluding to the caricature of the *New Yorker's* view of the world. I shall conclude by pointing out that Constantinople was the equivalent, in modern terms, of New York and Washington combined, and that both those cities are deeply abhorrent to the moral majority of the United States. Let me close with the following question: who is the real insider – is it the slick urban sophisticate, the *politikos*, as Kekaumenos would have called him, or is it the country boy from the Bible Belt and the ἔξω χῶραι, who comes to the big city, gets cheated by the immigrant traders and laughed at by the chattering classes, and goes away convinced of the moral superiority of small-town life?

12. Patron Imagery from the Fringes of the Empire.

Lyn Rodley

One of the most immediate and compelling sources of information for both the appearance and the personal aspirations of individuals from the Byzantine past comes from the representations of themselves with which they embellished the works of art and architecture they commissioned. Such images have a wide chronological range, appearing at least by the sixth century and still evident well into post-Byzantine times, but most of the examples we have are from the middle and late Byzantine periods (particularly the eleventh to fourteenth centuries), reflecting the higher survival rate of works of this period generally. They are most often found in monumental art and illuminated manuscripts (probably because the common feature of these otherwise dissimilar vehicles is that of available space: an area of narthex or nave wall in the church, an extra page or two in the manuscript).[1] I shall be concerned here with the images in monumental art, since the chief relevance of this topic in the context of the 'Byzantine outsider' is that most of these are in churches of the Byzantine provinces, rather than the metropolis,[2] so it is on evidence from the outside, rather than the core, that exploration of this particular aspect of patronage depends. Further, the question of whether distance from the

---

[1]   Patron images occasionally appear in other contexts: on crosses, reliquaries, icons or their frames. See, generally, N. Ševčenko, 'Close Encounters: Contact between Holy Figures and the Faithful as represented in Byzantine Works of Art' in A. Guillou and J. Durand, eds, *Byzance et les images* (Paris, 1994), 257–285. For patron images in manuscript illumination, see I. Spatharakis, *The Portrait in Byzantine Illuminated Manuscripts* (Leiden, 1976).

[2]   The imperial images in Hagia Sophia form the main body of evidence for monumental patron imagery in Constantinople, and although certainly in the same stable, these form a special category. For these images, see T. Whittemore, *The Mosaics of Hagia Sophia at Istanbul* (Paris and Boston, 1933–1952); P.A. Underwood and E.J.W. Hawkins, 'The Mosaics of Hagia Sophia at Istanbul. The Portrait of the Emperor Alexander', *DOP* 5 (1961), 189–215; N. Oikonomides, 'Leo VI and the Narthex Mosaic of Saint Sophia', *DOP* 30 (1976), 151–172.

From *Strangers to Themselves: The Byzantine Outsider*, ed. Dion C. Smythe. Copyright © 2000 by the Society for the Promotion of Byzantine Studies. Published by Ashgate Publishing Ltd, Gower House, Croft Road, Aldershot, Hampshire, GU11 3HR, Great Britain.

metropolis had any bearing upon such imagery deserves to be asked (even though the answer is that it probably did not).

Patron images are often found in provincial 'pockets', such as in the cave churches of Cappadocia,[3] the small churches of central and northern Greece[4] (particularly in Kastoria[5]) and in churches on Cyprus.[6] This distribution of course reflects various circumstances which allowed the structures containing the images to survive, rather than the original distribution of patron images, but its widespread nature is relevant to exercises of comparison, in the sense that images made in areas so distant from one another are unlikely to have any direct connection (such as travelling artists, or even travelling patrons). Recurrent features, therefore, particularly when they appear over a long chronological period, probably represent empire-wide tradition rather than regional developments. Such comparison does, indeed, yield a common iconographic vocabulary for patron images, the most easily identifiable element of which is the figure of the patron, usually standing, holding a model of the church in which the image is located; he/she presents this model to a divine figure, usually Christ or the Virgin, sometimes a saint.[7] Another basic type shows the patron without a church-model, simply standing or kneeling in the presence of a divine figure, usually with hands raised in a gesture of supplication. In most cases, with or without church-model, the patrons are drawn to a smaller scale than the divine figure. Although, as noted above, most surviving patron imagery is middle late Byzantine, these iconographic types are of long pedigree and can be found in examples going back to the early Byzantine period.[8] The

---

[3] In Yusuf Koç Kilise (Avçılar); Karabulut K., Chapels 5a, 10, 18, 21, 22, 23, 28, 29, 33 (Göreme); Karşı K. (Gülşehir), Balkam Dere Chapel 3 (Ortahisar); Kırk Dam Altı K. (Peristrema valley), Selime Kalesi (Selime); Ballık K., Belli K., Canavar K., Karabaş K. (Soğanlı valley); Ayvalı K., Pigeon House Church (Çavuşin). For illustrations, see G. de Jerphanion, *Les églises rupestres de Cappadoce. Une nouvelle province de l'art byzantin* (Paris, 1925–1934) and M. Restle, *Byzantine Wall Painting in Asia Minor* (Shannon, 1967).

[4] S. Kalopissi-Verti, *Dedicatory Inscriptions and Donor Portraits in 13th-Century Churches of Greece* (Vienna, 1992).

[5] S. Pelekanides and M. Chatzedakis, *Kastoria* (Athens, 1985).

[6] A. and J.A. Stylianou, 'Donors and dedicatory inscriptions, Supplicants and Supplications in the Painted Churches of Cyprus', *JÖB* (1960), 97–128.

[7] A parallel iconography appears in manuscript illumination, where the patron presents a book: a famous example is found on f. 2v of the Bible of Leo the *sakellarios* (Vat. Reg. Gr. 1): Spatharakis, *Portrait*, pl. 1.

[8] For example, in San Vitale, Ravenna (548) Bishop Ecclesius presents a model of the church to Christ: A. Paolucci, *Ravenna* (Florence, 1971), 42. Several patrons, in various attitudes of supplication, were present in the sixth-century mosaic panels of the nave

nature of patronage recorded by means of a donor image varies, and is often something less than responsibility for the entire establishment. Thus, in many instances more than one patron figure appears in a single building, each in its own iconographical context: at Yusuf Koç Kilise in Avçılar (Cappadocia), for example, three patrons are shown in separate panels and probably represent three individuals who made contributions to the church.[9]

My interest in this imagery began over twenty years ago with an attempt to derive specific meanings for the various iconographical types found in the patron images of Cappadocian cave churches – the precise significance, for example, of a standing figure as opposed to a kneeling one (each of the three figures in Yusuf Koç Kilise is represented in a different attitude), or the relationship between the icongraphic type and the wording of supplicatory inscriptions. I found then, and continue to find, when widening the survey beyond Cappadocia, that the more examples scrutinised, the less likely it seems that any general taxonomic principles apply. It is not even possible to infer that a patron holding a model of the church was responsible for building it, since there are several instances in which an inscription clearly specifies that the model-holder simply renovated or decorated the church. (The model, in fact, designates the *ktetor*, who may be the initial founder of a church or monastery, and therefore responsible for its fabric, but could equally well be a re-founder, applying his resources to the patronage of an existing establishment, often one in decline or disrepair.[10]) This conclusion is not, however, a dead end: Stoppard's philosopher in *Jumpers* notes that all the observable phenomena associated with a train leaving Paddington could also be accounted for by Paddington leaving the train, and I find a similar adjustment of viewpoint useful in this context. Byzantine patron imagery certainly drew upon a standard iconographical vocabulary, but used it very flexibly to produce various meanings, reflecting a wide range of patron behaviour and, on occasion, the personality of individual patrons. (Perhaps this is nowhere so evident as in the late twelfth-century hermitage of St Neophytos at Paphos, Cyprus where, in addition to a

---

arcade in St Demetrios, Thessakonike: R.S. Cormack, 'The Mosaic Decoration of St Demetrios, Thessaloniki', *ABSA* 64 (1969), 17–52.

[9]   L. Rodley, *Cave Monasteries of Byzantine Cappadocia* (Cambridge, 1986), 157; dating of the church to the mid-eleventh century is based upon the style of its paintings.

[10]   Indeed, the phrase 'from the foundations' (ἐκ τῶν βάθρων), which is found in many dedicatory inscriptions, may be included specifically to avoid ambiguity as to whether a *ktetor* is a builder or renovator.

conventional image of Neophytos kneeling before Christ, there is another, unique one, showing Neophytos borne up to heaven by a pair of angels.[11])

A frequent elaboration of the basic vocabulary just noted shows the patron as part of a family group, with spouse, and sometimes children, and the circumstances of the commission are enlarged upon in inscriptions, either alongside the images, or elsewhere (often in a 'lintel' panel above the interior face of the main entrance), or both. This is the formula used at St Demetrios, Dali (Cyprus) where such a lintel panel states that the church was renovated and painted at the expense of Michael, son of Katzouroubes, and his wife and children in 1317. Michael offers a model of the church to Christ (a half figure in the top right-hand corner of the field) and his wife stands behind him (fig. 1); one inscription in the field names the pair and mentions their children (not depicted) and another, bottom right, makes a plea that Michael should be relieved of his heartburn.[12] It is usually the case that the man of the family is clearly the chief patron in groups like this, but there are exceptions, as in Kırk Dam Altı Kilise, Belisirma (Cappadocia) where figures of Basil and Tamar flank St George, but it is Tamar who holds the church model (fig. 2), and an inscription on the nave ceiling attributes to her also the donation of a vineyard.[13] The date of this church is given by the first inscription, which says that the work was done in the time of the Seljuk sultan Masut and the Byzantine emperor Andronikos, placing it somewhere between 1283 and 1295 (and also reflecting the political circumstances of late thirteenth-century Anatolia).[14]

Sometimes, however, more complex arrangements of family patronage are represented. At the cave church of Karabaş Kilise in Cappadocia, the lintel inscription says that the church was redecorated by Michael Skepides, *protospatharios*, Ekaterine the nun and Nyphon the monk, in 1060/61.[15] Each of these three is depicted in the church, and there are several more images of persons not named in the lintel inscription (fig. 3). Michael Skepides (a) in secular dress, is on the west face of an arch in the south wall (probably originally a niche, with a

---

[11] C. Mango and E.J.W. Hawkins, 'The Hermitage of St Neophytos and its Wall Paintings', *DOP* 20 (1966), 119–206, figs 66, 93, pl. facing page 166.

[12] A. and J.A. Stylianou, *The Painted Churches of Cyprus* (London, 1985), 425–426.

[13] N. Thierry, *Nouvelles églises rupestres de Cappadoce. Région du Hasan Daği* (Paris, 1963), 201–213, pl. 94.

[14] S. Vryonis, 'Another Note on the Inscription of the Church of St George of Beliserama', *Byzantina* 9 (1977), 11–22.

[15] Rodley, *Cave Monasteries*, 196–202.

divine figure in the main field, to whom Michael gestures); Ekaterine (b), dressed as a nun, is on the west face of a niche in the north wall, with a man in secular dress (d) opposite her on the east face (inscription lost), and St Katherine with small figures Eirene and Maria is in the main field (c). In a niche to the right of this one is a large figure of the Archangel Michael, with elderly figures of Nyphon the monk, and Eudokia kneeling at his feet (e). Yet another figure, Basil the priest (f), not mentioned in the lintel inscription, appears next to the Virgin and Child in a further small niche on the north wall. The church is part of a small complex, probably a hermitage which grew over a period of about one hundred and fifty years to accommodate a small monastic community, and it would appear that the Skepides family was responsible for the final layer of church decoration, which is the one bearing their images. The ages and groupings of figures suggest that Michael Skepides was the principal donor and the elderly couple Nyphon and Eudokia his parents; Ekaterine and Basil may have been Michael's siblings, and the others in Ekaterine's niche her husband and children. Whether or not every detail of this analysis is correct, the programme as a whole would seem to represent a family concern with the Karabaş site, with patron imagery adjusted to represent the differences of status of the various family members, in particular that two of them were in monastic retirement (or perhaps dead, having taken the monastic habit shortly beforehand).[16]

Another mid eleventh-century Cappadocian example may offer evidence of group patronage independent of family ties. Karanlık Kilise, the church of a cave monastery in Göreme valley, has, like Karabaş, several patron images (fig. 4): John *entalmatikos* and another man (possibly Genethlios) both in secular dress (a), kneel before Christ in a scene of the Benediction of the Apostles in the narthex; Nikephoros the priest and another man (b) kneel before Christ enthroned in the main apse. In the centre bay of the north wall two small figures, apparently male juveniles, flank the archangel Gabriel (c); this group is mirrored by a similar pair flanking the archangel Michael on the south wall (d).[17] Here, therefore, is a mixture of adults, secular and clerical, and children, but in this case all the figures are male. The programme therefore either

---

[16] For patronage of monasteries generally, see R. Morris, *Monks and Laymen in Byzantium, 843–1118* (Cambridge, 1995), 123–130 for the adoption of the monastic life in terminal illness. I think it unlikely that the two members of the Skepides family retired to the Karabaş Kilise complex itself, particularly since they were monk and nun.

[17] Rodley, *Cave Monasteries*, 53–56. Of the four figures with archangels, only one has the head surviving: this is beardless, without headdress.

represents an act of patronage in which the male members of a family acted alone, or one which was not associated with a single family at all, but represents a group of another kind, such as a confraternity.[18]

At Karabaş Kilise, the patron imagery indicated that some members of the family had entered monastic retirement at the time of the donation. At the church of the Anargyroi in Kastoria, the patron images actually seem to record such a transition. The church, which was renovated and repainted at the end of the twelfth century,[19] has an inscription on the east wall of the narthex, over the entrance to the *naos*, naming one Theodore Lemniotes as the patron responsible. An image on the south wall of the north aisle shows Theodore Lemniotes and his son John to the right of the Virgin and Child, and Theodore's wife, Anna Radene, to the left, all named in inscriptions next to the figures (fig. 5a). As it now appears, the painting shows Theodore offering a church model to the Virgin and Child, but this is an adjustment to the original painting, in which he simply had his hands raised in a gesture of supplication. Further alterations included overpainting the original secular robes of Theodore to represent a drab monastic habit and supply him with the tall headdress of a monk. Kyriakoudis suggests that the changes were made when a further image was added, in the south aisle, of an elderly man in monastic habit, inscribed Theophilos Lemniotes, monk, and holding a church-model (fig. 5b). The circumstances proposed to explain these changes are that Theodore and Theophilos are the same man: Theodore repaired and redecorated the church, an action recorded by the west wall inscription and the family patron image; later on, when in old age or near death he became a monk, taking the name Theophilos, the south aisle painting was added. The overpainting of the first image is thus explained as a measure to bring it up to date with Theodore's changed status by altering his costume; the church model was added so that his role as *ktetor* was evident in both images.[20] It may be noted before leaving this

---

[18]   For such groups generally, see P. Horden, 'The Confraternities in Byzantium', in W.J. Sheils and D. Wood, eds, *Voluntary Religion* (Oxford, 1986), 25–45.

[19]   A date at the end of the twelfth century is attributed on the basis of close stylistic similarity with the paintings of Kurbinovo, former Yugoslavia, dated 1199: T. Malmquist, *Byzantine Twelfth-Century Frescoes in Kastoria* (Uppsala, 1979).

[20]   E.N. Kyriakoudis, 'Ο κτίτορας τοῦ ναοῦ τῶν Αγ. Αναργύροι Καστοριᾶς Θεόφιλος Λημνιώτης', *Balkanika Symmeikta* 1 (1981), 3–23. A tall headdress was added also to the figure of Anna, perhaps indicating that both entered monastic life. The church of the Anargyroi demonstrates still further complexities of patronage: in both earlier and later phases of its several layers of painting there are more patron images: S. Pelekanides and M. Chatzedakis, *Kastoria* (Athens, 1985), pls 29 and 40.

example that although Theodore/Theophilos is clearly identified as *ktetor*, the figure of his wife Anna is much larger than those of her husband and son, and we may suspect that there was some reason for his prominence – perhaps that hers was the better pedigree?

Changing circumstances are also indicated by a patron image in the single-naved fourteenth-century church of the Anastasis in Veria, also in north-western Greece. A remarkably detailed lintel inscription on the interior west wall attests that the church was built by one Xenos Psalidas and that his wife Euphrosyne completed the work; the painter was Kallierges, declared the best in the region, and the church was consecrated by the patriarch, in the time of the Emperor Andronikos, in the year 1315.[21] The painted decoration contains no images of Xenos or Euphrosyne – a reminder that the inclusion of patron images was a matter of choice, and many monuments lack them – but on the south wall of the nave there is a figure of a monk, kneeling before St Anthony and St Arsenios (fig. 6), who stand side by side in the file of saints traditionally found in the lowest register in Byzantine painted churches. An inscription next to the monk appears to associate him with a stauropegic monastery (under the authority of the patriarch), but is too fragmentary to be reconstructed. Pelekanides adds to all this the evidence of patriarchal documents of 1314, now in the Great Laura of Mount Athos, which record the granting of a monastery of Christ Soter in Veria to an Athonite priest–monk Ignatios Kalothetos, to be administered by his father Andreas Kalothetos while Ignatios remained on Athos; he suggests, therefore, that the kneeling monk is Kalothetos (father or son).[22] A plausible sequence, therefore, has Xenos Psalidas as the initial patron of the Church of the Anastasis, who died (in 1314?) before the work was finished. His wife Euphrosyne then ceded the church to a patriarchal monastery and ensured the completion of the painted decoration, modifying the programme to include the image of the monk. Conceivably Xenos (or Euphrosyne) had kinship of some kind with the Kalothetos family – perhaps also with the patriarch (Nyphon), given that he consecrated the church. Whatever the relationship, the Psalidas family apparently derived some status-by-association from including the reference to the participation of the patriarch in the consecration of the church.

---

[21]   G.G. Gounaris, *The Church of Christ in Veria* (Thessalonike, 1991).
[22]   S. Pelekanides, Καλλιέργης ὅλης θετταλίας ἄριστος ζωγράφος (Athens, 1973), 12.

Reflected glory may also have been influential in the creation of a group of images in the north-west corner of the Pigeon House Church at Çavuşin, Cappadocia (fig. 7). At the centre of this programme is a large panel on the north wall, showing an archangel with male and female kneeling patrons, probably husband and wife, their inscriptions too damaged to yield names. In the north apse stand the emperor Nikephoros Phokas, his wife Theophano, his father, the Caesar Bardas, his brother Leo the Curopalates and a woman, probably Leo's wife. To the left of the archangel panel, on the north wall, are equestrian figures, also with inscriptions, of the *strategoi* Melias and, probably, John Tzimiskes.[23] The arrangement, and the wording of the inscriptions with the imperial group, suggest that the central couple with the archangel were the patrons of the church, and the inclusion of the imperial family and the generals in its decoration might have been a way of declaring their elevated associations – possibly the couple were relatives of Nikephoros, who came of a Cappadocian family.

'Status-by-association' may also explain cases in which a new programme of decoration acknowledges earlier patrons. At Asinou (Cyprus) a fourteenth-century redecoration of the church of the Panagia Phorbiotissa depicts the twelfth-century founder, on the interior lunette above the south door of the *naos*. Here, Nikephoros *magistros*, proffering a model of the church, is presented to Christ by the Virgin, and an inscription identifies him as the builder of the church (fig. 8a); a small female figure behind him – possibly his wife or daughter – is named as Gephyra, who died in 1099. Nikephoros is mentioned again in an inscription below the southwest lunette of the *naos*, which also dates his work to 1105/6.[24] As noted, both the images and inscriptions relating to this twelfth-century patron are part of a fourteenth-century refurbishment, but precisely who was responsible for this is unclear, since the church has several layers of painting, the dating of some of which is disputed, and there is no documentary evidence to elucidate its history. An inscription alongside a large figure of St George in the narthex credits it to a second patron named Nikephoros and indicates that by the time this work was done (perhaps in the late twelfth/early thirteenth century) the church belonged to a monastery. The narthex also contains a number

---

[23] Melias and John Tzimiskes were generals under Nikephoras Phokas; John Tzimiskes, of course, later became emperor himself. L. Rodley, 'The Pigeon House Church, Çavuşin', *JÖB* 33 (1983), 301–339 and N. Thierry, 'Un portrait de Jean Tzimiskès en Cappadoce', *TM* 9 (1985), 477–484.

[24] Stylianou, *Cyprus*, 114–117.

of patron images, of more than one period, most in separate panels with customary 'servant of God ... ' inscriptions (fig. 8b: three are secular figures: George (with St George), Anastasia Saramalina (with St Anastasia), Anna of Laha (with St Anne) and eight are monks (Kallinikos, Basil, Babylas, Leontios, Laurentios, Germanos, Barnabas and Theophilos)). A family group of husband, wife and son, in Frankish dress, appears with the Virgin and Child in the south lunette. Finally, a fragmentary inscription over the west door of the narthex gives the name Theophilos and the date 1332/3 for another phase of repainting; it is likely that the repainting of the original founder's portrait belongs with this phase.[25] In the absence of contextual information, the relationships of all the people depicted to each other, or to the monastery, are unlikely to be elucidated, but it would appear that, over a period of over two centuries, the monastery attracted the patronage of several individuals or families, some of whom, at least, wished to continue their association with the first founder.

Several components already described appear together in a final example which is very much on the 'fringes of empire'. The chapel of the Panagia Eleousa is built in the shelter of a large cave on the shore of Lake (Great) Prespa.[26] The style of its ornamental, if rustic, brickwork suggests a date no earlier than the fourteenth century for construction, and an inscription on the interior west wall (in a panel at the base of the Dormition of the Virgin) records that it was repainted for three patrons: Kyr Sabas, Kyr Iakobos and Barlaam, all priest–monks. The inscription also gives the date 1410 and the name of a ruler, the *authentes* Vlkašin, but without explaining his connection with the site. A further inscription (at the base of a niche in the south wall) names the priest–monk Ioanikios as painter. Depicted on the south wall of the nave, flanking the Virgin and Child, is a patron couple (fig. 9): a man to the right, presenting a church-model, and a woman to the left, but no inscriptions survive to identify these two.[27] The diversity of the arrangements already seen permits a range of conjecture here. Perhaps the depicted couple were relatives of one (or all?) of the priest–monks named in the west wall inscription. Or perhaps the man of the couple is actually one of those priest–monks, shown in his secular manifestation before adopting the monastic habit.

---

[25]   D.C. Winfield, *Asinou* (Nicosia, 1969), 26–27.

[26]   N. Moutsopoulos, 'Βυζαντινά μνεμεῖα τῆς μεγάλες Πρέσπας', 171–199, in Βυζαντινά Αρθρα καὶ Μελετήματα 1959–1989, *Analekta Blatadon* 51 (1990).

[27]   They may have existed once; the surface of the painting looks 'scrubbed', especially on the lower parts of the wall.

Alternatively, the image of the couple may commemorate the builders of the chapel, which the three priest–monks caused to be redecorated. The name of Vlkašin may have been included to place the commission chronologically, or to reflect the political circumstances of the time, or to establish some connection with an important local dignitary.[28]

In summary, therefore, it is the case that the simple formulas of patron imagery were not bound to prescribed meanings, but were deployed creatively to meet the particular circumstances of each commission, and evidence of such flexibility found from Cappadocia to Macedonia suggests that this was the norm throughout the empire. In most instances, the exact circumstances of patronage cannot be understood unless documentary evidence is available to enlarge upon that of the images themselves. On the strength of this, the question raised at the outset, as to whether provincial patron images differ from metropolitan ones, is likely to have a negative answer. The very small number of non-imperial metropolitan images makes it impossible to decide this with certainty, but the likelihood is that, since there is no rigid formula for provincial images, there was none for metropolitan ones either. The few non-imperial images known from Constantinopolitan churches are of Palaiologan date and conform to the 'basic vocabulary' noted above:[29] a lady kneels before a standing figure of the Virgin and Child in a painting done when the substructure of the tenth-century Myrelaion church was remodelled as a burial chamber;[30] a similar image, but with a male figure holding a scroll, was found in Kalenderhane Camii, in a passage between the *bema* and *diakonikon*;[31] finally, in the lunette of a tomb niche in St Euphemia of the Hippodrome, a cleric kneels to present a church-model to the Virgin and Child.[32] In all these cases the survivals are isolated fragments, the full pictorial context of which is unknown. The only church of the capital that has its decoration, including patron images, reasonably intact is that of the Chora monastery (Kariye Camii) which

---

[28] Even this was not without its problems: a ruler named Vlkašin died in 1371, but the inscription is dated 1410; possibly there was a later ruler of the same name. Moutspoulos, Πρέσπας, 189–192.

[29] And it may be noted in passing that a variety of meanings was also created for the several imperial images in Hagia Sophia, for which see above, note 2.

[30] C.L. Striker, *The Myrelaion (Bodrum Camii) in Istanbul* (Princeton, NJ, 1981), 31, figs 60–62; there may have been other such images in the substructure.

[31] C.L. Striker and Y.D. Kuban, 'Work at Kalenderhane Camii in Istanbul: Second Preliminary Report', *DOP* 22 (1968), 185–194, 192 and fig. 33.

[32] R. Naumann and H. Belting, *Die Euphemia-Kirche am Hippodrome zu Istanbul und ihre Fresken. Istanbuler Forschungen* 25 (1966), 189–193.

was refounded (and virtually rebuilt) by Theodore Metochites, *grand logothete* under Andronikos II, where work was finished by 1321. A famous mosaic lunette in the inner narthex, above the door to the *naos*, shows Theodore, wearing an extraordinary hat and kneeling before the enthroned Christ, presenting a church-model (fig. 10a). An adjacent larger panel to the right (thus on the east wall of the inner narthex) has large figures of Christ and the Virgin accompanied by two small figures (fig. 10b): one, to the right, next to the Virgin, is a kneeling woman, in nun's habit, identified by inscription as Melane the nun, a lady of the Palaiologos family (fig. 10b). This may be either the half-sister or the daughter of Andronikos II and her presence surely indicates that she is an auxiliary patron of some kind, possibly linked by kinship or marriage to Theodore's family. The other small figure represents Isaac Komnenos, son of the emperor Alexios I and a twelfth-century patron of the Chora monastery, and indicates that Theodore Metochites saw something to be gained in acknowledging an earlier imperial patron.[33] Here, therefore, we have a metropolitan example of patronage with several strands to it, much as was the case in the provincial examples noted above. Even what one might suspect to be a provincial trait in the 'status-by-association' pattern seen in some of those provincial examples appears also in the splendid commission of the emperor's chief officer. Perhaps it should be no surprise to find that manifestations of human nature are much the same, whether in the court of Constantinople or a cave on Lake Prespa.

---

[33] P.A. Underwood, *The Kariye Djami* (New York, 1966), I. 42–43, 45–48; pls 26–29, 36–41.

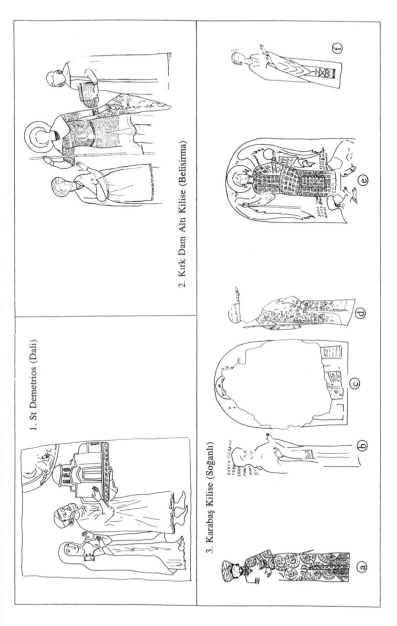

1. St Demetrios (Dali)

2. Kırk Dam Altı Kilise (Belisırma)

3. Karabaş Kilise (Soğanlı)

Plate 12: 1 St Demetrios (Dali) (drawing: Lyn Rodley)
Plate 12:2 Kırk Dam Altı Kilise (Belisirma) (drawing: Lyn Rodley)
Plate 12:3 Karabaş Kilise (Soğanli) (drawing: Lyn Rodley)

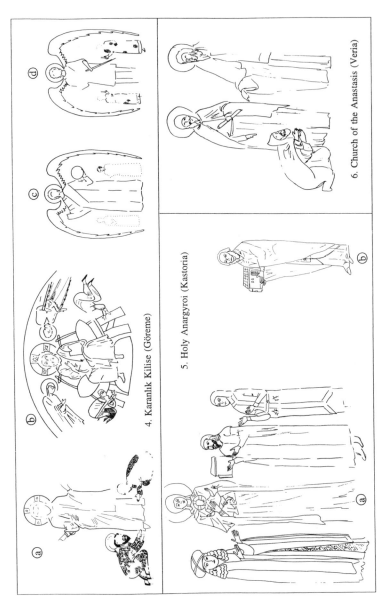

4. Karanlık Kilise (Göreme)

5. Holy Anargyroi (Kastoria)

6. Church of the Anastasis (Veria)

Plate 12:4 Karanlık Kilise (Göreme) (drawing: Lyn Rodley)
Plate 12:5 Holy Anargyroi (Kastoria) (drawing: Lyn Rodley)
Plate 12:6 Church of the Anastasis (Veria) (drawing: Lyn Rodley)

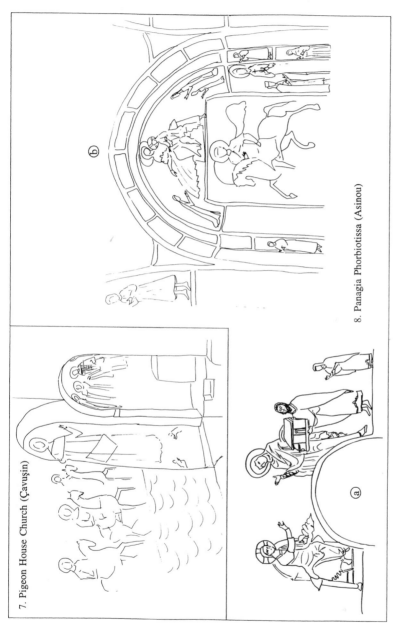

7. Pigeon House Church (Çavuşin)

8. Panagia Phorbiotissa (Asinou)

Plate 12.7 Pigeon House Church (Çavuşin) (drawing: Lyn Rodley)
Plate 12.8 Panagia Phorbiotissa (Asinou) (drawing: Lyn Rodley)

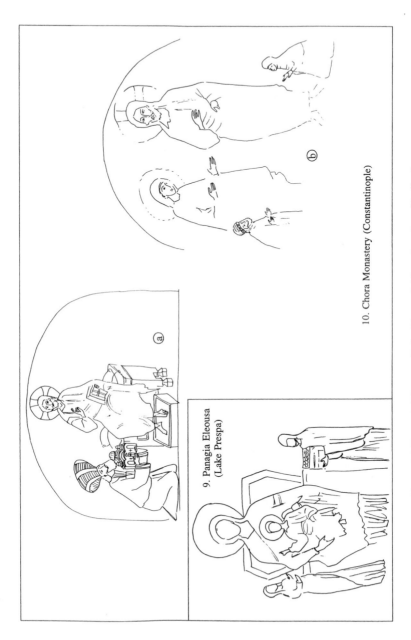

9. Panagia Eleousa
(Lake Prespa)

10. Chora Monastery (Constantinople)

Plate 12:9 Panagia Eleousa (Lake Prespa) (drawing: Lyn Rodley)
Plate 12:10 Chora Monastery (Constantinople) (drawing: Lyn Rodley)

13. The World of Fiction and the World 'Out There': the Case of the Byzantine Novel[*]

Roderick Beaton

The Byzantine novels of the twelfth century,[1] with their recurring story-pattern of elopement, estrangement, exotic trials and eventual homecoming, ought to be revealing of Byzantine attitudes towards these matters. Each one of these novels sends its characters out into a world where the character, formerly an insider in his own, familiar environment, himself becomes the outsider in a series of environments which are variously exotic, strange, and – especially – threatening.

---

[*] I am grateful to Dr Ruth Webb and Professor Elizabeth Jeffreys, both of whom looked over and commented on a version of this paper before it went to press, and additionally to Dr Webb for letting me have the full text of her paper given at the 1995 BSC conference in New York, of which only an abstract has been published (see note 2).

[1] Probably composed between the 1130s (Elizabeth Jeffreys: personal communication) and the 1150s (for this consensus and bibliography see R. Beaton, *The Medieval Greek Romance*, 2nd ed., revd, (London, 1996) 211–112. The four texts are: Prodromos, *Rhodanthe and Dosikles*; Niketas Eugenianos, *Drosilla and Charikles*; Konstantinos Manasses, *Aristandros and Kallithea*; Eustathios Makrembolites, *Hysmine and Hysminias*. The first three are in verse, the fourth in prose; the third survives only in excerpted fragments, and will not be discussed in this paper. For texts of all four, with introduction, notes, and parallel Italian translation, see F. Conca, *Il romanzo bizantino del XII secolo*, Classici UTET (Turin, 1994). All citations in this paper are to this edition. There are also serviceable modern editions of Prodromos's and Eugenianos's novels: see, respectively, M. Marcovich, ed., *Theodori Prodromi, de Rhodanthes et Dosiclis amoribus libri IX* (Stuttgart, 1992); F. Conca, ed., *Nicetas Eugenianus, de Drosillae et Chariclis amoribus*, London Studies in Classical Philology no. 24 (Amsterdam, 1990). Makrembolites's novel has been translated into French and German: see, respectively, F. Meunier, trans., *Eumathios: Les amours homonymes* (Paris, 1991); K. Plepelits, ed. and trans., *Eustathios Makrembolites, Hysmine und Hysminias. Eingeleitet, übersetzt und erläutert*, Bibliothek der griechischen Literatur, no. 29 (Stuttgart, 1989). However, there has been no critical edition of the Greek text since that of Hilberg in 1876. An English translation of all four novels has been prepared by Elizabeth Jeffreys, and is expected to be published shortly.

But if these fictional texts are to be read in this way, we have to eschew any expectation that the novels represent directly the everyday world of their authors and readers. Even when the principal characters are on their home ground at the beginning and end of the story, theirs is a world with which the implied reader is assumed to be familiar, not from daily experience, but from reading. In addition, we have to make full allowance for the fact that these novels are predicated on a genre or type of fiction which had last flourished almost a full millennium before the twelfth-century writers took up the pen. This is not to reiterate the now discredited view that they are nothing more than 'imitations' of the Hellenistic novel.[2] However, in order to see how these novels reinterpret the world for their own time, we have to make full allowance for the generic allusion which is built into every one of them. To make sense, these novels have to be read *against* their Hellenistic predecessors – with which, it is very clear, not only their authors but surely their intended first readers also, were deeply familiar.

We must not therefore expect these novels to give us a direct picture of insider–outsider relationships as they were perceived by educated Byzantines of the twelfth century. Instead, in order to penetrate how these texts conceive of such relationships, we have to read them for their *differences* from the models of the genre which were exemplary for writers and first readers alike.

In order to do this, I propose to use, in slightly modified form, the concept of the 'chronotope' as coined by Mikhail Bakhtin. Bakhtin, in his short book or long essay, 'Forms of Time and of the Chronotope in the Novel: Towards a Historical Poetics',[3] is rare among historians and theorists of the modern novel in the emphasis he places on the starting point of Hellenistic fiction. On the other hand, though he mentions the continuation of that genre in Byzantium, it is clear that even the

---

[2]   On the creative use of their Hellenistic predecessors by the writers of these novels, see, from differing perspectives: M. Alexiou, 'A Critical Reappraisal of Eustathios Makrembolites' *Hysmine and Hysminias*', *BMGS* 3 (1977), 23–43; F. Conca, *Il romanzo* (introduction); C. Jouanno, 'Nicétas Eugénianos, un héritier du roman grec', *Revue des Etudes Grecques* 102 (1989), 346–360; S. MacAlister, 'Ancient and Contemporary in Byzantine Novels', in J. Tatum, ed., *The Search for the Ancient Novel* (Baltimore and London, 1994), 308–322; Beaton, *Romance*, 52–88; R. Webb, 'Re-Writing and Re-Reading the Greek Novel: Eustathios Makrembolites and the Metamorphoses of the Text' (BSC Abstracts, 1995).

[3]   M.M. Bakhtin, *The Dialogic Imagination: Four Essays*, in M. Holquist, ed. and trs. C. Emerson and M. Holquist, University of Texas Press Slavic Series no. 1, (Austin, TX, 1981), 84–258.

prodigiously read Bakhtin had not looked at the twelfth-century texts, and is content to repeat the dismissive verdict of Erwin Rohde.

Bakhtin's definitions are notorious, but the chronotope, as I understand it, stands for the distinctive configuration of time and space that defines 'reality' within the world of a text, *as conceptualized within that world itself*. It is in this sense that Bakhtin characterizes the Hellenistic novel as 'the adventure novel of ordeal'.[4] Its plot takes place in 'adventure-time';[5] the world in which the hero and heroine endure their adventures is 'an alien world in adventure-time';[6] it is because this world of adventure is so 'abstract' that it appears to be ruled (as all commentators on the genre agree) by Chance.[7] This chronotope (or subgenre: Bakhtin does not distinguish) is summed up in terms of affirmation through test. And it is a sufficiently basic chronotope that it is frequently revived, or used in multifarious ways, according to Bakhtin, throughout the whole subsequent history of the European novel.

It is characteristic of this perceptual configuration of space and time, as Bakhtin conceives it, that within it, space is interchangeable ('what happens in Babylon could just as well happen in Egypt or Byzantium and vice versa'), and so is time ('adventure-time leaves no defining traces and is therefore in essence reversible').[8] It is in this way, although Bakhtin does not make this fully explicit, that 'adventure-time' is distinguished from biographical or historical time. And this is not a distinction between fiction and fact, imagination and truth, as becomes clear when Bakhtin contrasts the 'adventure-time' which makes up almost the whole of the narrative in the Greek novels with the no less fictional moments of what he calls 'biographical life' and 'biographical time' that frame it. Such are the meeting and falling in love, at the beginning of the hero's and heroine's adventures, and the marriage at their end, moments to which Bakhtin attributes 'biographical significance'. The entire chronotope of adventure, then, lies in the 'gap, the pause, the hiatus that appears between these two strictly adjacent biographical moments'.[9]

---

[4]   Bakhtin, *Dialogic Imagination*, 86.
[5]   Bakhtin, *Dialogic Imagination*, 87 and passim.
[6]   Bakhtin, *Dialogic Imagination*, 89; 102.
[7]   Bakhtin, *Dialogic Imagination*, 101; 95ff.
[8]   Bakhtin, *Dialogic Imagination*, 100.
[9]   Bakhtin, *Dialogic Imagination*, 89. Compare J.J. Winkler, who approaches the ancient novel from a quite different perspective: 'In fact the entire form of the Greek romance can be considered an elaboration of the period between initial desire and final consummation', J.J. Winkler, 'The Invention of Romance', in Tatum, ed., *Search*, 23–38, citation from page 28.

'Biographical time' and 'adventure-time' may therefore each be more or less fictional. The former has no necessary connection to any *real* biography or historical context, but is distinguished from the latter by the way the relations of space and time are conceived.

Let us now see how the conceptualization or construction of space and time in the Byzantine novels compares with the equivalent phenomenon in their generic models of Hellenistic times.

Modifying Bakhtin's account of the ancient novel only slightly, we can show that it actually depends on the contrast between two different time-spaces, which are marked by a radical disjunction between them. These, to stay so far as possible within Bakhtin's terminology, we can term 'adventure time-space' and 'biographical time-space'. The first (adventure time-space, which is the characteristic domain of all the Hellenistic novels and defines what Bakhtin calls their 'chronotope') can be glossed as that in which 'anything can happen anywhere, in any order'. In adventure time-space all is ruled by Chance (or the whim of the author, which for the inhabitants of that time-space is the same thing), but nothing, not even apparent death, is irrevocable. That is what Bakhtin means by describing this construction of time as 'reversible'. By contrast, in 'biographical time-space', events have what Bakhtin terms 'significance': they have irreversible consequences, they define the movement of a biographical subject through time, which in turn is part of the uniquely unfolding process of history. (Once again, it is of no importance whether the biographical subject is a real person or an invented one; what matters is that for that subject, events have consequences.) Not surprisingly, of these two time-spaces, the one which is the more familiar to the reader, as it is also the one in which the fictional characters are at home, is biographical time-space. (Even in the ancient novel, this time-space is placed at some historical and usually also geographical distance from the production of the text itself.) Biographical time-space is fictional time-space, but it functions more or less *like* the time-space in which the story is being narrated and (it is to be assumed) also read.

To simplify the pattern somewhat, in each of the five Hellenistic novels that we possess entire,[10] hero and heroine set out at the beginning of their adventures from a given point in space and time. At the end of all

---

[10] Chariton of Aphrodisias, *Chaireas and Callirhoe*, Xenophon of Ephesus, *Ephesiaca*; Longus, *Daphnis and Chloe*; Achilles Tatius, *Leucippe and Clitophon*; Heliodorus, *Aethiopica* (English translations of these and other related and fragmentary works collected in B.P. Reardon, *Collected Ancient Greek Novels* (Berkeley, CA, 1989)).

the mishaps and trials of their love for one another, they return to the same place and the (according to Bakhtin) 'adjacent' moment of time in their 'real', biographical lives, at which point the narrative ends.

How, then, is this pattern modified by the Byzantine continuators of the genre?

With varying degrees of fictionality, and of emphasis, the world in which the heroes and heroines of the twelfth-century novels are at home (the world of their biographical time-space) is an antiquarian construct, a composite Greek world which precedes Christianity and knows nothing even of the Roman Empire, of which Byzantium was the official continuation. As many textual allusions make abundantly clear, this is a world 'familiar' to writers and implied readers through the classical education of the Byzantine élite; and just as in the ancient novels, it stands in implicit contrast with the world of adventures into which the protagonists are precipitated when once they have transgressed its boundaries.

By contrast, the world of adventure time-space in the three twelfth-century novels which we possess complete presents a surprising amount of variation. Theodore Prodromos in *Rhodanthe and Dosikles*, once he has launched his pair of lovers into an alien world of adventures, seems almost relieved to be able to forget them altogether for almost a third of the length of the text, as he concentrates his efforts on the intrigues, embassies, speeches and battles of their successive captors. The effect, in *Rhodanthe and Dosikles*, is to marginalize the protagonists: the love that is all-important to them in their own biographical time-space, in the fictional adventure-world 'out there', in which battles and cities are won and lost, comes to seem almost insignificant. There are good reasons for thinking that whatever motivated the prolific and versatile Prodromos to take up the challenge of writing in this genre, it was not an overwhelming dedication to the 'love interest' of his theme.

Niketas Eugenianos, in *Drosilla and Charikles*, who in many respects follows Prodromos faithfully, conspicuously puts this to rights: both in biographical and adventure time-space the lyrical element is brought to the fore, and for much of the extended sabre-rattling and bloodthirsty episodes of Prodromos's adventure-time Eugenianos substitutes the bathos and buffoonery of a Theocritan idyll gone wrong. But the most radical departure, in this as in much else, as we shall, is made by Eustathios Makrembolites in *Hysmine and Hysminias*. This time, it is not until more than half-way through the text that the conventional elopement displaces the hero and heroine from their own familiar world into that of adventure-time.[11] And just over one book later, all the obligatory episodes of violence and terror having been compressed into that space, the hero is returned to a time-space (still in adventure-time, to be sure) in which places and events will closely and ironically mirror those of his and the heroine's lives in their familiar, (biographical) world.

The strict formal organization of space and time in the fictional world of this novel has been noticed before.[12] Summarizing the action solely in these terms, the novel's structure can be divided into three parts:

> I (Books I–VI = 54% of text). Hysminias, chosen by lot as herald as part of a religious festival, travels from his home town of Eurykomis to Aulikomis where he is entertained by the family of Hysmine with whom he falls in love. Both families return to Eurykomis for the conclusion of the festival, at which point it is announced that on her return to Aulikomis, Hysmine is to be married off.

> II (Books VII–VIII 15 = 15% of text). The pair elope from Hysminias's home town by ship; at sea they are separated and Hysminias is a victim of piracy and warfare before becoming a slave in a well-to-do household in the town of Dafnepolis.

> III (Books VIII 16–XI = 32% of text). It is festival time again, and Hysminias's master is sent as a herald to another town, Artykomis. Hysminias, as a slave, goes along to serve him in the household of his hosts. In this household, he finds Hysmine, also a slave. As slaves, the pair reclaim their love for one another and finally, thanks to the timely intervention of their respective parents, Hysminias and Hysmine regain

---

[11] This happens at VII 4. The novel is divided into eleven books of roughly similar length; or by a count of pages, 54% of the way through the text.

[12] See Alexiou, 'A Critical Reappraisal', which also contains the fullest plot-summary in English. Alexiou adopts the methodology of Tomas Hägg, *Narrative Technique in Ancient Greek Romances* (Stockholm, 1971), for the Hellenistic novels, to demonstrate how the greater part of the text represents the events of only a small number of days, with an interval of a year in the middle. For the dislocation in time and space that separates the first part of the novel from the events of its third part that run in parallel, see Beaton, *Romance*, 83–84.

their freedom and return to the latter's home town to be married.

Just over half the entire length of this novel is devoted to representing a time-space that in Bakhtin's terms can only be termed biographical. The action of Books I–VI is markedly without adventures of the kind that traditionally characterize the kind of 'adventure-time' traditional to this genre. With unprecedented psychological subtlety, the stage-by-stage progression of the biographical (and irreversible) experience of falling in love is represented in these books. Although marked off from the routines of daily life by the ceremonial of a religious festival, and involving a complementary displacement of first the hero and then the heroine (in the ritual journeys first from Eurykomis to Aulikomis and then from Aulikomis to Eurykomis), none the less the environment in which this process of falling in love takes place cannot be equated with the exotic, threatening world of adventure-time, but belongs rather to the world in which these characters have led their lives so far. The exotic and the adventurous do indeed exist in this long first half of the novel; but they are located not in a never-never world 'out there', but in the dreams experienced by the hero–narrator Hysminias.

In terms of space and time, then, the journeys in the first part of this novel (between the home towns of hero and heroine) belong to biographical, not to adventure time-space. Hysmine's home town of Aulikomis, to which Hysminias travels as herald and from which he returns home again, with Hysmine, before the elopement that will finally open the door to adventure time-space, is strange and wonderful to Hysminias (as perhaps Eurykomis is to her, although, since it is Hysminias who tells the story, we are not told this); but the heroine, throughout most of this first part of the novel, is on her own home ground. And since what Hysminias experiences there is the carefully staged process of falling in love, Aulikomis, no less than Eurykomis, turns out to belong decisively to biographical time-space for him too. What happens to him is not 'reversible'. Neither could it be happening just as well at any other place or any other time than this.

If we look back at the schematic division of the novel above, two unprecedented characteristics of the adventures which follow the lovers' elopement are immediately apparent. The first is the almost perfunctory extent into which many of the longest-established types of adventure in the genre are compressed: only one and a half of the novel's eleven books, or 15% of the text. By half-way through Book VIII, Hysminias's travels are largely over. All the remaining adventures, which traditionally take the form of trials of his and Hysmine's constancy, are distributed, in space, between the alternating sites of Dafnepolis and Artykomis, until the final return to the familiar, biographical axis (Eurykomis/Aulikomis) at the very end, and concentrated, in time, into a finite number of days.

There is a strong hint, in the compressed second part of the novel, that the traditional components of the lovers' ordeal in adventure time-space are for the first time in the genre *explicitly* (and playfully) understood to be what, at a certain level of interpretation, they perhaps always were: namely externalizations of inner experiences or processes.

This hint is confirmed when we move on to the third part of the narrative. Structurally speaking, the second half of Book VIII is transitional, explaining as it does how Hysminias comes to be a slave in the household of the unnamed herald at Dafnepolis, and, significantly, both specifying and mystifying the precise dislocation in both time and space which separates the festivals at Dafnepolis and Artykomis (which belong to the alien world of adventure time-space) from those of the protagonists' familiar world of Eurykomis and Aulikomis.

The third part of the narrative gets into its stride with the start of Book IX, when Hysminias's master is chosen to be the herald and to travel to another town (Artykomis) as part of another religious festival. It has already been noticed that the action which begins here, and continues up to the end of the novel, mirrors closely the developing action of the first part, with the significant and frequently signalled difference that, in the first part, hero and heroine were free but enslaved to Eros, whereas now they are degraded as the slaves, not only of Eros, but of human masters as well.[13]

Book IX begins almost exactly as the first book did, with a description of the festival, the drawing of lots, and the journey of the herald and his entourage. But whereas at the ritual banquet in the first part, Hysminias the herald had been the object of advances by Hysmine, the daughter of his host, here, as a slave, he is importuned by Rhodope, the daughter of his *master's* host. Rhodope's advances, it is assumed, are improper not only because Hysminias is already the slave of Eros, who has betrothed him to Hysmine (this Rhodope could not have been expected to know!) but also because the object of her attentions is literally a slave in her father's house (something which Rhodope can see for herself, and here lies the superficial, external proof of her transgression). The symmetry is

---

[13]   Cf. Beaton, *Romance*, 81–84; 212–214.

compounded when Hysminias discovers, on the second day in the house at Artykomis, that one of Rhodope's slavegirls, whose resemblance to Hysmine had troubled him on the first, is indeed Hysmine (how she came there Hysminias, and we, will only learn much later). As the action develops, and on Hysmine's initiative, Hysminias finds himself responding nominally to the advances of Rhodope, but using Hysmine as the pretended intermediary for a progressive affirmation of love which is of course destined for Hysmine alone.

There is much play, in all this, with the ironies and symmetries of freedom and slavery, which certainly has a symbolic dimension, whether or not it is truly allegorical in the Western medieval sense. But, restricting the argument, for present purposes, to the construction of space and time in the narrative, it is clear that the world of 'adventure-time' depicted in Books IX and X, and which becomes re-connected to the world of biographical time and space in the course of Book XI, has been artfully constructed so as to mirror, across a crucial displacement, the characters' own familiar world. The household in which Hysminias finds himself a slave is the mirror-image of the one that he has lost. Similarly, the household of Sostratos and his daughter Rhodope in which he finds Hysmine a slave no less closely mirrors that of her father Sosthenes at Aulikomis. And both Hysminias and Hysmine, as slaves, work their way towards freedom and the affirmation of their love in an environment almost identical to that which they have left behind. The exotic, 'other', or testing element, here, lies not in the strangeness of the adventures which lie in wait for the pair, but in the reversal of *their own* condition, as they experience what is essentially their own familiar environment in an unfamiliar, and highly disadvantageous role.

Conclusion

In *Hysmine and Hysminias*, then, the exotic and the other are to be found no longer in the never-never world of adventures, in the 'gap' between moments of biographical time, as Bakhtin termed the chronotope of the Hellenistic novel. Instead, the traditional ingredients of adventure time-space are downgraded to an almost perfunctory role, and also portrayed with knowing humour.[14] The true – and quite new – territory of the 'other' is to be found, in the first part of the novel, in the dreams and the

---

[14]   This aspect is well analysed by both Alexiou, 'A Critical Reappraisal' and Webb, 'Re-Writing'.

subjective, irreversible, biographical experiences of the individual; in its third part in a world which is the exact mirror-image of the protagonists' familiar world back home, but which is made strange, threatening and testing only by the fact that *they themselves have changed*. They experience as 'other', and are tested (as is traditional in the genre), by a world that is essentially identical to their own, but experienced, this time, from the position not of masters but of slaves.

What we see in the chronotope of the Byzantine novel is a marked domestication of the 'other', which in its inherited, fabulous form is treated to affectionate ridicule, while the true 'other' is seen to reside in the consciousness of the hero–narrator (the dreams of the first part), and in the reversal of status that defamiliarizes an otherwise familiar world (in the third part). The first of these chronologically anticipates, and bears an intriguing relation to, what Bakhtin terms the chronotope of Western medieval fiction.[15] The second (an otherness which consists in the reversal of status) seems to anticipate even later developments in the genre of fiction.

So in this way, based on a reading of the Byzantine novels and especially *Hysmine and Hysminias*, it *is* possible to extrapolate a perception of the 'other' as conceived by a talented and educated writer of the Comnenian court around the middle of the twelfth century. That perception of the 'other', which deserves to be regarded as a radical conceptual innovation at that time, may be succinctly summed up in the phrase of the twentieth-century poet George Seferis:

τὸν ξένο καὶ τὸν ἐχθρό τὸν εἴδαμε στὸν καθρέφτη
the stranger and the enemy: we saw him in the mirror.[16]

---

[15] It is in the context of the chivalric romance ('a miraculous world in adventure-time') that, according to Bakhtin, the strict literal linearity of time begins to be challenged by the subjective, inner experience of dreams. As he puts it: 'Time begins to be influenced by dreams; that is, we begin to see the peculiar distortion of temporal perspectives characteristic of dreams. Dreams no longer function merely as an element of the content, but begin to acquire a form-generating function' (*The Dialogic Imagination*, 154). The kind of writing that Bakhtin describes here did not begin in the West, so far as is known, until the time of Chrétien de Troyes in the 1170s and 1180s, almost certainly some decades after Makrembolites's novel was written.

[16] Giorgos Seferis, *Poiemata* (8th ed., Athens, 1972): 'Mythistorema', sect. 4.

14. Akritis and Outsiders[*]

Elizabeth Jeffreys

In the Byzantine poem *Digenis Akritis*, at the end of the hero's life, Digenis makes a speech of farewell from his deathbed to his beloved wife. He is concerned for her in her coming widowhood. In the Grottaferrata version of the poem he cries out:

> But, my most longed-for Girl, what grief of yours shall I lament?
> How shall I console you? Where am I to leave you, the foreigner?
> (G8.129–130)[1]

Digenis's reference to his wife as a *xene*, a foreigner, a stranger, an outsider, raises questions about the poem's concepts of familial and social relationships. In an earlier passage, which has been more discussed, Digenis is said to choose to live alone (*monos*):

> And he chose to spend his time in solitude on the frontiers,
> taking the girl with him and his own servants.
> For he had a boundless desire to spend his time alone
> and to walk alone with no companion. (G4.956–959)

In the following lines it becomes plain that his desire for solitude, which is also emphasized elsewhere in the poem, does not exclude the presence of his *agouroi*, 'youngsters', a group of fighting retainers, as well as his wife and servants already mentioned. Here again we have a term which demands examination for its implications about the place of an individual in the family and society. This paper proposes to look at lexical clusters in *Digenis Akritis* connected with the words *xenos* and *monos*. Incidentally, it

---

[*] My gratitude, as always, to Michael Jeffreys for his willingness to read and comment.

[1] All translations and quotations are from E.M. Jeffreys, *Digenis Akritis. The Grottaferrata and Escorial versions* (Cambridge, 1998).

will add to recent explorations of the poem's nature through comparison of the very different forms in which it has survived.

Digenis Akritis is preserved in six Greek manuscripts. In the following discussion the four later versions (T, A, P and O), interesting though they are, will be ignored. The focus will be on G and E, the primary versions which, it is now well understood, lie behind the compiled version christened Z by Erich Trapp, from which TAP and O derive.

G – the Grottaferrata version – and E – the Escorial version – are very different from each other and scholarly debate continues over the relationship of the one with the other. It is important to remember, however, that the manuscript in which G survives is to be dated to some time around 1300 and the manuscript in which E survives to some time around 1480. Both versions tell much the same story though there are major variations: G, for example, does not know about Digenis's first encounter with the *apelates*, the unruly band of guerrillas, while E says nothing about the emperor's visit or Digenis's dealings with the daughter of Aploravdis. Set out opposite is the framework of the poem's plot, divided up into the five sections which can be perceived as common to both G and E. The similarities include much wording: there are a dozen or so lines that are virtually identical in each and very many more that reflect each other lexically, syntactically or thematically. From this I, and others, draw the conclusion that a proto-*Digenis*, a simple written text, stands somewhere behind both G and E and is reflected in both. However, blurred as it has been by the transmission processes that have led to the present forms of G and E, this proto-*Digenis* cannot be recreated in any detail. Recent papers have discussed the restricted possibilities available for the reconstruction of particular episodes.[2] It seems to me to be a valid principle that where G and E agree, whether at the level of wording, plot sequence or overall structure, then this common element may be claimed as part of proto-*Digenis*. Where they disagree, then the situation is more complex. It remains a challenge to explore the relationships between these two primary surviving versions and to attempt to glimpse the proto-*Digenis* that lies behind them.

Reverting to the words with which I began, there is a difference in the uses of *xenos* in G and E. E uses it once and G fourteen times, as both

---

[2]   On the opening scenes: R. Beaton, 'An epic in the making? The early versions of Digenis Akrites', in R. Beaton and D. Ricks, eds, *Digenes Akrites: new approaches to Byzantine heroic poetry* (London, 1993), 55–72; on the closing scene: E.M. Jeffreys, 'Digenis and Charos: G and E reconsidered', in C.N. Constantinides et al., eds, *Φιλέλλην, Studies in honour of Robert Browning* (Venice, 1996), 117–131.

Episode	G	E
Lay of the emir		
The emir raids, carries off the girl; her brothers pursue and defeat the emir	1.1–197	[lacuna in E] 1–55
They cannot find girl, emir produces her, converts, marries; birth of DA	1.198–337; 2.1–49	56–224
Emir's mother writes, he quarrels with the brothers, leaves his bride, returns to Syria, converts his mother and returns	2.50–300; 3.1–343	225–609
Romance of DA		
Education of DA	——	610–620
DA visits Philopappous and asks to join the guerrillas	——	621–701
Emir's exploits;	4.1–47;	702–791
education and first hunt of DA	4.48–253	
DA serenades the girl and carries her off	4.254–855	[lacuna in E] 792–1065
The wedding of DA and the gifts	4.856–952	1066–1088
DA on the borders with the girl	4.953–970	1089–1094 1095–1096 DA's parents die
Visit from the emperor	4.971–1093	——
DA's exploits (1st pers. narrative)		
DA's meeting with Aploravdis's daughter	5.1–289	——
Meadow in May, the encounter with the serpent, lion and guerrillas	6.1–175	1097–1196
Defeat of the three guerrillas	6.176–310	1197–1315
Guerrillas summon Maximou and Melimitzis	6.311–475	1316–1420
DA defeats guerrillas and Maximou	6.476–713	1421–1351
DA defeats Maximou again and commits adultery	6.714–805 [lacuna at 785/6]. (6.795–798 kills Maximou)	1352–1605
(end of exploits and 1st p. narrative)		
Palace and garden		
Garden and palace by Euphrates; DA keeps peace on borders	7.1–229 (7.106–55 death and burial of father; 7.189–198 mother)	1606–1659 1660–1694 tomb on bridge
Death		
DA falls ill, recalls his past life with the girl, advises her; they both die	8.1–141 8.142–198	1695–1793 1794–1867
Funeral and mourning	8.199–313 (8.238–244 tomb at Trusis)	——

adjective and noun. As an adjective it has the meaning 'extraordinary', 'marvellous', or even 'bizarre', and is applied to Digenis's appearance, the girl's singing, a garden, a room and so on. E normally has no equivalent phrase at these points (G's descriptions are regularly more elaborate) though *xenocharagos* (1632) appears once, referring to the wall around Digenis's garden.

As a noun G uses *xenos*, or rather *xene*, twice to refer to the girl, Digenis's bride; both references occur in the deathbed scene. The first I quoted just now; the passage goes on to explain that the girl will have no parents to advise and support her. The second comes just as Digenis expires, with a prayer of gratitude that, through the girl's death, he has been spared the unendurable pain of imagining her fate as a *xene* in his absence (G8.194). For Digenis, the status of *xene* that he attributes to his wife is entirely negative.

G also uses *xenos* of the emir, Digenis's father, a convert to Christianity who came to live in his wife's Christian family. When his plans for returning to Syria are discovered, 'he was ashamed because he was found out and frightened because he was a *xenos*' (G2.173). Again a negative condition; the implication is that the emir is frightened because he is vulnerable, since he has no advocates. However, a little later (G2.225) the classical ambiguity of this word emerges. His bride pleads with her brothers for their sympathy; the emir should not be harmed precisely because he is a *xenos*. He is an outsider, a stranger, but also a guest deserving of hospitality, the dual element present in this word from the Homeric poems onwards. There is nothing of this in E: we are simply told that the emir was frightened.

Later, however, Digenis and the girl approach his father's house after their successful elopement and are met by a great procession, made up of all the members of the household. The girl has no idea who the huge crowd is and fears the worst. If these are *xenoi*, she says, then they are going to separate us. The wording is almost identical in both G and E, so this line may be attributed to proto-*Digenis*.[3] The sense of *xenoi* here must be 'not one of us', 'people who do not know us', 'people we can't trust'.

Of related lexical items the most obvious is *xeniteia*, that is, the condition of being a *xenos*, a term whose uses in the spiritual life are examined elsewhere in this volume. There are no examples of this word in E, but in G it appears twice. We find it in connection with the girl, Digenis's wife, where in the deathbed scene she prays for pity on her

---

[3]   E1038 and G4.804.

xeniteian, on her state of being a *xene* (G8.171). The girl thus accepts Digenis's negative interpretation of her situation. And we find it used in an interesting way in connection with the emir earlier in the poem (G3.266), where he refers to his absence in Syria to fetch his mother as his *xeniteia*, that is, he experiences *xeniteia* in his absence from his bride and his new family.

G's usage of *xenos* and *xeniteia* looks somewhat paradoxical. The term *xenos* is applied both to the emir and to Digenis's bride after they have married into a family unit – in other words they are being identified as extraneous elements that have been introduced into an enclosed group. The emir, however, has been sufficiently integrated into the group for him to regard his temporary separation from it when he goes to fetch his mother as a *xeniteia*. His incorporation has been complete, marked by his own conversion and baptism; we see him later functioning on equal terms with his wife's brothers in the education of the young hero. His incorporation into a new family is much more significant than his rejected origins. Digenis's bride, on the other hand, especially when her new family is about to disappear on Digenis's death, still remains an alien element, in need of the support of her birth familial unit; she needs her fathers and brothers. We are beginning to see something of G's usages and concepts. To be a *xenos* is to be outside a supportive family unit, a condition not usually perceived as desirable. Margaret Mullett has emphasized just how important family ties were to the functioning of Byzantine society:[4] they involved, as we see here, an ambivalence towards outsiders who were brought in perforce, as brides and grooms, in order to allow the blood line to continue. Parallels from the post-Byzantine period are legion in the values of traditional Greek society as recorded in folksong: in the *Bridge of Arta*, for example, the luckless bride is an expendable *xene*.[5] The question of relationships between spouses and the families into which they marry becomes a major subject of anthropological study in twentieth-century Greece.[6]

Let us now consider the second set of words and phrases. Digenis himself, as we have seen, famously wants to be alone. How does this fit in with exclusion from a family unit which, in G's usages elsewhere, is to be

---

[4]   M. Mullett, 'Byzantium: a friendly society?', *P&P* 118 (1988), 3–24.

[5]   R. Mandel, 'Sacrifice at the Bridge of Arta: sex roles and the manipulation of power', *Journal of Modern Greek Studies* 1 (1983), 173–183; M. Alexiou, 'Sons, wives and mothers: reality and fantasy in some Modern Greek ballads', *Journal of Modern Greek Studies* 1 (1983), 73–111, especially 78–79.

[6]   As it is, for example, in J. Du Boulay, *Portrait of a Mountain Village* (Oxford, 1974).

a *xenos*, a negative condition? The relevant lexical items are the adjectives *monachos*, *monos*, both meaning 'alone', 'on one's own', and *monogenis*, 'only child', which is tied up with *monos* and *monachos*, and the noun *monaxia*.

These words are spread across G and E. So *monos*, in all cases, is found 64 times in G, 25 times in E. *Monachos* is preferred by E where it occurs 16 times, as opposed to twice in G. *Monogenis* is found 4 times in G and twice in E. *Monotatos*, the superlative of *monos*, is found twice, in G only. *Monaxia* occurs twice in G and once in E.

Many instances are absolutely straightforward, as in the dozen or so examples of *monon* functioning adverbially to mean 'only'. Adjectivally *monos* more often than not also simply means 'only'; as in G4.303: Τοῦτο δὲ μόνο εὔχομαι, εἴπερ ἀποδεκτόν σοι ('I make this prayer only, if it is acceptable to you'). The word *monachos*, preferred by E, often functions in the same way, and often parallels *monos* in G: as in E1250 καὶ μοναχὸν τὸ κράτημαν ἀπόμεινεν στὸ χέριν and G6.220 ἐν τῇ χειρὶ τὸ κράτημα μόνον μοι ἀπελείφθη, both meaning 'only the handle was left in his (my) hand'. *Monos* used in this way is found applied to a chamber, a prisoner, flight, comfort, love, God and so forth. No value judgements are implied.

The remaining occurrences carry the meaning 'alone', 'on their own' and are applied, in descending order of frequency, to Digenis, the girl, Maximou, the *apelates*, Aploravdis's daughter, the emir and his bride and his bride's brothers, more often than not appearing to imply a value judgement of some kind. Interestingly, according to my lists, *monos* and its cognates are not used of the two generals and their wives or of the emir's mother.

Let us deal with the least intricate cases first. The emir and his bride are alone (*monoi*) in their chamber as he prepares to depart to Syria (G2.266); E simply puts them in the chamber – a straightforward statement of fact. The *apelates* are warned not to set off on their own against Digenis (3 occasions in G, one in E);[7] they are being warned that he is a dangerous opponent. The brothers of Digenis's mother are said to have acted alone (*monoi*) when rescuing their sister: by implication they are commended. This is G's phrasing (G2.232); E simply has a generally approbatory remark (E404–6). Aploravdis's daugher is on her own when Digenis finds her (G5.127, 156; an episode only in G). This has obvious implications: it means that she lacks protectors since the faithless Roman youth in whom she had put her trust had gone off with the horses; she is

---

[7]   G6.464, 6.488, 6.255; E1358.

vulnerable and Digenis rapes her. A pattern is developing which becomes clear when Digenis, the girl and Maximou are considered. Males are admired and commended for actions taken independently; females are not.

If we consider the case of the girl, there is one use of *mone* which is irrelevant to this argument: at E954 (not reflected in G), as her father pursues them, she urges Digenis to make his escape since she alone has been responsible for their predicament. Otherwise the point of the statements in which *mone* is applied to the girl is that when she is on her own, she lacks protection, or the prestige of a suitable retinue, the support of her kinsfolk and in particular of her male relatives, her father and brothers. This comes up when the elopement (or abduction) is being planned, in both G and E (G4.808; 4.814, cf. E1048–9), and when her mother first hears of the abduction (in E1024). It is a disgrace, not to be mitigated by claims that her family's status, and so hers also, is self-evident. The consequences for a female of being 'on one's own' become apparent when the *apelates* catch sight of the girl 'on her own', when Digenis has fallen asleep in the meadow (G6.126): they immediately plan an abduction, exactly as Digenis had reacted on encountering Aploravdis's daughter. In this passage it is G which has the word *mone* while E has the sense but not the word: E1151 the *apelates* wondered at the ἡδονὴν τῆς κόρης. At G8.82, as Digenis reflects on his past life with the girl, he comments that the *drakon* had attempted to rape her when she was *mone*. These attitudes and their results are fully in accord with the legal discussions of where moral responsibility lies in the case of assaults on lone females, as recently examined by Angeliki Laiou.[8]

There are two sets of phrases which are rather more complex. One concerns Digenis's claims that he took the girl *mone*, for herself alone, and not for her *proika*, her dowry. The claim is made twice in E (1008 and 1300) and once in G (8.77), in lines whose wording is very similar, though the contexts are different. In E the claims are made in connection with the abduction and the marriage arrangements; in G the claims are made directly in the deathbed speech, referring to a refusal that had taken place at the time of the marriage. In E the claim is that the dowry is renounced in favour of the girl's brothers, in G that it is in favour of the girl's father. Digenis, by initially refusing the dowry, opted out of full integration into

---

[8]   A. Laiou, 'Sex, consent and coercion in Byzantium', in A. Laiou, ed., *Consent and Coercion to Sex and Marriage in Ancient and Medieval Societies* (Washington, DC, 1993), 109–221.

his bride's kin group, and remained outside it.[9] (The status of the gifts subsequently offered and accepted is ambiguous.) This can be contrasted with the situation of his father, the emir, in connection with whom no dowries or marriage contracts are mentioned, who plainly accepted his new family's demands and became fully integrated. If later in his dying speech in G Digenis laments for his wife that she is *mone kai xene*, then it is through his actions that she has been brought to this condition. He has refused integration into her family, thus creating a unit of two persons which will become one on his death. E was seen earlier to be less explicit than G in acknowledging the concept of a *xenos* as being outside a family unit, and in the placing of Digenis's bride in this category; the statements about the dowry seem, however, to show that E shares the view expressed in G.

The other phrase concerns the girl's status as a *monogenes*, an only child. This word is also used in connection with Digenis, as will be discussed later. The two occurrences referring to the girl, in G only (G4.601, 603), are used by her mother, as part of her outburst of grief at the abduction. The word is used in a strained sense: the girl is in fact merely her only daughter, for there are five brothers. But the status of being an only child, a naturally emotive concept, is close enough to the truth to be used as a justification for extra sympathy.

But when we turn to actions performed on her own, the girl gains no commendation for them, in fact the reverse, as can be seen by the uses of *monaxia*, which is found only in connection with her, in both G and E. Whether used by Digenis to refer to her lack of an appropriate escort when they first meet his family (G4.813, E1049) or by the girl herself of herself in her final prayer (G8.172), *monaxia* is a condition to be pitied and excused. We should note that we have no comments about Digenis's mother, the female figure who is a parallel to the girl, being alone or on her own; for, although she was abducted from her home by the raiding emir in the absence of her father, her brothers immediately sprang into action and to her defence, while her abductor was integrated into the family unit by conversion and marriage. In the case of Digenis's bride, he, the abductor, by rejecting the dowry, refused to be integrated completely, thus leaving the girl without access to her male relatives.

---

[9]   For a discussion on the legal background to Digenis's marriage, see M. Angold, 'The wedding of Digenes Akrites: love and marriage in Byzantium in the eleventh and twelfth centuries', Ἡ καθημερινὴ ζωὴ στὸ Βυζάντιο (Athens, 1989), 201–215.

Next Maximou, who is quite unlike the female characters considered so far, apart from the sinister element of cross-dressing which she shares with Aploravdis's daughter. Maximou spans the genders, a female in a male role. It is to this that is usually attributed her defeat and rape, and in G her death. And this is surely correct. However, this is not apparent in terms of the lexical combinations that are being discussed. The comments that Maximou plans to go *mone kai monache* against Digenis (in both G and E; G6.566, E1523) seem to be statements of fact. And in G's great set-piece description as she stands in all her brilliance alone on the battle-field: ἰδοὺ μόνη ἡ Μαξιμοὺ ἐφάνη ἐν τῷ κάμπῳ, there may even be a positive force to the adjective. Up to this point the female seems to be succeeding in the man's role. The folly of her actions becomes apparent only later and only through deeds, not through lexical slanting. Thus there is an ambiguity about Maximou – an admiration for her prowess combined with a need to see that her non-conformity did not go unpunished. This ambiguity must have been present in proto-*Digenis*.

So to the hero himself. It is around Digenis that most of the references to being 'alone' and 'on one's own' cluster. We may categorize them in two types: when he is completely on his own, and when he claims to be on his own but is accompanied by the girl and some attendants, a situation which at times strikes a modern reader as bizarre. The semantic content of the phrases used of Digenis being *monos* is positive, with only one exception; at the outset of their elopement where in both G and E the girl fears that Digenis's rashness will lead to his death and in E (869) the fact that he is *monachos* is an element in her fear. One suspects that she may be using a categorization more appropriate for a female.

Digenis is an unarmed and unsupported warrior. We first meet his claim to be this when he has just caught sight of the girl and is planning her abduction. In both G and E (G4.374, E793) this is emphatic and the wording very similar: 'since I wish to travel completely on my own' (G), 'since I am alone and wish to journey on my own' (E). At this point there is a further element in E to which we will return to in a moment. This is Digenis's first independent action, and his preparation for it has been made in the course of his hunting exploits, in the company of his father and uncles, where he has pursued and slain bears and a deer with his bare hands and a lion with his sword. If the girl is to be seen as the most challenging prey available to him (as his comments to his mother indicate and as David Ricks has surely been right to emphasize),[10] then it is entirely fitting that he should match this with an equally challenging method of pursuit. Later, too, his lack of support is a matter of amazement to all those he encounters, whether the Arab raiders in G5, or the *apelates*, the *drakon* or Maximou in his later adventures. The clearest statement comes in his defninitive clash with the *apelates* (G6.315–6, E1323–4), where he is said in G to be 'unarmed, on foot and with only his stick' and in E to be 'on his own, on foot and in boots, and in a simple tunic'. There are 18 other occasions on which Digenis is said to be on his own, and all have positive implications. He is a heroic figure, to be admired and feared. He is to be contrasted with the other heroic warrior of the poem, the emir, his father, who is supported constantly by his troop of *agouroi*, young men. We should note that when in the deathbed scene in E Digenis summons his *pallikaria* to make his final bequests and give his advice, none of the actions that he attributes to their shared pasts can be matched to the previous narrative, and these *pallikaria* play no part in G's version of the scene; in G Digenis addresses only the girl. It is arguable that here E has departed quite radically from the proto-*Digenis*.

The most striking example of Digenis claiming to be on his own, yet being in the company of the girl, has been mentioned before. It comes when the narrative of his exploits has concluded and in both G (4.956, 5.22) and E (1096) he and the girl set off on their life together on their own. In E it is simply stated that they live in a house, but in G we are told about the tent in which they live their solitary lives, while there are other tents at a discreet distance in which their attendants are housed. All is done with due domestic decorum. The point is presumably that there were no other military forces, no squadron under his command. The *agouroi* are never shown playing a military role, until the deathbed speech in E:[11] they are a small group of retainers quite inadequate for the lofty status of their lord. Nevertheless, the only occasions in the poem when we see Digenis as a truly solitary roaming warrior are when he sets off to hunt the girl and when he is ranging around the desert and encounters the daughter of Aploravdis.

The reason that Digenis gives for wanting to take up this solitary existence is intriguing. He is *monogenes*, an only child. This is the extra element referred to just now which in E first appears when he sets off to

---

[10] E809; D. Ricks, 'The pleasures of the chase: a motif in *Digenes Akrites*', *BMGS* 13 (1989), 290–295.

[11] The discrepancies in this speech are discussed in E.M. Jeffreys, 'Digenis and Charos'.

hunt the girl but which occurs subsequently in both G and E. In Book 6 of G we find his claim, 'I do not wish to rule but to live alone, since I am the only child born to my parents' (6.298–9); and at the equivalent point in E 'But I am an only child and wish to make my way alone' (1299). By such statements he seems to justify his decision to live on the frontiers (cf. G4.958), though the logic behind this decision is not clear to me. In E at times the preference for solitude is explicitly linked to Digenis's refusal of the girl's dowry: 'I want to live alone and I took the girl on her own and I want nothing else' (1300). While this might be due to E's habit of aural association (that is, the use of *monos* has triggered other parts of the poem's thought- and word-pool that use *monos*), Digenis's refusal of the dowry is, as pointed out earlier, a major element in both G and E, and so of proto-*Digenis*. E's assertion should not be dismissed too quickly. It is a re-statement of Digenis's wish to have no links and obligations. The ultimate statement of this wish to be alone comes in G's scene of the emperor's visit where Digenis *monotatos*, that is, absolutely on his own (4.1012), approaches the emperor, makes deep obeisance and lectures him on the correct performance of imperial duties.

The concept of Digenis as a lone figure, an outsider, with no access to social units, is thus deeply embedded in proto-*Digenis*. The term *xenos* is not applied to him, though his actions are such that he puts himself into positions where he could be classed as *xenos* by the social groups with whom he interacts, much as he finds himself referring to his wife as *xene*. Perhaps *xenos* is an adjective which can have no positive meaning apart from that involved with the concept 'guest'.

'Outsider' implies the existence of groups from which the outsiders are perceived to be exterior or extraneous. The discussion so far is predicated on these groups being family units. But *xenos* in Modern Greek refers to a division between 'us' and 'them', between *dikoi mas* and *xenoi*, which begins from the family unit but which may be transposed upwards at a lower level of intensity to cover other levels – for example, the village, the district, the modern nation state.[12] May we see examples in the poem of these other applications?

There is, first, the Christian East Roman frontier society as a whole, represented by the family units of the conglomerate households of the two generals (Digenis's maternal grandfather and his father-in-law),

---

[12] These divisions are implicit, for example, in the argument of P.S. Cassia and C. Bada, *The Making of the Modern Greek Family* (Cambridge, 1992), or M. Herzfeld, 'Within and Without: the category of "female" in the ethnography of Modern Greece', in J. Dubisch, ed., *Gender and Power in Rural Greece* (Princeton, 1986), 215–233.

made up of parents, offspring, kinsmen, retainers – several generations within the one community. Exterior to this society can be seen three elements – the *apelates*, mostly Christian presumably and with elements of a cohesive social group, but neither functioning as a regular kin group nor centred round particular buildings, despite Philopappous's patriarchal role; the Arab communities, represented by the emir, his mother and his family in Syria, and by Aploravdis's daughter; and the emperor from Constantinople, who in G only appears abruptly from some totally exterior area. It is perhaps more likely than not that he is an insertion, not part of proto-*Digenis*.

Secondly, these sub-elements also have their own boundaries and loyalties, and operate their own sets of inclusions and exclusions. Thus, as we have seen, the family unit of Digenis's mother transforms the *xenos*, the emir, by baptism and marriage, to the extent that he feels *xeniteia* when he is forced temporarily to leave it. The family unit of Digenis's bride seeks to bring Digenis within its boundaries, but fails when he (at least initially) refuses the dowry. He sets up an establishment that is, again at least initially, free from ties with the previous generation, though he later brings in his father's tomb and his mother (certainly in G, and by implication in E). Maximou, part of the *apelates* group, is an interesting case. She is within the group, by virtue of kinship; but from the authorial perspective she is an outsider, and doubly so – the group is not the norm and neither is her role as a cross-dressing female warrior, which leads to her fate (which is not good in E and worse in G).

I end with the figure of Digenis himself. He made himself an outsider first by rejecting normal methods of combat and adopting idiosyncratic weapons and garments and then by rejecting the normal methods of setting up a household unit. Yet with the passage of time he is beginning to re-integrate himself – his palace has space for his kinsmen; he took in his mother in her widowhood; he buried his father.

As Catia Galatariotou has pointed out on several occasions,[13] the *Digenis* text, especially the Grottaferrata version, is constructed out of a series of oppositions: Christian/Muslim; palace/tent; enclosed space/open space. When looking at the way in which outsiders function, in the sense of those who place themselves or are placed outside the accepted norms, then the male/female opposition becomes crucial. The

---

[13] C. Galatariotou, 'Structural oppositions in the Grottaferrata *Digenes Akrites*', BMGS 11 (1987), 29–68; C. Galatariotou, 'Open space/closed space: the perceived worlds of Kekaumenos and Digenes Akrites', in M. Mullett and D. Smythe, eds, *Alexios I Komnenos. I. Papers* (Belfast, 1996), 303–328.

isolation or independence which in a male may be interpreted heroically, in a female is automatically unacceptable to the *mores* dominant in the poem. These are attitudes which are in accordance with late Roman legal practice where females have very little independent status.[14] Hence we find both Digenis's bride as *xene* and the fate accorded to Maximou.

The concept of standing outside the regular norms will have been fundamental to proto-*Digenis*. Proto-*Digenis* would have been a poem set in the Euphrates frontier region, written from the perspective of the frontiers themselves, from outside the cultural centre. The environment that it presents is that of the Byzantine ruling adminsitrative élite of that area, with their estates, retinues and their decorated houses. Urban centres are referred to largely as points on a raiding itinerary. Digenis visits an urban centre only when he deposits Aploravdis's daughter in Chalkourgia. From the point of view of Constantinoplitan culture, the poem is a graphic representation of an aristocratic outsider's world.

Part of the poem is expressed in the first person, and must have been so in proto-*Digenis*. In G the interlocutor is a Cappodocian, which is entirely of a piece with the authorial focus of the rest of the poem. Out of this Roderick Beaton has recently tried to argue for a context for the poem's composition, different from the one put forward here: he is certainly right to highlight the alien elements in the poem's structure.[15] Given the extent to which *Digenis* stands outside so many Byzantine cultural and literary norms, we should certainly ask how he ever came to be inside, how his poem survived. What need of the establishment did the text supply? I tend to return to a point I have made before – that Digenis was used by an imperial propaganda machine which itself was trying to show its attachment to the Euphrates frontier, and was willing to portray the emperor Manuel himself as a strangely dressed outsider.[16] The moment could have been when, in 1151–1152, Manuel returned Byzantine arms to the heartland of the epic by purchasing the County of Edessa from the widow of its last count in a last, brief and futile gesture

---

[14]   A. Laiou, 'The role of women in Byzantine society', *JÖB* 31.1 (1981), 233–260; J. Beaucamp, 'La situation juridique de la femme à Byzance', *Cahiers de civilisation médiévale* 20 (1977), 145–176.

[15]   R. Beaton, 'Cappadocians at court: Digenes and Timarion', in M. Mullett and D. Smythe, eds, *Alexios I Komnenos*, 329–338.

[16]   As in the Ptochoprodromic poems where Manuel is referred to as 'Akritis' in language reminiscent of *Digenis Akritis*. Compare with Ptochoprodomos, 4.190–1; H. Eideneier, ed., *Ptochoprodromos: Einführung, kritische Ausgabe, deutsche Übersetzung, Glossar* (Cologne, 1991).

of defiance against the forces of the Arabs of Aleppo and the Seljuks of Ikonion.

15. Defining the Foreign in Kekaumenos

Charlotte Roueché

The purpose of this paper is to consider the extent to which 'foreignness' is an issue in the text which we call 'Kekaumenos' or 'The Strategikon of Kekaumenos'. The nature of this text is such that it is often called in aid to support arguments about 'Byzantine attitudes'; but it will be helpful to consider the specific characteristics of the text itself.

The Consilia et Narrationes

The text under consideration survives in only one manuscript, Moscow Synodalis 298 (Vlad. 436) ff. 136vo–229ro, probably copied in or near Trebizond in the fourteenth century; it was first published in 1881.[1] When it was copied it was already in a fragmentary state, and the name of the author had been lost. He does, however, mention his father, called Kekaumenos, (72.22) which is also the name of a grandfather (65.11), so that it is not extravagant to assign this name to the author as well. While the text that we have contains a variety of material, it all appears to come from the same author. The bulk of the work is made up of moral and practical advice, on the conduct of public and private life, supported by anecdotes. Many of these are drawn from recent or contemporary affairs; recent editors, therefore, have rejected the title of the work used by the

[1] V. Vasiljevskij, 'Sovety i rasskazy vizantijskoo bojarina XIv', *Min. Nar. Pros.* 215 (1881), 242–299, 216 (1881), 102–171, 316–357; the full text published as *Cecaumeni Strategicon*, ed. B. Wassiliewsky and P. Jernstedt (St Petersburg, 1896). The most recent full edition by G.G. Litavrin, Cecaumeni *Consilia et Narrationes* (Moscow, 1972) is used as the basis of the recent edition with Modern Greek translation, by D. Tsougarakis, *Κεκαυμένος, Σρτατηγικόν* (Athens, 1993). The most important commentary is the study by P. Lemerle, *Prolégomènes à une édition critique et commentée des Conseils et Récits de Kékaumenos* (Brussels, 1960); there is also a German translation by H.G. Beck, *Vademecum des byzantinischen Aristokraten* (Graz, 1964). References here are to the pagination of the 1896 edition, which is still the mostly widely available.

scribe, *Strategikon*, in favour of *Consilia et Narrationes*, 'Advice and Anecdotes'.

The work itself appears to have been written during the reign of Michael VII Doukas (73.18, 73.25), and after the death of the patriarch John Xiphilinos in August 1075 (72.13); the bulk of the stories date from the period 1034–1054.[2] The only mention of events later than 1054 is in the story of Nikoulitzas Delphinas (66.19–73.26). Much of the scholarly attention paid to this text has come from historians, concerned to learn from such narratives.

The family of the author

A great deal of effort has also been applied to trying to determine the possible identity of the author – a subject which has developed a large bibliography.[3] This task is made more difficult because the author refers surprisingly seldom to his own career. He does, however, recount several anecdotes involving members of his family, or connections by marriage. Before examining these in detail, there is one general point to be made. One story, which is disproportionately long and not particularly apposite, is about the author's cousin, Nikoulitzas Delphinas, who became unwillingly involved in an uprising against the emperor in Northern Greece in 1067 (66.19–73.26). The account seems to be based on a first-person narrative by Delphinas. Our author seems to have included it partly because he had it already to hand, but perhaps also because the story was clearly told to explain and justify Delphinas's conduct. It may well be that a desire to show the conduct of various members of his family in the best light, in what were, in some cases, rather ambiguous circumstances, underlies the inclusion of some of the other anecdotes about the author's relations – particularly those at 26.21f., 29.2f, 65.11f, and 96.5f. Perhaps for the third, and certainly for the fourth of these he used documents from the family archives; but it seems likely that some other criterion, beyond the availability of such documents, must have operated in the selection of these particular stories, each of which presents, in favourable terms, actions by his relations which could well be interpreted otherwise. In view of the neatness with which the justification

---

[2]   Analysed by Lemerle, *Prolégomènes*, 56–77.

[3]   For recent work on this topic, see A.G.C. Savvides, 'The Byzantine Family of Kekaumenos', *Diptuxa* 4 (1986), 12–27, and A.G.C. Savvides, 'The Armeno-Byzantine Family of Cecaumenus: addenda et corrigenda', *Journal of Oriental and African Studies* 2 (1990), 224–226, with very full bibliographies.

for telling the Nikoulitzas story is inserted (66.12–18), we should not underestimate the subtlety of our author, or his ability to use his subject matter for his own ends.

It is also important to bear in mind that the casual way in which our author introduces references to members of his family (in particular, the references to Nikoulitzas at 65.10, 66.10 and 71.18) apparently suggests that he assumes his reader to be already aware of the relationships involved. This is perhaps of especial importance in considering the most difficult of the genealogical problems presented by our text, which is that, in the four passages mentioned above, the relatives whom the author describes are referred to as πάπποι, of whom at least three are definitely separate individuals. The references are:

A.   ὁ τοῦ Τοβίου τοπάρχης καὶ πάππος μου (undated; 26.21f.)
B.   ὁ πρὸς μητρὸς πάππος μου Δημήτριος ὁ Πολεμάρχιος (fl. between 976 and 1018; 29.2f.)
C.   ὁ μακαρίτης μου πάππος ὁ Κεκαυμένος (circa 980; 65.11f)
D.   ὁ πάππος μου ὁ Νικουλιτζᾶς (fl. 959-963, 980; 96.5f).

This situation raises several questions. The most basic one is, how should we interpret the word *pappos*? Kekaumenos uses the term in its normal sense of 'grandfather' on one occasion, where he uses and juxtaposes the two terms πάππου and προπάππου (95.26). There have been attempts to combine some of these individuals, to reduce them to two; but none of these are satisfactory, and it seems far easier to accept that *pappos* cannot mean 'grandfather' in each of these examples. In all four cases, the *pappos* is introduced simply as protagonist in a story that illustrates a point which Kekaumenos is trying to make. What is remarkable is that, of those four characters, two are presented in anecdotes where they are fighting against the Byzantines – and winning. Their ingenuity and their success (in each case they win by a ruse) is far more interesting and important than what side they are on.

The first alien *pappos* was a commander on the Eastern border, against the Byzantines. His story is told in the context of advice to a frontier commander to be suspicious:

> Frontier-commander, guard your fortresses and the land entrusted
> to you, and don't trust the toparchs near you, even if they profess
> vehemently that they are your friends. Let me tell you a story of
> this sort.

There is a fortress in the region of Greater Armenia; it is in a high place, with, above it, a good-sized plateau, sufficient, even abundant, for the people who live in the fortress as arable land and as pasture for their livestock, and for all their needs; it is made secure on every side by cliffs and ravines, and does not admit of being attacked by anyone from any side. For it's not even possible for anyone to get up there unless by one narrow road, and then to enter first through the gate of the fortress – and that with considerable difficulty. So there was nothing safer than this strong-hold. The toparch of Tobion, who was also my grandfather, was longing to get possession of it. So what does he think up? By many gifts he makes a friend of the general in command of this fortress, having declared to him that, whatever he needed, he should boldly send and get from him. So the general was enchanted by all this; he happened to come in need of corn, and then informed the toparch, who said, cheerfully: 'As much as you demand'. He sends him a thousand animals carrying corn; a man followed each pair of donkeys, as if indeed to take care of them. The general reckoned: 'If my fortress is victualled by the very enemy of Romania, what do I deserve?' Then, when the corn arrives, he cheerfully opens the gates for the animals and the men attending them to come in. But the men were armed for fighting, and had their swords, hidden. As soon as they came in they wrenched open the gates; they kill the spearmen and take possession of the fortress. And so a friendship becomes a cause of misfortune, and deserves to be remembered. So you should protect yourself from your friends more than from your enemies. If the general had not trusted those he thought were his friends but had ordered them to unload the corn outside the gate, he would have benefited from them, and their cunning would have come to nothing, and the general would have had no worries. (26–27)

There is no attempt to name the fortress held by the Roman commander, and the *pappos* is not named; but the name of his command is given. Although the manuscript tradition is difficult, it appears to be a reference to Dvin. Of the four *pappoi*, this unnamed man is a good candidate for being a *propappos*, and so active in the mid-tenth century. Between 927 and 966, Dvin was ruled by a series of commanders, of whom we know very little.[4] These could with equal probability have been Arabs, Kurds,

---

[4]   The account by V. Minorsky, *Studies in Caucasian History* (London, 1953), especially 'Vicissitudes of Dvin', 116–124, was further developed by A. Ter-Ghévondian, 'Chronologie de la ville de Dvin (Duin) aux 9ᵉ et 11ᵉ siècles', *JEA* NS 2 (1965), 303–318. For a summary see

or Armenians; Dvin was a very mongrel city, with large Christian and Muslim populations.[5] Kekaumenos's ancestor could well have been an independent commander who held Dvin during this period, and later fled to the Byzantines;[6] similarly, when the Arab adventurer Muhammed b. Shadded was driven out of Dvin by another Arab commander in 953, his first move was to appeal to Byzantium for help.[7] This *pappos*, therefore, could have come from a wide range of different backgrounds. Kekaumenos sees no need to enlighten us, or to present him as anything other than an enterprising soldier.

The same is true of *pappos* II, further defined as being the author's maternal *pappos*, who was active in northern Greece. He is actually given a name – Demetrios Polemarchios; that name is itself so grandiose, that it is tempting to see Polemarchios as a translation of some foreign term. He is not presented as belonging to any particular ethnic group – he is merely a prominent man in the area, clearly fighting for Samuel of Bulgaria – but Kekaumenos does take pains to tell us that after the war he was rewarded by the Byzantine emperor. This very mention does suggest a little embarrassment – but not enough to make Kekaumenos omit the story.

> Serbia is a strong city in Bulgaria. A Roman general was guarding it, named Magerinos, and two taxiarchs with their thousands. My *pappos*, on my mother's side, called Demetrios Polemarchios, was a prominent chief in that area near the frontier; after the pacification of Bulgaria the Emperor, Basil the Porphyrogennetos, of blessed memory, raised him to the rank of patrician, having also made him a *mystikos*. So this man, after labouring indefatigably for a whole year in order to take this invincible city, wasn't able to capture it; so that all that labour was in vain. For [the fortress] obtained its security from cliffs and terrifying ravines. Below the fortress, under the cliff, was the bathing-place, and there the general used to go, and the taxiarchs, when they wanted to, and bathed. So he devises this device: he went by night, and took up position opposite the fortress, with his men – the place was wooded, with bushes – and ordered the men with him to take large bushes and hold them in front of them, and overshadow and hide the horses

G. Dédéyan, 'Les Arabes au Caucase', in *Il Caucaso: cerniera fra culture dal Mediterraneo alla Persia, Settimane* 43 (Spoleto, 1996), I, 169–192, 175.

[5]   Minorsky, *Studies* , 8, 121, 135; Ter-Ghévondian, 'Chronologie', 313.
[6]   Minorsky, *Studies*, 119–120.
[7]   Minorsky, *Studies* , 11–12.

and their riders, so as to look not like men, but like some wood growing on the spot. He had two *chonsarii* (scouts) near the fortress on the ridge, who, directly the general and the taxiarchs went down and began to wash, made a signal which they had been ordered to make. The others spurred down and surrounded the bathing-place, and captured the people in it. For the man who doesn't take care, but walks unguardedly, often falls, even into misfortunes. So when they had been captured he took the fortress without bloodshed. So take care over these things. (28–29)

This background to our author has left the field open to the historians. Of the other two *pappoi*, one bears the name Kekaumenos, and is found commanding Larissa in the reign of Basil II: he may well be a real grandfather. The name Kekaumenos is found in the East, and the famous general, Katakalon Kekaumenos, came from Koloneia, in the Armeniac theme. It seems clear that Kekaumenos could be used as a soubriquet for persons with darker skin; an eleventh-century text recycles an earlier phrase to describe a man from Armenia as 'burned black' διακεκαυμένον εἰς τὸ μελάντατον.[8] It may be, therefore, that not all Kekaumenoi were related to one another. An attempt to identify our author's Kekaumenos *pappos* in an inscription found in Armenia, first put forward by Vasilievskji and developed by Paul Lemerle, has been eliminated by the work of N. Oikonomidès.[9] The dynamic energy of Armenian historiography, however, means that the Kekaumenoi have been appropriated as Armenian fairly consistently;[10] Kazhdan and Epstein describe our author as of 'hellenized Armenian stock'.[11] But, on the other side of the family, Demetrios Polemarchios, who has a name for which I

[8]　　P. Gautier ed., 'Le *de daemonibus* de pseudo-Psellos', *REB* (1980), 133–177, l.443; the phrase is borrowed from Lucian, *Hercules* 6.1.

[9]　　N. Oikonomidès, 'L'organisation de la frontière orientale de Byzance aux Xᵉ–XIᵉ siècles et le taktikon de l'Escorial', *Actes du XIVᵉ Congr. Int. des Et. Byz.* (Bucarest, 1974), 285–302, reprinted in N. Oikonomidès, *Documents et études sur les institutions de Byzance* (London, 1976), XXIV, 291 and n. 35.

[10]　　See C. Toumanoff, *Studies in Christian Caucasian History* (Washington, 1963), 224–225; A. Kazhdan, *Armjane v sostave gospodstvuscego klassa Vizantijskoj imperii v XI–Xii vv* (*Armenians in the ruling class of the Byzantine empire in the XIth–XIIth centuries*), (Yerevan, 1975; reviewed by W. Seibt, *BS* 38 (1977), 50–51); the discussion is summarized in A. Kazhdan, 'The Armenians in the Byzantine ruling class, predominantly in the ninth through twelfth centuries', T. Samuelian and M. Stone, *Mediaeval Armenian Culture* (University of Pensylvania, 1984), 439–451.

[11]　　A. Kazhdan and A. Epstein, *Change in Byzantine Culture in the Eleventh and Twelfth Centuries* (Berkeley, 1985), 180.

can find no parallel, clearly functioned in the northern part of the Greek peninsula. The fourth *pappos*, Nikoulitzas, bears a name also associated with northern Greece; he had held office in Hellas 'for life', for some time under Basil II, and so might well be of an earlier generation. His name is less widely attested than Kekaumenos, and only in the western part of the empire. A Nikoulitzes is known as *chartularios* and *ek prosopou* of the imperial stables, from a seal dated tenth–eleventh century.[12] A Nikolitzas is attested as a landowner of Kephallenia before 1264,[13] and another as a landowner near Ohrid at the end of the fourteenth century.[14] The name Nikolotzopoulos is found at Mistra in the fourteenth century.[15] Litavrin, quite reasonably, sees our Kekaumenos as coming from northern Greece; but there is no modern historiographical tradition that needs to assert this point of view.

What is perhaps most striking, however, is that the text should be capable of such varied interpretation. Even if the stories, as has been suggested, may have been included to show his family members in the most favourable light, it is still remarkable that Kekaumenos does not pass over his 'foreign' relations in silence.

Kekaumenos on 'foreigners'

Kekaumenos was apparently unconcerned to present himself – or his ancestors – in terms of their 'ethnicity'. He seems to see himself as 'a Roman', and to see Romanness as something that was not jeopardized by having foreign forebears. But, although Kekaumenos may be unembarrassed by his ancestry there are two passages where he is famously critical of foreigners. The first is the passage in the *Advice to an Emperor* recommending against over-promotion of foreign officers.

> Don't promote foreigners, who are not of royal birth in their own land, to great honours, nor entrust great offices to them; for you will certainly injure yourself by doing so, as well as the Romans who are your officials. For whenever you honour the foreigner of the vulgar class, who arrives, as *primikerios*, or general, what worthy command do you have to give to the Roman? Certainly you will make him an enemy. But, also, in this man's country,

---

[12] V. Laurent, *Corpus des sceaux de l'empire byzantin* II (Paris, 1981), 929.

[13] E. Trapp, *Prosopographisches Lexikon der Palaiologenzeit* (Vienna, 1976–), 20581.

[14] Trapp, 20580

[15] Trapp, 20582, for Joannes, a *paroikos* at Mistra in 1366.

when they hear that he has reached such an honour and office, they will all laugh, and say: 'We considered him here worth nothing, but, going off to Rome, he has met with such honour. As it seems, in Romania there is not a competent man, and, for this reason, our man has been exalted; if the Romans were efficient, they would not have promoted this man to such a great height'. Don't let your Majesty say: 'I benefited him for this reason: so that others would see and come as well'. For this is not a good aim; if you wish, I will bring you as many foreigners as you wish, for a bit of bread, and clothing. It is greatly to the advantage of the Romans, master, not to bestow great honours on foreigners; for, if they serve for clothing, and bread, be assured, they will serve you faithfully and wholeheartedly, looking to your hands to receive trifling coins, and bread. But, if you honour a foreigner beyond the rank of *spatharokandidate*, from then on he becomes contemptuous, and will not serve you correctly. Ask and learn, master, how they came in many times of trouble to the previous Emperors, to the lord Basil, the porphyrogennetos, to his father, his grandfather and his great-grandfather, and those further back. And why do I speak of ancient [emperors]? Not even the lord Romanos Argyropoulos, nor even any of those emperors, of blessed memory, promoted a Frank or a Varangian to the honour of patrician, but [none of them] was even prepared to make any of them a consul or a *stratiotophylax*, and scarcely [to make] any of them a *spatharios*. All these served for bread and clothing, but the Romans took the great honours and the jobs, and Romania was in a state of prosperity. (95–96)

This is also one of the better-known passages in the work; but it is interestingly different from other contemporary passages on foreigners. Kekaumenos is not attacking foreigners in terms of their characteristics; he is apparently proud to have served with Harald Hardrada. He makes instead a specific point about the professional interests of Roman soldiers. His comments focus on the implications for the pay and conditions of Roman soldiers, rather than suggesting anything unsatisfactory about the foreigners – except that they are not the emperor's own subjects. This is a definition by allegiance, not by race. There is also an odd inconsistency here: what about the ranks given to Demetrios Polemarchios? All this suggests that Kekaumenos is able to define foreigners as it suits him, without any very strong sense of a fixed and immutable boundary.

The best passage for illustrating xenophobia in Kekaumenos is his description of the Vlachs. This passage has less context than the others; it is appended to the story of Nikoulitzas Delphinas and is an unremittingly hostile account of the Vlachs:

I give you, and your offspring, this advice. Since the race of the Vlachs is entirely untrustworthy, and corrupt, and keeps true faith neither with God nor with the Emperor, nor with a relative or a friend, but endeavours to do down everyone, tells many lies and steals a great deal, swearing every day the most solemn oaths to its friends, and violating them easily, performing adoptions of brothers and baptismal alliances, and scheming by these means to deceive simpler people, it has never yet kept faith with anyone, not even with the earlier emperors of the Romans. After being fought by the emperor Trajan, and entirely wiped out, they were captured, and their king, the so-called Dekabalos, was killed and his head was fastened on a spear in the middle of the city of the Romans. They lived formerly near to the Danube river, and the Saos, the river which we now call the Sava, where Serbs live now, in secure and inaccessible places. Being confident in these [places], they pretended friendship and service to the earlier emperors of the Romans, and used to go out of their strongholds and plunder the lands of the Romans; as a result they were angered with them, and, as has been said, destroyed them. They left those parts, and were scattered throughout all Epiros and Macedonia, but most of them inhabited Hellas. They are very cowardly, with the hearts of hares, but with bravado – and even this comes from cowardice. So I advise you not to trust these people at all. And, if a revolt ever takes place, and they pretend friendship and trust, swearing by God to keep it, don't trust them. It is better for you not to make them swear at all, nor to give them an oath, but to watch them, as evil men, rather than swearing or receiving an oath. So you mustn't trust them at all; only, pretend yourself to be their friend. But, even if, sometime, an uprising takes place in Bulgaria, as has been said before, even if they profess to be your friends, or even swear, don't trust them. But, even if they bring their women and their children into the fortress belonging to Romania, encourage them to bring them, only let them be inside the citadel; let [the men] be outside. If they wish to go in to their households, let two or three go in; when they come out, you let others in turn come in. Pay great attention to the walls and to the gates. If you do so, you will be in safety. But, if you allow many to go in to their households, the fortress will be betrayed by them, and you will be bitten by them as if by an asp, and then you will remember my advice. But, if you observe this,

you will have them as your subjects, and will also have freedom
from worries. (74–75)

The narrative has had a lively history; it is the earliest significant mention
of the Vlachs, whose history, from the late nineteenth century onwards,
has been debated, according to Robert Lee Wolff, 'between chauvinist
Bulgarian and Romanian scholars': the former downplay the role of the
Vlachs; the latter 'are eager to show ... above all, that it was the Vlach
portion of the population who led the revolt of 1186 and brought new
glory and independence under a Vlach dynasty to the submerged and
apathetic Bulgarians. ... In the Balkans mediaeval data accumulated by
scholars are often regarded as providing strong arguments for the settling
of present day controversies.'[16]

But, in order to understand this passage, it is necessary to remember
that Kekaumenos was trained in the basics of rhetoric, and had studied at
least the early stages of the *progymnasmata*.[17] It seems very likely that the
description of the Vlachs is modelled on a *psogos*, 'invective' (exercise
number 7); the first headings – origin, development, activities – are all
covered, although there is no comparison. It is the historical references –
which are what have really excited the modern historians – which most
strongly suggest a rhetorical construct; they draw on Dio Cassius, whose
work we know to have been in circulation in Constantinople in the
second half of the eleventh century.[18] That is not, of course, to say that
Kekaumenos really liked Vlachs, and that rhetoric should be equated
with falsity. But it does mean that the function of this passage may have
more to do with his trying out a rhetorical technique, and applying it to a
particular group of people; it does not reflect an overall attitude to 'the
foreign'.

---

[16] R.L. Wolff, 'The "Second Bulgarian Empire". Its origin and history to 1204',
Speculum 24 (1949), 167–206, 174–175; see also T.J. Winnifrith, *The Vlachs. A History of a
Balkan People* (London, 1987), 39–56.

[17] On the *progymnasmata* see G.A. Kennedy, *A New History of Classical Rhetoric*
(Princeton, 1994), 202–208 (very general); R.F. Hock, 'General Introduction' in R.F. Hock
and E.N. O'Neil, *The Chreia in Ancient Rhetoric* (Atlanta, 1986), 3–60; and, for Byzantium, H.
Hunger, *Die Hochsprachliche profane Literatur der Byzantiner* I (Munich, 1978), 92–120.

[18] So M. Gyóni, 'L'oeuvre de Kékauménos, source d'histoire roumaine', *Revue
d'Histoire comparée* 23 (1945), 96–180, 129–167. The most recent discussion is N. Djuvara,
'Sur un passage controversé de Kékauménos', *Revue Roumaine d'Histoire* 30 (1991) 23–66.

Kekaumenos and 'the foreign'

Perhaps this very passage can help us to understand this author's attitude to 'the foreign', which enables him to pour invective on the Vlachs, and yet acknowledge ancestors who were enemies of Romania. Kekaumenos's work is grounded in a particular set of educational values; it is written according to rhetorical guidelines, to be read by people from a similar background. This is a work of advice – a work about conduct. It is deeply rooted in a very old tradition, and above all by the norms of the Hellenized East of the Hellenistic period – the world of his two most influential sources, the Wisdom of Sirach and Pseudo-Isocrates. Since the expansion of Hellenism under Alexander, the cultures of the eastern end of the Mediterranean had been seeking and building a common code of conduct, and a shared culture. That shared culture can be found, for example, in the Aesopic tradition, or in the Eastern texts translated into Greek precisely in the eleventh century – the *Syntipas* and the *Stephanites and Ichnelates* (both transcribed in the same manuscript as the text of Kekaumenos). Those texts transferred very easily into the thought-world of Byzantium. It is this ancient cultural tradition, shared by people both sides of the frontier, that made it easy to move from one allegiance to another. Such admonitory texts passed swiftly into Slavonic languages, to facilitate the same process at the other end of the empire; this was the basis for the manual of advice that Photios sent to Michael of Bulgaria.[19] It was entirely well suited to assimilating men to a shared set of values, compatible with, but not based on, Christianity; Photios, in his letter to Michael, had to add on a specifically Christian section. This literary tradition parallels the visual tradition of an achievable culture that Byzantium exported so effectively to its neighbours over the same period – a process dazzlingly documented in the *Glory of Byzantium* exhibition at the Metropolitan Museum in 1997.[20] There, too, it could be seen that apparent immutability and the confident reassertion of an established *taxis* are necessary constituents of a cultural package to which outsiders can aspire.

Peter Charanis, writing on 'The formation of the Greek People', quoted Isocrates in the *Panegyricus*: 'the title Hellenes is applied rather to

---

[19] Photius, *Epistulae et amphilochia*, ed. B. Laourdas and L.G. Westerink (1983) Ep.1.

[20] Helen C. Evans, ed., *The Glory of Byzantium: Art and Culture of the Middle Byzantine Era, AD 843–1261, Catalog* (New York, 1997); see the review by Peter Brown, *New York Review of Books* (July 29, 1997), 19–24.

those who share our culture than to those who share a common blood'.[21] Over many centuries, manuals of education and admonition – including one appropriately attributed to Isocrates – made 'Hellenism' or *Romanitas* a condition which could be acquired; a cultural identity with no connection to ethnicity.[22] It is this attitude which makes Byzantine texts so unhelpful to those modern politician–scholars who have tried to mine them for support for fictitious modern identities for the pernicious – and now, we hope, moribund – construct of the nation-state.

---

[21] Sp. Vryonis ed., *The Past in Mediaeval and Modern Greek Culture* (Malibu, 1978), 87–101, 88; for a discussion of Kekaumenos on the Vlachs cf. 95–96.

[22] On this see the important observations of Glen Bowersock, *Hellenism in Late Antiquity* (Ann Arbor, 1990).

16. Procopius the Outsider?[*]

Geoffrey Greatrex

Two ways in which the historian Procopius of Caesarea might be viewed as an 'outsider' will be examined here. On the one hand, the composition of three so different works as the *Wars, Buildings* and *Anecdota*, marks Procopius off from all other writers of antiquity or Byzantium; for while others tried their hand at both history and panegyric – the example of John the Lydian is perhaps the most obvious – no other author is known to have produced anything comparable to the *Anecdota*.[1] On the other hand, there is Procopius's position in the sixth century: was he a lone critic vainly fighting the currents prevailing in Justinian's reign? It will be argued that although Procopius was not alone in his criticisms of the imperial regime, it is very doubtful whether he should be associated with any senatorial group; it will further be suggested that the notion of a particular genre of criticism, *Kaiserkritik*, is of little help in considering this issue.

The *Anecdota* has long perplexed scholars. For the proponents of *Kaiserkritik*, it represents a blueprint for the type of criticisms which could be levelled at an emperor – the fullest instance of the genre we have available.[2] The range of criticisms of the imperial couple and their associates

---

[*]   This paper is dedicated to Katherine Adshead on the occasion of her retirement from the University of Canterbury, Christchurch.

[1]   On John the Lydian, see M. Maas, *John Lydus and the Roman Past* (London, 1992), 9. The title *Anecdota* is a modern one, cf. J. Haury and G. Wirth, *Procopii Caesariensis Opera Omnia*, III (Leipzig, 1963), xxv. The suggestion of M. Angold, 'Procopius' portrait of Theodora' in *Philellen. Studies in honour of Robert Browning* (Venice, 1996), 22, that the genre of *Anecdota* was invented by Theopompus of Chios can therefore hardly be accepted. Although Theopompus's critical style bears similarities to Procopius's, there was nothing unpublished or secret about his *Philippica*, which were published after the death of both Philip and Alexander. Cf. M.A. Flower, *Theopompus of Chios* (Oxford, 1994), 36.

[2]   B. Rubin, 'Zur Kaiserkritik Ostroms' in *Atti dello VIII congresso internazionale di studi bizantini*, I (Rome, 1953), 453 = idem, *Das Zeitalter Iustinians* I (Berlin, 1960), 235; cf. F. Tinnefeld, *Kategorien der Kaiserkritik in der byzantinischen Historiographie von Prokop bis Niketas Choniates* (Munich, 1971), 29. See also A. Cameron, *Procopius and the Sixth Century* (London,

From *Strangers to Themselves: The Byzantine Outsider*, ed. Dion C. Smythe. Copyright © 2000 by the Society for the Promotion of Byzantine Studies. Published by Ashgate Publishing Ltd, Gower House, Croft Road, Aldershot, Hampshire, GU11 3HR, Great Britain.

is wide and set out in (apparently) no particular order; there is some repetition and a promise of a treatment of religious affairs is left unfulfilled. It is therefore possible, as has been suggested, that the work was not completed and that the *Anecdota* was assembled in the form in which it has survived at a later point.[3] Two points concerning the work will be examined here: first, its unpublished (or secret) nature, and second, the type of criticisms it offers.

In his preface to the *Wars*, Procopius stated that he had 'not concealed the failures (*ta mokhthêra*) of even his most intimate acquaintances, but [had] written down with complete accuracy everything which befell those concerned, whether it happened to be done well or ill by them'. With this assertion may be compared his words at *Anecdota* 1.10, 'I shall proceed to relate, first, all the base deeds (*ta mokhthêra*) committed by Belisarius; and afterwards I shall disclose all the base deeds (*ta mokhthêra*) committed by Justinian and Theodora'. Despite the inconsistency of Dewing's translations, the *Anecdota* clearly represents the fulfilment of Procopius's brief as set out in the *Wars*. The close relationship between the *Wars* and *Anecdota* (especially chapters 1–5) has never been in doubt, and it is most likely that Procopius was at work on both throughout the 540s.[4] It is less clear, however, whether Procopius, as he wrote up his account of Belisarius's campaigns during the 540s, actually intended to produce two works, one for the contemporary public and one for posterity. The prefaces to both works, quoted above, are significant in this regard. At the most obvious level they may be seen as one instance of Procopius's clever references to his secret work, which most, if not all, contemporaries would not understand.[5] But the reference to *mokhthera* at the opening of the *Wars* should alert us to a further point. Procopius did not think it inappropriate

---

1985), 16–17 and 49, with A. Cameron, 'Early Byzantine *Kaiserkritik*: Two Case Histories', *BMGS* 3 (1977), 15.

[3]   Cf. Rubin, *Zeitalter*, 469–470 n.621, Cameron, *Procopius*, 52–53 and, most recently, K. Adshead, 'The Secret History of Procopius and its Genesis', *B* 63 (1993), 19–28, esp. 28 on the problematic preface to the *Anecdota*. See also now J.A.S. Evans, 'The dates of Procopius' works: a recapitulation of the evidence', *GRBS* 37 (1996), 308–309. In the light of these points, it is surely overconfident to suppose (as A. Carile, 'Consenso e dissenso fra propaganda e fronda nelle narrative dell' età giustinianea' in G.G. Archi, ed., *L'imperatore Giustiniano. Storia e Mito* (Milan, 1978), 62, does) that the work was composed according to the rules of invective (*psogos*) prescribed by Aphthonius.

[4]   The initial quotation is from *Wars* I.1.5. On the timing of Procopius's composition, see Cameron, *Procopius*, 9, 15–16, 50. Evans, 'The dates', 312, argues, however, that the *Anecdota* was only started after the *Wars* was completed.

[5]   On these cross-references, see (e.g.) Cameron, *Procopius*, 16.

to indulge in criticism in this work too; on the contrary, it was part of his brief to write the truth. And in fact it is not hard to find examples of criticism, some of it remarkably trenchant, in the *Wars*. One of the most obvious examples is his bitter attack on John the Cappadocian and Tribonian at *Wars* I.24.11–16 and the whole chapter which follows, concerning John's fall from power.[6] It is clear that Procopius thought that criticism – in some cases, verging on invective – had a role in his history. The view according to which 'Procopius was a highly self-conscious writer who imposed artificially severe restraints on himself by adopting so classicizing a literary form [in the *Wars*]' therefore requires modification: Procopius did not pigeon-hole what he had to say, reserving invective and criticism for the *Anecdota*, classicizing history for the *Wars* and panegyric for the *Buildings*.[7] There is classicizing history in the *Anecdota* and invective in the *Wars*; and this is because the division between these two works is a contingent one, dependent on circumstance.

Classicizing history, far from being a straitjacket, gave ample scope to the historians of the later Roman Empire. If Thucydides had been the only classical model, classicizing historians might well have felt restricted; but the more loosely constructed narrative of Herodotus, with its digressions on the most diverse topics, allowed great flexibility while remaining faithful to classical models. Furthermore, right from Herodotus (and to a lesser extent, Thucydides), judgements, favourable or hostile, had been passed by historians on the important figures in their works.[8] In the Hellenistic period, and then under the Roman emperors, it is not surprising to find that the tendency to focus on individuals increases. Theopompus in the fourth century concentrated his work on Philip of Macedon; and although a separate tradition of imperial biographies grew up in Roman times, a genre which remained popular in Late Antiquity, the writing of history itself could not remain unaffected by the enormous power now wielded by one man and his ministers.[9] Ammianus Marcellinus did not hesitate to

---

[6] Cf. Procopius's criticisms of Bessas, *Wars* VII.19.13–14, VII.20. On John's fall from power, cf. G. Greatrex, 'John the Cappadocian and the composition of Procopius' *Persian Wars*', *Prudentia* 27 (1995), esp. 9–13.

[7] Quotation from Cameron, *Procopius*, 17, cf. 25.

[8] See S. Hornblower, ed., *Greek Historiography* (Oxford, 1994), 30–33, referring (e.g.) to the 'chatty, judgemental and Herodotean Xenophon', (31). Note (e.g.) Herodotus, *Historiae* IX.116 (condemnation of Artayctes) or VII.135 (praise for the Spartan heralds sent to Persia). Cf. M. Whitby, *The Emperor Maurice and his Historian* (Oxford, 1988), 41 on the flexibility of classicizing history.

[9] Hornblower, *Greek Historiography*, 32–33, on the tendency to focus on individuals, perhaps already visible in Thucydides (on Alcibiades). See A. Momigliano, 'The historians of

condemn or praise emperors and officials, as well as the Senate and people of Rome.[10] This tendency is even more marked in the strong criticisms voiced by Ammianus's near contemporary Eunapius of Sardis, for instance against the author of the *Breviarium* Festus.[11] Similarly, Priscus feels at liberty to indulge in criticism of Theodosius II and the *magister militum* Ardaburius, while Malchus is still more forthright in his attacks on Leo, and, to a slightly lesser extent, Zeno.[12] In the early sixth century, Zosimus included some remarkably personal allegations in his treatment of previous emperors, particularly concerning Constantine, alongside more serious criticisms of the way in which the empire was governed.[13] It is clear therefore that most of the *ad hominem* invective which Procopius deploys in the *Anecdota* would not have been out of place in a classicizing history.[14]

How then is the division between the *Anecdota* and the *Wars* to be explained, if there is little or nothing to distinguish them in terms of genre? The answer lies in factors extraneous to the two works. Their separation is a matter of circumstance, as the case of John the Cappadocian illustrates. John fell from power in 541, and even the death of his arch-enemy Theodora in 548 failed to bring about a restoration of his position. Procopius was therefore able to give full rein to his skill at invective in the *Wars* on this occasion, and so there remained almost nothing for him to report about John in the *Anecdota*; much the same could be said for Tribonian.[15] At work on the *Wars* during the 540s, Procopius can hardly have supposed that the

---

the classical world and their audiences: some suggestions', *Sesto contributo alla storia degli studi classici* (Rome, 1980), 371–372, on the impact of the imperial system on Roman historiography; also J.F. Matthews, *The Roman Empire of Ammianus* (London, 1989), 231.

[10] E.g. 14.1 (criticism of Gallus and his wife), 14.6 (criticism of the Roman Senate and people, cf. 28.4), 27.6 (praise for Valentinian's minister Eupraxius).

[11] Eunapius, frg. 39.8 (Blockley). Cf. 46.1 (criticism of Theodosius I) and 5.1–2 (invective against the Emperor Carinus). See Blockley, *FCH* I, 8, on Eunapius's tendencies towards biography (expressed also in his preface, frg. 1).

[12] Priscus, frg. 3.1–2 and 19; Malchus, frgs 1 and 3 (on Leo), cf. 16.2 on Zeno (with 20.191 for some criticism).

[13] Zos. II.8.2, cf. II.32. Cf. II.32.2–34 for more general charges.

[14] Even the demonization of Justinian and the explicit detail concerning Theodora's sexual habits need not be viewed as incompatible with the genre: Eunapius (frg. 5) condemned Carinus for his sexual misdemeanours with noble youths, while Malchus (frg. 8) described how Zeno's son Zeno was led into all manner of vices by his attendants. Note also the allegations of sexual misconduct aimed at John the Cappadocian, *Wars* I.24.14 and cf. the attacks on Philip of Macedon's private life by Theopompus (*FGH* 115.224, 225b), with Flower, *Theopompus*, 104–111 and 218–219.

[15] See above, note 6 on John. On Tribonian, cf. *Wars* I.24.16, 25.2 and *Anecd.* 13.12 (adding nothing of substance).

emperor he so disliked would outlive him and reign for another twenty years: Justinian was already forty-five when he became sole emperor in 527. Of average build, he ate sparingly and slept little; in the 520s he suffered from a serious illness, and in the early 540s he contracted the plague.[16] The victim of one illness and two serious plots in the 540s alone seemed unlikely to remain on the throne for very much longer. Yet Justinian not only lived to see the publication of *Wars* I–VII in 550/1, but was still firmly in control of the empire in 554, when the final instalment of the *Wars* appeared. The date of Procopius's death is unknown, but there is no reason to doubt that he died before Justinian.[17] Had the emperor succumbed to old age or a plotter's dagger in 549 or 550, it is likely that there would be no *Anecdota*: all the criticisms that could be incorporated from the *Anecdota* would have been inserted into the *Wars* at some point, even at the cost of some coherence to the chronological (and geographical) structure – just as was done with the material on John. The resulting work, one might speculate, would have had a far more Herodotean feel than the *Wars* does, but would undeniably still have been classicizing history.[18] If Justinian had survived a little longer and died before *Wars* VIII was completed, it would have been possible for Procopius either to revise the *Wars* or to incorporate still more digressions and corrections in Book VIII than it contains already.[19]

---

[16]   *Anecd.* 9.35 for the illness in the 520s, 4.1 on his contraction of the plague (in 542). He was also seriously ill with a headache in 560, Theophanes, *Chronographia*, C. de Boor, ed. (Hildesheim and New York, 1980), 234, and at another time suffered problems with one of his knees, *Aed.* I.7. Mal. 425, *Anecd.* 8.12 on Justinian's appearance.

[17]   Cameron, *Procopius*, 15, cf. Evans, 'The dates', 301–302. Cameron rightly rejects the unlikely identification of the historian with the city prefect Procopius (Procopius 3 in *PLRE* III). Evans, 'The dates', 301–313, puts both *Wars* VIII and the *Buildings* in the late 550s, but cf. G. Greatrex, 'The dates of Procopius' Works', *BMGS* 18 (1994), 101–114.

[18]   The chronology of the last chapters in *Wars* I is notably askew, on which see Greatrex, 'The Composition', 5–9. J.A.S. Evans, *Procopius* (New York, 1972), 54, sees the placing of the episode on John as an emulation of Herodotus. The work produced would certainly have contained inconsistencies, as it already does in relation to John the Cappadocian, who is praised by Procopius at *Wars* III.10.7 and criticized at I.24–25. Cf. the differences in tone between Thuc. II.65.11 and VI–VII with S. Hornblower, *A Commentary on Thucydides*, I (Oxford, 1991), 348.

[19]   John of Ephesus took a more critical line on Justin II after his death, as he makes clear at *HE* III.1; cf. J.J. van Ginkel, 'John of Ephesus on Emperors: The Perception of the Byzantine Empire by a Monophysite', in R. Lavenant, ed., *VI Symposium Syriacum* (Rome, 1994), 328, 330. The description of the Black Sea at VIII.1–6 is the most obvious example of digression in *Wars* VIII; it incorporates (implicit) corrections of earlier material, e.g. on the rivers Boas and Phasis (cf. *Wars* II.29.14–16 and VIII.2.6–9, 27), as well as additions (VIII.14.38–40, omens which preceded the outbreak of war in 540).

Procopius therefore differs from other classicizing historians only in his misfortune to have passed his entire career during the principate of one man. Unlike Zosimus or Eunapius, he did not delve into much earlier history, in which his taste for invective could be exercised quite openly; Tacitus too had preferred not to extend his history into current affairs. Whereas Ammianus, Eunapius, Priscus, Malchus, Candidus or Menander were able to write about events within their own lifetime in candid and critical terms – though not without caution – Procopius was not; for in all of the above cases, the historians were writing under a new emperor, and often one whose policies were at odds with those of his predecessor.[20] When at last Justinian died, a wave of criticism was unleashed, expressed most vigorously by Evagrius (writing some decades later, however), but visible in Agathias, Menander, Corippus and even the first novel of Justin II himself.[21]

So far, then, Procopius remains well within the conventions of classicizing historiography: the existence of the *Anecdota* does not mark him off as some sort of particularly bilious outsider, more disenchanted with imperial rule than any previous historian had ever been. It remains to assess whether, like Ammianus Marcellinus in the phrase of Arnaldo Momigliano, he might be described as a 'lonely historian', difficult to place in context among his contemporaries in the sixth century.[22]

It is impossible to consider Procopius's place in sixth-century society without confronting what might be termed the '*topos*' of Byzantine *Kaiserkritik*, a literary genre first proposed by Berthold Rubin and the subject of a detailed study by Franz Tinnefeld in 1971.[23] The term has gained wide acceptance, and seems to be interpreted as denoting a range of charges which might be levelled at emperors, regardless of their appropriateness.[24] Therefore, since *Kaiserkritik* is a literary genre,

---

[20] This point is well brought out by Tinnefeld, *Kaiserkritik*, 192, cf. Menander, frg.4.6; also Ammianus 26.1.1 with Matthews, *Ammianus*, 204–205.

[21] Cf. Carile, 'Consenso', 79–83, Tinnefeld, *Kaiserkritik*, 37–40. See also A. Cameron, *Agathias* (Oxford, 1970), 125–126.

[22] A. Momigliano, 'The Lonely Historian Ammianus Marcellinus' in *Essays in Ancient and Modern Historiography* (Oxford, 1977), 127–140. Procopius's classicizing style certainly in itself does not mark him out as an outsider, since there were so many practitioners of the genre in this period; Cameron, *Procopius*, 17 and ch. 7, rightly points out that his general attitudes were also quite typical of his time.

[23] Rubin, 'Zur Kaiserkritik', Tinnefeld, *Kaiserkritik*.

[24] Rubin himself, *Zeitalter*, 233, did not believe that the allegations which constituted *Kaiserkritik* were in themselves unworthy of credence; and Tinnefeld, *Kaiserkritik*, 15, argues that the *Anecdota* is a work of history, however rich in the *topoi* of *Kaiserkritik*.

accusations which can be so labelled may almost instantly be dismissed for that very reason. In this respect, the notion of *Kaiserkritik* appears particularly unhelpful, since the evidence of panegyrics, another well-known and comparable literary genre, is regularly put to use by historians, albeit with circumspection.

However, as Katherine Adshead has pointed out, 'the existence of a separate and single genre of *Kaiserkritik* has yet to be demonstrated'.[25] The difficulty in defining a separate genre of *Kaiserkritik* arises as soon as one tries to pin it down. Rubin firmly believed in the existence of a *Senatspartei* in constant opposition if not to the imperial system of government, then at least to the methods by which it operated and to the emperor of the day. This opposition group could trace its roots back to Tacitus, via Dexippus, Eunapius and Zosimus; and it even employed a certain vocabulary in voicing its criticisms, detectable not only in the *Anecdota*, but also in Evagrius's *Church History* and John of Antioch's *Chronicle*.[26] If the existence of such a group could be demonstrated, then the *Kaiserkritik* evident in the *Anecdota* would be of great interest in reflecting the views of dissident senators in the Constantinople of Justinian. But the conclusions of Tinnefeld's wide-ranging study do nothing to vindicate Rubin's theories. Echoes of Procopius may be found in later authors, but these are by no means confined to the criticisms of emperors; and, as Averil Cameron has pointed out, it is highly doubtful whether any authors had access to the *Anecdota* before the tenth century.[27] Moreover there are, by Tinnefeld's own admission, considerable variations within the range of criticisms levelled by practitioners of *Kaiserkritik*: Procopius is, for instance, unique in castigating the emperor for excessive harshness to religious minorities. And since phrases which Rubin thought exemplified the genre could be applied to

---

[25] 'The Secret History', 22. It should be noted that Tinnefeld's treatment of *Kaiserkritik* is more nuanced than Rubin's, and he departs from his predecessor's more literary approach (*Kaiserkritik*, 180–182).

[26] Rubin, 'Zur Kaiserkritik', 453–457, *Zeitalter*, 133, 233, 235, 240–245 and 447 n. 546, cf. C. Gizewski, *Zur Normativität und Struktur der Verfassungsverhältnisse in der späteren römischen Kaiserzeit* (Munich, 1988), 59–60. Tinnefeld, *Kaiserkritik*, 13 and 180, is more sceptical, particularly concerning the notion of senatorial phrases. It is clear, however, that Procopius was not opposed to the imperial system of government, as Rubin, *Zeitalter*, 173 and Cameron, *Procopius*, 246, note; but he may have believed in a more restricted role for the emperor, like the author of the *Peri Politikes Epistemes*, cf. Cameron, *Procopius*, 249–250 and Gizewski, *Zur Normativität*, 142.

[27] Cameron, *Procopius*, 16 and n. 88, cf. Tinnefeld, *Kaiserkritik*, 180–181 and Adshead, 'The Secret History', 19–23. Rubin, *Zeitalter*, 240, argued that Evagrius and Zonaras were both (directly) influenced by the *Anecdota*.

individuals who were not emperors, one may begin to wonder just how useful the term *Kaiserkritik* is.[28] Furthermore, the scope of the proposed genre is peculiarly narrow. Tinnefeld views *Kaiserkritik* as the product of writers of high social standing, and he does not hesitate to conclude that Procopius was expressing the views of sixth-century senators and large landowners; he goes so far as to identify Procopius with the aristocracy which had prospered under Anastasius and now found itself threatened by the change in regime which had taken place in 518.[29] Yet there is criticism – and praise – of emperors in works not associated with the élite in Byzantine society, a good instance of which is the *Oracle of Baalbek*, which reports with approval the popularity enjoyed by the Emperor Zeno because of his love for the poor and his humiliation of the aristocracy, and is equally critical of his successor.[30]

The concept of *Kaiserkritik*, if it is to survive, requires extensive modification and refinement. It seems doubtful whether it is worth the effort involved; but it may have proved useful, if its legacy is to draw attention to the fact that 'not even the best contemporary critics were able to throw off the habit of interpreting politics in terms of the behaviour of the emperor', or at any rate of the emperor and his closest associates.[31] What we are left with therefore is no more than a certain tendency to focus criticism on the ruler(s) of the empire, and for the same charges – such as avarice, weakness and corruption – to recur constantly. This is, of course, extremely

---

[28]   Tinnefeld, *Kaiserkritik*, 180–181.

[29]   Tinnefeld, *Kaiserkritik*, 185.

[30]   P.J. Alexander, *The Oracle of Baalbek. The Tiburtine Sibyl in Greek Dress* (Washington, DC, 1967), lines 159–161 and 167–170, cf. 93 and 95–97, with Cameron, 'Early Byzantine *Kaiserkritik*', 16; cf. the favourable remarks on Zeno in the *Anonymus Valesianus*, 9.40, 44, on which see A. Laniado, 'Some problems in the sources for the reign of the emperor Zeno', *BMGS* 15 (1991), 162–163. As Cameron notes, 'Early Byzantine *Kaiserkritik*', 1 n. 5, Tinnefeld also fails to take into account less 'mainstream' writers, such as John of Ephesus; and, given the doubtful worth of the dividing line between 'élite' and 'popular' literature (cf. Cameron, *Procopius*, 24–26), it is unclear why *Kaiserkritik* has not been perceived in the work of chroniclers and hagiographers.

[31]   Quotation from Cameron, 'Early Byzantine *Kaiserkritik*', 16. Praetorian prefects were the usual alternative (or additional) focus of criticism: note Eunapius's criticisms of the praetorian prefect Rufinus (frg. 62.2), as well as Zosimus's (V.9–12) and John the Lydian's of Marinus (see 225 below). John the Lydian's invective against John the Cappadocian contains accusations similar to those brought against emperors, yet, since not directed against Justinian and not in a historical work, it is passed over by Tinnefeld.

broad, and has no evident benefits for the interpretation of sources, particularly since almost any emperor was vulnerable to such accusations.[32]

Notwithstanding the limitations of the notion of *Kaiserkritik*, Procopius's position in sixth-century society must be considered. Here again it appears difficult to view him as an outsider, for there was no shortage of malcontents under Justinian's regime.[33] Hence, although Procopius is probably the fullest source on the disastrous consequences of the emperor's policies, his contemporary John the Lydian echoes many of his criticisms. Further attacks on Justinian's conduct of affairs followed under later emperors; and as late as the twelfth century Zonaras appears to have had access to an earlier (unknown) source critical of Justinian.[34] Thus Procopius was by no means an outsider in reacting negatively to the developments in imperial policy introduced by Justinian and his ministers. But was he a 'lonely' outsider? It would be much more interesting if he could be associated with a particular group in sixth-century society, as exponents of the genre of *Kaiserkritik* seek to do: as has been noted, they regard him – and other classicizing historians – as spokesmen for an aristocratic group, comprising senators and wealthy landowners. According to this view, the accession of Justin I in 518 caused consternation among the élite which had risen to prominence during the reign of Anastasius, and who resented the sudden rise to power of the parvenu Justin (and Justinian).[35] There was therefore a significant pool of former high officials and senators eager to unseat Justin and Justinian. They placed their hopes for a change in regime in Belisarius, but were consistently disappointed by his singular loyalty both to the emperor and to his own wife; this disappointment is reflected in the attacks on Belisarius in the *Anecdota*, which are directed chiefly at his uxoriousness.[36]

---

[32] The *Anecdota* may, however, stand out from such standard accusations to a certain extent: Roger Scott has argued persuasively that the work represents a considered riposte to particular initiatives undertaken by the government: 'Malalas, the *Secret History* and Justinian's propaganda', *DOP* 39 (1985), 99–109.

[33] In general see M. Maas, *John Lydus and the Roman Past* (London 1992), 34–36 and Cameron, *Procopius*, 21–22.

[34] Rubin, *Zeitalter*, 213, 230–231, 240 with Carney, *Bureaucracy in Traditional Society* (Lawrence, KS, 1971) II, 163–176, for a detailed comparison of John and Procopius. Although Zonaras XIV.6.1–9 contains criticisms of Justinian and Theodora similar to those of the *Anecdota*, those at 6.31–2 are clearly different.

[35] See above, note 26; also Rubin, *Zeitalter*, 61, 203, Tinnefeld, *Kaiserkritik*, 23, and cf. Angold, 'Procopius' portrait', 30.

[36] Rubin, *Zeitalter*, 199–200, 218.

Such a picture cannot, however, be sustained for a number of reasons. First, the extent of aristocratic discontent under Justinian is very difficult to gauge. The only readily available figure is that of the eighteen patricians, *illustres*, and consulars who had their property confiscated as associates of Hypatius in the wake of the Nika riot. Although the Senate of Constantinople in the sixth century was much smaller than it had been in the late fourth century, this is not a large number.[37] Furthermore, by the time Procopius was writing, the number of senators who owed their appointment to Anastasius must have been very low indeed, for in addition to the eighteen punished after the Nika riot, others had succumbed to persecutions of pagans and heretics in the late 520s and mid-540s.[38] Hence, as time passed, the ranks of senators will have come to be dominated by men promoted by Justin and Justinian; and so it is not surprising that the two plots against Justinian later in his reign failed to attract much support and were swiftly betrayed.[39] Second, it overemphasizes the discontinuity between the reign of Anastasius and his successors. The situation for the senatorial aristocracy did not suddenly worsen in 518; on the contrary, it actually improved. For according to John of Antioch, late in his reign, 'Anastasius, having turned for the worse, exiled the entire aristocracy of the state at one stroke', and the prosopographical record confirms the thrust of the assertion: the 510s saw the disgrace and exile of the former praetorian prefect Apion, as well as that of the former military commanders Philoxenus and Diogenianus, not to mention the civil war fought in the Balkans against the former *magister militum* Vitalian.[40] All were restored to favour as soon as Justin ascended the throne, even if Vitalian was

---

[37] Theophanes, *Chronographia*, 185–186; the three ranks were those held by senators, cf. G. Greatrex, 'The Nika riot: a reappraisal', *JHS* 117 (1997), 80 n. 99.

[38] Cf. (e.g.) Maas, *John Lydus*, 70–71, on the persecutions. Yet others will no doubt have have fallen victim to the plague, as Tribonian probaby did; cf. T. Honoré, *Tribonian* (London, 1978), 61–64.

[39] Cf. P.J. Heather, 'New Men for New Constantines' in P. Magdalino, ed., *New Constantines* (Aldershot, 1994), 13–14 and 20 on the new 'aristocracy of service' which emerged in the fourth century. This remained true in the sixth century, with the modification that only those reaching the pinnacles of a career in the bureaucracy gained entry to the Senate: cf. Rubin, *Zeitalter*, 233 and Jones, *LRE*, 529 (noting that a hereditary element managed to perpetuate itself none the less).

[40] Joh. Ant. frg. 215. *PLRE* II, Apion 2 (he was exiled in 510), Diogenianus 4 (date of exile post-493), Philoxenus 8 (date of exile unknown), Vitalianus 2. Diogenianus was a relative of the empress Ariadne (Mal. 393), while Apion's family was among the most distinguished of Egypt: both might therefore be viewed as members of the 'hereditary aristocracy'. Cf. G. Greatrex, 'Flavius Hypatius, *quem vidit validum Parthus sensitque timendum*', *B* 66 (1996), 138–140, on the conservatism of Justin's reign in particular.

assassinated not long afterwards.[41] Moreover, the family of Anastasius continued to prosper: Hypatius's career in particular reached its acme under Justin and Justinian. Even after the Nika riot, Probus was soon pardoned, and the reputation of Hypatius and Pompey rehabilitated. The next generation of Anastasius's family was actually united with Justinian's, when the emperor's niece Praiecta married John, the son of Hypatius, in 546/8.[42]

Anastasius's reign cannot then be portrayed as a golden age for the established senatorial aristocracy. The fragment of John of Antioch cited above relates numerous abuses of the emperor's regime, including the appropriation of funds from the wealthy. A similar picture emerges from the biography of St Theodosius compiled by Theodore of Petra, as well as from John the Lydian. Although John is usually regarded as a critic of John the Cappadocian, and indirectly of Justinian, he clearly believed that the decline of the praetorian prefecture at any rate started under Anastasius; as in the case of Justinian and John the Cappadocian, he prefers to blame the prefect Marinus than to criticize the emperor.[43] The image of a powerful circle of disgruntled aristocrats throughout the reigns of Justin and Justinian thus has little to recommend it. Discontented senators there certainly were, such as the former praetorian prefect Julian, who joined Hypatius and Pompey during the Nika riot, and the unknown Origenes; but there were unhappy senators under any emperor, no less so in the case of Anastasius than in that of his successors.[44] According to both Victor Tonnennensis and Zonaras there were senators actually enthusiastic for Justinian: it was apparently only in response to pressure from them that Justinian was raised to the rank of *nobilissimus*, then Caesar, by his uncle.[45]

---

[41] Mal. 411; cf. Vasiliev, *Justin I* (Cambridge, MA, 1950), 108–114, with Greatrex, 'Flavius Hypatius', 132–136.

[42] Cf. A.D.E. Cameron, 'The House of Anastasius', *GRBS* 19 (1978), 259–276, on the fortunes of Anastasius's family under Justin and Justinian; also Greatrex, 'Flavius Hypatius', 121 on Hypatius's career. *PLRE* III, Praiecta 1 for the date of her marriage to John.

[43] *Der Heilige Theodosios*, ed. H. Usener (Leipzig, 1890), 54–55; note the accusation of *philargyria* at 55.12. John the Lydian, *De Mag.* III.36, 46, 49, 51, with Maas, *John Lydus*, 86–87. Cf. Laniado, 'Some problems', 164–165, pointing out that the panegyricists of Anastasius make very similar complaints concerning the later years of Zeno's reign.

[44] Tinnefeld, *Kaiserkritik*, 39 n. 77, cites Joh. Eph. *HE* VI.24, in which both Senate and people are said to have been critical of Justinian's gifts to the Avars (late in his reign), cf. Agathias, *Historiae*, V.14. But one cannot infer from the complaints of Procopius and John the Lydian that there was general senatorial discontent in the latter half of Justinian's reign, as Carile, 'Consenso', 61, does. On Julian, see Cameron, 'House of Anastasius', 264–267.

[45] Vasiliev, *Justin I*, 94–95, citing Zon. XIV.5.35 and Victor Tonnennensis, *Chron.* a.525 (ed. Mommsen, 197). Gizewski, *Zur Normativität*, 124–125, notes how Justinian sought to support

Finally, Procopius himself. There is no evidence that he was a senator, although he was rewarded with honorary *illustris* rank at some point.[46] In this he is no different from other classicizing historians, such as Ammianus or Priscus. This need not have precluded him, however, from voicing complaints made by senators: the proudly republican author Titinius Capito, who (with Trajan's permission) displayed busts of Brutus and Cassius in his house, clearly took a senatorial line in his commemoration of the great men of earlier times, and was neither a senator nor a knight himself.[47] Both Ammianus and Zosimus, to name but two examples, are critical of the harsh treatment of the Senate under certain emperors.[48] Procopius was thus by no means unusual in singling out this aspect of Justinian's reign for criticism; and in other areas of policy, his accusations resemble those of earlier historians – such as Zosimus and John of Antioch concerning the oppression of the cities and the curial class or Malchus on the sale of offices.[49]

At one level, Procopius was a 'lonely historian': 'unable to have confidence even in the most intimate of [his] kinsmen', he composed a work destined – so he claims – for the eyes of posterity alone.[50] Yet it is clear from

---

the Senate in some of his legislation; cf. *ibid.* 145 and 146 n. 186 on senators aligned with Justinian and criticized by Procopius. On the other hand, see also *Anecd.* 9.52, 10.7, 10.9, noted by Rubin, *Zeitalter*, 125 (attesting hostility to the succession of Justinian among senators).

[46] Gizewski, *Zur Normativität*, 126 n. 165, asserts (from *Anecd.* 12.14) that Procopius was a senator, although the passage certainly does not allow such an inference. Procopius was an *illustris* according to the Suda (cf. *PLRE* III, Procopius 2), but (despite Evans, *Procopius*, 38), the rank (at any rate at honorary level) was bestowed fairly widely during Justinian's reign, cf. Stein II, 712 and n. 1.

[47] Cf. R. Syme, *Tacitus* I (Oxford, 1959), 92, from Pliny, *ep.*1.17. Ammianus was not a senator: see A. Cameron, 'The Roman friends of Ammianus', *JRS* 54 (1964), 15–16. Cf. Rubin, *Zeitalter*, 431–432 n. 425, on the similarity between Procopius's 'senatorial' attitudes and those of Tacitus and Ammianus; also Angold, 'Procopius' portrait', 29.

[48] Zos. V.13.1 (under Arcadius), Ammianus 28.1 (trials at Rome under Valentinian); cf. Momigliano, 'The Lonely Historian', 133, on Ammianus's sympathy for the *curiales* and propertied classes generally. Zosimus was not a senator: cf. *PLRE* II, Zosimus 6. Note also Joh. Ant. frgs 106 (Domitian), 189 (Eutropius) and Priscus, frg. 9.3.

[49] Zosimus IV.29, Joh. Ant. frgs 215, 216 (on the cities and curial classes); cf. Malchus frg. 3; Malchus frg. 10 and Joh. Ant. frg. 215 on the sale of offices.

[50] *Anecd.* 1.2 (tr. Dewing). Rubin, *Zeitalter*, 470 n. 621 regards the work as destined for a (contemporary) opposition movement, however; cf. J.A.S. Evans, *The Age of Justinian* (London, 1996), 5, surmising that 'it must have found some appreciative readers' for it to have survived. I would be less inclined to dismiss Procopius's preface so lightly, especially given what he goes on to report concerning the frequency of betrayals; the case of the patriarch Paul of Antioch, reported by John of Ephesus (*HE* II.2), shows how dangerous the composition of a critical work could be; cf. van Ginkel, 'John of Ephesus on Emperors', 328.

other sources that he was by no means a lone voice or outsider in inveighing against the emperor's policies.[51] And like all other classicizing historians, he was certainly a member of the 'sub-élite', a member of the landed classes of the eastern empire, with the typical prejudices of his rank. As an *assessor* of the most successful general of his age, he was well informed about intrigues in the palace and the army; he was undoubtedly an 'insider' in this respect.[52] It has been argued here, however, that Procopius's criticisms of Justinian's rule should not be interpreted as the manifesto of some sort of senatorial grouping.[53] Nor should he be seen as a spokesman for a party which favoured the deposition of Justinian in favour of Belisarius. Such a body of opinion may have existed, since he was frequently implicated in conspiracies.[54] But in fact Belisarius did not command the loyalty of even all the military, as is clear from his campaigns in Italy. Thus the (not unwavering) enthusiasm of Procopius for his patron by no means implies the existence of a *Belisariuskreise*.[55]

In conclusion, Procopius should not be regarded as an outsider, either in terms of genres, or as someone isolated from contemporary opinion. He worked within the conventions of classicizing historiography and, as a well-born and successful official, had good connections in the upper échelons of the empire. The existence of the *Anecdota* as a separate work has, regrettably, rather confused the picture. On the one hand, it has inclined scholars to see it as the antithesis of the *De Aedificiis* (*psogos* against panegyric), rather than as a historical companion to the *Wars*. On the other,

---

[51] Note also Procopius's claim to be reporting the opinion of 'most people' at *Anecd.* 13.1. See note 34 on Zonaras's critical source and cf. Rubin, *Zeitalter*, 227 on John the Lydian (and later critics).

[52] Cf. Cameron, *Procopius*, 71 (on his knowledge of the plot to entrap John the Cappadocian) and J. Haury, 'Prokop und der Kaiser Justinian', *BZ* 37 (1937), 8–9. Cameron, *Procopius*, 240, 245, 264 on Procopius (and John the Lydian) being members of the 'sub-élite' and their attitudes.

[53] Cf. Momigliano, 'The Lonely Historian', 133: 'Ammianus does not belong to a "party" or "faction"' *contra* (e.g.) Rubin, *Zeitalter*, 200: 'Der Mitarbeiter Belisars fühlt sich als Sprecher einer Gruppe...', cf. ibid., 198 and Tinnefeld, *Kaiserkritik*, 21–22. Procopius's criticisms actually go beyond the scope of the charges usually brought against emperors and powerful figures, and thus seem more individual than conventional; see above, note 32.

[54] Stein II, 480–482, 779 on Belisarius's implication in plots in 541 and 562, cf. Procopius, *Wars* III.8.1–2. Tinnefeld, *Kaiserkritik*, 21, Rubin, *Zeitalter*, 200–201, and Carile, 'Consenso', 64, clearly envisage some sort of Belisarius-party. It should be stressed that whatever opposition groups there were are unlikely to have been either united or organized: see J. Karayannopoulos, *Gnomon* 31 (1961), 670 and Maas, *John Lydus*, 7.

[55] The allegations against Belisarius and Bouzes in 542 (*Anecd.* 4.1–4) point to his isolation in the military: it was two fellow commanders who laid the accusation.

it has tempted others to infer the existence of factions of conspiring senators and generals, although neither the *Anecdota* nor any other sources permit such extrapolations. Both these tendencies, it has been argued, should be resisted.

17. Foreigners in tenth-century Byzantium: a contribution to the history of cultural encounter

Liliana Simeonova

Europe, and the Hellenistic Roman world before it, have always been concerned with cultural encounter and cultural appropriation in ways that other cultures perhaps have not.[1] 'How to deal with the Other?' was a question to which the European seemed never to be able to find a simple answer. In his book entitled *The Conquest of America. The Question of the Other*, Tzvetan Todorov wrote: 'The first, spontaneous reaction with regard to the stranger is to imagine him as inferior, since he is different from us: this is not even a man, or if he is one, an inferior barbarian; if he does not speak our language, it is because he speaks none at all, or *cannot* speak, as Columbus still believed.' It is in this fashion, according to Todorov, that the European Slavs call their German neighbours 'mutes', the Mayas of Yucatan call the Toltec invaders 'mutes', and so on.[2] It was in a similar fashion that the ancient Greeks started calling foreigners 'barbarians' on account of their inarticulate manner of speaking. In due time, the pejorative 'barbarian' spread out to include the foreigners' dress, mannerisms, food and customs which, from a Hellenic point of view, seemed quite 'barbaric'.

Byzantines inherited their ancient Greek predecessors' attitude toward foreigners. To them, the foreigner was a distorting mirror in which they were able to contemplate a wholly unrepresentative image of themselves: thus the foreigner was uncouth, simple, and uncivilized; Byzantines, on the other hand, were sophisticated and refined. This attitude served consistently to assure the Byzantines that their civilization was superior to all other civilizations and deserved to dominate the *oikoumene*; that

---

[1]   See A. Pagden's review of J. Fontana, *The Distorted Past: A Reinterpretation of Europe*, trans. by C. Smith (Cambridge, MA, 1995), in *AHR*, 102 (1997), 1469–1470.

[2]   T. Todorov, *The Conquest of America. The Question of the Other*, trans. by R. Howard (New York and Cambridge, 1984), 76–78.

their empire's proper place in the world was that of the benefactor and
the master of all the others; and that, bearing primary responsibility for
everybody's salvation, the Christian Roman emperor had the divine task
of spreading Orthodoxy on a world-wide scale.

As its critics have insisted, Byzantium was aggressive and overbearing
in its attitudes toward outsiders, whether these were foreigners or
minorities. At the same time, however, the Byzantine policy-makers,
diplomats, merchants and generals seem to have been well informed of
the real world that stretched beyond the imperial borders; more often
than not, they were capable of making the right decisions in their
dealings with foreigners. The Byzantines' attitude toward foreigners
could, therefore, be described as ambivalent: in their collective mind, the
long-term perspective of conquering the whole world in order to bring it
in harmony with God's sacred purposes went hand in hand with a certain
amount of flexibility and compromise, which their empire showed in its
day-to-day dealings with other nations.

In a sense, the tenth century marked a peak in the Byzantines'
awareness of the role which their empire played in the contemporary
world. Thanks to Constantinople's increased significance as a cultural,
religious and commercial centre, as well as the emperors Leo VI's and
Constantine VII's love of multiculturalism, the imperial capital and the
imperial court hosted great numbers of foreigners, Christian, Muslim,
and pagan. In the eyes of the tenth-century Byzantines as well as in those
of their foreign contemporaries, Constantinople was more or less an
epitome of the Eastern Roman Empire, representing the entire complexity
of the empire's power structures, social practices, religious norms and
artistic canons. The surviving sources provide evidence of at least
fourteen visits of foreign heads of state or other high-ranking visitors to
the imperial capital in the course of the century.[3] At the same time, in
Constantinople, there always was the possibility of a rise of xenophobia,
due to a growing number of foreigners presented with titles and gifts by
the emperor.

Much has been said and written about Byzantium's self-
representation which has found reflection, at various levels and in
various ways, in its religious and imperial propaganda. Audiences with
the emperor, lavish diplomatic receptions at the palace, tours around the

---

[3]   L. Simeonova, 'Semiotika na uniženieto: visokopostaveni čuždenci v imperskata
stolica prez X vek' ('Semiotics of Humiliation: High-Ranking Foreigners in the Imperial
Capital in the Tenth Century'), *Rodina* 1996/4, 29–43 (in Bulgarian).

capital, religious processions, military triumphs and games in the Hippodrome were used by the Byzantines as a means of impressing, and intimidating, the foreign visitors. Life in Byzantium – in fact, every aspect of it – was loaded with layers of symbolism, and the average Byzantine was highly apprehensive of the language of symbols. But how far were foreigners able to read into the symbolic language of Byzantine ceremonies? Did Byzantine symbols 'work' within a Christian cultural context only or were there any universal, 'trans-cultural' symbols that 'worked' in a wider cultural context? And how much of this propaganda was actually designed for purely domestic consumption?

In the first place, there was a large group of symbols that transgressed the boundaries of the Roman Christian symbolism and were easily understood by most foreign visitors to Constantinople. The large amounts of delicious food served at imperial banquets, the endless demonstrations of wealth, the ample decoration of the palace and the streets, and the rich gifts of silk, valuables and money certainly formed a 'universal' language that no Christian, Muslim, or pagan would fail to understand.

Thus, scholars have argued whether Liutprand's *Relatio* is a true account of his diplomatic mission to Constantinople or an angry pamphlet presenting a distorted picture of what he saw and experienced in the imperial capital.[4] Whatever the case, the bishop of Cremona did not fail to appreciate the good food served at the palace, as could be seen from the following episode. In his own words, after he made a fuss because an uncouth Bulgarian ambassador was given precedence over him, the illustrious ambassador of Emperor Otto I angrily left the banquet; his anger, however, was soon mollified thanks to the delicious dish which was sent to him by the emperor:

> But the pious emperor relieved my grief through a generous gift by sending me, out of his most refined dishes, one fat kid of which he himself had consumed and which was deliciously filled with garlic, onions, and leeks and was soaked in fish sauce. At that point, I was wishing you were at my table, so that you, who do not believe that the refined pleasures of the pious emperor lead to favorable solutions, would, just by seeing this, believe it.[5]

---

[4] On the nature of Liutprand's *Relatio*, see M. Lintzel, *Ausgewählte Schriften*, Bd 2 (Berlin, 1961), 371 and following. Cf. B. Karageorgos, Λιουτπράνδος. Ο επίσκοπος Κρεμώνης ως ιστορικός και διπλωμάτης (Athens, 1978), 62–65.

[5] Liutprand, *Relatio de legatione Constantinopolitana*, in *MGH SS* III, 350.30–351.39.

As Thomas Weber's study of the descriptions of food and beverage in Liutprand's accounts of Constantinople has shown,[6] the bishop made fun of the Greek wine but seemed very much to like Byzantine cuisine; he described, in detail, the Greek food and spices. Translated into the language of signs, Liutprand's references to the excellent Byzantine food provide an example of how easily the 'us vs them' gap could be bridged by feasting which 'worked' as a trans-cultural sign.

Muslim guests at imperial banquets did not fail to appreciate the Greek food, either. Harun-ibn-Yahya seems deeply thankful to the Byzantine masters of ceremonies for their going as far as to swear, by the head of the emperor, that in the dishes served to the Arabs there was no pork at all; he was further impressed by the fact that the food was served on large golden and silver plates.[7]

To discuss the importance which, since its earliest days, Western civilization has assigned to the ritual of feasting is not one of my objectives here. Suffice it to say that, to the ancient Greek *symposion*, the Byzantines added a large number of meaningful elements. Thus, the arrangement of the great number of guests at the imperial tables was a reflection of the hierarchy at the imperial court and the one in Heaven.[8] And because Christian society is a society valuing ritual and sacrifice, the

---

[6] J. Koder and Th. Weber, *Liutprand von Cremona in Konstantinopel. Untersuchungen zum griechischen Sprachschatz und zu realienkundlichen Aussagen in seinen Werken, Byzantina Vindobonensia* Band XIII (Wien, 1980), 73–99.

[7] A.A. Vasiliev, 'Harun-ibn-Yahya and His Description of Constantinople', *Seminarium Kondakovianum* 5 (Prague, 1932), 149–163, esp. 157. Vasiliev believes that ibn-Yahya's journey to Constantinople took place in the second half of the ninth century and, still more exactly, after 881: ibid., 149–152. I am more inclined to attribute his journey to the very end of the ninth or, rather, the very beginning of the tenth century. The *terminus post quem* of his trip to Byzantium seems to be the late 890s: ibn-Yahya describes the participation of Arab prisoners of war (of which he was one) in the Christmas banquets; yet inviting POWs to the palace seems to have been an innovation introduced to the Byzantine court ceremonial on the initiative of Leo VI; most probably, it was this as well as some other changes in the ceremonial that made the imperial *atriklines* Philotheos abandon the existing *kletorologia* and compile a *kletorologion* of his own (Sept. 899). Cf. L. Simeonova, 'In the Depths of Tenth-Century Byzantine Ceremonial: the Treatment of Arab Prisoners of War at Imperial Banquets', *BMGS* 22 (1998), 74–103, and esp. 77 and 103. The *terminus ante quem* of ibn-Yahya's visit was the first decade of the tenth century: ibn-Rosteh seems to have written ibn-Yahya's story down *c.* AD 903, according to M.J. de Goeje, or no later than 913–914, according to other Orientalists: see Vasiliev, 'Harun-ibn-Yahya and His Description of Constantinople', 149, n. 1. This narrows the dates of ibn-Yahya's journey down to a period of several years, i.e., between the late 890s and 903 (or 914).

[8] See the above-mentioned *Kletorologion* of Philotheos, in N. Oikonomidès, *Les listes de préséance byzantines des IXe et Xe siècles* (Paris, 1972), 81–235.

food served at these banquets played the double role of a means of social interaction and ritual food. Inasmuch as the Byzantine court ceremonial was loaded with secular and religious elements, banquets at the palace were closely linked with the ritual of eating sacrificial food on the main feasts of the liturgical calendar (Christmas, Easter, Pentecost, the Feast of the Holy Apostles, etc.). Through a seemingly friendly gesture of compromise, which amounted to swearing that they were not feeding their Muslim guests on pork, the Byzantines actually succeeded in securing the Muslims' unconscious acceptance of a Christian ritual of eating sacrificial food on Christmas.

That, at banquets, certain guests were given precedence over others was a gesture that was not hard to decipher, at least in most cases. Muslims, pagans and recent converts, however, were not always able to read into this type of coded language. Much harder to decipher were such complex ceremonies as, for example, a foreigner's spiritual adoption by the emperor, or an act of quasi-baptism of infidels, or the extravagant colour-and-number symbolism encoded in some triumphs, processions and other public events. Let me adduce several instances of this type of lack of understanding, or misunderstanding on the foreigners' part, of Byzantine ceremonies.

For example, the meaning of what happened to Princess Olga of Kiev during her stay in Constantinople is explained, in divergent ways, by the Byzantine and Russian authors.[9] Constantine Porphyrogennetos, for one thing, tells us that, upon being received at the palace, Olga was decorated with a waistband and thus became one of the empress's ladies-in-waiting. Later, at the banquet, she was seated at the empress's table. While this episode is described, in *The Book of Ceremonies*, in the context of the great honours accorded to the foreign princess,[10] the fourteenth-century editor of the *Russian Primary Chronicle* (the so-called *Laurentian text*) does not mention it at all. What followed Olga's baptism is described, by this Russian chronicler, in terms of folklore rather than historic fact:

---

[9]   For more details concerning Olga's trip to the imperial capital, see D. Obolensky, *The Byzantine Commonwealth. Eastern Europe 500–1453* (New York, 1982), 238–239; and also S. Franklin and J. Shepard, *The Emergence of Rus 750–1200* (London and New York, 1996), 133–138.

[10]   Constantine Porphyrogenitus, *De cerimoniis aulae byzantinae libri duo*, ed. I. Reiske, vol. II (Bonn, 1830), 594–598. See also J. Featherstone, 'Ol'ga's Visit to Constantinople', *Harvard Ukrainian Studies* XIV/3–4 (1990), 293–312.

> After her baptism, the emperor summoned Olga and made known
> to her that he wished her to become his wife. But she replied, 'How
> can you marry me, after yourself baptizing me and calling me your
> daughter? For among Christians that is unlawful, as you yourself
> must know.' Then the emperor said, 'Olga, you have outwitted
> me.' He gave her many gifts of gold, silver, and various vases, and
> dismissed her, still calling her his daughter.[11]

Although, somewhat later in the text of the *Primary Chronicle*, Olga's trip
to the Byzantine emperor is likened to the Queen of Ethiopia's trip to
King Solomon in search of wisdom, the fourteenth-century Christian
editor of this Russian saga did not consider it necessary to revise his
earlier folklore-style explanation of what happened when the Russian
princess was baptized. An earlier, tenth-century version of the same
chronicle, the so-called *Perejaslavl'-Suzdal'* text, informs us that the
emperor wanted to make Olga an empress but eventually made her his
daughter. Another Russian source, the *Chronicle of the Russian Princes* (the
twelfth-century *Perejaslavl'-Vladimir* text) says that, upon seeing Olga's
beautiful face, the emperor 'spoke to her in words of love and told her
that he wanted to marry her'.[12] Referring to the same episode, Olga's
Russian hagiographer emphasizes the princess's spirituality which was in
sharp contrast with the emperor's sinful taste for worldly pleasures.[13] In
fact, most Russian sources say that the Greek *tsar* then was Tzimiskes but
the name of the emperor does not really matter.

During her visit to Constantinople, Olga was accompanied by an
impressive number of people, both men and women; maybe it was their
narrative of what they thought they had *seen* happen that was used, by
both contemporary and later Russian writers, as an explanation of what

---

[11] *The Russian Primary Chronicle. Laurentian Text.* Tr. and ed. by S.H. Cross and O.P.
Sherbowitz-Wetzor (Cambridge, MA, 1953), 83. Cf. *Povest' vremennykh let. Po Lavrent'evskoj
letopisi 1377 goda*, ed. D.S. Likhachev and V.P. Adrianova-Perets (Leningrad, 1950), I, 241–
242, and commentary in ibid., II, 306–308.

[12] On the above texts, see N.I. Prokof'ev, *Russkie khozhenia XII–XV veka* (Moscow,
1970), 5–30, and esp. 19–24. Prokof'ef believes that 'love' in Olga's case is used in a political
rather than romantic context, all the more that the princess must have been about 67 years
old at that time. According to Prokof'ev, the word 'love' was part of the traditional formula
used in the tenth-century Byzantine–Russian peace treaties: e.g., 'to create love with the
Tsar himself, and with all the boyars, and with all the Greek people'.

[13] I. Malyshevsky, 'Proiskhozhdenie russkoj velikoj kn'agini Ol'gi sv.', *Kievskaja starina*
(1889), 4–5.

had *really* happened upon the princess's conversion to Christianity.[14] Thus, while Constantine Porphyrogennetos saw himself as an intermediary between man and God who stood as Olga's sponsor before the altar, Russian authors depicted the foreign *tsar* as the failed suitor of Slavic folklore.

Another example of foreigners not being able to decode the language of Byzantine ceremonial is presented by the participation of Muslim prisoners of war in the Christmas Day and Easter Sunday banquets at the palace. The obvious part of the story is that Emperor Leo VI, and Constantine VII after him, may have wanted to add to their imperial universalism by inviting people of as many nationalities to these banquets as possible. The less obvious part, at least from a Muslim's point of view, is that these Arabs, selected from among the prisoners kept in the Great Praetorium, may have been subject to a coded ceremony of baptism which remained concealed from their eyes.

Alterity resulting from religious differences seems to have bothered Byzantines more than any other type of alterity, whether originating in ethnicity, class distinction, or gender. Byzantines were prepared to do everything humanly possible in order to secure the salvation of other people's souls on the day of the Last Judgement. At the same time, they felt that it was their duty to punish severely everybody who had apostatized or had refused to adopt Christianity. Thus, during a Cretan campaign in the 870s, Niketas, the commander-in-chief of the Byzantine forces, showed great cruelty in his dealings with prisoners: those who had apostatized from Christianity were skinned alive and their property was confiscated; those who were Muslims were dropped into a vessel filled with boiling resin and were told that it was in this painful and gruesome fashion that they were being baptized.[15]

Under Leo VI and his son, this type of 'conversion' of Muslims to Christianity was no longer possible. Both emperors showed great interest in the Arab world and felt a certain degree of respect for Arab customs and warfare. Consequently, Arab POWs began to be treated in a more

---

[14] Likhachev argues that the *Russian Primary Chronicle* was greatly influenced by Russian folklore. See D.S. Likhachev, *Izbrannye raboty v trekh tomakh* (Leningrad, 1987), II, 43–133. Furthermore, the motif of a smart woman, who succeeds in outwitting a stranger making advances to her, is one of the most exploited motifs in the vast body of Slavic moralistic tales, the so-called Slavic *paterika*. On the central themes running through these tales, see S. Nikolova, ed., *Pateričnite razkazi v bălgarskata srednovekovna literatura* (Sofia, 1986), 5–17.

[15] Theophanes Continuatus, *Chronographia*, , ed. I. Bekker (Bonn, 1838), V.61.

humane fashion by the Byzantines while Arab delegations were given lavish receptions at the palace;[16] ordinary Muslims were encouraged to convert to Christianity in return for a comfortable settlement in the empire.[17]

Because the prisoners kept in the Great Praetorium were most probably members of the Arab nobility, the Byzantines did not dare to make them openly apostatize; they went for a coded baptismal ceremony instead. In an earlier article of mine, I examined the multi-layered meaning of the Muslim prisoners' participation in the Christmas Day and Easter Sunday banquets.[18] By a comparative study of contemporary sources, I tried to prove that the white dresses, which the Arabs were given to wear for the occasion, were, in fact, the so-called 'robes of sinlessness' worn by catechumens, or newly enlightened; and that these Arabs were invited to partake of Christian feasts that were directly associated with the baptismal season in the East Orthodox liturgical calendar (and especially with the days when baptism of adult catechumens took place).

Furthermore, at both banquets, the Muslim captives were seated next to the low-ranking members of the Bulgarian delegation.[19] In the language of Byzantine ceremonies, this may have been a hint that Arabs will soon become 'Bulgarians', that is, tame Christian 'friends and subjects' of the Roman emperor. As a result of this meaningful ceremony, the emperor must have scored points in the eyes of his own subjects and his Christian guests: he was seen as a truly universal ruler capable of securing everybody's salvation through baptizing them, whether openly or secretly.

Harun-ibn-Yahya, who seems to have participated in at least one of these imperial banquets, does not suspect the Byzantines of any wrongdoing; this only confirms my assumption that the Arabs were unaware of the hidden meaning of the ceremonial of which they were partaking. Neither does he mention the fact that the banquet hall was brightly lit and that, from time to time, the lights went off: after all, Muslims were not familiar with the meaning of light in the Christian metaphysical sense.

---

[16] Const. Porph., *De cerim.*, II, 584.

[17] Const. Porph., *De cerim.*, II, 694–695.

[18] See above, note 7: Simeonova, 'In the Depths of Tenth-Century Byzantine Ceremonial'.

[19] Oikonomidès, *Les listes de préséance*, 169.8–20, 203.13–15.

As his description of the twelve-day Christmas banquet shows, however, ibn-Yahya did not thoroughly fail to decode the symbolic language of the ceremony. For example, he writes that the emperor sits in front, and four richly decorated tables are brought to him; the first one is said to have belonged to Solomon, the second to his son, David, the third to Korah (a personage to be found in *Numbers*, 16), and the fourth to the Emperor Constantine.[20] On the other hand, the Arab writer does not say that, at his table, the emperor was surrounded by twelve dignitaries, after the fashion of Jesus and the Twelve Apostles (a fact mentioned in Philotheos's description of the emperor's table[21]). Once again, this example of what Muslims understood, and what they failed to understand, shows that non-Christians were able to decipher only those cultural signs that transcended the narrow context of Christian symbolism and 'worked' in a wider cultural context. As a Muslim, ibn-Yahya understood the symbols that were drawn from the Old Testament but not the ones borrowed from the New Testament.

In Byzantium, Arabs did understand the meaning of the display of wealth; they also knew what gold and purple stood for.[22] Other elements of the Christian colour-number symbolism, however, remained hidden from Muslim eyes. Thus, there is no evidence that the prisoners who took part in General Nikephoros Phokas's triumph of 960/61 were aware of the symbolism encoded in this event. Instead of riding in a chariot, the victorious general chose to walk; behind him walked the emir of Candia, his family and the rest of the Arab prisoners; all of them were clad in white.[23] A closer look at Pseudo-Symeon's description of the parade shows that the general, who was known as an extremely pious man, must have made his triumph resemble a scene from the Book of Revelation:

---

[20] Vasiliev, 'Harun-ibn-Yahya and His Description of Constantinople', 157.

[21] Oikonomidès, *Les listes de préséance*, 167.10–18.

[22] N.El Cheikh-Saliba, 'Byzantium Viewed by the Arabs' (Unpublished PhD dissertation, Harvard University, 1992), 166–190, and esp. 185 and following. Western civilization has consistently viewed purple and gold as symbols of supreme authority and power for thousands of years: cf. M. Reinhold, *History of Purple as a Status Symbol in Antiquity* [*Collection Latomus*, vol. 116], (Brussels, 1970). As for the meaning of gold in the system of Byzantine symbols, see S.S. Averincev, 'Zoloto v sisteme simvolov rannevizantijskoj kul'tury', in *Vizantija, iužnye slavjane i drevnjaja Rus'* (Moscow, 1974), 48 and following.

[23] Pseudo-Symeon, *Chronographia* in *Theophanes Continuatus, Ioannes Cameniata, Symeon Magister, Georgius Monachus*, ed. I. Bekker (Bonn, 1838), 759–760. Cf. M. McCormick, *Eternal Victory. Triumphal Rulership in Late Antiquity, Byzantium, and Early Medieval West* (Cambridge, London and New York, 1986), 168.

this was the so-called *Triumph of the Elect* (Rev. 7).[24] This public event, with its apocalyptic connotations, must have been designed mostly for domestic consumption; it ought to convince the Byzantine observer that it was his empire that would shepherd, on the day of the Last Judgement, people of various nationalities into salvation.

Another example of a Muslim attempting to read into Byzantine symbols, and being only partially successful in this task, is ibn-Yahya's description of a public procession to the Great Church, which was led by the emperor.[25] Obviously, ibn-Yahya was well aware of the importance which Byzantines attached to the ample decoration of the streets, the bright colours of the clothes of the participants in the procession, the display of gold, silver and arms, the use of censers and the endless acclamations. He pays special attention to the colour and fabric of which the clothes of each group of people were made; he also describes their arms and the accessories to their clothes; and he mentions the number of people included in each group.

The Muslim author, however, does not endeavour to explain the meaning of any of the colours or numbers. He makes a passing remark about the emperor's two different shoes – one was red, the other black – but does not say that, while the red shoe symbolized the man's imperial status, the black shoe was a reminder of the emperor's being only mortal, like the commoners.[26] In fact, the colour black had a different meaning in the contemporary court ceremonial of the caliphate: it was the royal colour of the Abbasids.[27] In the eyes of a tenth-century Muslim observer of Byzantine ceremonies, black was, therefore, a status symbol of royalty rather than commonality.

---

[24] On the apocalyptic connotations of the triumph, see Simeonova, 'In the Depths of Tenth-Century Byzantine Ceremonial', 101. After they were paraded in the streets in the guise of martyrs, the emir of Candia and his family received lavish gifts from the emperor (Romanos II) and were given an estate in the country. According to Pseudo-Symeon, the emir was not promoted to senatorial rank because he and his family declined to receive baptism. This episode shows that Byzantines did not dare to convert forcefully high-ranking Muslim captives to Christianity.

[25] Vasiliev, 'Harun-ibn-Yahya and His Description of Constantinople', 158–160.

[26] That black shoes were worn by commoners is known thanks to several middle-Byzantine sources: see, for example, Leo Diacon. VII, 6 D; Anna Comnena III, 4 C. Pseudo-Codin., *De offic.* IV, B 69 writes that all the *archontes*, except for the *sebastocrator* and the *despotes*, wear black shoes too.

[27] According to Masoudi, among the precious gifts which tenth-century caliphs gave to high-ranking Muslim visitors to their court was the black banner of the Abbasid dynasty. Cf. A.A. Vasiliev, *Byzance et les Arabes*, II/2 (Bruxelles, 1950), 60.

Being a Muslim, ibn-Yahya is keen on telling us that Byzantines introduced horses into the Great Church; the horses were let loose on Christian consecrated grounds in order to show, by taking or not taking the bridles into their mouths, what the outcome of the Christians' war on Islam would be.[28] While the horse (also: horseman, or charioteer) was one of the most powerful Roman images of victory, bridling (or putting on reins, or a yoke) was a popular metaphor that was used by Byzantine authors of all epochs when referring to 'barbarians' who were brought under Roman control, or pagans being brought into the Christian fold. Obviously, in Arab culture, horsemanship was loaded with similar symbolism, so ibn-Yahya was able to decode the meaning of the above-mentioned act.

In his description of Constantinople, ibn-Yahya pays special attention to statuary art and architecture. Once again, however, he is able only to partially decipher the meaning of what he saw. Some of the statues which ibn-Yahya mentions seem to have been regarded as talismans by the city-dwellers of Constantinople. For example, in the middle of a central city square, there were two statues which, according to ibn-Yahya, were 'talismans' (maybe talismans against crime): they were said to be able, by waving their hands, to show which criminal deserved to have his life spared and which one was to be executed. Ibn-Yahya does not say what kind of a public ritual was associated with these two statues and how it fitted with the existing Byzantine legal practices.[29]

Another sculpture, three brassy figures of horses which were a 'talisman for horses', was placed above the gate of the imperial palace (most probably, above the arch of the *Chalke* vestibule); its function was to prevent horses from neighing and fighting each other; it was said to have been 'made' by the sage Apollonios. Ibn-Yahya mentions this talisman in connection with the excellent, in his opinion, training of Roman horses which were very calm and well-behaved during ceremonies.[30] For the

---

[28] Vasiliev, 'Harun-ibn-Yahya and His Description of Constantinople', 159–160.

[29] Vasiliev, 'Harun-ibn-Yahya and His Description of Constantinople', 161.

[30] Vasiliev, 'Harun-ibn-Yahya and His Description of Constantinople', 160–161. This 'talisman' was, most probably, the group of three horses which was brought, by order of Justinian I, from the temple of Artemis in Ephesus. Cf. C. Mango, *The Brazen House. A Study of the Vestibule of the Imperial Palace of Constantinople*. Arkaeol. Kunsthist. Med. Dan. Vid. Selesk. 4 (1959), 98–102. It is mentioned by other Arab authors too: while al-Harawi (twelfth century) believes in its ability to calm down nervous horses, Masoudi (tenth century) refuses to accept this legend and attributes the tame nature of Roman horses to the hot and humid climate of Constantinople. Cf. A.A. Vasiliev, 'Quelques remarques sur les voyageurs du moyen âge à Constantinople', in *Mélanges Ch. Diehl* (Paris, 1930), I, 296.

Muslim observer, it was easy to 'understand' the 'magical' functions of this sculpture for two reasons: (a) the horse, as I mentioned before, seems to have been a symbol that 'worked' in a similar fashion in both the Byzantine and Arab cultural contexts; and (b) like the famous *Horologion* (which too is mentioned in ibn-Yahya's narrative[31]), the horse talisman was believed to have been made by Apollonios.

In the Eastern Mediterranean, Apollonios of Tyana (called *Balinâs*, or *Balinûs* by Arab authors) was honoured as the 'benefactor of cities'. As the legends of the 'miracles' performed by this first-century vagrant philosopher grew and spread throughout the Byzantine and Arab worlds and, in the course of time, the sage himself turned into something of a mythological figure, the number of 'works' attributed to him multiplied. Christians and non-Christians came to share the view that the figures 'made' by Apollonios and scattered throughout most of the Eastern Mediterranean were, in fact, city talismans capable of warding off evil.[32] Apollonios and his talismans thus became 'trans-cultural' signs that 'worked' across the Christian–Muslim cultural and religious border.

Harun-ibn-Yahya's sightseeing of Constantinople altogether deserves to be subject to a special study. Of particular interest to the student of symbols are ibn-Yahya's descriptions of the honorific column of Theodosius/Justinian (which later came to be regarded as a monument to Byzantine victory over the Saracens) as well as of the numerous figures of animals and birds, both in the Hippodrome and in a churchyard, whose symbolism the Muslim observer failed to decipher because of the different meanings encoded of the same animals and birds in Muslim culture. For the purposes of the present study, I will briefly mention only two of all the remaining descriptions of statuary art in Constantinople which can be found in ibn-Yahya's narrative: these are the famous Serpent column in the Hippodrome and the Golden Gate in the Theodosian wall of the city.

The Serpent column seems to have been one of at least two sculptures in the Hippodrome that were perceived as talismans against snakes.[33] In

---

[31] Vasiliev, 'Harun-ibn-Yahya and His Description of Constantinople', 160.

[32] Cf. W. Speyer, 'Zum Bild des Apollonios von Tyana bei Heiden and Christen', *Jahrbuch für Antike und Christentum* 17 (1974), 47–63; and W.L. Dulière, 'Apollônios de Tyane dans Byzance et Antioche. Evolution de son mythe', *Byzantinische Zeitschrift* 63 (1970), 247–277. On Apollonios's role as a benefactor of Constantinople, see G. Dagron, *Constantinople imaginaire. Études sur le recueil des 'Patria'* (Paris, 1984), 191–314.

[33] The other talisman protecting the city from snakes was a bronze eagle with a snake in its claws: Nicetas Choniates, *Historia*, ed. I van Dieten (Berlin, 1972), 651. In the

the words of ibn-Yahya, these were 'four snakes made of brass whose tails were in their mouths as a talisman against snakes that they may not do any harm'.[34] Ibn-Yahya seems to have taken quite literally the Byzantine explanation of what the snakes stood for.[35] It seems, however, that the medieval Greeks had endowed the brass snakes with some additional meaning. As the Byzantine and Slavic medieval works dedicated to the interpretation of dreams and visions show, the Viper (or Snake) signifies a Muslim and above all a Saracen.[36] In other words, the Serpent column was probably seen, by the inhabitants of Constantinople, as a city talisman against Muslim evil as well.

The iconographic type of a Christian emperor in military attire trampling upon a snake with a human face (that is, upon the Satan) was widely spread in Late Antiquity.[37] This symbol of Christianity's victory over paganism was borrowed from the ancient ritual of *calcatio* which amounted to ritual trampling upon a subdued enemy. Maybe it was not accidental that this ritual, or some revised version of it, was revived in the tenth century, under Constantine Porphyrogennetos.[38] While Arabs may have known the meaning of ritual trampling upon a high-ranking

---

Hippodrome, there was yet another sculpture of a monster-snake, the famous *Drakontaion*; this was a replica of a famous sculpture in Rome which was sent to Arcadius by his brother, Honorius. The *Drakontaion*, however, does not seem to have been endowed with any apotropaic functions. Cf. Dagron, *Constantinople imaginaire*, 131, n. 19.

[34] Vasiliev, 'Harun-ibn-Yahya and His Description of Constantinople', 161.

[35] In actual fact, the snakes were not four but three. Originally, this column commemorated the Greek victory over the Persians at Plateia and Salamis in 478 B.C.; it was erected in Apollo's temple at Delphi; the column owed its serpentine form to the myth of Apollo thrashing the monster-snake Python. Constantine the Great ordered that this column, together with some other works of art, be brought to Constantinople: Zosim., II (Bonn, 1837), 31.1–2; Socrat., I.16, *PG* 67, col. 717 A. Cf. Sozomen., II.5.

[36] V. Tăpkova-Zaimova and A. Miltenova, *Istoriko–apokaliptičnata knižnina văv Vizantija i v srednovekovna Bălgarija* (Sofia, 1996), 103–104, 216: in the system of Christian symbols, the Snake stands for the Antichrist (Gen. 3; Isa. 27:1); in the visionary literature, the Snake symbolizes the infidels (Saracens, Turks, Tartars, etc.) who were enemies of the Christians.

[37] On the early Byzantine coins and mosaics displaying this iconographic type, see Mango, *The Brazen House*, 23–24.

[38] Cedrenus, ed. I. Bekker (Bonn, 1839), II, 330–331. Cf. McCormick, *Eternal Victory*, 159–161. In 956, during a triumph celebrated by his general Leo Phokas, Constantine VII put his foot on the head of a high-ranking Arab, a captured emir kneeling before him. Cedrenus, however, does not make it clear whether the emperor believed that he was trampling upon an infidel who personified the Satan-Snake. Upon enduring this public humiliation, the emir received great honours and lavish gifts from the emperor.

captive,[39] it is not clear whether they were aware of the fact that Byzantines identified them with the biblical image of the Satan-Snake.

When speaking of Arabs' ability, or willingness, to read into the symbolic language of Byzantine triumphs, one must mention ibn-Yahya's description of the Golden Gate. He has faithfully recorded the fact that this was the gate from which one went to Rome and that it was guarded by guardians. And further: 'On the gate there are five figures in the form of elephants and one figure of a standing man who holds the reins of those elephants.'[40] What ibn-Yahya does not say is that the Golden Gate also played the role of a Triumphal Arch of Constantinople; victorious generals and emperors followed by their trophies and prisoners entered the city through that gate.[41] The Roman iconographic type of the Invincible Sun riding in a chariot which is drawn by four elephants (or horses) persisted, in Byzantium, as late as the early seventh century.[42] The triumphal chariot drawn by elephants (or horses) was an image that was certainly known to the Arabs; yet ibn-Yahya does not elaborate on the symbolic nature of the chariot and the elephants on the Golden Gate.

That Arab authors may have been unwilling to elaborate on the imagery of Byzantine triumphs could be seen from Masoudi's description of the same city gate: he admires its beautiful bronze doors[43] but does not say that they were the doors of Mopsuestia, which Nikephoros Phokas had managed to recapture from the Arabs during his campaigns in the East.[44]

---

[39] In 260, Emperor Valerian was captured by the Persian King Shapur I. Cf. E. Kettenhoffen, *Die römisch–persischen Kriege des 3. Jahrhunderts n. Chr.* (Wiesbaden, 1982), 59 and following. Arabs must have known the reliefs at Naqsh-I-Rustam and Bishapur (Persia) which celebrate Shapur's triumph over the Roman emperor; in these reliefs, however, it is not the Persian king but his horse that is trampling upon the subdued Valerian.

[40] Vasiliev, 'Harun-ibn-Yahya and His Description of Constantinople', 154–155.

[41] R. Janin, *Constantinople byzantine. Développement urbain et répértoire topographique* (Paris, 1950), 252–255. In reality, the elephants were not five but four; Dagron has recently proved that they were brought, by order of Theodosius II, from the temple of Ares in Athens. Cf. Dagron, *Constantinople imaginaire*, 128, n. 7. The Golden Gate should not be confused with the Triumphal Arch of Theodosius which was located in the *forum Tauri*.

[42] H.H. Scullard, *The Elephant in the Greek and Roman World* (Ithaca, NY, 1974), pl. XXIV h: coins of the emperors Maurice, Justin II and Phokas.

[43] *Les Praires d'Or*, ed. and tr. B. de Meynard and P. Courteille (Paris, 1863), 261.

[44] The same emperor, Nikephoros Phokas, had yet another gate, that of St Barbara, decorated with trophy doors: these were the doors of the city of Tarsos which he had recaptured from the Arabs. See Cedrenus (Bonn, 1839), II, 363.

In the tenth century, money, luxury goods, silk and arms made up the usual Byzantine gifts to important foreigners; in return, emperors and other high-ranking Byzantines received money, furs, arms, wax, slaves (including castrated boys), exotic animals and birds, and spices. For comprehensible reasons, in this article I cannot afford to discuss the symbolism vested with gifts, or whether both parties were always able to read into the coded language of the exchanged presents. Other interesting cases of visitors' understanding, or misunderstanding, of Byzantine ceremonies in the tenth century are provided by foreigners' reactions to the performance of *proskynesis*, the waiting periods which preceded the audiences with the emperor, and the treatment which the important visitors' servants and horses received at Byzantine hands.

As I mentioned at the beginning, Byzantines made skilful use of their guests' understanding, or lack thereof, of the language of Byzantine ceremonies. It is also important to point out that, whenever Byzantines wanted to make sure that certain acts of international importance would not be misinterpreted by foreigners due to the foreigners' lack of knowledge of Byzantine ceremonies, they resorted to rituals and symbols borrowed from the foreigners' native culture. For example, as ninth- and tenth-century sources inform us, in their dealings with pagan Bulgarians or Russians, Byzantines sealed the mutual oaths of peace by publicly practising Bulgarian, or Russian, pagan rites which were borrowed from the barbarians' own culture.

By using a variety of sources, I have tried to shed some additional light on the question of how far foreigners of various ethnic and religious backgrounds were able to read into the symbolic language of the tenth-century Byzantine court ceremonial, public processions, military triumphs and diplomatic receptions as well as into Byzantine colour and number symbolism, veneration of 'city talismans', gestures of hospitality, and so on. The Byzantines' attitude toward foreigners was, no doubt, ambivalent. At the same time, it would hardly be an exaggeration to say that the foreigners' attitudes towards Byzantium were ambivalent, too: foreigners seem to have been intimidated by the Byzantines, they feared the empire and they hated it; and yet, they were impressed by its riches, admired its architecture and enjoyed its delicious food.

The present study is not so much the result of unearthing of new texts or facts as an interpretative shift in the meaning of medieval culture that has emerged as a consequence of a refocusing from older styles of cultural history to one that is, in the words of Eugene Vance, 'a science not of things and deeds but of discourses; an art not of facts but of encodings of facts'.[45] Such studies aim at bringing novel insights into our understanding of well-known events by helping us see how events functioned symbolically, and not just practically; and they help us get at the complex relations between symbolic events and cultural mind-sets, or *mentalités*.

---

[45] E. Vance, 'Semiotics and Power: Relics, Icons and the *Voyage de Charlemagne à Jérusalem et à Constantinople*', in *The New Medievalism*, ed. M. Brownlee et al. (Baltimore, MD, 1991), 227.

18. Byzantine conceptions of Otherness after the Annexation of Bulgaria (1018)[*]

Paul Stephenson

In 1018 the emperor Basil II extended Byzantine political authority across the whole Balkan peninsula, and advanced the empire's frontier once again to the Danube. Bulgarians, at once barbarians and Christians, were brought within the *oikoumene*, the civilized world. Even as they were, a new threat to the integrity of the *oikoumene* appeared on the northern bank of the lower Danube: the Pechenegs, fierce steppe nomads who would prove a consistent threat to the empire's Balkan lands for much of the eleventh century, and make a profound impact on all who suffered by their raids and invasions. Only after the battle of Levounion on 29 April 1091 was the threat diminished, and the Pechenegs who had settled independently within the empire's borders were baptized and resettled in smaller groups according to the wishes of the emperor Alexios I Komnenos (1081–1118). The purpose of this paper is to explore how peoples in the northern Balkans, particularly the Pechenegs and Bulgarians, were portrayed by Byzantine authors after 1018, and to consider why.

In the early 1080s, several years before he was appointed as archbishop of Bulgaria in Ohrid (in modern Macedonia), Theophylact Hephaistos wrote in praise of the weather in Constantinople, where 'winter does not rebel, nor rush the frontiers and fall upon us in Scythian fashion, freezing the blood of living creatures and laying crystalline fetters upon the rivers'.[1]

---

[*]   I acknowledge with gratitude the support I received from the British Academy and from Keble College while I was working on this paper. Averil Cameron and Alex Drace-Francis read drafts and offered welcome advice and encouragement.

[1]   Théophylacte d'Achrida, I, *Discours, traités, poésies*, ed. and tr. P. Gautier, CFHB 16/1 (Thessalonike, 1980), 181.5–8. The translation is from Margaret Mullett, *Theophylact of Ochrid. Reading the Letters of a Byzantine Archbishop* (Birmingham, 1997), 44. The sentiment,

His chosen subject is prophetic, for he would later write often and at length of his exile from Constantinople, and his choice of imagery is fascinating. The winter outside the most civilized of cities is personified as the archetypal barbarian, the Scythian, launching sudden raids across the limits of the *oikoumene*.

Complementary imagery was used a century later by Gregory Antiochos, a military functionary posted to Bulgaria who felt sensations akin to Theophylact's seasonal affective disorder. For Gregory, who appears to have suffered from acute depression as a consequence of his feelings of geographical and cultural alienation, disease attacked the human body as barbarians assaulted the frontiers of the body politic. Thus, he wrote, 'barbaric illness invades the small town of our body, takes over the acropolis of the head, takes us alive like prisoners to a distant land, away from health and beyond the borders'.[2]

For both Theophylact and Gregory barbarism threatened all aspects of civilization. It constantly circled the frontiers, the political and conceptual limits of the Christian Roman Empire, and threatened to fall suddenly and swiftly upon those not standing vigilant guard. As is now well known, the notion of the barbarian was articulated in fifth-century Athens.[3] The barbarian was the universal anti-Greek against whom Hellenic culture was defined. The two identities were polarities and together were universal: all that was Greek was civilized; all that was barbarian was uncivilized. *There was nothing else.* Since Herodotus, the Scythian was considered the archetypal barbarian, and most northern peoples were regarded, at various times, to be Scythians.[4] Early in the tenth century, the patriarch of Constantinople, Nicholas I Mystikos, wrote to Tsar Symeon of Bulgaria (c.894–927) to warn him of past or future

---

if not the exact wording, follows closely Ovid's *Tristia*. See, for example, *Ovid Tristia Ex Ponto*, ed. and tr. A.L. Wheeler (Cambridge, MA, 1953), 68–69, 107–108.

[2] J. Darrouzès, 'Deux lettres de Grégoire Antiochos écrites de Bulgarie vers 1173', I, *BS* 23 (1963) 276–284; II, *BS* 24 (1963), 65–86, at 67.107–10. See also C. Galatariotou, 'Travel and perception in Byzantium', *DOP* 47 (1993), 221–241, at 229 (on sickness when leaving Constantinople), and 237 (Gregory away from the healthy, civilized *oikoumene*).

[3] E. Hall, *Inventing the Barbarian: Greek Self-Definition through Tragedy* (Oxford, 1989).

[4] On universal familiarity with Herodotus see *ODB* II, 922; N.G. Wilson, *Photius. The Bibilotheca* (London, 1994), 8, 15, 42. See also the *OED* definition of 'archetype': '(in Jungian psychology) a primitive mental image inherited from man's earliest ancestors, and supposed to be present in the collective unconscious.' For a full and stimulating treatment of Herodotian Scythians see F. Hartog, *The Mirror of Herodotus. The Representation of the Other in the Writing of History* (Berkeley, CA, 1988).

assaults by 'Magyars, Alans, Pechenegs, Rus or other Scythian peoples'.[5] Symeon, known to his own nobles as 'half-Greek' because of his classical education in Constantinople, would have understood the allusion, and would have known that not long before the Bulgarians themselves were considered Scythians by the Byzantines. The use of the term to refer to numerous northern peoples alludes both to their origins (as far as the Byzantines were concerned) in ancient Scythia, and to their way of life, which resembled that of the Scythians portrayed by Herodotus. According to Michael Psellos in the mid-eleventh century the Pechenegs were archetypal Scythians: they had a loose social structure, fought as individuals (not in ordered regiments), and lived as nomads with swift horses; worse still, they observed no law and they were pagans.[6] It is clear that Psellos was defining the Pechenegs as the polar opposite of civilized Byzantines; he was drawing a distinction between stereotypes, between nature and culture.[7]

Psellos's contemporary, John Mauropous, produced orations to celebrated a 'victory' by Constantine IX Monomachos (1042–1055) over the Pechenegs who had crossed the Danube in 1046/7.[8] Victory was not achieved by the slaughter of barbarians, but by their voluntary conversion to Christianity after they observed a simple cross in the sky as

---

[5]   Nicholas I Patriarch of Constantinople, *Letters*, ed. L.G. Westerink, and tr. R.J.H. Jenkins, CFHB 6 (Washington, DC, 1973), 160.

[6]   Michael Psellos, *Chronographia*, VII.68–9; *Chronographie, ou histoire d'un siècle de Byzance (976–1077)*, ed. E. Renauld, 2 vols (Paris 1926–1928), II, 126. See also *Michaeli Pselli orationes panegyricae*, ed. G.T. Dennis (Stuttgart and Leipzig, 1994), 63, where the Pechenegs are described as a 'simple nomadic people, who lead an undisciplined (*automatizon*) life and do not recognize the higher rule of law'. His descriptions show great similarities with Leo VI's *Taktika* on the Magyars and to Maurice's *Strategikon* on the Avars. See E. Malamut, 'L'image byzantine des Petchénègues', *BZ* 88 (1995), 105–147, at 121–122. Skylitzes, whose work was not within the tradition of classicizing history, used contemporary ethnonyms, and refers to the Pechenegs as '*Patzinakoi*'. Nevertheless he presents a similar excursus on the 'Scythian Pechenegs', who favour life on the hoof and dwell in tents: *Ioannis Skylitzes Synopsis Historiarum*, ed. J. Thurn CFHB 5 (Berlin and New York, 1973), 455. See also A.P. Kazhdan and Anne Wharton Epstein, *Change in Byzantine Culture in the Eleventh and Twelfth Centuries* (Berkeley, Los Angeles and London, 1985), 205.

[7]   C. Lévi-Strauss, *The Savage Mind* (London, 1966), 20, 124–125, 129; E. Leach, *Lévi-Strauss* (London, 1970), 21, 36, 85, 88, 112–119. See also J. Le Goff, 'Lévi-Strauss in Broceliande. A brief analysis of courtly romance', in his *The Medieval Imagination*, tr. A. Goldhammer (Chicago, 1988), 107–131, for an approach to contemporary Western conceptions of the distinction between nature and culture, and the representation of the 'wild man'.

[8]   For the date of the invasion see A. Kazhdan, 'Once more the "alleged" Russo-Byzantine treaty (ca. 1047) and the Pecheneg crossing of the Danube', *JÖB* 26 (1977), 65–77.

they crossed the Danube. The barbarians had passed into the Christian empire and at that moment they witnessed the same sign as had appeared to the first Christian Roman emperor Constantine, namesake of Mauropous's hero; immediately they threw down their weapons and sued for peace.[9] The orator regarded Constantine IX's greatest victory as the transformation of wild beasts into men, fierce nature transformed by orthodox culture. However, the transformation was not total: these Pechenegs were allowed to live within the frontiers as nomadic pastoralists and roving border guards; thus they retained characteristics of a 'Scythian lifestyle'.[10]

In the turmoil of the early 1070s the Pechenegs broke their treaty with the empire and took control of the lands between the Haimos (Balkan mountains) and the lower Danube. From there they launched frequent raids south of the mountains, striking deep into Byzantine Thrace. Theophylact Hephaistos was familiar with the Pechenegs, and with the widespread terror caused by their raids. In an oration delivered on 6 January 1088, he spoke in praise of Alexios I Komnenos's bloodless victory over the Pechenegs, referring to a treaty negotiated in autumn 1087. It is clear that at this time Alexios had suffered a significant defeat, and was obliged to recognize the Pechenegs' independent settlement of the lands north of the Haimos. Unlike Mauropous, Theophylact does not dwell on the baptism of barbarians. Their brute nature was transformed, instead, by the emperor's rhetoric, persuading them to recognize the force of law. For Theophylact, Alexios was a Homeric hero, now Odysseos booming, now Menelaos speaking in softer tones, briefly but fluently (*Il.*, iii.214–222). Beguiling everyone with his rhetoric, he enchanted philosophers and orators with his sharp wit and the clarity of his speech. In this way Alexios exposed the Scythians' secret plans, and forced them to sue for peace. 'Those who previously solved their disputes by spilling blood, swore their faith in writing and with a treaty.' The emphasis is on the triumph of imperial order (*taxis*), in the form of written law (*nomos*), over the undisciplined barbarian nature (*physis*). Once again nature and culture are explicitly contrasted, and by choosing justice, rather than the

---

[9] *Ioannis Euchaitorum metropolitae quae in cod. Vat. gr. 676 supersunt*, ed. P. de Lagarde (Göttingen, 1882), 142–147, at 145 (§13); J. Lefort, 'Rhétorique et politique: trois discours de Jean Mauropous en 1047', *TM* 6 (1976), 265–303, at 266–267.

[10] *Michaelis Attaliotae historia*, ed. I. Bekker, *CSHB* (Bonn, 1853), 205.

judgement of battle, the enemy were no longer acting entirely as Scythians.[11]

So barbarism could be brought within frontiers and modified by the contacts with the civilized. Even in defeat the civilized could triumph by the extension of its defining characteristics: by baptism, soothing the brutish nature of the barbarian; or by treaties, obliging barbarians to recognize the force of law. Both were the triumph of culture over nature, and both made the Pechenegs now settled within the *oikoumene* not entirely Scythians. It is fascinating to see how imperial rhetoric was brought to bear on a political reality: the Pechenegs had settled in the heartland of what had until so recently been the Bulgarian Empire. This had to be explained, and it had to be lauded. In doing so writers modified the polarity of civilized and barbarian, allowing for an intermediate category, the semi-civilized world which was not entirely barbarian.

This was not a unique sentiment. Both Theophylact and Gregory Antiochos, with whom we began, indicate that barbarism was already present within the frontiers of the *oikoumene*, in Byzantine Bulgaria. Theophylact is notorious – too notorious, Margaret Mullett has recently demonstrated – for his condescending attitude towards his barbaric Bulgarian flock, who stank of sheep- or goatskin.[12] Gregory was similarly appalled by the stenches and noises of Bulgaria, by the ethnic preferences for red meat over fish, and for dressing in animal skins and felt hats.[13] But the barbarism within Bulgaria was quite different to that without: it had been modified by years of contact with the civilized, and in particular with the greatest gifts of civilization: Christianity and law. Thus, in a further letter to Tsar Symeon, Nicholas Mystikos had acknowledged that, as fellow Christians, both Bulgarians and Byzantines were Christ's

---

[11] Theophylact, *Discours, traités, poésies*, ed. Gautier, 222–7. On the civilizable barbarian, see now T. Habinek, *The Politics of Latin Literature. Writing, Identity and Empire in Ancient Rome* (Princeton, NJ, 1998), 151–169.

[12] *Théophylacte d'Achrida*, II, *Lettres*, ed. and tr. P. Gautier, CFHB 16/2 (Thessalonike, 1986), 141; Mullett, *Theophylact of Ochrid*, 266–274, esp. 270.

[13] Darrouzès, 'Deux lettres', I, 279.25–27, 280.70–71. The barbarian love of red meat was an enduring *topos*. For example, Rousseau used classical allusions to condemn the dietary habits of eighteenth-century savages in his *Essay on the Origin of Languages*: J.J. Rousseau, *The Discourses and other Early Political Writings*, ed. V. Gourevitch (Cambridge, 1997), 270, 'To get a notion of the meals of the ancients one need only consider the meals of present-day savages; I almost said those of Englishmen.' However, Strabo, *Geography* 7.3.3, offers a fascinating contrast between carnivorous Scythians and vegetarian Mysians; cf. *The Geography of Strabo*, ed. and tr. H.L. Jones, 8 vols (London and New York, 1917–1932), vol. III, 178. We shall return to Mysians below, 255–256.

'peculiar people, his inheritance'.[14] Shortly afterwards, in a speech to celebrate the marriage in 927 between Tsar Peter (927–969) and Maria Lekapena, who was the daughter of the ruling emperor Romanos I (920–944), Theodore Daphnopates declared that the Bulgarians 'are no longer called Scythian or barbarian ... but may now be named and shown to be Christians'.[15]

The *History of the Fifteen Martyrs of Tiberioupolis*, a work attributed to Theophylact of Ohrid, expands upon this theme in considering the conversion of Bulgaria: 'What was previously not a people but a barbarian race (*ethnos*) became and was called a people (*laos*) of God ... the Bulgarian people have become, as it is written, a royal priesthood, a holy nation, a peculiar people.'[16] Theophylact stresses the Pauline nature of the mission by using a Pauline quotation. He is more explicit in his *Vita Clementis* (xxii.66), where we find a people called into being and given a recognized identity through conversion by Clement, 'a new Paul to the new Corinthians, the Bulgarians'.[17] Thus, Theophylact demonstrates a grudging respect for distinct Bulgarian institutions in the Cyrillo-Methodian tradition, including the Slavonic language.[18] As Obolensky says: 'A language which serves as a medium for the Christian liturgy becomes a sacred one. Hence every people which acquires a sacred tongue is raised to the status of a nation consecrated to the service of God, with its own legitimate place and particular mission within the family of Christendom.'[19] The Bulgarians had been granted something denied other northern peoples: a distinct Christian identity, not Roman, but then not entirely Scythian.

---

[14] Nicholas I, *Letters*, 124.66–69.

[15] R.J.H. Jenkins, 'The peace with Bulgaria (927) celebrated by Theodore Daphnopates', in *Polychronion. Festschrift für Franz Dölger zum 75 Geburtstag*, ed. P. Wirth (Heidelberg, 1966), 287–303, at 289, 293.

[16] *Historia martyrii XV martyrum*, PG 126, 152–221, at 200–201. For a translation of this passage and further commentary see D. Obolensky, *Six Byzantine Portraits* (Oxford, 1988), 71–77; and also see now Mullett, *Theophylact of Ohrid*, 235–239.

[17] N.L. Tunickij, *Monumenta ad SS Cyrilli et Methodii successorum vitas resque gestas pertinentia* (London, 1972), 66–140, at 126. D. Obolensky, 'Theophylaktos of Ohrid and the authorship of the *Vita Clementis*', in *Byzantium. A Tribute to Andreas N. Stratos*, 2 vols (Athens, 1986), II, 601–618, has convincingly argued for Theophylact's authorship; also see now Mullett, *Theophylact of Ohrid*, 235–239.

[18] Although he notoriously parodied Slavonic terms and place-names, Theophylact knew and used them: see Mullett, *Theophylact of Ohrid*, 272–273.

[19] Obolensky, *Six Byzantine Portraits*, 67.

Certainly, Bulgaria was rustic and rough, and Theophylact complained that 'having lived for years in the land of the Bulgarians, the bumpkin lifestyle is my daily companion'.[20] The phrase he uses is adapted from Euripides's *Orestes* (485) and it is fascinating that Michael Choniates used the same phrase more literally a century later to describe his 'becoming a barbarian by living a long time in Athens'.[21] The Athenians may have appeared provincial and parochial to their archbishop, but he certainly did not mean to imply that they were pagan and lawless. Theophylact's attitude to his own flock was similar, and when he wrote that he was 'a Constantinopolitan, and, strange to tell, also a Bulgarian',[22] he perhaps considered himself the most refined resident of a second, lesser *oikoumene* with an autonomous but inferior church with its own liturgy and hierarchy. In a letter to the Caesar Nicephoros Melissenos, Theophylact even coins the phrase '*barbaros oikoumene*' to refer to Bulgaria, and this appears to sum up his attitude of ambivalence and grudging recognition.[23]

Before Obolensky and Mullett, scholars could not believe that Theophylact, the author of letters which contained such vitriolic outbursts against the Bulgarians, was the same man who wrote so sympathetically about the Bulgarian church and its founding fathers. Now we can see that the contradictions between Theophylact's hagiography and letters reflect the inherent contradictions of the two traditions in Byzantine thought and literature: the precepts of the orthodox world-view which was ecumenical and hierarchical; and the classical Greek vision of polarity. And we have also seen that these two ideas came together in the northern Balkans, which was at once within the frontiers of the civilized world, but also the realm of barbarians who were also Christians.

Having said this, as the eleventh century progressed the orthodox notion of hierarchy ran a poor second to the classical vision of otherness. It is surely of significance that this development parallels the decline in the popularity of hagiography even before Theophylact began writing.[24]

---

[20] Theophylact, *Lettres*, ed. Gautier, 243.17; Mullett, *Theophylact of Ochrid*, 276; Obolensky, *Six Byzantine Portraits*, 58.

[21] *Michael Akominatou tou Choniatou ta sozomena*, ed. S. Lampros, 2 vols (Athens 1879–1880), II, 44.

[22] Theophylact, *Lettres*, Gautier, ed., 141.58–60; Mullett, *Theophylact of Ochrid*, 274.

[23] Theophylact, *Lettres*, Gautier, ed., 171; Mullett, *Theophylact of Ochrid*, 274–275, 298.

[24] Although see the qualifications offered by P. Magdalino, 'The Byzantine Holy Man in the Twelfth Century', in *The Byzantine Saint*, ed. S. Hackel (London, 1981), 51–66, at 52.

Other genres flourished, and we have several collections of letters, an unrivalled corpus of encomia, and some fine historiography, each drawing on classical models and language to portray northern peoples. For example, Niketas Choniates provides a description of the brutish Cumans, a nomadic people who occupied lands beyond the Black Sea.[25] He relies on Ammianus Marcellinus's account of the Huns and the Alans (XXXI.2), which in turn makes use of Herodotus's *excursus* on Scythia (IV.1–144). We are thus confronted with the problem of deciding whether any of Choniates's information (like that of Psellos more than a century before) was based on contemporary observation. And if for Choniates barbarian behaviour was so standardized as to be a *topos*, John Tzetzes went a stage further by constructing fictitious ancestries; for example he drew a direct line between the Kievan Rus and the ancient Taurians.[26]

For Choniates and Tzetzes, as it had been for Psellos, the first principle in selecting an appropriate ethnonym was not contemporary accuracy, but literary style and the demonstration of erudition. Our picture of the Balkan peoples is thus presented through Cyril Mango's famous 'distorting mirror'.[27] But, as Margaret Mullett has written very recently, 'If we once accept that Byzantine literature is a distorting mirror we must try to understand (even if we cannot correct) that distortion, because (apart from a few documentary texts) we have no alternative.'[28] We cannot be satisfied with the explanation, now universally acknowledged, that Byzantine authors were composing for each other in an élite code; we must ask why they did so.

First a proviso: I do not mean to suggest that the use of classical language and learning was absent before 1018.[29] However, as Alexander Kazhdan has written, 'There was a fundamental change in attitude

---

[25] *Nicetae Choniatae historiae*, ed. J. van Dieten, *CFHB* 11/1 (Berlin, 1975), 94.

[26] *Ioannis Tzetzae historiae*, ed. P. Leone (Naples, 1969), 463.872–876; Bohumila Zástěrová, 'Zur Problematik der ethnographischen Topoi', in *Griechenland – Byzanz – Europa*, eds J. Hermann, H. Köpstein and R. Müller, *Berliner byzantinische Arbeiten* 52 (Berlin, 1985), 18. An analogous practice, also the result of a quest for continuity and the desire to establish authority, was the construction of fictitious ancestries for individuals and aristocratic families.

[27] C. Mango, *Byzantine Literature as a Distorting Mirror*. Inaugural Lecture delivered before the University of Oxford on 21 May 1974 (Oxford, 1975).

[28] Mullett, *Theophylact of Ochrid*, 4.

[29] Mango's principal examples are from the sixth, tenth and eleventh centuries; Wilson has emphasized the admiration for Attic Greek from Lucian to Photios: Mango, *Distorting Mirror*, 6–7 (Procopius), 10–11 (Psellos), 14–15 (Constantine Porphyrogennetos); Wilson, *Photius. The Bibilotheca*, 13–17.

toward ancient culture from the ninth to twelfth centuries. The corpus of classical literature was gathered and transcribed in the ninth and tenth centuries; in the eleventh and twelfth centuries the process of assimilation and reflection began.'[30] We must ask, therefore, what were the motivations for this assimilation and reflection? Why did it manifest itself in accentuated classicism in eleventh- and twelfth-century Byzantine literature? And what might it tell us about the attitudes of the authors to the world around them, both within and beyond the borders of the *oikoumene?*[31]

To answer these questions it is worth considering briefly how another classically educated member of an élite conceived of and represented others. In 1784 Count Louis-Philippe de Ségur was appointed minister plenipotentiary and envoy extra-ordinary of Louis XVI to the court of Catherine II of Russia. As he journeyed from France he passed from the civilized world into the realm of the barbarian, recording his sentiments in his *Mémoires*. 'When one enters Poland', he wrote, 'one believes one has left Europe entirely, and the gaze is struck by a new spectacle ... a poor population, enslaved; dirty villages; cottages little different from savage huts; everything makes one think one has moved back ten centuries, and that one finds oneself amid hordes of Huns, Scythians, Veneti, Slavs and Sarmatians.'[32] Ségur was a product of the Enlightenment, the age which coined the neologism 'civilization', whose conceptual bounds were the frontiers of Western Europe. Eastern Europe, which one entered at Poland, was a semi-barbarian hinterland between civilization and the truly barbaric world of the south Russian steppe; and like Byzantine authors of the eleventh and twelfth centuries Ségur chose to represent the world of the barbarian in classical terms.

According to Larry Wolff, the notion of Eastern Europe was an invention of Western Europe, constructed by people of learning and action like Ségur. He proposes the institution of a 'philosophic geography', a framework of representation designed to dominate,

---

[30] Kazhdan and Epstein, *Change in Byzantine Culture*, 136.

[31] C. Mango, *Byzantium: The Empire of the New Rome* (London, 1980), 237, relates the change to the re-emergence of cities as centres of learning, contemplation and literary production. This is a crucial element in the expansion of the empire, and I see no contradictions between my explanation and his.

[32] Louis-Philippe, Comte de Ségur, *Mémoires, souvenirs, et anecdotes, par le comte de Ségur*, I, in *Bibliothèque des mémoires relatif à l'histoire de France pendant le 18ᵉ siècle*, ed. M.F. Barrière (Paris, 1859), XIX, 300. Cited in L. Wolff, *Inventing Eastern Europe. The Map of Civilization on the Mind of the Enlightenment* (Stanford, 1994), 19.

restructure, and have authority over the uncivilized; and here Wolff acknowledges his intellectual debt to Edward Said's *Orientalism*, the seminal study of this system of thought and practice. In its many guises Orientalism arises from a sense of cultural superiority, but this sense arises from insecurity and a consequent desire to regain control through the imposition of a constraining framework of representation. Therefore Orientalism is self-referential, having no bearing on the objective reality it seeks to portray. In many historical contexts we find the learned attempting to reinforce perceived differences between their civilized world, a world of erudition and order, and the world of the barbarian. We also have examples of the articulation of a semi-barbarian hinterland, somewhere between the civilized and the barbarian. So authors in eleventh- and twelfth-century Byzantium were not the first, nor would they be the last, to see Scythians instead of Pechenegs (or Poles). But the distorted reflection of others in the mirror of Byzantine literature after 1018 was a form of Orientalism specific to the situation in which authors found themselves.

The accentuated classicism in works of the eleventh and twelfth centuries was closely related to the increased sense of unease which arose among the literate élite in Constantinople as they struggled to come to terms with new economic and political circumstances. The empire had expanded rapidly and there were new provinces that had to be put in order and governed; and after an initial period when attempts were made to put the empire on a peacetime footing, there were suddenly new external threats on all sides. Theophylact Hephaistos and Gregory Antiochos were members of the literate élite who were posted as administrators to the semi-barbarian world of the northern Balkans, where they encountered Bulgarians and Pechenegs. They wrote of their experiences and communicated them to friends and colleagues, and in doing so they forced contemporary places and peoples into an antiquarian framework. Certainly, they distorted the mirror into which we now peer for factual information, but their aim in using classical language was not deliberate obfuscation, but rather to create a veneer of order and continuity over the disorder and discontinuity they experienced.[33]

For others living and writing in Constantinople the restoration of 'Roman' political authority across the whole Balkan peninsula was unambiguously a good thing; order (*taxis*) was re-established where

---

[33] Zástěrová, 'Zur Problematik', 16–19.

disorder (*ataxia*) had reigned for centuries. The restoration of the empire's frontier at the Danube was central to the articulation of continuity with the ancient world, since the river was regarded as New Rome's 'natural' frontier in the West, the boundary which should delimit the *oikoumene*, and mark the point of transition from the civilized world to that of the barbarian.[34] We have already seen how crossing this line affected the Pechenegs in 1046–7, and the conceptual boundary had been reinforced since Byzantine troops first overran Bulgaria and recovered the fortresses on the lower Danube in 972. In an epitaph to John I Tzimiskes (971–976), the poet John Geometres remembered the emperor's victories over the Kievan Rus, recently imperial allies against the Bulgarians, but now once again truly Scythians sent back across the Danube.[35] Geometres also praised Nikephoros II Phokas (963–969) for extending his reach 'to the Roman borders in east and west', and for advancing 'the five frontiers'.[36]

Basil II (976–1025) considered it the emperor's duty to add to imperial lands, particularly to recover what was rightfully 'Roman'.[37] And as he recovered the former Roman provinces of Dalmatia and Moesia (Superior and Inferior), authors began to refer to the contemporary inhabitants of those regions as Dalmatians and Mysians (although not Moesians).[38] In her *Alexiad* Anna Komnene refers to the Serbs of Duklja as Dalmatians and their land as Dalmatia,[39] while John Kinnamos refers to the Serbs of Raška as a 'Dalmatian people'.[40] Bulgaria was frequently called Mysia

---

[34] P. Stephenson, 'The Byzantine frontier at the lower Danube in the late 10th and 11th centuries', in *Frontiers in Question: Eurasian Borderlands c.700–1700*, eds D. Power and Naomi Standen (London, 1999), 80–104. The Euphrates fulfilled the same role in the East (*ODB* III, 1797–1798). On the highly politicized notion of 'natural' frontiers see P. Sahlins, 'Natural frontiers revisited: France's boundaries since the seventeenth century', *American Historical Review* 95 (1990), 1423–1451.

[35] John Geometres, *PG* 106, 806–1002, at 919–920. A Russian force under Svyatoslav Igorevich had invaded Bulgaria shortly after campaigning there as imperial allies and occupied several important cities on the lower Danube.

[36] John Geometres, 902.

[37] Towards the end of his reign Basil issued an edict which recorded that 'among the many and great benefits which God has lavished upon Our Majesty ... the one preferred above all else is that there should be addition to the Roman empire'. See J. Zepos and P. Zepos, eds, *Ius graecoromanum*, 8 vols (Athens, 1931–1962), I, 272. I am grateful to Jonathan Shepard for drawing my attention to this reference.

[38] J. Kabakčiev, 'Mysia or Moesia?', *Bulgarian Historical Review* 23/i (1995), 5–9, for the origins of this practice and further references.

[39] *Anne Comnène, Alexiade*, B. Leib, ed., 3 vols (Paris, 1937–1945), I, 60, 155; II, 166–167.

[40] *Ioannis Cinnami epitome rerum ab Ioanne et Manuelo Comnenis gestarum*, ed. A. Meinecke, *CSHB* (Bonn, 1836), 12. The use of the name Dalmatia and its geographical limits

and the Bulgarians Mysians by Byzantine authors.[41] Rarely was this qualified, as for example in the *Short Life of St Clement*, where it is remarked that the saint 'drew his origins from the European Mysians, who were also known to most people as Bulgarians'.[42] In calling Bulgarians by the name of an ancient subject people they were not merely described, they were acquired; the polity which dominated the northern Balkans for three centuries preceding Basil II's reconquest was denied a contemporary identity; its distinct origins and development were masked by a rigid framework of representation. For the same reason Peter and Asen, the founders of the 'Second Bulgarian Empire', were known throughout Choniates's account of their insurrection as Mysians.[43] This has provoked a heated and artificial debate between Bulgarian and Romanian scholars concerned with their ethnic origins.[44] Neutral commentators have attempted to calm the waters by avoiding commitment.[45] If we restore the references to Mysians to their original context it is clear that Choniates's concern was not to ascribe an accurate ethnic tag, but to bolster the empire's façade of immutability. Choniates was a historian seeking continuity in the discontinuity which followed the sack of Constantinople in 1204.[46]

Thus, it is generally clear from the context to which people an author is referring, and in each case the practice reflects an attempt to categorize and control the turbulent world that lay to the empire's north and west. Nevertheless, the Byzantine quest for ethnic continuity has led to confusion. The compilation of lists of names known as *metonomasiai* which accompanied certain texts (notably Constantine Porphyrogennetos's *De Thematibus*) suggests that as early as the thirteenth century

---

in this period have been the subject of some discussion: see J. Ferluga, 'Dalmatien – Wandlung eines verwaltungsgeographischen Terminus in den byzantinischen Quellen des 12 Jahrhunderts', in, *Europa Slavica – Europa Orientalis. Festschrift für K. Ludat*, eds K.D. Grothusen and K. Zernack (Berlin, 1980), 341–353.

[41] For example, *Leonis Diaconi Caloensis historiae libri decem*, ed. C. B. Hase, *CSHB* (Bonn, 1828), 103; *Skylitzes*, ed. Thurn, 385, 399.

[42] A. Milev, *Grutskite zhitiyana Kliment Ohridski* (Sofia, 1966), 174–182, at 174; cited by Obolensky, *Six Byzantine Portraits*, 12.

[43] Choniates, 369, for the appearance of Peter and Asen.

[44] For example, S. Brezeanu, '«Mésiens» chez Nicétas Choniate. Terminologie archaïsante et réalité ethnique médiévale', *Etudes byzantines et post-byzantines* 2 (1991), 105–114, who argues for Choniates's 'correct' application to the Romanian Vlachs.

[45] C.M. Brand, *Byzantium Confronts the West, 1180–1204* (Cambridge, MA, 1968), for example at 88–89, refers to 'Vlach-Bulgars'.

[46] On the context for Choniates's composition see P. Magdalino, *The Empire of Manuel I Komnenos 1143–1180* (Cambridge, 1993), 4–14.

readers required clarification of who was called what, now and then.[47] Modern observers have similarly sought exact and consistent translations for ancient names, attempting to correct rather than understand the distortion. Such corrections often introduce modern concerns and prejudices which act as further barriers to understanding.

When he identified the distorting mirror of Byzantine literature in 1974 Cyril Mango believed that the task of the historian was 'to sift out all the antiquarian passages before he obtains a residue that may be applicable to the [appropriate] century'. While the historian seeking facts about peoples in the northern Balkans after 1018 may still operate in this way, finding the distortion a hindrance, the historian seeking insights into the attitudes of Byzantine authors as their society confronted new and real threats may find that the mirror is an asset. Moreover, dealing with distortion is a problem Byzantine historians share with historians of other periods and places, which is also an asset in so far as it invites us to consider life beyond medieval Constantinople – something Byzantinists often seem as unwilling to do as the people with whom they are principally concerned.

---

[47]   A. Diller, 'Byzantine lists of old and new geographical names', *BZ* 63 (1970), 27–42. Mango, *Distorting Mirror*, 15, called the *De Thematibus* 'an extraordinary mosaic of snippets, most of which have no relevance to the tenth century'.

19. Afterword by an Art Historian

Robin Cormack

The art historian who is offered an afterword on a symposium about the Byzantine outsider is likely to feel out of place. Is not Byzantine art one medium within the culture which entirely colluded with the cultural élite to communicate the 'norm', the centre, the insider? Is it not so often treated as the vehicle of 'official' attitudes that to suggest that art acts as more than a definition of the conventions of the 'establishment' might seem a perverse exercise? Byzantine art so regularly features as the 'orthodox' art of the Orthodox church, and is assumed so naturally to be state art, that any question of 'otherness' might seem out of place. In exploring how far the papers in this volume might be able to subvert this traditional art historical attitude, it will be useful to ask first how the contributing art historians treated the issues, and then move on to the cultural historians.

Lyn Rodley treats 'other' as art in the provinces rather than the capital; but she finds it is operating in the same way. By pragmatically listing a number of examples where patrons of churches are self-referentially represented in their churches, she asks whether there is any difference in the imagery used in the provinces from that in the capital; and finds none. Even if the artists working on the fringes of the empire in north Greece or in Cappadocia are different people from those employed in the capital, they collude with the dominant élite in their use of visual conventions. They represent power and status in the same way. Indeed in the case of Neophytos at Paphos who is included in this survey, the artist of the wallpaintings of the *Enkleistra* which were executed in 1183 has been widely accepted as a painter trained in Constantinople. The fact that Theodore Apseudes recorded his name in the paintings on the wall has been seen as a reflection of the new practices of Constantinopolitan

From *Strangers to Themselves: The Byzantine Outsider*, ed. Dion C. Smythe. Copyright © 2000 by the Society for the Promotion of Byzantine Studies. Published by Ashgate Publishing Ltd, Gower House, Croft Road, Aldershot, Hampshire, GU11 3HR, Great Britain.

artists.[1] Only geographical location distinguishes the centre from the periphery.

Nancy Ševčenko treats the question in a different way and looks at the representation of the 'other'. She treats as the 'other' not the hermit in the desert, but his environment and his relationship with his everyday companions, the wild and dangerous animals around him. The desert fathers co-existed with nature and found a Christian way of life which included safe cohabitation with lions and other threatening beasts. What is explored here is the dichotomy between culture and nature, and the portrayal of the differences. But again the pictorial strategies are the conventional ones and the lions are entirely recognisable as wild beasts – they are not anthropomorphised.

One might therefore raise the question how far art historians in treating the question of the 'other' can go beyond the investigation of its *representation*. Is this an issue of the art historian using pictures as windows instead of using them as artefacts in their own right?[2] How far is a patron like Neophytos at Paphos using the conventions as part of a subversive exercise to transform himself from an outsider into an insider? Put in this way, one notices that the modern literature on Neophytos has indeed treated him as a provincial oddity and eccentric, witnessed for example by the representation of himself as ascending to Heaven, like Christ, an image which has no parallel in Byzantine art.[3] Yet while the cycle of paintings which Theodore Apseudes carried out may be an individual and personal attempt to communicate the place of Neophytos in the Christian order of things, Neophytos successfully emerges in his portrayal as a Byzantine insider and his use of art was conventional in its strategies, even if not in its individual choice of imagery and its arrangement in a church space. The community of monks who sub-sequently worshipped in the *Enkleistra* and viewed the images were equally transformed from membership of a rural and provincial cave-monastery into a regular establishment with a saint for its first abbot. It was the power of art and its traditional conventions which both promoted Neophytos as a saint and acted to regularise the community within the conventions. Unlike his western contemporary, St Francis of

---

[1] C. Mango and E.J.W. Hawkins, 'The Hermitage of St Neophytos and its Wall Paintings', *DOP* 20 (1966), 119–206.

[2] The imagery is used of text by J. Davidson, *Courtesans and Fishcakes*, (London, 1997), especially xxiv ff.

[3] R. Cormack, *Writing in Gold* (London, 1985), 215–51.

Assisi, neither the decoration nor the cave monastery environment attempted to reach out to the people on the fringes of society.

Similarly the various types of group patronal images are seen in Rodley's paper to work within the established conventions. Male patrons with their families make it visually evident that the wife is the 'other' in the relationship. For the art historian to confront the 'other' becomes in part a question of methodology, and of examining how Byzantine visual arts carry meanings, both within the culture and for us – as of course the outsiders. A recurring fallacy in this field of study is that the modern 'Orthodox Christian' scholar has a privileged 'insider' view of the Byzantine world which must be inherently superior to the analysis of the 'outsider' historian from another background. The fallacy is to ignore that all historians have different advantages and disadvantages in their attempts to visualise the past, and it is in this difference that the dynamic of history resides. The question explored in this volume is how far the concepts of insider and outsider can be justifiably attached to the culture. Several of the historical papers set up ways of handling this question.

Liliana Simeonova treats texts in different languages of the ninth and tenth centuries as evidence of the ways in which the public ritual and symbolic displays of Constantinople might be misunderstood by foreigners (the 'other'). This gives specific clues to the areas in which decoding was difficult for those with different cultural and religious backgrounds. She also gives examples where the Byzantines themselves, acting on the basis of their own acquired knowledge of foreign customs, adapted their symbolic messages to harmonise with the anticipated perceptions of foreigners. The methodology of her paper is to analyse what the symbolic codes were, and to distinguish between foreigner and Byzantine by their expertise in reading them. A qualification here is that we cannot assume that the codes were themselves without ambivalence, or that all Byzantines would read them in similar ways. The dichotomy of insider/outsider does not necessarily coincide with foreigner/Byzantine, as there must have been diversity of thinking between individuals and groups who resided in the capital.

This issue of the nature of the 'multiculturalism' of Constantinople is examined by Paul Magdalino, especially with reference to the twelfth century, arguing that around 1200 was a time of exceptional insularity in the attitudes of the inhabitants of the city. He argues that at face value Constantinople was a homogeneous community, which as New Rome gave its citizens the title of *Romaioi*. Yet underneath the façade the population was multifarious and always in flux. It was the 'place where outsiders became insiders'. An alien who saw this was Michael Attaleiates whose elevation to insidership was publicly asserted in his membership of 'the senatorial aristocracy, a senior judge loaded with public honours'. Yet this case, no doubt repeated in many others, shows the subjective nature of our terminology. The emperor above all might fit this pattern of an outsider becoming an insider; yet he might feel himself always to be an outsider in the court. The 'loneliness of power' is the traditional description of any ruler as powerful as the Byzantine emperor. The infinite regress in our terms is signalled by Margaret Mullett, in suggesting that all Byzantines were outsiders, exiled from Paradise, and by John McGuckin who reminds us that *xeniteia* (detachment?) is an ingredient of the monastic life discussed in the *Heavenly Ladder* of John Klimakos. On this evidence we might be able to define 'foreigner' from external information, but to be an 'outsider' is in part a psychological state, which may not necessarily have recognisable external signs.

The embedded ambivalence between foreigner/Byzantine and outsider/insider dichotomies emerges again when David Jacoby sets out the evidence of Byzantine and Western traders. The paradox suggested is that the decision of Alexios I Komnenos to give sweeping trade and maritime privileges to Venice in 1082 had the consequence that the western trader in the empire, and particularly in Constantinople, was the insider. The Byzantine traders, although in the majority, had fewer privileges and exemptions, and were effectively the outsiders. The frustration and resentment felt on the Byzantine side accounts for the increasingly violent rhetoric against traders and westerners. Magdalino and Jacoby easily found authors producing all the stereotypes of the greedy trader and hostile expressions of ethnic and cultural difference. In the case of traders, then, a functional definition would define the foreigners as insiders; it is other aspects that allowed the Byzantines to continue to see themselves as the 'real' insiders.

Another group in the empire, forming perhaps one per cent of the population of Constantinople according to Nicholas de Lange, was the Jews. It has been argued in an art historical study by Corrigan that there was extensive verbal and visual polemic against the Jews in the ninth-century Khludov Psalter, and that this was because they were regarded as a threat.[4] She argues that their facial appearance was distorted and caricatured to be recognisably 'Jewish'. It follows from the scepticism of

---

[4]   K. Corrigan, *Visual Polemics in the Ninth-Century Byzantine Psalter*, (Cambridge, 1992), 43–61.

de Lange that 'clothing and customs apart, there was nothing in the physical appearance or physiognomy of the Jews that distinguished them from the gentiles', that the Byzantine artists were producing a pictorial and symbolic image of the 'other' rather than mirroring reality. This would seem to offer a case of the artefact constructing and communicating the idea. Nevertheless the Jews do offer us a specific case of an ethnic group within a complex empire, whose religion taught that they, and not the Orthodox Christians, would at the end of time be the triumphant people of God.

Whereas the historical analysis of texts helps to illuminate the complexities of the population of Byzantium and their perceptions of the foreign, the literary picture as analysed in this volume creates a wider frame. It is however complicated by the question of genre or mode, and how those genres and modes were used within the historical circumstances of specific periods in Byzantine history. The understanding of the different productions of Procopius, according to Geoffrey Greatrex, involves exploring a balance between the fashionable attitudes of his period and the conventions of classicising historiography. In this scenario, Procopius was not a lone critic of the reign of Justinian, but might appear so, since he happened to choose to give a critical account of the events of his own lifetime and died before his views became repeatable in public (as they soon did in the next reign with its backlash against Justinian). Procopius, it follows, must be treated in a very different way from a later writer such as Michael Psellos in whose life the turnover of emperors was rapid enough to protect the critical writer from social isolation.

For Charlotte Roueché, the text known as 'The Strategikon of Kekaumenos' matches the rhetoric of the visual arts of the Middle Byzantine period in its aim to convey to the world at large the claims of Byzantium to represent unchanging good order (*taxis*). Similarly the materials reviewed by Jane Baun show that the literary expression of the supposed circumstances in which the soul existed after death changed in the period of the ninth to eleventh centuries, although it involved the reworking of the Late Antique genre of Jewish and Christian literature of the 'tour of hell'. Such a literature of the description of dreams and near-death experiences must be innately moralising and a powerful tool of the social construction of the insider and outsider at the moment of its production. The various versions of the poem of *Digenis Akritis* and the question whether they can be related to an 'original' model are covered by Elizabeth Jeffreys both as a way of illuminating the concept of an outsider hero operating on the eastern frontier lands between the Christian and Islamic world and also as an example of a way of using literature in twelfth-century Constantinople to evoke a Byzantine presence in the east. Perhaps the most complex imagery of all the twelfth-century literature is in the novels covered by Roderick Beaton, in which it is again emphasised that the modern reader must distinguish the Byzantine narrative patterns from those of the Hellenistic models which lie behind this genre.

The outcome of this symposium was to splinter the monolithic image of Byzantium, yet its exploration of its parts did not construct any clear categories of who might be insiders and who might be outsiders. The terms themselves became central to the discussion. Did this mean that Byzantium was a society where the insider/outsider dichotomy was irrelevant, or was it that the papers add up to a deconstruction of the concept?

Index